Steamboats, Shoshoni, Scoundrels and Such

Seldom-Told Tales Of The Western Frontier

BOOKS BY JAMES F. VARLEY:

Brigham and the Brigadier

*Lola Montez; the California Adventures
of Europe's Noted Courtesan*

*The Legend of Joaquín Murrieta;
California's Gold Rush Bandit*

Steamboats, Shoshoni, Scoundrels and Such

SELDOM-TOLD TALES
OF THE WESTERN FRONTIER

by

JAMES F. VARLEY

BIG LOST RIVER PRESS
TWIN FALLS, IDAHO
2001

Copyright 2001 by
JAMES F. VARLEY

All rights reserved, including the rights to
translate or reproduce this work, or parts
thereof, in any form or by any media.

LIBRARY OF CONGRESS CONTROL NUMBER: 2001118978
ISBN 0-9647747-2-0

To John Hensley, of *Brother Jonathan,*
and other brave seamen who have given
their lives that others might live.

Contents

Preface	ix
1. Josefa and the Senator	1
2. Brother Jonathan	15
3. Sagebrush Steamboat	59
4. Old Kale	85
5. A Hard Road to Jordan	135
6. Slaughter at Bear River	191
7. The Last Battle	215
8. First Family	261
9. Uncle Billy	291
Notes	315
Bibliography	339
Index	349

Preface

Herein is a mixed bag of stories chronicling some little-known events that took place during the opening of our Western frontier. They are engrossing tales and, despite their relative obscurity, have long deserved a fuller recital. Most are set in early Nevada or Idaho, and several describe just how difficult and dangerous it was to get goods and American citizens to those wilderness regions.

One of the yarns is about *Brother Jonathan*, a Gold Rush steamship with a hex. Another is the story of the little steamboat *Shoshone* that sailed on the upper Snake River, and once went hurtling, pell-mell down through Hell's Canyon of the Snake River. Still another recounts the antic history of Caleb Lyon, the foppish territorial governor who started a "diamond" rush in the Owyhee region of Idaho, who twice fled the territory out of fear for his life, and who stole treaty money meant for the Nez Perce Indians.

And here, for the first time, in full, is chronicled the short, melancholy life of Colonel Charles McDermit, who played such a large part in early Nevada military history. The protagonists of another tale set in Nevada—the Haws brothers—are a pair of hoodlums who rediscovered their religion after spending their younger days in league with Indians, robbing emigrants.

Nearly all of these accounts deal, in part, with the deadly clash between white and red men that took place during the middle years of the nineteenth century, and demonstrate, I think, the damage done to both races, by corrupt, carpet bagging politicians. Two of the stories deal exclusively with White-Indian animosity—one tells of a massacre of Shoshoni on the Bear River in Idaho, and another recounts the "last battle" between the two races which took place 45 years later, possibly as a consequence of that massacre.

Many of the incidents depicted in this collection took place in the backwash of America's great Civil War, when events in the West were largely overshadowed by that conflict. This perhaps, is one reason they are so little known.

In each story, I have attempted to chronicle the harshness of life, and its tenuous nature, that was part and parcel of opening a new country. I hope to have also shown the restless energy that existed in America in earlier times—the hustle, and that overwhelming desire to see what lay farther west, or at the newest mining camp.

I have relied heavily on contemporary newspapers, with their rough, cynically humorous editors, who weren't afraid to state their opinions or prejudices, and who didn't clothe their reporting or opinions in political correctness or an appearance of impartiality. By a thorough examination of these early newspapers, and the discovery of various other untapped primary sources, a number of facts have surfaced which have made new interpretations possible.

I owe a large debt of gratitude to the many who have so generously helped in my research. Special thanks are due to Donald Knight of Diamond Bar, California, Arlen Call and the staff of the Twin Falls, Idaho public library, the Del Norte County Historical Society, Peter Pelkofer of the California State Lands Commission, Sheri Allen of the Humboldt County Library, Nevada, and Barbara Bernauer of the Reorganized Latter-day Saints Church historian's office.

Mackay, Idaho   JAMES F. VARLEY
2001

Josefa and the Senator

We begin with a story about that cherished American institution, the lynching. Not a run-of-the-mill lynching, mind you, but one in which the lynchee was a woman. This incident had a hat full of scoundrels.

The sensitivity of modern man does not abide hanging. Though many people favor capital punishment—so long as they don't have to watch any executions—most of them prefer the antiseptic method wherein the criminal is given a lethal injection. But, for many years, in a less-squeamish world, public hanging was the preferred means for disposing of murderous criminals. Most states in America didn't discontinue the practice until the early decades of the twentieth century. The English hung their last murderer in 1954.

In earlier days, of course, long delays or appeals were not tolerated. Justice was administered summarily by the courts, and—in the American West—by vigilante committees or lynch-law mobs. And, just about every conceivable apparatus has been used to "string up" and strangle unfortunate victims—the gallows, tree limbs, wagon tongues, pole tripods, and, in the case of the subject of this story, the timbers of a bridge.

Hanging—or more precisely, lynching#—flourished during the early crime-ridden days of the California Gold Rush. The discovery of the precious metal in 1848 at Sutter's Mill triggered a huge influx of fortune seeking men from around the world. While most of these newcomers to California respected the law, a significant number from every country were the dregs of society.

Once in California, these mostly young and immature men lived the hairy-chested life. To celebrate their masculinity, a good many gave up shaving, wore buckskin and flannel clothing, and ornamented themselves with broad-brimmed felt hats, revolvers, and Bowie knifes. Often a pair of foot-long animal skins could be seen slung from the hips of these two-fisted fellows come to seek their fortune.

They sought a variety of diversions. Sunday was their day for raising hell in the mining camps but, in the towns, the pleasure seeking went on non-stop. Fights of all kinds were popular amusements–man versus man, dog against dog, dog against bear and, of course, that most delightful sport of all, wherein a bull and bear were chained together to do mortal combat. If occasionally the chain would break and the animals run amok, it could only add to the thrill of the occasion.

Tents and halls, in which a lonely miner might drink, gamble and carouse, were to be found everywhere in abundance. At night, these emporiums were packed with a heterogeneous mass of men, milling about under a blaze of lights. Often such places were lavishly ornamented and decorated with salacious pictures, and were fitted up with a splendid bar at one end of the room. Usually, gold scales were at hand, so that a miner might get coin for his dust, and then, at "two-bits" a glass, build up his courage before wagering away the earnings of months of hard toil and privation.

At many of the plentiful gaming tables around the room—all piled high with money—could be found reckless, fearsome men dealing the Mexican game of monte, a particular favorite in those days. It always drew large crowds of spectators, hoping to see someone "tap the bank," that is break it by betting all it was worth.

The "forty-niners" of the Gold Rush were almost entirely untempered by any of the refining influences of home or female society. One early county census shows a typical imbalance of the sexes, listing, as it does, only 1,200

The punishment of presumed crimes or offenses, usually by death, without due process of law. Probably after Charles Lynch, a former justice of the peace who, in 1780, presided over an extra-legal court to suppress Tory activity in Virginia.

Sunday in the California Diggings. From San Francisco *The Wide West*, December, 1854
(Author's Collection)

females of all nationalities for a male population of 30,500. John Daggett, who was in Mokelumne Hill in those days, described such of the fairer sex as were available. The town's several saloons and two dance halls were always in full swing, he said, "with grandily [sic] dressed Spanish women, not particular in regard to an introduction, but ready to go the rounds of a dance if the [patron] had the necessary 'four bits' to 'liquidade' a bill for two drinks at the bar..."[1]

In daily life the slightest offense, real or imagined, might be cause for violence. Franklin Buck, a young businessman of Marysville, spoke of the "California Code," which required that if one man struck another without provocation, the offended party had a perfect right to shoot the aggressor. Everyone went armed and, at the smallest provocation, out came the revolvers. Someone would yell, "Don't shoot," the crowd would surge back, and the combatants would blaze away. "A man's life is but little thought of," Buck lamented.[2]

Aside from the foregoing factors, the significant surge in crime seen during California's first, formative years was abetted by the remoteness and isolation of the gold-bearing regions, poor police organization and a scarcity of honest and competent civil officers. Citizens complained most about the quality of the judiciary, which often allowed those few murderers who were apprehended to pass and re-pass before the bench, unpunished.

Many magistrates had little knowledge of common law, and just as many were not hesitant about taking an occasional bribe. Some conducted their business from gambling saloons where the majesty of the law had to compete with men drinking grog and "bucking" against monte dealers. In Mokelumne Hill, one judge of the first instance (county judge) even owned the saloon in which he ran his court. Another judge, in a Stockton gambling house, set up shop at the end of a counter, such that he could receive his brandy toddy without ever having to leave his seat. During one particular case being tried, a lawyer who sat close to the judge gave him "an unmistakable nudge in the ribs to call his attention to a whisper that he softly insinuated in his ear."[3]

Racial divisions also significantly increased crime. The diggings were crowded with large numbers of Mexicans, Chileans, Frenchmen, and other races and nationalities. In the summer of 1849, with about three-fourths of the men working in the mines being foreigners, there arose a determination among Americans to expel these "vagrants of other nations."[4]

In many of the rough-and-tumble mining towns along the Tuolumne, Stanislaus and Mokelumne rivers, resolutions were passed ordering all aliens to leave. A few who resisted were forcibly evicted from their claims. Anyone looking or sounding remotely foreign became a likely candidate for such treatment. The Mexicans bore the brunt of the animosity. It had only been a few months since America's war with Mexico had ended, and there was no love lost between the two nationalities.

In April 1850, strong pressure on the California legislature resulted in passage of a so-called "Greaser Act," which imposed a tax of $20.00 per month, in the form of a license, upon all foreign miners. Tax collectors, appointed by the governor in each county, were allowed to skim $3.00 for themselves from every license issued, and were authorized to call upon sheriffs for help in enforcing the law.

Twenty dollars was an onerous impost—more than some miners earned in a month. Consequently, there was a certain amount of open and violent resistance to the law, and, by summer, the incidence of robbery and murder had increased so much in the mining regions that a state of terror prevailed.

In one instance, a dozen naked corpses were found lying in a remote ravine near Double Springs. In another, the keepers of two different ferries across the San Joaquin River were murdered for their money. Other victims were found stabbed, or with their throats cut, or with heads severed and bodies hacked up by sabers. Still other men were found in their tents, shot or axed, or with their skulls crushed by rocks. While many of the assailants went unidentified, often the crimes were known or suspected to have been committed by small groups of Mexicans.

In August, another general cry arose against foreigners. Mass meetings were held at Sonora and the various diggings along the Stanislaus at which resolutions were passed, aimed at ridding the camps of the "Peons of Mexico," the "renegades of South America," and the "convicts of the British Empire"[5]—the latter being the Australian criminals known as "Sydney Ducks." All foreigners, except persons in permanent business and of respectable character, were ordered to turn over their firearms and leave the county within fifteen days. Three citizens at each camp would decide who could stay and who must leave. As a consequence, over 15,000 Mexicans left the southern diggings.

Many merchants, gamblers and saloon-keepers blamed the increasing crime rate—and their decreasing business—on the mining tax, believing it to have driven the worst of the foreigners into a wayward life. An editor at the San Francisco *Daily Alta California* reckoned that if this were the case, then it was high time for every man in the region to "carry 'Colt's Common Law' and 'Bowie's Practice' at his girdle" so that he might "quote those unquestioned authorities at a moment's notice." With life having become so tenuous, a great many men took that advice.[6]

Finally yielding to pressures from businessmen, the legislature would repeal the foreign miner's tax in the spring of 1851. But havoc had been loosed during that long summer of 1850. In all, from the beginning of the trouble in May, until October 19—the day when the steamer *New World* reached San Francisco with the news that California had been admitted as a state into the Union—about 60 unsolved killings occurred. And, sadly, robbery and murder would remain a harsh fact of daily life throughout California for more than a decade.

By the time 1851 rolled around, many ordinarily-reasonable men—fed up with unchecked murder, arson and robbery—became convinced of the need for citizens to take the law into their own hands. One respected Grass Valley author and businessman, Alonzo Delano, expressed well the existing sentiment, writing to deplore the many murders throughout the state during the past year, for which only one legal execution had taken place.

In a nation where "the force of early education and of public example had tended to the observance of the law," Delano said, a state now existed "which bordered on anarchy and threatened to dissolve the social compact of the community." All of California, he noted, was beset with unprincipled men, and everywhere there was distrust of authority. The point had been reached where "strong individual combinations"[7] were needed to protect life and property.

And so, beginning that year, vigilance committees became fashionable. San Francisco's Committee of Safety would set the example. Formed June 12, 1851, not many weeks after a huge, devastating fire—thought to be the work of arsonists—the committee began its work with the hanging of two men accused of murder. By July, so many other towns and mining camps in the state had formed their own committees to meet threats, real or perceived, that an alarmed Governor John McDougall issued harsh proclamations denouncing their formation. For this, and for interfering in the hanging of three more men at San Francisco, the governor was himself hung there—in effigy.[8]

In the mining camps, sometimes even the formality of a vigilance committee was dispensed with, and raw, primitive lynch law prevailed. Whether by mob or committee, harsh punishments were meted out promptly to American and foreigner alike. These might vary from a few lashes or a head shaving for minor larcenies, to ear cropping, branding or peremptory hanging for the more serious offenses of livestock theft and murder.

Sometimes, the mood turned especially vicious. A committee at Columbia once seized a seventy-year old insane woman accused of stealing $1,200, stripped her, and administered 100 lashes and "other outrages" before

Cradle Rocking on a California River
(From *Harper's Magazine*, December 1859-May 1860)

discovering that she was wholly innocent.⁹

Even more brutal was the disposition of a well-known cutthroat and scoundrel at Yankee Jim Knowlton's dry diggings on the American River. This man—"Jim Ugly"—was accused of stabbing to death a fellow patron of a bordello. While being taken by the vigilance committee to a place of trial, he, in turn, was stabbed in the back by one of a wrathful mob of miners. The ill-fated Jim was then placed on a cot and his wound examined. Though the injury was thought to be a mortal one, the indignation of the mob was too great to let the matter rest there. The dying man was taken to a nearby tree and hoisted up by the neck, and everyone present agreed that justice had been done.¹⁰

Another story, perhaps apocryphal, displays the black humor that sometimes sprang from the sad business of lynch law. At Hangtown—later to be known as Placerville—a fellow called "Irish Dick" had been convicted and sentenced to death by a people's court for murder. When he was taken to a tree, and the rope tied around his neck, he asked for, and was granted, a favor. Instead of being hauled up, the apparently ungrudging Dick was allowed to climb the tree with the rope in hand, fasten it to a horizontal limb and—at the drop of a handkerchief—jump off. Thus, his neck was broken cleanly and he died without a struggle.

Perhaps the most sensational instance of lynch-law in California's history was the hanging of a Mexican woman named Josefa, at Downieville, about the time such behavior first became popular.

Downieville, in Sierra County, was sometimes called "The Forks" in its earliest days. By 1851 the remote little community could boast only some 200 rude structures—tents, adobe or log huts and shanties, several sawmills, a tiny theater, and a surfeit of that standard refinement of life in a gold rush mining camp, the gambling saloon. Only twenty miles from the summit of the Sierra Nevada, there was, as yet, no road to the place, and all necessities had to be packed in by mules for the final fifty miles.

But, the hike to reach this highly productive placer-mining camp was worth it. At its legendary "Tin Cup" diggings, owners of the claim divided up their plenteous take every day by measuring it a plain tin cup. Just up the north fork of the Yuba from town was a deposit of gravel, rich with gold, known as the Blue Banks. A bit farther up, the biggest nugget ever found in California was dug up at the mouth of Sailor Ravine.

Independence Day—July 4,1851—had seen a wild, and brawling celebration in Downieville. Colonel John B. Weller, who was campaigning in the mining regions for a U. S. Senate seat, had been the featured speaker, and his presence had drawn a large crowd from the surrounding camps. Weller, 39-years old, was a former state legislator from Ohio who, during the Mexican War, had risen from the rank of private to colonel.

All that day and into the night the revelry continued, the frolic given added impetus by the fact that this was the first Independence Day to be celebrated in the new state of California. One of the drunkest of the revelers that night was a huge, popular Scot named Jack Cannon. He had spent the evening hours celebrating with friends, having drinks and supper in a small, rude cabin on a back street. A former sailor, Cannon spoke Chinese fluently, and he had entertained his friends by singing and enacting Chinese love songs, using different tones of voice to play, in turn, the various characters in the song. At about midnight, Cannon left this party and fell in with a crowd of drunken revelers on a spree, staggering through the streets, all the while hooting, howling and emitting oaths. Here and there the giddy miners paused to awaken sleepers by assailing doors and windows with kicks and

Downieville, California in 1852
(California State Library)

blows.

A young Mexican woman, Josefa, was living in an adobe hut on Main Street with her paramour, a monte-dealer named Jóse. Josefa—who somehow down through the years has come to be known as "Juanita"—was most likely a prostitute, but at least one writer has romantically portrayed her as living in domestic tranquility as Jóse's wife—taking in washing to make ends meet, baking bread, crafting fine embroidery and, in the evenings, strumming her guitar while singing love songs to Jóse. Whatever the true case, Josefa was, as one observer noted, "proud and self-possessed, her bearing graceful, almost majestic." And she was, in the miners' parlance, "well put up."[11]

As Cannon and his friends staggered past Jóse's house, one of them either fell through, or deliberately broke down, the rickety door which opened directly into the room where Josefa and Jóse were sleeping. Some said it was dark inside and that the revelers fixed the door and left without speaking. Others would accuse Cannon of going shamelessly into the room and coming out with "an article of female attire"[12] on his head. In any event, the revelers soon moved on, distracted by a stray mule in the street, which they drove into another nearby house.

Eventually one of Cannon's friends, a certain Lawson, convinced Cannon to go down to the river for a wash and to sober up a bit. An hour or so after the breaking down of Jóse's door—about 7 A.M.—the two miners were once again walking near his house, toward a barber shop. Seeing the pair, Jóse came out and demanded that Cannon pay for the damage he had done. When Cannon said he wasn't aware of having broken anything, and refused to pay, the quarrel grew heated. Lawson thought Jóse was about to draw a pistol, and warned him against it.

Josefa came out and talked to Lawson, who said he wanted no quarrel. Jóse, apparently seeing no point to further talk, tried to get her back into the house. In a few minutes, as she stood at the door, Cannon approached her as though they were old friends, and offered his hand and his endearments to make up. When she refused, Cannon, who spoke Spanish fairly well, called her a "whore" in that language.

At this, Josefa disappeared into a side room, leaving Cannon leaning with a hand on each side of the doorway, conversing with Jóse. Cannon seemed about to reach into the house and take hold of Jóse—who was a boy in strength compared to the huge miner—when Josefa reappeared, with a long Bowie knife hidden in the folds of her dress. Before Cannon could react she rushed up and stabbed him in the heart with all her strength. Cannon fell, mortally stricken.

Almost before the blood stopped flowing from Cannon's wound, a gong was sounded in the street, accompanied by cries of "to the Plaza! to the Plaza!"[13] The news of the murder spread like wildfire among the many miners strung out for miles up and down the river. They dropped their picks and pans and hurried into town where Cannon had been laid out in a large tent, like a saint, so that all might view the ugly, death-dealing wound in his breast.

Josefa and Jóse had fled up the street to a nearby saloon for protection. The gamblers there tried to shield the two against the threatening mob, but soon had to give them up to the constable.

Urged on by the friends and drinking companions of the deceased—who were still under the influence of their carousal—the Mexican couple were hurriedly taken for trial to the Plaza, where John Weller had delivered his oration the previous day. Once there, a certain Mr. Thayer—a relative newcomer to Downieville—volunteered to defend the pair. Bar owner John Rose was named judge, and William S. Spear, a friend of Cannon, was selected to prosecute. Other friends of Cannon would later say that foreman Amos Brown and the other Americans picked as a jury by the crowd, were sober, intelligent and honest men.

Without being sworn, prosecution witnesses were called forth to tell the story of the killing. After this, at defender Thayer's request, Jóse and Josefa were allowed to make statements. But, because of their poor English, neither was able to converse with Thayer, and their statements had to be made through an inefficient interpreter.

Josefa admitted the killing, but deemed it justifiable in view of the provocation and her fear of the men who lived near her house. When she told of being tormented a day or two previously by one of the witnesses, and having drawn her knife in self-protection, prosecutor Spear cited this as proof of her violent character. Some of those present remembered that she had previously stabbed other inhabitants of Downieville.

The defense was exceedingly unpopular. It was said that scarcely a dozen persons present could see the slightest injustice to the proceedings. Foreseeing what was to come, Thayer stood on a barrel and argued against the enormity of hanging a woman. But this just further angered the crowd, and they kicked the barrel out from under him, his hat flying in one direction and his spectacles in another. Then, he was seized and carried at least a hundred yards, before he touched the ground, and was released.

One man would later recall that it was the hungriest and craziest mob he had ever seen, requiring rope lines to keep the men back. From time to time during the trial, the crowd would make a rush at Josefa, and Spear would have to intervene, asking them to remember their wives, mothers and daughters.

A young doctor, Cyrus D. Aiken, in a bold and magnanimous move, attempted to save Josefa by testifying that she was pregnant, even though he probably had no knowledge that she actually was. At this, a howl of incredulity was raised by the crowd, and one of the jury shouted, "Damn her, we do not want any more of the race."[14]

Other physicians were called for to examine Josefa, including one who was a close friend of the deceased, Cannon. She was taken into a house nearby, but the consultation was broken up within just a few minutes by the loud demands of the crowd to bring Dr. Aiken out. The would-be savior, however, had the good sense to leave the house by another door just before his fellow doctors returned with the opinion that Josefa was not with child. Incensed that Aiken had tried to shield the woman from justice, the crowd voted to banish him from the town.

Other witnesses were privately asked to go on the stand in defense of Josefa but they refused, having seen the mood of the crowd and its treatment of Thayer and Dr. Aiken. Some have said that there were also a number of

John B. Weller
(*California State Library*)

men—prominent or destined to become so—who watched the whole affair without protestation: Hank Monk, the famous stage coach driver; Stephen J. Field, afterwards Chief Justice of the U. S. Supreme Court, and William M. Stewart, later a U. S. Senator from Nevada.

Speech-maker John B. Weller was still in Downieville, and he attended the trial that day. When it became evident how things were going to end, if allowed to continue, he was solicited to use his considerable influence and popularity to prevent it, but he "coldly declined."[15] It would be later said that he came to regret not having spoken up in Josefa's defense, when he learned that he would have been supported, had he simply raised his voice.

The jurors retired barely long enough to write down a verdict. At 2 P.M. they pronounced Jóse innocent, but found Josefa guilty, and sentenced her to hang in two hours. Jóse was retained in custody until the affair was over, thus cutting off Josefa's only opportunity of communicating with those who knew her. There was no priest in town to take her confession.

As a crowd of some six hundred spectators gathered, a makeshift gallows was built on one of the two bridges that crossed the Yuba. The hangman's rope was fastened to one of the projecting upper timbers, while, beneath it, a six-inch wide plank was pushed out over the stream and lashed to the lower framework of the bridge.

At a quarter to four, the judge, accompanied by prosecutor William S. Spear, led a procession to the gallows through the obscene shouts of the mob. Josefa walked with a firm step onto the bridge. With a perfect calm, she surveyed the crowd and spoke pleasantly to several of her friends, asking that her remains be decently cared for. Unrepentant, she admitted she would kill again if similarly provoked.

After bidding her friends adieu, Josefa used a small ladder to climb up onto the plank. Then the proud woman took off a straw hat she had borrowed, and sailed it over the heads of the crowd to its owner, bidding him good-bye in Spanish. Next, she loosed her long, raven-black tresses, allowing them to fall over her shoulders and graceful figure. When hangman "Big" Logan seemed unable to proceed, Josefa adjusted her hair to make room, then took the rope in her own hands and placed it around her neck.

A blindfold was fastened over her face and her hands tied behind her back. At each side of the plank stood a man, ax in hand, ready to cut the lashings. At six minutes to 4 o'clock, as a signal that she was ready, Josefa dropped a handkerchief she was holding in her hand. A pistol was fired, down came the axes to cut the ropes, the plank dropped and Josefa fell three or four feet to her death. Her body twisted in mid-air for twenty-two minutes before being lowered and given to friends, who buried it. Jack Cannon's remains were placed in an adjacent grave on the same day.

News of the hanging electrified the state. Indeed, many newspapers at first couldn't believe a woman had been hung, and denounced the story as a fiction. For six months afterwards, the morality of such an act would be debated in the prints. One paper would label it the "most savage and infamous deed ever yet committed in California."[16]

Defenders of the vigilante action called the murder of the peaceable Jack Cannon entirely unprovoked. One Downieville resident said those who had conducted the trial and execution of the murderess, Josefa, weren't "bloodthirsty monsters," but simply Americans "too magnanimous to admit any favoritism" in administering justice.

But many who witnessed the affair, like John S. Fowler, thought it a "blot upon the history of the state." It had reflected "infinite disgrace" upon all involved. Josefa—a "friendless and unprotected foreigner"[17]—he said, had been provoked by a man who persisted in making a disturbance in her house.

Of John Weller's failure to intercede in the hanging, one editor said: "Poor Josepha! [sic] of noble, though Mexican blood, neither you nor California owe the aspirant to Senatorial honors much gratitude!"[18] Weller's defenders held that his influence would not have availed in the least to save the condemned woman.

Weller weathered the storm of criticism and, six months later, was chosen by the California legislature to succeed John C. Frémont in the U.S. Senate. In 1858 he became California's governor. Two years later he was appointed by President Buchanan as minister to Mexico, but, being a pro-slavery Democrat, was recalled the following year by Lincoln. He was excoriated during the Civil War for his Copperhead tendencies, and was jailed for a time on Alcatraz Island for refusing to take an oath of allegiance to the Union.[19]

Like Josefa, William S. Spear, the Downieville lawyer who had prosecuted her, would meet a violent end. When gold was discovered in Nevada he went there, along with many other Californians, to try his hand. At the outbreak of the Paiute War of 1860, he joined a small armed force hurriedly thrown together by William Ormsby, of Carson City, bent on wreaking vengeance on the Indians. Ormsby and his men were soundly defeated near Pyramid Lake in May, and Spear was killed, along with some 46 other whites. His bleaching bones were discovered six months later.[20]

At Downieville, the bodies of Josefa and Jack Cannon lay, side-by-side, undisturbed, until about 1870, when the cemetery grounds were "mined off." At that time, so goes the story, someone stole Josefa's skull, and for years it was used as a prop in initiation ceremonies by a secret society.

Thus, perished the courageous and defiant Josefa. One old pioneer would come to recall how she had faced death with a bravery "that made us men ashamed." And, he lamented, "girls were so scarce in those days too."[21] Downieville has had to live with the memory of the incident, somewhat defensively, ever since.

Brother Jonathan

This next tale is about a notoriously unlucky Gold Rush steamship, recently in the news.

Traveling on the water in the early days of steam propulsion was a chancy business. Nowhere was this more apparent than on America's Pacific coast, following the 1848 discovery of gold in California. Whether at sea or on the rivers, ships collided with one another, were run onto rocks, caught fire, or "exploded through the reprehensible passion for racing, the inferior boiler material and the lack of efficient engineers."[1]

In just the first two years that fortune-seekers were carried between the Isthmus of Panama and San Francisco, eleven steamships were lost on that route. Further experience in Pacific waters didn't seem to help much, nor did the passage of a steam propulsion safety law. During the first half of 1854, for instance, there were sixty-four steamer calamities, involving a loss of 548 lives. Seventy souls perished when the boilers of the *Pearl* blew up during an 1855 race with another steamboat on San Francisco Bay. Another thirty persons were killed on the Bay, and many maimed—including that venerable California pioneer, John Bidwell—when the steamer *Belle* exploded.

The dangers of steamer travel were reflected in the songs of the era. "I Do Not Want To Be Drowned,"[2] was the title of a plaintive tune inspired by the escape of a lad named Addio Manchester from the burning wreck of the *Golden Gate* in 1862. A renowned comic actor of the day, "Yankee" Robinson, made light of the hazards in a jingle he sang from the stage of a San Francisco theater. Called "A Ripping Trip," and adapted to the tune, "Pop Goes the Weasel," the ditty began like this:

> You go aboard a leaky boat, and sail for San Francisco,
> You've got to pump to keep afloat, you have that by jingo!
> The engine soon begins to squeak, But nary a thing to oil her;
> Impossible to stop the leak—**Rip** goes the boiler![3]

Pacific waters were considerably more dangerous than those of the Atlantic, despite having generally better weather, and fewer shoals upon which to go aground. But the Pacific coast was, for the most part, poorly charted, and, up until 1856, there were only two lighthouses from San Francisco northward. Neither of these even had a light, however, until someone discovered two new Fresnel lanterns that had been sitting in a San Francisco warehouse for several years.

Safety was also lessened by the tendency of Western men of that era to be in a hurry. One observer—in noting how captains ran along, within gunshot of the coast, for hundreds of miles, just to gain a few hours time—blamed the practice on "an over-confidence—a kind of recklessness which leads men to run risks...in California, which they would never dream of doing elsewhere."[4]

Then too, in the rush to make fortunes, ship owners were often careless about the maintenance and seaworthiness of their ships. Albert Richardson, of the *New York Tribune*, wrote that when an inspection was to take place, the owners and officers often knew about it in advance, and they borrowed "hose, boats and other needful articles of outfit."[5]

It was a deadly combination of the above-named factors that led to one of the most tragic of calamities in Western waters—the grounding and loss of the steamship *Brother Jonathan*.

Today our remembrance of the expression has all but faded, but, before America had "Uncle Sam" as an enduring national symbol, we had "Brother Jonathan." George Washington first used the term in referring to

Brother Jonathan, M. D.

Uncle Sam: "Pesky little critters! What they need is a leetle o' this, I reckon!"¹

Brother Jonathan, as depicted in 1902, about the time the icon metamorphosed into Uncle Sam. (Author's Collection)

Jonathan Trumbull, governor of Connecticut. During the Revolutionary War, Washington depended heavily on Trumbull for material and moral support and, according to tradition, when faced with a difficult decision, he would say, "we must consult Brother Jonathan on the subject."⁶ Before long, "Brother Jonathan" came to personify the American nation.

Early political cartoons depict Jonathan as a tall, hawk-faced man, clothed in a suit adorned with stars and stripes. Eventually this homespun, anthropomorphic symbol of America would be transfigured into "Uncle Sam," but, in the mid-nineteenth century, "Brother Jonathan" was still very much a part of the American idiom. The name was bestowed on a variety of objects—

animate and inanimate—including the ship that is the subject of our story.

The ocean-going steamship *Brother Jonathan* was built in the shipyard of Perrine, Patterson and Stack at Williamsburg, New York, for Edward Mills. She was launched on November 2, 1850 and completed early in the following year. By today's standards, Mills' new steamer was a small one, displacing a mere 1,300 tons, with a 220-foot keel, a thirty-six foot beam and a draft of 14 feet. But, according to report, she was sturdily built of yellow pine and white oak, with a copper-fastened hull.

Propulsion was furnished by a 400-horsepower, 72-inch cylinder engine, of the walking-beam type, with an 11-foot stroke, driving two 33-foot diameter side paddle wheels. Steam for the engine came from two 12 by 28-foot coal-fired shell boilers. And—as was usual for a ship built in the days of transition from wind power to steam—*Jonathan* was also fitted-up as a sailing ship, with two masts, the forward of which was square-rigged. Her bow was ornamented with a carved billethead and trailboards, and her paddle wheel boxes and stern bore decorative gilded eagles.

As built, *Jonathan* had accommodations for 365 passengers, most of them in steerage. The main saloon—a general-purpose area used by cabin passengers—was on the level below the main deck, toward the stern. It measured 80 by 20 feet, and was decorated elegantly, with white and gold-painted paneling, a deck covered with bright, colorful oil-cloth carpeting, and furniture adorned with crimson cushions. On each side of the saloon were twelve staterooms.

Edward Mills expected to quickly recoup the $190,000 his ship had cost him, by using her to carry gold-fevered, California-bound passengers to Chagres on the Isthmus of Panama. In those earliest days of the Gold Rush, travelers crossed the Isthmus on foot, or by mule, to the Pacific side, where they took another ship to San Francisco.

Brother Jonathan was started on the New York to Chagres run at the end of March 1851, under Captain Charles Stoddard. In the beginning, there were some people who considered her to be one of the "fleetest packets on the Atlantic Coast."[7] But, from the outset, the ship was so beset with troubles that many others thought she was jinxed.

On her maiden voyage a paddle wheel was badly damaged; on the second outing she had to return to New York because of a broken engine crosshead; and on her sixth trip she struck and sunk a schooner off the coast of North Carolina. Perhaps *Jonathan's* hex—if such it was—had been transmitted, virus-like, when her builders installed, as her engine, one salvaged from the 1846 wreck of the Long Island Sound steamship *Atlantic*.

Despite the puffery in the press—customary in those days for any new

***Brother Jonathan* ca. 1851**
(*San Francisco Maritime National Historical Park*)

endeavor—the ship had been too poorly designed and fitted out to handle the large numbers of passengers the owner stuffed aboard her. There were frequent complaints about over-crowding and unsanitary conditions, and, during a November, 1851 return trip to New York, disease infiltrated the ship. One who survived that voyage described *Jonathan* as "...a moving pestilence, whose putrid carcass was strewn with the dead and the dying during the passage, and we happen to be spared, as monuments of God's mercy, to tell the tale."[8]

Sometime between August, 1851 and March, 1852—the record is confused as to just when—Mills sold his steamer to Cornelius Vanderbilt. "Commodore" Vanderbilt controlled the Nicaragua Line of steamers, as well as the Accessory Transit Company, which had been given a charter by the government of Nicaragua to run ships out of San Juan del Norte (Greytown), on the Atlantic coast, and San Juan del Sur on the Pacific. The company also had been given approval to build a canal and roads to transport passengers across the Nicaraguan Isthmus.

Initially, Vanderbilt ran *Brother Jonathan* between New York City and San Juan del Norte. But, in February, 1852, one of his Pacific coast steamers

—the *North America*—ran aground and was wrecked near Acapulco, Mexico, and *Jonathan* was chosen as her replacement.

Vanderbilt added superstructure decks to increase her passenger capacity to near 500, gave her a third mast—a fore and aft rigged mizzen—and then, on May 14, sent her off from New York to San Francisco under command of Captain C. H. Baldwin. For her 288 passengers, the boredom of the four-month voyage was broken only by the terrors of rounding Cape Horn, where relentless storms ultimately tore the ship's wheelhouse from its foundation and washed it overboard.[9]

Over the next few years, *Jonathan* ran regularly from San Francisco to Nicaragua, making a good profit, and with no further tribulations. Her advertised rates for the sea passage and Isthmus transit were: upper saloon, $275; main saloon, $220; lower cabin, $200; and steerage, $135.

In early 1853, Vanderbilt transferred a large part of his Nicaragua Line and Transit Company holdings to others, in return for bonds and a share of future profits, and the corporations were reorganized under new directors. In 1854, these new principals—Charles Morgan, William Garrison and C. K. Garrison—combined with the Pacific Mail Steamship Company to purchase the steamers of a competitor, the Independent Line, and they then conspired to set prices and ships' schedules.

This new monopolistic arrangement resulted in *Jonathan* being laid up at San Francisco in favor of larger, more seaworthy ships. Her final trip was made in October to San Diego, under Captain James H. Blethen, Jr., to retrieve survivors from the wreck of the steamer *Yankee Blade*, which had grounded on the coast of southern California.

Jonathan didn't make another voyage until March 1856, when she ran once to San Juan. Apparently she was to have begun regular service again, but, during her long period of inactivity, factors had come into play to prevent it.

First of all, a revolution had begun in Nicaragua, sustained by an American filibuster, William Walker, and a large force of mercenaries. Walker and his allies gained the upper hand in the conflict just about the time of *Jonathan's* intended resurrection, and, because of its failure to pay him a share of the profits, Walker revoked the Accessory Transit Company's charter, and seized its property in Nicaragua.

Added to this, Commodore Vanderbilt was waging a legal battle with the directors of the Nicaragua Line and the Transit Company, to regain control of his former shipping empire. By April, all of the companies' Pacific coast ships—*Jonathan, Uncle Sam, Cortez and Pacific*—were laid up at Vallejo, California, in possession of the U. S. Marshal for northern California.

Both Vanderbilt and his opponents had attached the ships, and the state of California was also trying to gain possession of them, arguing that, since they were within California waters when Walker's government revoked the company's charter, they had reverted by escheat to the state. A three-way legal duel continued until February, 1857, when the district court in San Francisco ruled in favor of Vanderbilt.

And so, after a long period in mothballs, *Brother Jonathan* was once again prepared for service. Perhaps to burnish her bad-luck image, she was given the new name, *Commodore*, an appellation no doubt meant to honor Vanderbilt.

But, as events proved, it would take more than a name change to rid the ship of bad *karma*. On February 25, 1857, as she was being brought from anchor to Pacific Wharf at San Francisco, a decayed wooden cathead, used to secure the anchor, gave way. The anchor let go with a run, the chain breaking the leg of one seaman, and causing another to be swept overboard and drowned.

In March, both *Commodore* and *Pacific* were sold to Captain John T. Wright, an independent operator doing business as the Merchant's Accommodation Line. Wright began running the two ships to Portland and other northern ports, offering reduced rates for freight and passengers.

Commodore's very first trip came near to proving fatal, she leaked so badly. And, when getting underway on April 11 for a second voyage, her lubberly commander, W. H. Fauntleroy, ran her into the sailing ship *Alexander*, damaging a paddle wheel housing. Then, for about ten months she ran without incident, carrying passengers, farm products and other freight.

Command was given, in February, 1858, to Captain George W. Staples, a competent sailor who had previously been skipper of the *Pacific*. Due to increased competition from the Pacific Mail Steamship Company, *Commodore* had been running less frequently during the winter, but with spring came the discovery of gold along the Fraser River in British Columbia. The ensuing boom led shipping companies to put every vessel they could spare—seaworthy or not—into the northern service. *Commodore* had the distinction of being the first ship to reach Victoria, B. C. with American miners, debarking 450 passengers on April 25, 1858.[10]

During the peak of this Canadian gold excitement, the steamers running northward were often grossly overloaded, and *Commodore* was no exception, though the much-neglected steamer was by then regarded as a second-rate affair. She stopped at nearly every port along the route—Mendocino, Trinidad, Crescent City, Victoria, Port Townsend, Nanaimo—carrying freight and a class of less-affluent passengers.

Commodore had barely gotten started in this flourishing service, when, in May, Captain Staples ran her onto a rock in Puget Sound. He had the ship patched up enough to limp back to San Francisco Bay, where John Wright had her dry-docked at Mare Island for hurried repairs. However, despite a San Francisco newspaper having warned that she was unseaworthy, avarice prevailed and the ship was underway just four days later.

Two more trips were made after the dry-docking without incident, but the third voyage was a near-disaster. *Commodore* sailed for Victoria on the afternoon of Thursday, July 8, 1858, heavily laden with freight and over 400 passengers, many of whom were required to sleep on deck. These people, as one newspaper observed, had become "so desperately reckless," excited as they were by the gold reports, "that they would doubtless have taken passage on a paper ship, had one been advertised."[11]

By the time Cape Mendocino was reached, on Saturday afternoon, strong winds from the northwest were blowing and seas were rising. Staples knew that the side-wheeler's shallow draft and high center of gravity made her quite unstable in heavy weather, so, as a precaution, he had everything topside battened down, and the lifeboats re-positioned for easier access.

Conditions continued to worsen and, when Sunday morning dawned, the winds had reached gale force, causing *Commodore* to labor heavily and become nearly unmanageable. Captain Staples ordered the storm trysail close-reefed, to help keep the ship into the wind, while he worked her inshore as much as possible.

At noon, there was a bit of a lull in the wind, but the seas were much higher, and had burst in several of the running lights. At 5 P.M. the wind picked up again, blowing fiercely and more westerly. By now the seas were breaking against the side of the ship with tremendous force; water was pouring across the main deck, and the hull had begun to hog and sag severely. At 10:50 P.M., a heavy lurch caused a leak in a boiler, but not enough to disable it.

Just after midnight, as Monday began, the wind increased to a perfect hurricane. The engine and trysail together were barely able to keep the ship from falling off into the trough of the frightful sea. By 2 A.M., *Commodore* was almost entirely at the mercy of the waves, and straining terribly under her heavy burden of freight. The boilers were displaced from side to side with each roll, and the hull was beginning to leak. With water rising in the bilges, the pumps were started, but the main steam-driven unit only worked a short time before clogging up with fine coal.

Within another 30 minutes, a crack appeared in a flange of the main steam pipe, causing a major leak. Soon after this, the entire bilge piping system became plugged with coal dust, rendering all pumps useless, except for several portable, hand-operated units. With the water rising ever closer to the boiler fires, the passengers were formed into gangs and put to work with buckets, bailing from the fireroom and forward steerage.

By five A.M. the ship had become altogether unmanageable and was lying helpless in the trough with the gunwales nearly underwater. To save her, Staples decided he must lighten ship, so he ordered the crew and passengers to begin throwing the cargo overboard. First to go was the deck load, which included some twenty horses, by now frantically apprehensive.

As he was being led to the deck's edge, one fine bay broke loose from the man holding him and plunged overboard. As another of the horses was being led out, its owner stepped up to Capt. Staples and with tears in his eyes, said that the animal was all he owned in the world, and that it provided the livelihood for himself and family. The softhearted captain ordered the horse to be retained, saying that if he, Staples, could manage to save the ship, the horse would be saved also.

After most of the deck load was disposed of, the forward and after cargo hatches were opened, and over the side went sacks of flour, kegs of nails and, finally, even the passengers' trunks. A few of the owners personally tossed their luggage overboard, jokingly declaring that they would begin life afresh.

Shortly after sunrise, enough cargo had been removed from the forward hold to allow the rigging of whips and barrels for bailing. But, by this time, the water had reached the firebox of the lee boiler and extinguished its fires. There was now much alarm, but passengers and crew alike were kept busy at the tasks of bailing and getting rid of more freight, leaving no time to panic. In all 500 tons of cargo were jettisoned.

Commodore was then just a bit south of Crescent City, California, but Staples didn't think he could reach that port safely. With the wind so fierce, and the ship so unmanageable, he thought it surely would have been dashed to pieces on the rocks. He had tried several times to turn downwind, but had failed, tearing the topsail to tatters in the process. Thus, he had no choice but to try and weather the storm offshore.

In mid-morning the steamer *Orizaba* was sighted, bound southward, and a distress flare was sent up, but, the weather being hazy, the signal was not noticed. When, as a precaution, Staples ordered the lifeboats readied, several passengers stood alongside them, with pistols and rifles, prepared to shoot the first officer who might attempt to desert the ship.

At about 2:30 P.M. another effort was made to get the steamer before the wind. As the passengers would later tell it, one of their number, an experienced Russian sailor, was given the helm and, taking advantage of a rising wave, he made *Commodore* spin round like a top. After the ship's head was turned, all danger vanished, and she made for San Francisco, "flying before the wind like a race horse,"[12] the passengers bailing and pumping most of the way. The horse that had jumped overboard at 6 A.M. was passed at 4 P.M., still swimming.

The hapless ship limped into port in the wee hours of July 14. The passengers, who considered their escape from death almost miraculous, immediately set about venting their wrath upon the owner, Captain Wright, for his "wanton trifling with human life by overloading a vessel notoriously unfit." At sunrise, Pacific Wharf was crowded with excited passengers and their friends—many of them tough miners—damming his name. When Wright came down on the wharf, about 10 A.M., they surrounded his carriage and demanded a return of their passage money. Wright's answer being unsatisfactory, they hauled him out onto the street, dragged him on board *Commodore*, and, with drawn revolvers, threatened vengeance unless he disgorged the cash.

To cries of "Hang him! hang him!," Wright broke loose and fled to the safety of a cabin. There he remained until San Francisco's chief of police arrived on the scene to restore order and help resolve the matter. Finally, after promising to refund the passage money, Wright was allowed to come out. Encircled by the crowd, he coolly marched to his office on Sacramento Street where, by noon, he began repaying $12,500 in fares to passengers.

Afterward, the passengers published a "card" in the newspapers labeling *Commodore* an "unseaworthy, floating coffin,"[13] and calling attention to the faulty pumps and the overloading. The card contained words of praise, however, for George Staples and his officers, as well as those passengers and seamen who had promptly and efficiently executed Staples' orders.

The editor of Portland's *Oregon Weekly Times* was cynical about any hope for improvement in the steamer's condition. Said he:

> So the Commodore is again laid up for lamp-black and putty, and soon we shall hear of the rotten unseaworthy craft going down forever and carrying with her a few hundred souls...[14]

This near-calamitous voyage would be *Commodore's* last for Captain Wright's Merchant Accommodation Line. The ship was sold, in December 1858, to the California Steam Navigation Company for $40,000. She was given a brief, cosmetic overhaul, which included installation of some iron bolts to strengthen the hull, and the now-tarnished name, *Commodore*, was discarded in favor of the original one, *Brother Jonathan*—only slightly more respectable. George Staples was retained as her commander, and she continued in the northern service.

On her first voyage, in this latest incarnation, she arrived at Portland on March 15, 1859, via Crescent City, carrying the welcome tidings of Oregon's admission to the Union. An advertisement appeared in Portland attesting that the ship had been "thoroughly refitted," was "now in perfect order, and not surpassed by any ship on the coast."[15]

In 1860, Samuel J. Hensley, an official of the California Steam Navigation Company, bought *Brother Jonathan* and *Pacific*, and formed the Oregon and San Diego Steamship Company. He ran *Jonathan* for several months and then, in March, 1861, started her through a lengthy overhaul at John G. North's San Francisco shipyard at Steamship Point, beyond Mission Rock.

With one of Hensley's captains, Aaron M. Burns, in charge of the work, the ship was hauled out of the water and the hull almost totally rebuilt, using timber from Port Orford, Oregon. Of the framework, only the diagonal iron braces, the keel and those bottom timbers which were deemed to be sound were retained. Two solid new bilge keelsons were installed. Thinking it would increase the ship's speed, the bow was changed so as to reduce its flare. Two modern Martin patent tubular boilers were installed, each with six furnaces, but the old walking-beam engine was retained.

The ship's entire interior and upper works were also made new. One of her two superstructure decks was removed, and a new 120-foot long saloon was built on the remaining one. Accommodations were provided for total of 350 passengers, in cabin and steerage. The saloon on the main deck was converted to carry freight, increasing cargo capacity to 900 tons.

Two months into the overhaul, the editor of the *Alta California* wrote enthusiastically about this first attempt to rebuild a seagoing ship on the Pacific Coast. He declared that not two ships in California had as strong a bottom as *Jonathan's*, and he recommended that his readers take a buggy ride out to the shipyard, to see the steamer, "looking for all the world like the skeleton of some antediluvian...mastodon."[16]

With *Jonathan* drydocked for a lengthy overhaul, Captain George W. Staples was once again given command of the company's steamer *Pacific*, which also ran on the route north of San Francisco. In light of what befell him in this new assignment, one could posit that perhaps the 37-year old captain had been infected with the *Jonathan* hex.

On October 4, 1861, Staples brought *Pacific* up the Columbia and

Willamette rivers and tied her up at Couch and Flander's wharf in Portland. The return trip to San Francisco was to be his last voyage as skipper of a passenger steamer, inasmuch as he had received a commander's commission in the United States Navy, and was eager to go East, join in the nascent Civil War, and find himself some Rebels to fight.

Pacific was to sail in the early hours of October 11. Prominent among its scheduled passengers were the ship's owner, Samuel Hensley, and Oregon Senator James Nesmith, the latter of whom was returning to Washington, D. C. with his family. On the evening of the tenth, Portland citizens fired gun salutes to honor both Nesmith and the popular Captain Staples.

Afterward, the captain joined a number of his old friends, and some of *Pacific's* passengers, at the bar of the Bank Exchange to do some serious drinking. As midnight approached, most everyone in the saloon was thoroughly soused, bellowing out patriotic songs and making toasts to "Old Abe" Lincoln and the Union.

As it happened, there was also in the bar a certain roughneck gambler from The Dalles, Oregon, named Ferd Patterson—he being of Southern persuasion—who was overheard to be damning the Union and its supporters. One of Captain Staples friends, a certain Mr. Dodge, took umbrage at Patterson's grumbling and asked the gambler, reprovingly, if he were a Secessionist. Patterson quietly replied that he had no desire to talk to Dodge on that subject.

But Dodge persisted, bragging that he, himself, was a good Union man. In response to this Patterson coldly instructed Dodge to "shove your Union up _____."[17] Dodge retorted with the same expression, substituting the word "secession" for " Union."

Inevitably, Dodge got the fight he was seeking. Patterson struck him with fist and cane, and then the two men scurried to opposite ends the bar and began throwing glasses, soda bottles, decanters—everything not fastened down—at one other. Captain Staples—said to be a "powerful and fearless man"—intervened by grabbing Patterson by the collar, and calmly asking him what was going on. Just as calmly, Patterson told the captain that it was none of his damned business.

Staples and Dodge, with most of the men in the bar helping them, forced Patterson into the back room, all the while calling him a "damned Secessionist," and howling "Kill him." Patterson was cornered for several minutes, but one of his friends opened the back door, allowing him to run out onto the wharf and disappear.

Their game having bolted, Dodge, Staples and some of the others went down to the steamer for a while, but, at 2. A.M.—being restless—they came ashore again for a few more drinks and songs. Unhappily, they chose the bar at the Pioneer Hotel, on Front and Washington streets, the place where Ferd Patterson was living.

When Staples' group enter the bar, they found Patterson there, drinking quietly and minding his own business. Arrogantly, Dodge renewed the argument, causing Patterson's anger to quickly resurface. The gambler made a move to draw his navy Colt revolver, but Staples laid his hand on the man's shoulder and told him not to do it. He insisted that Patterson and Dodge should, instead, remove their coats and have a fair fist fight.

Patterson said that was not his way of fighting and, seeking to end the business, he left the bar to go upstairs to his room. But, seeing that he was being followed by Dodge, Staples and about ten other men, the gambler ran up the two flights of stairs, firing warning shots as he neared the top. He yelled down to his pursuers, who had halted on the first landing, that he was not going to be mobbed, and would stand his ground and shoot the first man to come up any farther.

S. N. Arrigoni, the proprietor of the hotel, came out, talked to Patterson and got him to agree to go quietly to his room, subject to his pursuers leaving him alone. Arrigoni went down and told the mob of this, and asked them to back off and commit no violence.

But, Arrigoni's pleas were to no avail. Dodge, Staples and the others were still in full cry, drunk and awash in patriotic fervor, and they refused to let up. Dodge—the most clamorous—grabbed the hotelier by the lapels and hooted with delight that he was going to "kill that secessionist son of a bitch, and you a sympathizer with him."[18]

Foolishly, Captain Staples said—referring to Patterson—"Get me a pistol and a candle, and I will arrest him!" A certain O. B. Brown got a light, and another fellow handed Staples a pistol, but a few men with clearer heads tried to hold the captain back. Undeterred, however, up the stairs he went. He had only taken a step or two when Patterson fired three shots, one of them ripping a fatal wound in Staples' gut. Thickly, Staples said, "I am shot," and told Brown to "take the pistol and arrest the fellow."[19] Brown, instead, went to find a doctor.

Within minutes, Sheriff Addison M. Starr arrived and found Ferd Patterson hiding in a privy on the second story balcony, where he was arrested without further trouble. But the ringing of Portland's fire bell drew an immense crowd of citizens who clamored for an immediate hanging. Starr was obliged to procure a cannon and plant in it front of the jail, and make earnest appeals to the crowd, assuring them that Patterson wouldn't escape.

Captain Staples died on the morning of October 12 at the hotel, his ship having sailed without him, under command of First Officer Samuel De Wolf. For two days the flags in Portland, and on the ships in the river, were flown at half-staff out of respect for the captain. Patterson was released on bail, and was tried at the next session of the circuit court. His three lawyers made a convincing case of self-defense, and the jury pondered only a short time before pronouncing him not guilty.

After his release, Patterson went to Idaho, where he killed, in cold blood, Sumner Pinkham, a former sheriff of Boise County. He was also acquitted of that crime by reason of self-defense—his friends testifying for him—and with the congratulations of the judge, was discharged. Fearing reprisal, Patterson left for Walla Walla, and there, while sitting in a barber chair, he was gunned down by a double-barreled shotgun in the hands of a former Portland policeman whom Patterson had threatened at the time of the Staples murder.[20]

A few months after the Staples assassination, on the morning of December 14, 1861, the rejuvenated *Brother Jonathan* was taken out to the Farallon Islands for sea trials under command of Captain Aaron Burns. Owner Sam Hensley invited a group of prominent men to take the cruise. After returning to San Francisco Bay for a festive luncheon, Burns personally took the wheel to race his ship against the Sacramento steamer, *New World*. Making about 18 knots, *Jonathan* easily won the dash between Alcatraz and Angel islands.

The steamer was put back to work on the San Francisco-Portland-Victoria run, with an occasional trip to San Luis Obispo and San Diego. Advertisements declared her to be a "new and splendid steamship" built expressly for the northern route "with unequaled accommodations for passengers and freight." One Oregon editor proclaimed that she was "one of the staunchest vessels on the coast."[21]

Hensley figured he had the enormous sum of $100,000 invested in the ship, but there was plenty of business to be had, thanks to Civil War traffic and new gold discoveries in the region that would become northern Idaho. *Jonathan* was kept running on a regular schedule, carrying troops, miners, and substantial cargos of freight and agricultural products. By now, however, there were more ships running on the route, Ben Holladay and others having formed the California and Oregon Steamship Line.

Captain Burns commanded the steamer for its first two runs, but, on the second of these, in January, he got her stuck in the ice of the Columbia River, just below St. Helens. One of the stranded passengers—a newlywed who was anxious to get back to his bride in San Francisco—wrote a friend that the ice

***Brother Jonathan* after 1861 refit**
(*Author's Collection*)

was seven inches thick, and that everyone expected "to get away sometime between now and the Fourth of July next." It was necessary to go to bed at dark, since the coal oil and candles were all used up; the provisions were expected to give out soon, requiring that rations be reduced to "three baked apples and two ounces of beans per day," taken from the cargo.[22] Over two weeks passed before a thaw arrived and released the ship.

Perhaps because of this incident, Burns was replaced by a new commander, Samuel J. De Wolf, who had been running the steamer *Pacific* since Captain Staples' death four months earlier. The new captain, 37 years of age, was a competent and sober seaman with twelve years of Pacific coast experience.[23]

During the first years of Captain De Wolf's tenure, *Brother Jonathan* seemed to have shaken off her old gremlins. The only trouble of note had been the discovery, in the fall of 1863, that the first mate was smuggling opium between Victoria and San Francisco, for which he was dismissed.

In January and February 1864, extensive modifications were made to increase passenger accommodations. A new hurricane (upper) deck was installed along the full length of the ship, and a tier of rooms built into it. On the main deck, arrangements were provided for steerage passengers.

Captain Samuel De Wolf
(*Author's Collection*)

The ship made one trip after this refit under the ownership of Samuel Hensley, and then, in March, she and Hensley's other ships—*Senator* and *Pacific*—were sold or reverted back to the California Steam Navigation Company. Captain De Wolf was retained as commander.[24]

Business to Portland was sustained by a rush toward more gold discoveries, this time in southern Idaho. On one trip *Jonathan* took 800 passengers north; on another, in October 1864, she carried over a million dollars in gold and coin for Wells-Fargo and others, the largest shipment of treasure that had ever left Portland in a single ship.[25]

But, on that same trip, the steamer's bad luck suddenly returned. At Esquimalt, a man slipped from the gangplank and drowned. Another man—said to be deranged—fell overboard and drowned at the mouth of the Willamette River, just as the anchor was being hoisted for the return voyage to San Francisco. In December, at Portland, a strong current parted the ship's stern lines and tore out some cleats, nearly setting her adrift. Then, a few weeks later, her pilothouse and starboard paddle wheel housing were damaged in heavy seas encountered while approaching the bar of the Columbia River.

San Francisco waterfront, 1863. Brother Jonathan is at top center.
(San Francisco Maritime National Historical Park)

After this, *Jonathan* remained free of trouble for half a year, but this would prove a mere respite while the dreaded Fate, Atropos, sharpened her scissors.

The end came in July, 1865.
It began, ominously enough, in mid-month when *Jonathan* collided with the barkentine *Jane A. Falkenberg* on the Columbia River. The sailing ship was bound upstream at the time, against a strong current, and *Jonathan* was passing down under a good head of steam, making the crash a stunning one.

Falkenberg required extensive repairs, including replacement of her bowsprit and foremast, while *Jonathan* was reported to have been only stove in "somewhat" above the waterline. Since the steamer was scheduled for another trip from San Francisco on the twenty-sixth, the damage was hurriedly repaired at Astoria, allowing her to return to California in time to depart only two days late.[26]

As is usual with sailings, the mood was festive when *Jonathan* got underway at 10 A.M. on Friday, July 28, and steamed through the Golden Gate, bound for Portland and British Columbia. In a register, which was later found on his body, the purser recorded the presence aboard of 195 souls—a crew of 55, and 140 passengers, fifteen of them children. A few of the voyagers had jumped on and bought their tickets at the last moment.

They were a typical group of Westerners—miners, politicians, housewives, businessmen, civil servants, laborers, soldiers—with all of the usual human hopes and fears, longings and ambitions. While most of them were accustomed to the hardships and quirks of nineteenth-century life, it is likely that none of them dared think they had just booked passage to an ocean grave.

Several had lived through previous hair-raising steamship experiences. A few years before, George W. Pollock, a bookstore owner, had survived a boiler explosion on the riverboat *Washoe*. And, earlier in this very year, Victor Smith—the collector of customs at Puget Sound—had been aboard the *Golden Rule*, when she was wrecked on a reef near Aspinwall, Panama. No thanks to the ship's drunken officers, everyone aboard had been saved, but Smith had lost all his possessions, as well as a government safe in his charge containing a million dollars. The collector had planned to take an earlier steamer onward to Portland, but illness, caused by exposure during his *Golden Rule* ordeal, had required that he wait for *Brother Jonathan*.[27]

One group of passengers, at least—the family of Captain N. C. Brooks—was quite accustomed to a nautical regimen. Mrs. Brooks and her children were returning to Portland to resume their home life with Brooks aboard his ship, the *Cambridge*. They had been visiting her father in California.

Several well-known personages were aboard. Anson G. Henry was en route to assume the governorship of Washington Territory, having been appointed to the post by his friend, Abraham Lincoln, just before the latter had been assassinated.

Captain John Chaddock of the U. S. Revenue Service was returning to his duties at Puget Sound, and an Army paymaster, Major E. W. Eddy, was making one of his occasional trips to Fort Vancouver to pay the troops in the area. James Nisbet, distinguished editor and part owner of the *San Francisco Bulletin* was traveling to Victoria to obtain testimony in a lawsuit he had brought against the *San Francisco Chronicle* for alleged libel.

At the lower end of the shipboard social spectrum was Mrs. John C. Keenan, the keeper of a beer saloon at Victoria. She had no doubt sparked a great deal of comment when she boarded with seven "ladies" under her charge, none of whose name was given on the passenger list. Rumor had it that Keenan was also madam of a whorehouse, and that these girls, whom she had hired as "waitresses," were intended to satisfy the lustful appetites of British Columbia miners. One of the girls—sixteen year old Martha Wilder

> **FOR PORTLAND AND VICTORIA**
>
> The California Steam Naviga-
> tion Company's Steamship
>
> **Brother Jonathan,**
>
> S. J. DE WOLF .... Commander.
> **Will leave Broadway Wharf,**
> **FOR THE ABOVE PORTS,**
> **ON FRIDAY,** .... **JULY 28, 1865,**
> **AT 10 O'CLOCK A. M.**
>
> Bills of lading will be furnished to shippers, and some others signed.
> For freight or passage apply on board, or at the office of the California Steam Navigation Company on the northeast corner Front and Jackson streets.
> Jy22   **J. WHITNEY. Jr., President.**

**Advertisement for *Brother Jonathan's*
final voyage.** (*Author's Collection*)

—would later say that Keenan had engaged her to be a nanny in Victoria, and she was unaware, until after *Jonathan* had sailed, that it was intended she become a waitress in the saloon.[28]

Perhaps *Brother Jonathan's* most renowned passenger on this voyage was Brigadier General George Wright, a flinty soldier from Vermont, who had served his country well for forty-three years.

In a sense, it could be said that George Wright was a typical American "Brother Jonathan." He was not a large man, but had a masculine, dignified appearance and was universally admired for his gentlemanly traits, geniality, and keen sense of humor. As a youngster, Wright had been infused with all of those precepts of honor, integrity, and a reverence for God that Americans have long held in esteem. His forebears were pioneer settlers of Connecticut, some of whom had fought in the Revolution and the War of 1812.

George had entered the Military Academy at West Point at the unripe age of fourteen, and graduated in 1822 with one of the first classes to come under a new system of strict discipline and honor. At the start of his career,

America's small peacetime army had comprised only seven regiments of infantry. The young subaltern served on the western frontier during the ensuing years, working his way slowly through the commissioned grades.

While on duty at Fort Leavenworth, Kansas, he had married Margaret Wallace Forster, and started a family. A first child, Thomas, was born in 1830; a daughter, Eliza, in 1837 and a third youngster, John, had come in 1839.

Wright had first displayed his gallant spirit during the Mexican War, winning commendations and brevet promotions for his part in capturing Vera Cruz, Cerro Gordo, and Contreras. At Molino del Rey, he was wounded while leading a costly assault against the center of the Mexican position.

But George Wright was best known for his service in the far West. In the summer of 1852, he came by sea to the Pacific coast, and never left it again. As colonel of the Ninth Infantry Regiment, he was largely responsible for effecting a peaceful conclusion to the 1855 war with the Yakima Indians, which had been mostly caused by the ineptitude of the governors of Oregon and Washington.

Then, in the spring of 1858, the lawless actions of Oregon volunteer soldiers toward the tribes of the Northwest had led to another general Indian war, which had begun with an attack upon a peaceful army column, traveling in eastern Washington Territory, under command of Bvt. Colonel Edward J. Steptoe of Wright's regiment.

Feeling betrayed by the Indian chiefs who had made him promises during the preceding two years, Colonel Wright that summer exacted a terrible retribution for the Steptoe incident. Marching with a seven-hundred man force from Fort Walla Walla, in two successive and lengthy engagements near present-day Spokane, he soundly defeated a large force of Spokanes, Coeur d'Alenes, and Palouses without the loss of a single soldier.

Then, the colonel determinedly marched from one tribe to the next, forcing submission. A band of 800 horses was captured and destroyed, and sixteen natives were summarily hung, whom drumhead courts determined had been involved either in the Steptoe affair, or in the murders of several miners. None of the tribes that Wright dealt with subsequently raised a hostile gun, and the interior was opened for settlement.[29]

But despite his severity in dealing with the inland tribes, George Wright, like most regular army officers, was generally fair and even-handed in his dealings with Native Americans. Because of his beliefs, in fact, he had often been accused of coddling them. In one instance, he asked that Washington's governor pardon an accused chief, since several white volunteer soldiers had gone unpunished for their savage deeds. Said Wright: "Let impartial justice

Brig. Gen. George Wright
(*Nevada Historical Society*)

be meted out to both parties, or cast oblivion over all."[30]

When our great Civil War came, George Wright had been denied an opportunity to fight in the East, due to his age and the internecine workings of army politics. Also, to his great disappointment, he had been denied further promotion in the regular army. Instead, he was made a brigadier-general of volunteers and given command of the vast Department of the Pacific, embracing all of the states and territories west of the Rockies.

For three years, Wright's domain had included sixty military installations and some 5,000 troops, whose main job was to protect the citizenry, the overland mail and the telegraph from hostile Indians. The brigadier also had responsibility for dealing with periodic Confederate plots—both real and imagined—in a region largely populated by former Southerners, sympathetic to the Secessionist cause.

The general's biggest problem, however, had been in fending off radical Unionists. He had been given broad authority to suspend habeas corpus, and certain other civil liberties, and because he had only used these powers sparingly, he was severely criticized by the extremists. Wright, however, had had no desire to fill his forts with political prisoners, believing that such a policy would have led to a great deal of strife and bloodshed.

Brigadier Wright had been relieved of the Pacific command in mid-1864 by Major General Irvin McDowell, and he had served since then, under McDowell, as commander of the District of California, headquartered at Sacramento. Now, with the reduction of forces at war's end, he had been superseded by McDowell as California commander, and was taking passage northward in *Brother Jonathan* to assume command of the Department of Columbia at Fort Vancouver, Washington Territory.

The new assignment was perhaps welcome to the general and his wife Margaret, at this stage of their lives. They had many old friends in the area, and their daughter, Eliza, was married to Colonel Philip A. Owen, who commanded at Fort Vancouver.

General Wright's final weeks in Sacramento had been busy with official duties. At high noon, June 16, he had stood at the head of a contingent of troops at Camp Union to witness the hanging of a California cavalryman, who had murdered his lieutenant, after that officer had ordered him on the double-quick to sober him up.

Soon after this, the general helped entertain the Speaker of the House of Representatives, Schuyler Colfax, who was touring the West. On Independence Day, Wright had ridden in a parade, participated in the exercises at the Pavilion, and dined with members of the Pioneer Association at the Concert Hall on K Street. Here, a toast to "The Army and Navy" was responded to by Wright in a patriotic speech, which recalled the tension two years earlier when news was awaited of Grant's capture of Vicksburg.

The departing general was also honored at a dinner hosted by Governor Frederick F. Low, Leland Stanford and other dignitaries, and then, on July 26, he and Margaret, along with their retinue—an aide, Lt. Edward D. Waite; an orderly, Leach; a horse and a Newfoundland dog—had come to San Francisco in preparation for the departure of *Brother Jonathan*. In that pleasant custom of the era, the general had been serenaded by friends, on the evening of the twenty-seventh, at his rooms in the Occidental Hotel.[31]

As *Brother Jonathan* worked her way northward along the California coast, events began to unfold in a manner eerily reminiscent of that earlier, near-disastrous voyage of July, 1858. The month was the same, and, just as in that previous fiasco, *Jonathan* had once again been damaged and quickly repaired in order to keep a commitment. And, now, as she drew near

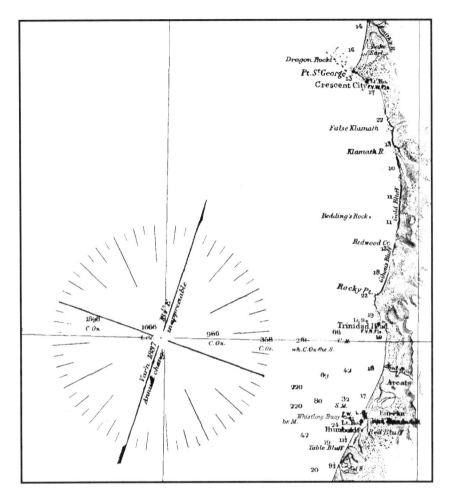

Northern California coast as shown on 1865 nautical chart.
(*Author's Collection*)

Crescent City, the locale of that previous trouble, a menacing storm began blowing, as before, square into her teeth.

By the morning of the third day, Sunday July 30, the wind was shrieking at near gale force through the standing rigging. Many passengers lay sick in their berths, and less than half felt well enough to take breakfast. It has been stated that a stop was made in Crescent City between 2 and 9:30 A.M., but there is no mention of it in any contemporary account, and one resident of Crescent

City would later recall that *Jonathan* gave her usual one-gun salute when passing that place about at mid day.

At local apparent noon, Captain De Wolf measured the sun's elevation and calculated his ship's latitude to be about four miles north of that of Point St. George. Seaman Jacob Gates, who had just taken over at the helm, described the sea at that time as running "mountain high."[32]

Seeing that little headway was being made, at 12:45 P.M., De Wolf decided to turn the steamer and run for Crescent City harbor, about sixteen miles to the southeast, where he could anchor until the wind subsided. Accordingly, he ordered the helm hard over, and the jib was set to help bring her around to the proper heading.

Lying between De Wolf and Crescent City is an extensive hazard, named St. George Reef, which extends northwestward from Point St. George for some six miles. A series of rocks rise sharply from the ocean bed, a dozen or so of which are large and visible, and several others that are usually either entirely under water or awash. At the time, this area of the coast had never been sounded in detail, but the superintendent of a cursory survey done in 1862 reported the reef's rocks to be "of a peculiar character, standing isolated like bayonets, with their points just below the surface..."[33]

A clear passage—St. George Channel—runs between the outlying impediments and those farther inshore. Another passage, now called Dragon Channel, approaches Crescent City along the southwest edge of the danger area, but to use it, a ship must be threaded through several of the occasionally submerged ledges. This latter path is the one De Wolf chose to take when, upon reaching tiny Northwest Seal Rock, he ordered a course of southeast by south.

Given his lengthy experience sailing along this coast, Captain De Wolf was surely familiar with the waters which lay inshore of the usual steamer coastal route, and, in particular, with the hazards of St. George Reef. And, he had commanded ships making frequent stops at Crescent City.

Visibility was somewhat obscured by smoke from forest fires burning along the coast but, despite this haze, De Wolf undoubtedly could have seen Castle Rock, and other large landmarks, as he approached the shore. A lighthouse had existed since 1856 at the northern tip of Crescent City Harbor, but the record is blank as to whether it was in operation that day.

Apparently, what De Wolf didn't realize—or chose to ignore—is that the tide might have covered the particular rock that was to be his undoing, or that the heavy seas might prevent its being seen. Now called Jonathan Rock, this ledge rises abruptly 190 feet from the sea floor, and, even at lower tides, only projects about three to six feet above the surface.

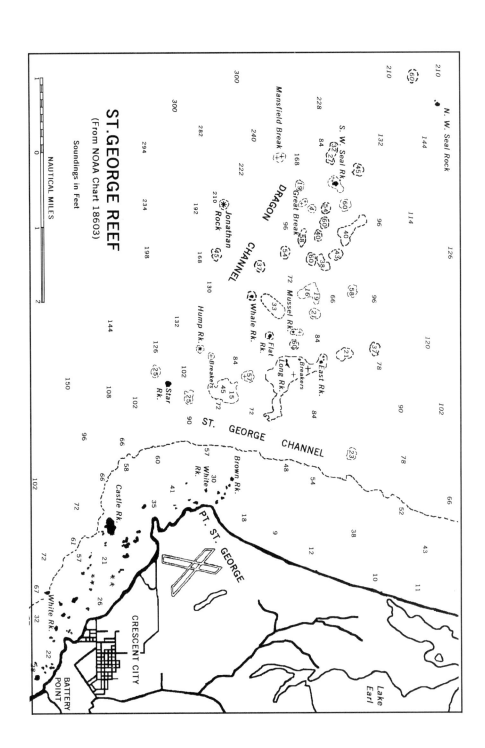

Some forty minutes after having changed course toward Crescent City, and when about four miles nearly due west of Point St. George, *Jonathan* struck this submerged pinnacle, with full force. So great was the impact that many people were knocked off their feet, and some of the ship's deck planks were badly skewed out of place. The jolt threw Mary Ann Tweesdale, an aged English lady, under the feet of General Wright's horse that was tethered on the main deck

Captain De Wolf stopped the engine and tried to back the ship off, but she was pinned securely, and would not budge. Mrs. Martha Scott, feeling a bit queasy after lunch, had remained on the hurricane deck, in company with her six-year old son and Mrs. Keenan's prospective young barmaid, Martha Wilder. They overheard another passenger remark to the captain that they would have a pretty rough time, at which De Wolf smiled, and said, "I guess it will be all right."[34] But, an instant afterward, he received a report that the boiler fires had all been extinguished by in-rushing waters.

Jonathan rolled for a few more minutes, her head slewing around until it came into the wind and sea. She worked off a little, then rose on a huge swell and came down with tremendous force onto the rock, tearing a large hole in the keel at the point where the foremast was stepped. With a terrible crash, the mast dropped right through the bottom, its yard coming to rest across the promenade deck. Simultaneously, the ship's rudder was torn loose.

Mrs. Nina Bernhardt, the widow of a Philadelphia printer, was bound for Seattle to start up a German newspaper. She had been lying sick in her berth, when she felt the fearful shock of grounding. This was followed by a laboring of the ship, a creaking of her timbers, and the distant roar of rushing waters.

Bernhardt sprang to a porthole and looked out to see pieces of rudder and keel come floating to the surface. Next, she noticed a man wearing a life preserver scurrying up a ladder to the hurricane deck. Now fully awakened to the danger, and her seasickness forgotten, she seized her two-year old son, Paul, with one hand, and a life preserver with the other, and ran out on deck. Other women—still in their nightclothes—were rushing from their rooms, their hair hanging loosely about them, and their faces pallid as death.

Just a few minutes prior to the grounding, the third mate, James Patterson, had been relieved as officer of the watch by the second officer, and had gone below. He had barely reached his bunk when the steamer struck. After a brief struggle to wrest open the door of his cabin, which had been sprung by the impact, Patterson raced back on deck just in time to see the foremast fall.

The ship remained pinned, swinging at the mercy of the waves, and settling by the bow. Seeing that she must surely sink, Captain De Wolf walked forward, ordering everyone aft, telling them to "look out for themselves, and he would do the best he could for them all."[35] He then ordered the boats to be manned, their plugs put in, and women and children to be loaded. In those days there were no lifeboat drills, nor even any instructions posted in living areas, directing passengers how to act in cases of imminent peril.

Jonathan had more than enough lifeboats—three of the Francis patent type and three surf boats, capable altogether of holding 250 people. But only three of these were routinely slung from the davits, located aft of the paddle wheels, ready for lowering. One of the large surf boats, on the port side, was the responsibility of first officer, W. A. Allen. Another, the forward most on the starboard side, was in charge of second officer J. A. Campbell. Third Officer James Patterson's boat—the smallest on the ship, but a Francis lifeboat—was rigged in the set of davits just aft of Campbell's.

It would later be stated that everything possible was done by officers, crew and male passengers to save the ladies, but that many of them were too sick in their cabins to be able to come on deck. Some who did come out could see that no boat could survive in such a sea, and they chose to remain on deck and face death there. Still other women, sobbing and crying, clung to their husbands, until forced from them to be thrown into a boat.

David Farrell was a steward for the steerage passengers, whose cabins were on the main deck, and his abandon ship station was as a crewman of Patterson's lifeboat. According to Farrell, Captain De Wolf—who was then standing on the hurricane deck just aft of the wheelhouse—told him to stay in the boat, keep men out of it, and load as many women as would consent to go.

But Patterson's small boat was apparently considered by the men to be unsafe. When a crewman, John P. Hensley, brought two ladies and tried to get them in, they begged off. A married couple standing close by were also asked to climb aboard, to which they gave their heads a toss and said they would go to a bigger boat. Mrs. General Wright came up to Patterson's boat and was about to get in when De Wolf took her by the arm and walked her forward to the second officer's boat.

Seeing this shunning of the small boat—so Farrell later would claim—he told John Hensley that he had better climb into the boat. But Hensley said no, he would stay and help others save their lives. At Farrell's request, Hensley got a fire bucket from the rack on the pilot deck of the wheelhouse and put it into the boat for bailing.

But other men were not so noble as Hensley. A number of the ship's company, not assigned as crew of Patterson's boat, were quick to get in and take a place. A few women and children were put in it—Martha Scott and her son; a Chinese woman and her child (the family of a Portland tea merchant) and Mrs. Tweesdale.

By now, about fifteen minutes had elapsed since hitting the rock, and the ship was beginning to break up. The captain ordered the three boats rigged in davits to be lowered. First officer W. A. Allen's surfboat, on the port side, was the first to be ready. It was full of women, including Mrs. Keenan—the madam from Victoria—who had been sick in her berth all morning.

As soon as Allen's lifeboat reached the water, it overturned, and most of the women disappeared in the heavy seas. Only Mrs. Keenan, who had two life jackets tied on, succeeded in crawling up onto the bottom of the boat. Clothed in nothing but a night dress, she held on desperately as it heaved to and fro, until the ship listed heavily and struck her on the head, at which she threw up her hands wildly, and slid off.

As this first lifeboat was foundering, the two boats in the starboard davits were being prepared for lowering. The one in charge of second officer Campbell was at the deck's edge, filled with a large number of female cabin passengers, including Margaret Wright. But, before it could be manned by seamen, or descend any farther, the steamer careened and smashed the boat's stem against the ship's side, upsetting the craft and throwing all on board into the water. One lady, clutching her infant with one hand, seized a boat fall (line) and swung at the ship's side, first born aloft, then disappearing into the sea as wave rolled on wave against *Jonathan's* side.

Campbell was able to climb into the ship's chains—the rigging on the outer hull to which a mast's shrouds are attached—and, with help from storekeeper Hensley, he rescued Mrs. Wright, young Martha Wilder, and a few other ladies he was able to reach. Captain De Wolf threw a plank overboard and a woman got on it, but a wave drove her head against the ship's side and, when last seen, she was sinking while pressing her wound with one hand.

John Hensley placed Martha Wilder in Patterson's boat, and Captain De Wolf and another officer began lowering it away. As it began to descend, Hensley bade goodbye to its occupants, telling them to "Keep cool and save yourselves!"[36]

At this moment, Mrs. Nina Bernhardt came crawling up from the main deck—little Paul tied on her neck with a shawl—calling out "Save my child!" One of the boat crew reached out and took the little boy, and Bernhardt began putting on a life preserver, thinking they would not take her. But one of the men asked, "Don't you want to come too?" She joyfully accepted, and two of the crew dragged her into the boat.

Just then, a man wearing a red jacket jumped into the boat, one foot landing upon the Chinese woman's shoulders and the other upon a child, but neither uttered a cry. The captain at the same time exclaimed, "Stay back! You'll all be drowned!"[37] Another poor woman, all dripping wet, ran up from below and rushed for Patterson's boat, but the ship's bartender, who was standing nearby, seized her around the waist and held her back, telling her that she would be drowned if she went in it.

One of the falls by which Patterson's lifeboat was being lowered became jammed, causing one end of the boat to tilt down at a frightful angle, threatening to plunge everyone into the sea below. But they clung to the boat, and to one another, until the barkeeper cleared the tangle, at which it went down with a splash, striking, however, right side up.

Once the boat was afloat, the rolling steamer threatened to engulf it, and the wild waves smash it to pieces. But the crew were strong men, and, with incredible difficulty they succeeded pushing the boat around under the ship's stern until the oars were clear enough to be used.

As the lifeboat passed *Jonathan's* stern, its passengers saw, for the first time, Allen's capsized boat. A man sat astride its bottom, and tough old Mrs. Keenan was still struggling in the water alongside. Although Patterson's boat was now surrounded by a shoal of drowning people, all struggling to clutch at any form of rescue, the third officer made no attempt to save another soul. The survivors later said the little boat was already too full, and that only three inches of freeboard remained.

As this only lifeboat to have survived its launching pulled away, Mrs. Bernhardt looked back and noticed one very beautiful lady, standing on deck with her husband and two children, looking wistfully after them. Bernhardt said she would long remember the expression on that sweet face.

Martha Wilder was able to make out Captain De Wolf, paymaster Eddy, Joseph Lord (the Wells-Fargo messenger), and the editor, Mr. Nisbet. Standing nearby, and wearing two life preservers, was Eddy's young clerk, Charles N. Belden, who had earlier offered the vests to Martha and another young lady.

General Wright was also seen, with his wife's arm locked in his, the other hand holding a life jacket. The general had draped his long uniform cloak around Margaret, who was wet and cold from the dousing received when her lifeboat had spilled. There they stood, brave and calm, awaiting their fate.

Once Patterson's boat was clear of *Jonathan*, its occupants took stock of the situation. The little craft was crowded with a total of nineteen persons. There were the above-named five women and three children, as well as eleven men—Third Mate Patterson; David Farrell; Henry Miller (a ship's baker); Edward Shields (a waiter); Stephen Moran (a cabin boy); two firemen and four black seamen, one of whom was Jacob Gates.

Most of the women were scantily clad and almost perishing with cold. As they huddled together, shivering and crying, Patterson took decisive command. First, he positioned his charges so as to trim the boat. Then, as he took off his life vest and put it on one of the sobbing women, he reassured all aboard by saying, "This is a life-boat, and if any can live in this sea, she can; so don't be afraid."[38]

Patterson steered directly for Crescent City, less than six miles distant, running with the seas on the quarter. Waves broke over the stern on nearly every crest, at times almost filling the boat, as she pitched incessantly, in and out of deep troughs. Bailing was begun using the hats of some of the men and the old fire bucket provided by the brave-hearted Hensley. Terribly frightened, Mrs. Bernhardt wished, for just a moment, that she was back aboard the sinking ship.

The lifeboat hadn't gone very far from *Jonathan's* side when two distress guns were fired from the ship. The survivors looked back and saw her flag flying upside down from the mizzenmast, as a signal of distress. Three lifeboats were seen to be still on deck, bottoms up, and it was thought that if the passengers had seen fit, they might have righted and launched them—but apparently no further attempts were being made because of the heavy seas.

The waves had earlier driven the steamer free of the rocks, and, within a few moments of firing the distress signals, *Jonathan's* funnel collapsed and she began settling more sharply by the bow. All of the passengers moved farther aft on the hurricane deck.

About fifteen minutes after Patterson's boat departed, the only part of *Jonathan's* hull still visible was a small portion of the stern, and that only when the lifeboat was borne up on the crest of a wave. Then, there was a sudden lurch and the steamer disappeared—the last thing seen being the distress flag at the mizzenmast as it quivered out of sight under the billows, forever. Seeing this, Patterson exclaimed: "There! The *Brother Jonathan* is no more! It is just forty-five minutes since she struck."[39]

It was now about 2:30 P.M. Under Patterson's command the crew bent to the task of rowing for shore, while simultaneously attempting to keep the lifeboat afloat by constant bailing. Several hours later, as the survivors approached Crescent City, anxieties were aroused again by seeing the huge breakers and frowning cliffs towering above them. But Patterson landed his charges safely, and they climbed out of the boat, cold and chilled, their scant clothing dripping and clinging to their shivering forms.

The first persons seen on the beach were some Indians, gaily decked in feathers, and Mrs. Bernhardt's initial thought was that she had been saved only to be "devoured" by savages on the strand. But, presently, the appearance of a broad-faced German man reassured the survivors that they were now completely out of danger. Before long, a throng of excited townspeople—who had seen the boat approaching—gathered and began offering help. The nearly naked women and children were taken to the town's hotel to be clothed, warmed and fed by attentive locals.

As it happened, the villagers had heard the two guns fired by *Jonathan*, but thought it was only some sort of signal from a ship headed northward. Now, a good many of them immediately set out on foot that afternoon to look for more survivors along the beach, while others pushed off in four boats—all of the surf boats and whale boats available in Crescent City—in the hope of rescuing any persons who might be floating alive.

Patterson would later claim that, notwithstanding the great fatigue of the day, he went along to guide them to the scene. But another report related that all of the surviving men exhibited a perfect indifference as to the fate of their comrades, and tried to dissuade anyone from going back. Whatever the truth of the matter, the boats that went out found it utterly impossible to go very far, and all returned shortly after dark.

Ben Holladay's great ocean steamer, *Sierra Nevada* had passed Crescent City, southbound, about noon on that day of the grounding. Its master, Captain Connor, had expected to meet *Brother Jonathan* and exchange newspapers, but due to the haze from forest fires, little more than *Jonathan*'s outline could be seen closer inshore. Albert D. Richardson, of the *New York Tribune*, a passenger, later described Captain Connor's face "wrinkled with anxiety" as *Sierra Nevada* threaded St. George's reef, hampered by the high winds and heavy following sea.[40] Meanwhile, Richardson and his companions were discussing what the odds of survival would be for anyone shipwrecked in such weather.

On the day following *Jonathan's* loss, August 1, boats from Crescent City tried once again to reach the scene of the grounding, but seas were still very high, and smoke continued to reduce the visibility. Later that day, some Indians reported seeing a number of people on a certain rock near shore, but sadly, the "people" proved to be a group of sea lions.

California volunteer soldiers at nearby Camp Lincoln began patrolling the beaches for survivors and bodies, and they built signal fires along the shore, clear into Oregon. On the afternoon of August 2, boats were finally able to reach the location where *Jonathan* had sunk, but, by then, there was nothing to be seen.

CRESCENT CITY, CALIFORNIA.

The news of this worst disaster in California maritime history was carried by a Camp Lincoln soldier to the nearest telegraph, at Jacksonville, Oregon, whence it went out to the world. The grim tidings of the sinking stunned people throughout the West. Flags in coastal cities, and on ships in their harbors, flew at half-staff to honor the dead.

The friends of L. J. Schwartz, a merchant from Idaho thought to be aboard, also grieved, until he turned up, safe and sound. Though "booked for the other world" on *Jonathan*, Schwartz had missed getting aboard by several minutes.[41]

As it happened, General Wright's son, Colonel Thomas F. Wright, was in command of the Second Regiment of Volunteer California Infantry at San Francisco's Presidio. He sailed for Crescent City on August 4 in the new Holladay Line steamer *Del Norte*, along with Captain Edwin Pollock of General Wright's Ninth U.S. Infantry regiment, and an undertaker who was to take charge of any servicemen's bodies that might be found.

While at Crescent City, Tom Wright# made arrangements at Camps Humboldt and Lincoln to have soldiers patrol southward along the coast as far as Eureka, and he furnished photographs and descriptions to aid in identifying any bodies found. Wright also offered rewards for the recovery of the remains of his father and mother, and the other army personnel. *Brother Jonathan's* owners likewise offered rewards for the bodies of the ship's officers.

In Portland, when Captain Brooks of the Cambridge learned that his family had been lost on *Brother Jonathan*, he set sail for the scene. Upon arrival, he located the submerged rock, which his soundings showed rose abruptly from the 25 fathoms of water all around it. But the only evidence of a wreck seen by Brooks was a mass of oily substance on the surface.

On August 7, *Del Norte* sailed from Crescent City, taking the survivors back to San Francisco. As of that date, only a shattered lifeboat, a mattress and a few buckets had been picked up—not a single body had been found. The drain hole of the stove-in lifeboat had been plugged with a copy of the *San Francisco Bulletin*.

The survivors' stories, and the apparent great loss of life in the sinking led to a torrent of fault-finding. An Oregon newspaper ripped into *Jonathan's* owners, alleging that "another wanton sacrifice of hundreds of valuable

---

Tom Wright was mustered out with his regiment in the spring of 1866. He subsequently became an officer in the regular army, and was killed by Modoc Indians, in the Lava Beds, California, in April, 1872.

lives" had been made "to the cool-blooded avarice of steamship companies." *Jonathan* had been "an old unseaworthy vessel," unfit for service "along this stormy coast." And, she had probably been insured for twice her real value.[42]

The editor of another Oregon sheet also questioned the steamer's seaworthiness, claiming that she had been seriously damaged by her prior collision with the *Jane Falkenberg*, which ship was still undergoing repairs. It was argued that *Jonathan* might not have broken up so easily if she had been thoroughly refurbished.[43]

In a second article, written from the safety of his armchair, the same editor tried to downplay the severity of the weather:

> Why did the Captain put about unless he was in fear lest with her heavy freight there was danger of her going down? There was no storm at all at the time, simply a brisk northwest wind, such as is quite common at this season of year.[44]

Patterson and the men in his boat were alternately praised for their bravery and criticized for saving themselves first. But, of the survivors, none uttered a bad word against them. As Mrs. Bernhardt put it, "...if there had been more of the passengers and fewer of the crew in that boat, it never would have reached the land, and none would have remained to tell the sad tale."[45]

Added to all this hand wringing, dark rumors flew in abundance. Captain Brooks of the *Cambridge* stated that one of the seamen told him that De Wolf had ordered Patterson to remain alongside the ship, and to this Patterson replied that his life was as valuable as that of anyone else. In another variation of this story, the boat crew are supposed to have told a resident of Crescent City that, after Patterson's boat had left the ship, De Wolf ordered Patterson to return, because there were too many sailors in the boat. Patterson wanted to start back, but, when the boat crew threatened to kill him if he did, he abandoned the idea.[46]

Word was also circulated that the husband of the rescued Chinese woman had been in the boat, but was killed by a blow from an oar in the hands of one of the crew. Mrs. Tweesdale wrote in later years that the Chinese man had simply been refused a place in the boat.

When the female survivors of the wreck reached San Francisco in *Del Norte*, they were given some money and basic necessities by *Jonathan*'s owners. The winsome Martha Wilder was one of a family of six children, with a widowed mother living in the city. She was taken home in one of William Taylor's Cosmopolitan Hotel carriages, and when the driver reported to Taylor how poor her family was, the hotelier immediately went to the house and returned the girl's fare, plus a donation he had collected.

Mrs. Bernhardt, having been left in destitute circumstances, received the proceeds of a benefit performance given in her behalf by Maguire's Opera Troupe in San Francisco. In a strange twist of fate, a few months later, some of this same troupe were killed when the steamer *Yosemite* blew a boiler, en route from Sacramento to San Francisco.

The old lady, Mrs. Tweesdale, who had been traveling in *Brother Jonathan* to join her son in Portland, bravely took passage in another steamer in a second attempt to reach that place. Having lost everything, she was put in steerage, and this caused the editor of the Portland *Oregonian* to berate the steamship company for not furnishing better quarters, and for its failure to provide even enough bedding to make her comfortable.

Finally, about August 10, the grisly residue of the wreck began to drive ashore, strewing a forty-mile stretch of beach with bodies, trunks, boxes, vegetables, spars, and mail sacks. Parts of *Jonathan's* superstructure were found, including the saloon, cabin doors and a spanker boom.

According to report, the large oaken ship's wheel was also found, with a passenger's body still clinging to it so tightly that it took the efforts of two men to break the death grip. The wheel is said to have been displayed, for 30 years afterward, in a saloon at Crescent City.

At Gold Bluffs, the corpse of Ed Cardiff, much bruised about the face, floated ashore on a forty-foot long, full-width piece of hull from near the steamer's wheelhouse. On Cardiff's person were found a few photographs of ladies, a memo book, and a twenty-dollar Confederate note. The discovery of his body led to further criticism of the steamship company, in this case for not having sent a ship to the scene as soon as they heard about the wreck. Seemingly, several persons had survived for a few days, and it was thought likely they might have been saved, had aid arrived in time.

The greatest sorrow resulting from the wreck came from the loss of the younger passengers. The body of a seven-year old boy was picked up at Gold Bluffs, clothed but barefooted; the remains of a five-year old boy, wearing a shoe with steel leg supporters, was found near Arcata.

Mary Berry was a pretty, 24-year old colleen, from Dublin, who had sailed without incident all the way from Ireland to San Francisco, and had been continuing aboard *Jonathan* to join her aunt and uncle in Portland. Her body was found not far from Eureka, clad only in nightclothes, and with a red blanket wrapped around her. From her neck hung a cross and a purse containing a Catholic amulet. Local parishioners of that faith temporarily buried her remains until they could be claimed by her uncle, Mr. Arrigoni—the same fellow who owned the Pioneer Hotel, and who, in 1861, had tried to intervene in the fracas leading to the killing of Captain Staples.[47]

General Wright's horse and a camel washed ashore north of Trinidad. The camel was one of two belonging to H. C. Lee, a well-known circus manager who was in Oregon awaiting the arrival of his wife, his child and the animals on *Jonathan*.

By August 16, thirty-eight corpses had been discovered, including three women wearing multiple life jackets. Word had it that most of the cash, watches and other valuable property found on the bodies was carefully catalogued and accounted for. There was, however, an unconfirmed story told by local Indians that a living male passenger had floated ashore below the Klamath River on a part of the wreck, and that Klamath Indians had killed him and stolen his considerable money.

Many of the bodies were buried where found on the beaches. One man's corpse, which was wedged in the rocks at the mouth of the Chetco River, and couldn't be gotten out, was covered up as best could be done. Some of the remains were interred at Chetco, more at Crescent City. Those being shipped elsewhere, and who had claimed a higher status while alive, were placed in zinc coffins, instead of simple pine. Wright's aide, Lieutenant E.D. Waite, was accorded zinc, as was the San Francisco journalist, James Nisbet.

Among the papers found on Nisbet's body was his last will and testament, written with a lead pencil on several sheets of notepaper, evidently inscribed as the ship was sinking. A certain George W. Russell found it, and, after taking it to his place of business to dry it out, he sent it to Nisbet's brother, Thomas, in San Francisco.

Apparently, even with the terror of sudden death staring him in the face, Nisbet was calm and thoughtful enough to write out the will. His partners at the *Bulletin* confirmed that it was in his hand, and was even "punctuated as accurately as if intended for copy." "Instead of being concerned for his own safety," they said, he appeared to have "coolly calculated the chances against him and to have employed his last moments as he had employed his life, in doing good to others."[48]

On the third page of the sheet, Nisbet wrote an affectionate note to his brother, giving him, in the fewest possible words, a schedule of all his property, naming his choice of an attorney, and sending a parting message to his only sister, to whom he was tenderly attached. Business being thus carefully attended to, and with still a spare moment before the fatal plunge, Nisbet wrote a few hurried lines to the wife of Caspar Hopkins, in whose home on Rincon Hill he had boarded for many years, and whose children fondly called him "Grandpa." Mrs. Hopkins had urged the old Scot not to sail on a Friday, especially in the ill-starred *Brother Jonathan*. It was in remembrance of her apprehensions that he wrote:

> My Dear, Dear, Ma.—A thousand affectionate adieus. You spoke of my sailing on Friday—Hangman's day—and the unlucky *Jonathan*. Well, here I am, with death before me. My love to you all—to Caspar, to Ditat, to Bella, Mellie and little Myra—kiss her for me. Never forget Grandpa.[49]

Nisbet's will eventually came before California courts but was refused probate on grounds of a lack of witnesses.

Neither Margaret nor George Wright having been found by August 17, General McDowell presumed them dead and issued orders honoring the couple. Pacific military posts flew flags at half-staff and fired gun salutes, and the men of Wright's Ninth Infantry wore emblems of mourning for thirty days. Wright's manifold good deeds, and his maintenance of personal integrity in an era of corrupt men, were widely praised. The passing of this Western pioneer, who had endeared himself to all who knew him, was greatly lamented.[50]

On August 23, Margaret Wright's body washed ashore at Trinidad, and was identified by finding her name inscribed in indelible ink on her underclothing. The general's remains were not discovered until September 27 when his badly decomposed corpse, minus both arms and covered with barnacles, was found near Shelter Cover, 140 miles south of the scene of the wreck. Though his features were not recognizable, Wright was clad in military attire, and, as in the case of his wife, his name was inscribed on some of his clothing.

Wright's corpse was temporarily buried on the beach, and then it was exhumed and brought to San Francisco, where a funeral for the couple was held October 20 at Calvary Church on Bush Street. Generals Henry Halleck and Irwin McDowell were among the couple's pallbearers. After the rites, a military cortege, followed by a large parade of civilians in carriages, escorted the caskets to the steamer wharf, to the mournful strains of the "Dead March."

An honor guard then accompanied the bodies on the steamer to Sacramento, where they lay in state for a day at the capitol building, while the whole city mourned. The entrance to the Orleans Hotel, formerly Wright's home and headquarters, was draped in black. On October 22, another cortege, stretching over a mile in length, escorted the remains to the city's old cemetery where both Wrights were given a military burial. There, one can still see the monument that was erected to mark their final resting place, inscribed with the touching sentiment, "Lovely and pleasant in their lives, and in their death they were not divided."

In all, 176 persons died in the *Brother Jonathan* tragedy, but only about 75 bodies ever came ashore, and many of these were never identified. Only two maritime disasters on the Pacific Coast have surpassed this loss of life. In November, 1875, the steamer *Pacific* collided with a sailing vessel north of Cape Flattery, Washington resulting in 275 dead; and, in 1918, the *Princess Sophia* ran up on Vanderbilt Reef, Alaska, resulting in the loss of 343 persons.

Undoubtedly the last to give up hope of ever finding a loved one lost in the *Brother Jonathan* sinking were the parents of Nathalie Shirpser, a beautiful and accomplished seventeen-year old. Refusing to believe that their daughter had perished, Isidor and Marie Shirpser cut up bolts of the cloth from which her dress had been made, and distributed bits of it, along with her photograph, to Indians and others along a two hundred mile stretch of the coast. Not until 1890 did they give up the search, finally conceding that Nathalie must have been locked in her cabin when the ship went down. Services were held that year in San Francisco's Jewish cemetery where a monument was erected to her memory.[51]

Captain De Wolf's widow, Marie, was another person affected by the calamity who seemed unable to put it aside. She spent years trying to clear her husband's name, fixing the blame on others.

According to Mrs. De Wolf, for months preceding *Jonathan*'s departure on her final voyage, the northern business had been exceedingly heavy, and steamers were obliged to leave freight behind for lack of capacity. She stated that, on the day before sailing, her husband had tried to induce the company agent to accept no more cargo, warning that the ship was already as deeply laden as she could safely run. He was also concerned that too much of the cargo was loaded on deck.

The agent is supposed to have paid no attention to De Wolf's remonstrance, telling the captain that if he didn't want to take the steamer out, he, the agent, could find a man who would. De Wolf said no more, though he expressed his misgivings to a friend on the dock a few minutes before sailing. Marie De Wolf further maintained that, when getting underway, the steamer was so deep in the water as to be stuck in the mud until the next high tide allowed a tug to free her.

But the truth of the matter is not clear. We know that on her fatal voyage *Jonathan* was transporting heavy equipment, consisting of machinery for a woolen mill being built in Oregon, a load of rails, and one or more quartz-crushing mills bound for the Idaho mines. And, a report from San Francisco, about a week after the fatal grounding, did say that the steamer was heavily laden with freight and low in the water, which, with the wind in her favor when she put about, caused her to drive hard upon the rocks.

But, in contradiction to the above allegations, other news reports of the disaster stated that, on her final trip, *Jonathan* had only 700 tons of merchandise, all closely under hatch, with nothing loaded on deck. This amount would have been well within her cargo-carrying capacity. Regarding the claim that there was a heavy demand for shipping, it is also a fact that, a few weeks after *Jonathan's* last voyage, the steamship *Sierra Nevada* left San Francisco for Victoria with only light freight.

De Wolf's widow further stated that her husband had not run his ship onto an uncharted rock, but that a heavy quartz mill had broken loose in the cargo hold and plunged through that part of the hull previously damaged in the collision with *Jane Falkenberg*. But, based on the testimony of multiple witnesses, there is no doubt whatsoever that *Brother Jonathan* ran aground.[52]

Her sinking caused no great rush to improve either steamer safety or coastal navigation. And, it would be years before work was begun on a lighthouse to mark the treacherous waters of St. George Reef. Completed in 1892, it sits on the small wave-washed Northwest Seal Rock, three miles from Jonathan Rock. The lighthouse—decommissioned in 1975—was considered to be a very dangerous duty station, because of its susceptibility to storm damage. The St. George Reef Lighthouse Preservation Society has started work to restore the old structure, a drawing of which can be found at the beginning of this chapter.

Interest remained high over the years in the possibility of finding fabulous treasure in the hulk of *Brother Jonathan*. A lack of surviving records make it difficult to confirm, but she is thought to have had aboard $40,000 in Wells Fargo funds, $76,000 belonging to the Northwest Fur Trader's Association, about $65,000 bound for the Norton Dexter Bank in Seattle, and a quantity of bullion belonging to the Canadian government. And, Mrs. Keenan supposedly had $7,000 worth of diamonds on the ship.

With more certainty, it is known that Major Eddy, the army paymaster, had with him some $200,000, but it was likely in 'shin plasters," the paper currency usually paid to troops. Also, the Indian agent from the Warm Springs Oregon reservation, William Logan, was on board with $10,000 or more of Indian Office money—believed to be in gold—which he had drawn in San Francisco.

In the years since the sinking, a good number of would-be salvagers have made unsuccessful attempts to locate the ship, based mostly on unreliable anecdotal evidence. Finally, in May, 1991 a private salvage company was formed for the express purpose of finding *Jonathan*. Called Deep Sea Research (DSR), its members included a fellow named Donald Knight, who had been trying to locate the ship for many years.

Optimistic about finding the hulk, DSR filed an admiralty action in the northern California United States District court, seeking title and salvage rights to the wreck and its cargo. But, just as it had in 1857, California intervened to try and gain control of *Jonathan*, despite having never made any effort on its own part to locate the wreckage.

The state argued that the wreck belonged to California in accordance with the Abandoned Shipwrecks Act (ASA) of 1987, under which the federal government asserts title to "abandoned" historic wrecks and transfers it to the states on whose submerged lands the wrecks are found. California also laid claim to *Brother Jonathan* under section 6313 of the state's public resources code, which gives the state title to abandoned shipwrecks on California's tidal or submerged lands.

When California intervened, DSR asked the district court to dismiss its action without prejudice, and the court did so in June, 1992. The company then began a systematic search for the hulk using modern magnetometers and side-scanning sonars, and, in October, 1993, discovered it about four and a half miles off the coast at Crescent City. The location confirmed that the ship had drifted two miles south of Jonathan Rock before sinking.

The hull is embedded in a sand and silt bottom at a depth of some 250 feet. Using a small submersible, DSR made videotapes which show the steamer to be eerily shrouded in an accumulation of old fishing nets. Only some 170 feet of the hull remains, the bow section having broken off and floated away when she sank. Most of the upper works have been consumed by marine organisms.

Lying exposed were the port paddlewheel shaft and hubs, the engine cylinder and bedplate, a boiler, and other machinery. Many domestic artifacts were also visible. A few of these—a dinner plate, a corked and full champagne bottle, an ale bottle, medicine bottle, and a brass spike—were plucked from the wreck to prove its identity.

In September, 1994, based on its possession of the artifacts and videotape, DSR went back to court once again to seek salvage rights to the ship and its cargo. As a further back its claim of ownership, the company had, by then, purchased the interests in the ship's cargo from the two insurance companies —of the original five—which had paid claims after the disaster. So far as is

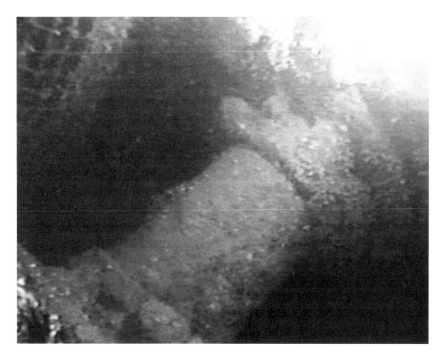

Paddlewheel drive shaft as seen on discovery dive. Note fishing net at top left. (*Courtesy of Donald Knight*)

known, the ship itself was not insured.[53]

California intervened once again, filing a motion to dismiss DSR's suit, but the court ruled in favor of the salvage company, reasoning that the ASA did not divest federal courts of the exclusive maritime jurisdiction conferred by Article III of the Constitution. The court also concluded that California hadn't demonstrated that the ship had been either abandoned, embedded in the sea floor, or was eligible for listing in the National Register, as required under the ASA. As for California's state law claim, the court determined that the ASA pre-empted it.

After finding that DSR had an adequate plan to protect the ship's historic treasures, the court issued a warrant for the "arrest" of *Brother Jonathan* and her cargo, and appointed the company as custodian and salvor of the wreck, pending the court's determination of the manner in which things were to be divided up. Meanwhile salvage work was allowed to begin.

California appealed the ruling all the way to the U. S. Supreme Court, which, in April, 1998, concluded that the constitution didn't bar the jurisdiction of a federal court over an admiralty action where the hulk was not within a state's possession. The high court therefore remanded the case back to the district court to settle the question of ownership.[54]

While the legal process was plodding along, Deep Sea Research had been busy salvaging, using a 210-foot ship in support of saturation divers. A hoard of 1,206 rare gold coins—mostly $20 double eagles—had been discovered in what had been the purser's office. No human remains were found.

On March 9, 1999, just one day before the ownership case was to be heard again in district court, the state of California and the company reached an accord that was subsequently approved by the court. Its terms provided that the company could keep 1,000 of the 1,206 coins thus far recovered, and the state would receive the rest. Any further treasure found is to be split 80% for the company and 20% for the state. The settlement also preserves the future claims of the Wells-Fargo Bank and the descendants of the H. C. Lee circus family, whose payroll supposedly went down with the ship.

The pact also gives the state title to all artifacts that are not gold, and the right to oversee the preservation process during the company's future operations. Some of the recovered artifacts, including many fine glass pieces, will be displayed at the Del Norte County Historical Society Museum. California's 200 coins will be distributed to that museum and others. The coins belonging to Deep Sea Research were auctioned off in Los Angeles in May 1999, and fetched 5.3 million dollars. Some of the trove of mint condition 1865-S ten-dollar golden eagles sold for as much as $115,000 each.[55]

And so, as of the date of this writing, the salvage operation continues, with a promise of yet more monetary and historical rewards. Still undiscovered is the ship's safe, which was bolted to a bulkhead in the purser's cabin, and which may contain the circus and army payrolls, and more gold coin and bullion.

We noted at the beginning of this story that songs were often written commemorating the maritime disasters of the day. And, sure enough, one was dashed off within a few days of the loss of *Brother Jonathan*. Entitled "The Sunken Rock," its melancholy verses proclaimed:

> A rock! a rock! our ship has struck
> A rock sunk in the sea,
> The white spray from the dashing wave,
> Rolls onward bold and free.
>
> But hear, oh hear the wailing sound,

Imploring aid to come;
No human help is near at hand,
O God, thy will be done.

Upon the deck our Gen'ral stands,
His eye on the blue deep cast,
Amazed he stood in silence bent,
He sank and breathed his last.

A boat! a boat! rides o'er the wave,
And safely gains the shore,
Go bear sad tiding of the wreck,
Of friends we meet no more.

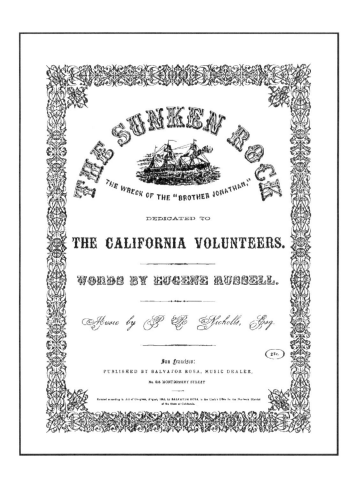

Sagebrush Steamboat

This is the first of several stories about Idaho's formative years, and is one of two examining the hazards faced by white pioneers in getting to the new territory across a hostile landscape. It also shows the irrepressible, sometimes reckless, energy and hustle of the era.

It rises in Yellowstone country. From alpine springs and tiny streams, it descends and flows across southern Idaho's sage-covered plains, gaining strength and volume, before turning northward to define more than 100 miles of the state's western border. Here, the Snake River's foaming, plummeting force has, over eons, sculpted America's deepest gorge.

Aptly named "Hell's Canyon," much of this great chasm is over 5,500 feet deep and, from one point on the Idaho rim, the river lies 7,900 feet below—making the gorge substantially deeper than the Grand Canyon of the Colorado. In the approximate 200 miles between Farewell Bend, in southwestern Idaho, and Lewiston in the north, the Snake drops some 1,400

Hell's Canyon of the Snake River
(Idaho State Historical Society)

feet, rapid after rapid coming in dazzling succession. And here, despite the building of dams upstream in recent years, can still be found some of the most turbulent white water in the world.

The character of the Snake, as it flows through Idaho, makes it an unlikely waterway for a steamboat. But, for a brief time in the 1860s, a little sternwheeled vessel named *Shoshone*—built on the verge of the river at great expense—not only carried passengers and freight on a stretch near Boise, but was also once steamed, higgledy-piggledy, down through Hell's Canyon. Later, there would be a few other such boats on the river, but none with such an intriguing history as *Shoshone*.

Steamers had been built and run on the lower Columbia River, from Portland to the Cascades, since the early days of settlement in Oregon, and, subsequently, operators began running them through the middle stretch of the river, above the Cascades to The Dalles. Even greater use of the Columbia came with the discovery of gold on the Clearwater River, and in the Salmon

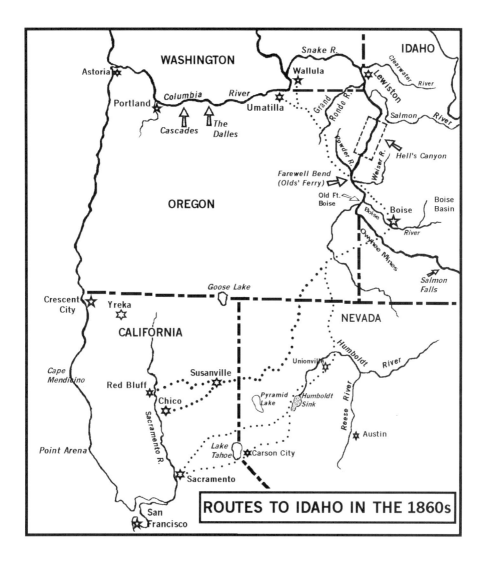

River country of what would become Idaho Territory. In the spring of 1861, to handle the huge rush of men and cargo to these mining districts, a number of small steamers—*Spray, Okanagan, Tenino,* and *Colonel Wright*—began running, during the ice-free months, up the Columbia and Snake to the thriving new village of Lewiston, which had sprung up at the confluence of the Snake and Clearwater.

The booming times motivated several steamship owners to combine as the "Oregon Steam Navigation Company." Under the leadership of Captain J. C. Ainsworth, and others, the O.S.N. soon gained a powerful monopoly over mail, passenger and freight traffic on the river system. High rates were levied, and enormous profits made. During this period—so it was said—the cost of building an upper-Columbia boat could be recouped in a single trip.¹

Commerce on the Columbia system was further increased by gold strikes made in the Boise Basin of southern Idaho during the summer of 1862. But, transporting people and goods to that region, via the Columbia, was both expensive and tiresome.

First, the freight or passengers had to get to Portland. Most traffic got there by sea on overcrowded, unsafe steamers, which, near the end of the voyage, had to cross the hazardous bar at the mouth of the Columbia. From Portland, it was necessary for goods and passengers to take several steamboats and make portages up the river to either Umatilla or Wallula, Washington Territory, the terminals for overland transportation to southern Idaho.

Finally, a long overland trek had to be made. At first, pack trains were used whereby, for $50, proprietors furnished "passengers" a horse to ride, and carried their baggage and provisions on pack animals. The journey from the Columbia took eight to eleven days, with stops each night at roadhouses or in rude camps, where the traveler did his own cooking.

Soon, better roads allowed wagons to replace the pack trains, but there were still complaints about the high cost of the "wretched meals and beds," and about having to walk "half the distance"² from Umatilla when the roads turned muddy.

Spurred on by the complaints of travelers and shippers (and the profits to be made) the O.S.N. and others made further attempts to provide better communication with the diggings. In particular, an interest was aroused in using the middle reaches of the Snake, above Lewiston, as an improved avenue to the rich new districts.

Little was known, at the time, about the middle Snake and Hell's Canyon. In April, 1819, four French-Canadian voyageurs—part of a British Northwest Company expedition under Donald MacKenzie—had floated a barge down through the canyon. Based on this trip, MacKenzie reported the river to be navigable for loaded boats without a single portage. Yet, due to the "force of the current, and the frequency of rapids," he recommended the continued use of land transport for the company's fur-trapping operations. There were two particularly threatening places "with bold rocks on either side [of] the river," where the great body of water was "compressed within a narrow compass."³

So far as is known, no further explorations were made until 1862, when a small company set out from Wallula in a *bateau*, to prospect in the region above Lewiston. By a generous use of the *cordelle* to drag their boats, some of this party got up as far as what is now called Pittsburgh Landing, about twenty miles above the mouth of the Salmon River. Unable to take their boat any higher, the group explored on foot toward the Boise Basin, and concluded that steamers could, at the least, travel with ease between the mouths of the Powder and Weiser rivers.[4]

In September of that same year, Captain A. P. Ankeney, who was running the small sternwheeler, *Spray*, in opposition to the O.S.N., joined with a group of Lewiston merchants in sponsoring another look at the Snake's navigability above Lewiston. Three "reliable men"—Charles Clifford, Washington Murray and Joseph Denver—were hired to float down the river.

Clifford and the others traveled overland from Lewiston, following up the western bank of the river as far as the mouth of the Grand Ronde. Here they struck out overland to intersect the emigrant road, and follow it to old Fort Boise.

There, the men built themselves a raft, and, after waiting until the Snake had dropped to its lowest stage—so the adventurers claimed—they lashed their provisions to it, pushed off, and came dashing down to Lewiston in just a few days. Though their account of the journey has the ring of truth to it, they grossly under estimated the distance traveled from old Fort Boise to the mouth of the Salmon River. They called it under 100 miles, when, in fact, it is nearly 175. Anyone who has sped through the churning labyrinth of Hell's Canyon will, perhaps, forgive these pioneer river rafters their error.

The results of this expedition were most gratifying to its sponsors, who now assumed that there was nothing whatever in the river to impede steamboat navigation at any season of the year, unless it be ice. The expedition had proven the Snake above Lewiston to be "much safer to travel" than the section from Lewiston to the Columbia.

Added to this, certain optimists thought the Snake might be unbroken by cataracts all the way to Salmon Falls (near present-day Hagerman, Idaho). And, if that point could be reached, even Nevada and Salt Lake City could be accessed by building relatively short roads.

Now, said John H. Scranton, the enthusiastic editor of the Lewiston *Golden Age*, and himself a former steamboat sailor:

> We shall penetrate Nevada and Utah Territory...[only] a few more suns will rise and set before the shrill whistle of the steamer will reverberate along the banks of this noble river, and its echo will be heard for ages yet to come through the ravines, gorges, canyons and on the mountain tops in our golden land, as a symbol of ambition, perseverance and goaheadative-ness.[5]

But, alas, that same autumn, Captain Ankeney was unable to take his steamer, *Spray*, any farther upriver than fifteen miles above Lewiston.

Nonetheless, the attempt to improve communication with southern Idaho via Hell's Canyon continued, and was given even more stimulus in 1863 by the discovery of placer gold, and rich silver ledges, in what is now Owyhee County. In the fall of that year, a group of businessmen in the new district, who were concerned about the O.S.N.'s high freight prices, sent six men, under Captain George Molthrop, to test the river's navigability.

Molthrop and his group started out from the mouth of the Boise River in a small, homemade boat, but got no farther than the head of Hell's Canyon, where they found "a series of rapids and falls, bidding defiance to any effort of man in the way of navigation."[6]

The following year, 1864, brought further activity. Captain Thomas J. Stump of the O.S.N., at the request of Lewistonians, made a test run upstream with a steamer, but got no farther than six miles below the mouth of the Salmon. Another group of men, thinking that a macadamized road and a railroad could be built, each running up its own side of Hell's Canyon, incorporated the "Snake River Portage Company." Not surprisingly, nothing came of this scheme.[7]

By 1865, the mines in the Boise Basin and Owyhee districts of Idaho were booming mightily, and the O.S.N. was hauling about 36,000 passengers and 21,000 tons of freight per year. Such a huge business had caused competing transportation interests to open direct overland roads from California to Idaho.

On one new route, freight and passengers were brought by steamer up the Sacramento River to Chico or Red Bluff, thence via wagon, pack or saddle train across Nevada and Oregon to the Owyhee mines on Jordan Creek. A plan backed by the influential John Bidwell of Chico called for a stage line to run over the same road. Another route—from Carson City, Nevada up the Humboldt River to Unionville, thence north to Owyhee—was also becoming popular for freight and travelers. Hill Beachy of Idaho had begun running stages on this road.

The threat posed by this activity forced the O.S.N. to act decisively in trying to improve their route. The company had by now abandoned the idea of routinely running steamers through Hell's Canyon. That hazard, as well as the now-moribund village of Lewiston, would be bypassed. Freight and passengers would be brought overland from Wallula or Umatilla, on the established roads, to Reuben P. Olds' Ferry, at Farewell Bend, from which point a steamboat would carry them upstream to Reynolds' Ferry, where the Boise-to-Owyhee road crossed the Snake (north of today's Murphy, Idaho). This would be within 30 miles of both Boise and the Jordan Creek mines.

Accordingly, in early summer, Captain Tom Stump was sent in the

Capt. Thomas Stump
(Author's Collection)

Colonel Wright to try once again to steam up through Hell's Canyon to Olds' Ferry, where the boat could be used in such service. *Wright* was a veteran steamer, whose namesake was George Wright—the same officer, much respected in the West, who would die that very year in the sinking of the steamship *Brother Jonathan*. The 110-foot long *Wright* had been built in 1858 to run supplies for the military above Fort Dalles to Wallula. Later, in June, 1861, she was the first boat ever to steam up the Snake to Lewiston.

The O.S.N. Directors had intended to mothball the steamer, but instead, decided to risk her in the attempt to stem the Snake. *Wright* was specially fitted up for the trip, with equipment to *cordelle* over the worst rapids.

The old boat left Lewiston on June 16. After landing some freight at Assotin Creek, she passed the mouth of the Grand Ronde River and anchored for the night at the foot of Cougar Rapids, about six miles below where the Salmon River joins the Snake. Two days were spent cutting wood for fuel, and in fastening the towline above these rapids, with their ten-foot drop.

The next few days were spent in utter frustration, trying to float the bitter end of the towline down from its upstream anchor point. In the process, one small boat was sunk, and another got away to float downstream. And *Wright's* hull was stove in twice by running onto rocks. Several times the pumps had to be set in the holds, the fuel wood hauled out and the steamer beached to make repairs.

Finally, on the morning of June 22, the ascent began. Capstan, gypsy, steam and muscle all strained to the hard pull and, after about four hours, *Wright* was at last tied up above Cougar Rapids, a mere 400 yards from her starting point. Stump had all the equipment gathered up, and started her off

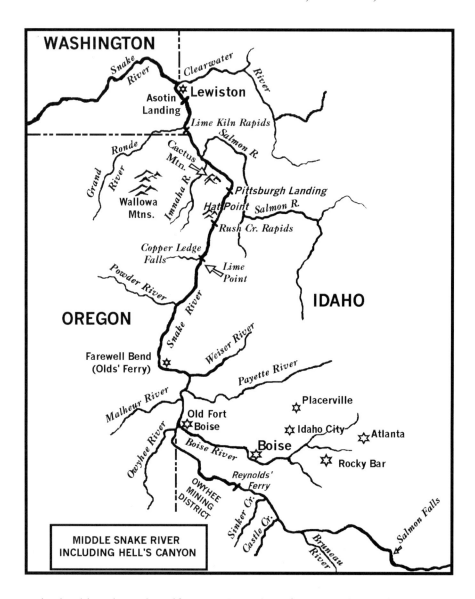

again, bucking through swift water. Late that afternoon, the towing line was used again to get over Frenchy Rapids, and camp was made for the night at the mouth of the Salmon River.

The following two days were spent cordelling through a series of strong chutes, including those known today as Mountain Sheep and Divide Creek rapids. While struggling up through one section of swift water, about five miles above the mouth of the Imnaha River, the towline parted, causing the steamer to drift ashore; another time the line caught in the paddle wheel, causing the boat to hit some rocks, slightly damaging the superstructure.

On Sunday, June 25, a line was used to get the steamer from the south to the north bank, where some driftwood could be cut for fuel. The crossing had to be made through what Stump named "Green Mountain Rapids." In the transit, *Wright* made a "nasty dive" and, for a few seconds, the crew thought it was a tossup as to which way she would go, but they were able to anchor her safely at what was dubbed "Colonel Wright's Landing."

After getting fifteen cords of wood aboard using the small boats, the steamboat was underway again on June 27. But, after going about a mile—probably at the rapids known today as Lower Dug Bar—Captain Stump and his crew found themselves in the strongest currents they had ever seen a boat enter.

The stern got caught in a bad eddy, causing water to come rolling across the decks. Over *Wright* went, almost on her beams' end, and then she swirled around to starboard until the stern ran up on the rocks. About ten feet of both garboard strakes, and about seven feet of keelson were ripped off by the impact.

With the situation desperate, Stump shouted down from the pilot house to get a line ashore and hold her to the rocks. His 19-year old assistant, William P. Gray, later described the "universal willingness" of those on board to get ashore with that line:

> Every deckhand, the mate, the chief engineer, the fireman and our two passengers, who were standing forward...seized the line by both ends, the middle and wherever they could get ahold of it and jumped ashore. The only people left aboard were Stump and myself in the pilot house, and the second engineer, who was below, and old Titus, the cook.[8]

Neither of two lines passed over could be made fast to a suitable place before the steamer began drifting downstream. The men remaining on board hauled back one of the lines, but the other had to be cut to prevent its fouling the paddle wheel. Despite one of the holds having flooded, Stump was somehow able to get his boat back down to "Wright's Landing," where she was anchored. And, fortunately, a large timber bracing, which had been torn from the paddle wheel housing, was seen floating in the water, and was retrieved with a small boat.

Soon the eager line handlers who had jumped ashore up above, came straggling down the bank. Pumps were set, and, by constant pumping and caulking, the hold was cleared of water by that evening. It took all of the next day to put ashore various stores and the twenty-five cords of wood that had been taken on board.

On June 29, the steamer was once again hauled out onto the beach to repair the hull and a bulkhead. Late that afternoon, a very discouraged Captain Stump decided to climb what he had named "Green Mountain," on the river's southwest side, and have a look at what lay ahead. This peak was probably today's Cactus Mountain, which lies a few miles above the mouth of the Imnaha.

Stump crossed the river and started climbing, taking along several crewmen, a gun, some food, water and blankets. After spending a night under the stars, the explorers reached the summit the next morning, June 30. In the distance, to the south, could be seen the Blue Mountains and the course of the Imnaha. Stump could also see about twelve miles farther up Hell's Canyon of the Snake, and, as he said, it looked "very rough."

Having decided the river was impossible to stem, Stump and his men returned to the steamer. By that afternoon, repairs had been completed and the cordwood reloaded. The crew began poling the boat off the beach, but the river had fallen enough to make it a difficult task. After much cursing and the breaking of straps and blocks, late that evening *Colonel Wright* was finally glided into the stream.

In the morning, while his engineer repaired a boiler safety valve, Stump nailed an oyster box to a board, which he stuck up in the rocks above the high water line. Inside was a note which said: "Steamer Col. Wright's landing. July 1, 1865."

Stump shoved off at 10:15 A.M. for what proved to be a wild ride back to Lewiston. Within ten minutes, the boat spun around in a bad rapid and grounded. This required repairs to the leaky forward bulkhead, and some timber braces abaft the wheel.

Then, about noon, it was off again. Eleven minutes later, *Wright* whizzed past the mouth of the Salmon. The Cougar Rapids, that had taken so long to stem, were cleared at 12:39; the mouth of the Grande Ronde was left behind at 1:22, and, by 3:15, the steamer was tied up safely at Lewiston.

It had taken eight days to get 76 miles above Lewiston—twenty-one above the mouth of the Salmon—and less than five hours to make the return trip. J. M. Vansycle, who related the above story of the expedition, said it was "an experience not very soothing to weak nerves."[9]

Though the attempt to get a steamboat up to Farewell Bend had failed, the Columbia River proponents remained optimistic. Samuel Bowles, editor of the Springfield, Massachusetts, *Republican*, was in the West that year, traveling in the entourage of Speaker of the House Schuyler Colfax. Bowles wrote from Portland on July 23 urging continued efforts to get a steamboat on the upper Snake. He believed the Columbia route was still a quicker way to reach southern Idaho than the new roads from California.

The officers of the O.S.N. needed no convincing. They were determined to hold their advantage in the commerce with Idaho, and, since they hadn't been able to get a steamboat up river into southern Idaho, they decided to build one there.

In August, Captain Stump was sent to Boise to examine the Snake in that region. A short distance above Reynolds' Ferry, where the road from Boise to the Owyhee mines crossed, he borrowed a small boat and floated downstream, taking soundings.

After this cursory exploration, the captain reported to his superiors in Portland that the river was navigable, for a steamboat of light draft, from a point four miles above Olds' Ferry to Reynolds' Landing. Stump called this distance 130 miles, though, in fact, it is more like 50. He said using this stretch of the river would save 95 miles of difficult land travel to the Owyhee mines, and about 50 miles in getting to Boise.

This was deemed satisfactory to the company so Stump made arrangements to build a stern-wheeled steamboat on a site near the ferry at the mouth of the Boise River. The plan was for the boat to be ready for the spring trade.[10] To connect with the boat, a contract was made with B. M. Durell and Company to begin daily passenger and "fast freight" trips in the spring, from Umatilla to Olds' Ferry and from Reynolds' Landing to Boise and the Owyhee mines.

Machinery was diverted that had been intended for building a Columbia River boat and, by mid-October, the boiler and some of the major components were on the road from Umatilla. In November, an O.S.N. representative, Reed Dorsey, contracted with the owner of a steam sawmill in Boise, A. H. Robie, for lumber to be delivered before December 4 at the building site. To fuel the steamer's boiler, Dorsey placed orders for 400 cords of wood. In all, the lumber, cordwood, and freight costs totaled $19,000. Said O.S.N. president Ainsworth: "These are frightful figures but there is no backout now."[11]

Poor Dorsey nearly lost his life in returning to Portland, when two Indians chased him, shot his horse from under him, and brushed his hair with bullets. Another O.S.N. official said "this was no fun" for Dorsey, and that he had "no desire to go back" to Idaho.[12]

Idaho's high-falutin' governor, Caleb Lyon of Lyonsdale, was active in drumming up enthusiasm for the steamer, motivated in large part by a desire to line his pockets. In a speech to the territorial legislature, delivered December 8, Lyon proposed a "branch Pacific Railroad," to connect with the steamboat.

Lyon's scheme called for Columbia River traffic from Portland to continue on from Wallula by railroad, across the Blue Mountains to Farewell Bend. From there the new steamer would run to Salmon Falls, whence another section of new railroad would carry goods and passengers to the north end of the Great Salt Lake. Finally, another steamer would run across the lake to Salt Lake City. To help sell his plan, Lyon made the bogus claim that "a careful series of soundings at low water"[13] had shown that the Snake River could be made navigable from Olds' Ferry clear to Salmon Falls, a distance of 250 miles.

The governor urged Idaho's legislators to memorialize Congress for charter rights and "Government bounty" to induce construction of the railroad. Then the Columbia, "the natural avenue of commerce, would attract the trade of the Orient as well as the Occident, and form the last grand link in this truly national highway."[14] The legislature sent off such a memorial, and also passed an act, signed into law by Lyon, that incorporated the "Idaho, Salt Lake and Columbia River Branch Railroad Company." The legislature also passed an act requiring that the Snake River from Olds' Ferry to Salmon Falls remain free of impediments to the navigation of steamboats, such as bridges, booms or other structures.[15]

It will perhaps be no surprise to the reader to learn that the incorporators of the proposed railroad company included Governor Lyon, and other prominent men of southern Idaho, as well as Overland Stage Line owner, Ben Holladay, and the O.S.N.'s John C. Ainsworth.

But Joe Wasson, one of the down-to-earth editors of the *Owyhee Avalanche* in Silver City, was skeptical from the beginning about these grand schemes, requiring a steamboat on the Snake. In a satirical piece, he announced that the new stern-wheeled boat would have:

> ...four paddles instead of the usual two, and they were to be extra long, and attached to a movable axle, so that they might be raised or lowered according to the depth of the stream. In deep water the [paddle] wheels would be raised so that the boat might be propelled in the manner of an ordinary steamer; in ascending rapids, and in going over shallow and rough places,—by a simple twist of the wrist, so to speak, the wheels are lowered so as to rest on the bottom of the stream, and, if necessary, raise the boat clear of the water, and carry it over in the manner of a wagon...
>
> The project is looked upon as entirely practicable by the friends of Capt. Stump, as it doubtless will be by any one up a stump. The boat will be

supplied with pushing poles...in case any assistance should be necessary in getting it up the rocky places, the passengers could get out and help shove it up.[16]

The skepticism of Wasson and others notwithstanding, the boat building began. Captain John Gates, chief engineer for the O.S.N., arrived at the building site about January 1, 1866 with twenty workmen. They had come overland from The Dalles on sleighs, inasmuch as the upper Columbia was frozen over.

Gates—described once as a "quiet genius"—was an inventor and renowned builder of Columbia River steamboats and, at the time, he held patents on at least 27 gadgets designed to improve boat operations. These included an hydraulic steering gear, several steam pumps, an automatic oiler, and a cut-off valve. In his lifetime, this busy man would supervise the construction of more than 21 boats.[17]

In those days, nearby "Boisé City" was thriving. It had grown from nothing, just two years earlier, into a town of some 250 houses. Its population now comprised 800 voters (all men, of course), about 600 women and children, and a floating community of some 300. The mile-long Main Street was fully occupied by businesses. There were three drug stores, a foundry, several hotels and restaurants, and a multitude of whiskey mills. Two schools were just getting started. A recently established tri-weekly paper, the *Boise Statesman*, was supported by a circulation of 500 and the contract for territorial printing.

Six stage lines serviced Boise. Greathouse and Kelly ran a daily coach to Idaho City; two companies ran daily, alternately to Umatilla or Wallula; Ben Holladay's line ran tri-weekly stages to Salt Lake City; William McWhirk ran to Rocky Bar; and Hill Beachy to Owyhee. The Wells Fargo express company had an agency in town, doing a lucrative business.

The best hotel in town was the two-story Overland, at the corner of Eighth and Main, operated since its opening in September, 1864 by Cram and Ellsworth. It had been built with a wide porch on the second story, running all around the building and extending over the sidewalk. From this lofty gallery every public speaker of note in those days addressed the citizenry.

But rooms were scarce, and it was not usual to enter any public place after 11 P.M., and find the floors covered with men asleep in blankets. Despite this crowding, one visitor deemed Boise to be "remarkably healthy," except for the occasional cases of fever and ague, "arising from the malaria from fresh plowed land." This overall state of good health gave the "poor medicine men" little to do; "their principal patients being *feet* [of mining ledges]."[18]

Nearby, about a mile back from the city, toward the foothills, sat Fort Boise. Its structures built of brown sandstone, just two years earlier, the post was manned by a small force under Lieutenant Colonel John M. Drake of the 1st Oregon Volunteer Infantry. The army's mission was to provide protection for the Boise Basin and Owyhee mining districts, and for emigrants passing through the area.

About the time the steamboat building began, a pioneer eight-person theatrical troupe opened at Sanderson's Hall, which had been specially fitted up for their use. In bitter cold weather, after a few freezing performances, the owners made the hall more comfortable by furnishing it with two large stoves.

Sue Robinson Getzler, the star of the company, had begun her acting, dancing and singing career as a little girl in California's Gold Rush towns. Among other roles, in Boise, Sue played Kate O'Brien in "The Irish Heiress" and Captain Daring in "The Captain's not A-Miss." Between plays she might dance a jig, or join in a duet such as "What are the Wild Waves Saying?"[19]

Probably no vessel was ever constructed in the northwest under greater difficulties, or at greater relative expense, than was Idaho's sagebrush steamboat. The cost was said to have been $80,000, which sum would have built several fine steamers closer to civilization. Hundreds of miles from any sophisticated foundry or machine shop, nearly all the iron fittings were transported a long distance by pack animals and worked into shape on the building grounds. Every piece of her steam propulsion system had to be brought from shops on the Columbia.

By late February, Gates had the boat's frame completed and ready for planking. In March, G. B. Underwood, arrived to put the engines in place. So confident were the directors of the O.S.N. that their enterprise would succeed, they began running advertisements in the papers promising to land freight at Salmon Falls from San Francisco in about seven days at $7\frac{1}{2}$ cents per pound, and to transport passengers from San Francisco, via the Columbia and Snake, to Salt Lake City, quicker and cheaper than any overland transportation.

But, Joe Wasson of the *Avalanche*, who favored the new direct routes from California, knew better. He said:

> 'Capital' is building a steamboat on Snake River, and 'blowing' is relied on to give it 'a sickly existence.' This concern is simply a bait to gull the unwary...and induce them to patronize the Columbia one more season. If the

scheme succeeds it will more than pay for several boats. The public shouldn't think the O. S. N. company have confidence in navigating the Snake simply because they are building a boat. It requires a considerable outlay of money to produce a profitable humbug.[20]

When news was received that Capt. John Mullan, John Bidwell and others had incorporated to run a stage line from Chico to Idaho, Wasson needled the O.S.N. once again. "Now whose steamboat's the biggest?" he asked.[21]

The boat was launched on April 20, and placed under the command of Captain Josiah Myrick. Named *Shoshone*, the little stern-wheeler was 138 feet long, with a 27-foot beam. She was equipped with 243-horsepower double engines, of 16-inch diameter and 48-inch stroke. The boat drew about 20 inches of water when loaded and was designed to carry about 175 tons of cargo. By way of comparison, steamers then running on San Francisco bay were usually ten to thirty feet longer, and a few feet broader than *Shoshone*. The *Colonel Moody*, shown at the beginning of this chapter, was almost identical in size and configuration to *Shoshone*.[22]

Invitations were extended to "representative men" of Owyhee and Boise to ride *Shoshone* and attend a "blow out." Wasson, of the *Avalanche*, who didn't get an invitation, and who didn't think much of the O.S.N. and the hazards of steam propulsion, wrote, sarcastically:

> Sorry we ain't 'representative,' etc. As for the 'blow out,' that'll come off sure, but it would have been better to have built two steamers...there would have been a bigger 'blow out'...Steamboats are good things...[We] Are glad the O.S.N. Co. are building some. They'll be handy for emigrants in case of a storm...Recent examinations show that the steamer can run up Sincker [sic] Creek to the N.Y. and O.F. [crushing] Mill as easily as to its mouth.[23]

Sinker Creek, of course, is a small stream.

One of the true believers in the steamboat was the energetic and fearless James S. Reynolds, 42-year old principal owner and editor of the *Boise Statesman*. Reynolds was a former New Yorker, who stood six feet four inches high, had enormous hands and feet, sandy hair, and kindly blue eyes.

Having received an invitation, he boarded one of Hill Beachy's stages at 2 A.M. on May 16 for the dreary, dusty journey to Reynolds' Landing, where the O.S.N.'s guests were to be picked up. As usual, a "jehu" named Charles W. Barnes was at the reins of the coach.

Charlie Barnes was quite a character. In the 1850s he had run a pack train out of Placerville, California distributing provisions and booze to miners in remote locales. After coming to Idaho he had, for a time, owned a part interest in Leach's Owyhee Stage Line, which had since been taken over by Beachy. In the winter of 1864-65, Charlie had built a sleigh and run it to the Owyhee mining camps, carrying passengers, mail and express items. On at least one occasion he had been required to carry the mail on his back over the summit to Silver City.

For part of the next winter, he had worked as an express man between Boise and Rocky Bar, riding the stagecoach as far as the Junction House, where he strapped on 12-foot long "snow-shoes"—skis, in fact—to get to Rocky Bar. On scheduled mail days, those at the isolated mining camp eagerly awaited the sound of Charlie's bugle, announcing his arrival. Running the gauntlet "of the long, lonely trail of ice and snow, in the storm and cold," he was their "messenger to and from the outer world...Bringing and taking messages of love, news and trade." And, the sound of his bugle was "as sweet music" to the ears in Rocky Bar, as "the bagpipes were to the besieged of Lucknow [India].[24]

One man who met Barnes called him "one of those eccentric, devil-may-care individuals" who "seem to have a general license to say and do whatever the whim of the moment may prompt them to do." Charlie, he said, had "but one great fault, his voice was cracked; he couldn't sing, but was eternally humming the tune "Never buy tripe on a Friday."[25]

Reynolds had previously ridden with the waggish Barnes on this same desert route to the Owyhee mines. One mile out from the center of Boise was the "miserable little one-horse"[26] rope ferry which crossed the Boise River. Then came 30 or so miles across the broken sagebrush plain to Snake River, with only Charlie's drolleries to amuse the passenger who sat beside him on the driver's bench. Said editor Jim Reynolds of his earlier trip with Barnes:

> I am inclined to think that if the Universal Architect had any definite design in making that patch of country, it was on purpose for Charley Barnes to drive stage over. I am sure no other man living could do so and keep his temper even...
>
> Charley has several stations on this road, for the names of which...he must have drawn heavily on his imagination. After breakfast [at Record's Station], the next station was to be 'Forest Grove.' To the stranger the name is suggestive of shady bowers and babbling brooks affording a pleasant escape from this insufferable dust and cloudless sun.
>
> Charley helps the imagination of the traveler by repeating his contract with the O.S.N. company to furnish them vast quantities of fuel for the steamer that is to navigate the tortuous Snake. In two hours after you have given up looking for any tree, Charley introduces you to a patch of the plain

where sage brush won't grow at all, as 'Forest Grove.'

Forest Grove station sat on a small hill just above the river, about a mile up a ravine from Reynolds' Landing. It consisted of a stone hut for the herdsman, and a stone horse corral, upon the walls of which a grinning human skull lay perched.

On his previous trip, Jim Reynolds had crossed the Snake on the man-powered ferry and continued on to the Owyhee mines. We include his impressions of the next station, just to give the reader a more vivid glimpse of the colorful Charley Barnes:

> The sun is scorching hot and there is not a drop of water to be seen, but Charley informs us that the next station is 'Cold Spring.' This is exhilarating news, and after extracting courage from our 'pocket companions,' we talk of quartz, and mills, and feet, and think of the 'spring.' After a while, coming to a spot more barren and dry than any we have yet seen, with not a stick, or stone, or brush more than a foot high, a *ranchero* with half an inch of alkali on him, holding four wild mustangs, tells us to halt. He and Charley commence exchanging horses, and we inquire if this is 'Cold Spring,' to which Charley nods affirmatively.
>
> Innocent passengers ask 'where is the house?' Charley looks in all directions and says it's here. We couldn't see it. The next query, 'where's the water?' to which Charley replies that there is a slough about four miles over the top of the next hill at right angles to the road. We just then recollected that 'Cold Spring Station' is on the same road with 'Forest Grove,' and Barnes drives it.[27]

But, on this particular morning of May 16, 1866, James Reynolds was going just as far as the Snake River. The stage arrived the ferry landing just in time for him to hear "the music of the steam whistle reverberate for the first time along the sagebrush solitudes of the Snake." It was pleasant music, he said, "to those of us who have for two years heard no other than the whoa-haw, driver's whip, or the Jehu's horn."

Captain Myrick had started *Shoshone* up river from her construction site on the previous afternoon, running with 50 pounds of steam. He had laid over at dark and then come up the rest of the way that morning.

Myrick served Reynolds and his other guests plenty of liquor and a hearty luncheon, and then took *Shoshone* down river, running back to the mouth of the Boise River in five hours, including time to take on wood. Strong desert winds were blowing that day and it was difficult to keep the lightly-loaded steamer on her course. Several times, strong gusts turned her completely around, in spite of the use of helm and engine.

The following day, Myrick took his passengers downstream to Olds' Ferry at Farewell Bend. It was a beautiful day and the trip was made without incident in just under five hours. Very much impressed, Reynolds hailed this "first link in the chain of steam communications to be made continuous... between Salt Lake and the Columbia River..."[28]

At Olds' Ferry, all of the passengers except Reynolds boarded one of B. M. Durell's stagecoaches and returned to Boise. Reynolds was upset that his companions had abandoned him, but said he had "enlisted for one round trip," and so would "stay with the *Shoshone* til it is finished if Captain Myrick and Engineer Underwood do not desert."[29]

Carpenters and painters were still putting the finishing touches on the boat, which Reynolds thought had been built in as fine a style as any on the Columbia. Usually, he said, the first vessels built on newly navigated waters were of inferior quality, but, in this instance, the company had taken the risk of constructing a first class item. *Shoshone* had already shown that her running time was excellent.

Captain Myrick kept the steamer tied up at Olds' Ferry all of May 18, giving editor Reynolds a chance to learn more about activities in the area. In March, William Packwood and his partners had moved the ferry down the river a mile or two to a more convenient point, where J. J. Smith was starting a public house and small store. The O.S.N. intended moving their shops there from old Fort Boise, and would also erect a small warehouse convenient to the steamer landing.

Shoshone required large amounts of fuel, and, with nothing but sagebrush hills for miles around, cordwood had to be hauled from the distant mountains. The discovery of coal in February at Olds' Ferry had aroused hopes that it might be used. Packwood's company had driven a 250-foot tunnel into the mountain, at a right angle to the river, where a seven-foot thick vein of coal had been discovered, of good enough quality to have been used by local blacksmiths.

Reynolds thought it a blessing that the fuel had been found "at the very place where it is most wanted." As soon as it could be mined, he said, nothing would hinder its use on the boats that would "hereafter ever navigate the Snake River from Olds' Ferry to Salmon Falls..."[30]

On May 19, Gates, the chief engineer of the O.S.N., arrived via the Umatilla stage to put *Shoshone* through her paces. After a brief trial, he was satisfied that the steamer was ready to explore the balance of the route for which she was intended—the water upstream of Reynolds' Landing, as far as Salmon Falls. Accordingly, she was taken back to the mouth of the Boise, where forty cords of wood were loaded.

With Gates and editor Reynolds riding as passengers, Captain Myrick began the ascent on the morning of May 21. No one aboard had ever seen the river above Reynolds' Landing, or had heard anything reliable concerning it, but there was an unconfirmed report of a canyon about seven miles above the landing, through which the steamer likely could not pass.

Indeed, at that point, Jim Reynolds later wrote, there began "one of the wildest and grandest canyons in the world," some ten miles long, and extremely crooked. In it, the river narrowed and deepened, and was contained by perpendicular bluffs of an almost uniform height of 600 feet. This canyon now marks the beginning of Idaho's famous Birds of Prey Natural Area.

A strong, smooth current ran through the gorge, but there were no impassible rapids. Myrick took her without difficulty by the mouth of Sinker Creek, out of the canyon, and past Castle (Catherine) Creek to the mouth of the Bruneau River.

This area is now covered by the waters of the C. J. Strike reservoir, but in those days, just above the Bruneau, there was another canyon, not so deep as the first, but full of rapids. Six miles into this second canyon, *Shoshone* came to swift rough water, which, even with 80 pounds of steam, brought the boat to a halt. The captain backed out of the situation, tied up and proceeded to explore by land. Ahead he could see two miles of a swift, rough rapid, with a considerable fall at its head.

With some doubt as to the feasibility of going any farther, Captain Myrick ordered and got a full head of steam—110 pounds. Up the rapid *Shoshone* went, with ease, until her prow touched the fall, where she faltered. Steam was raised a bit more, and the boat held to her work for over half an hour, but the fall was too much to overcome, and no reliable line with which to *cordelle* was aboard.

Accordingly, Myrick spun *Shoshone* around and took her darting back down the river. The run back to the landing was made in about four hours, which included a brief stop to investigate a possible silver vein seen in the canyon wall.

Reynolds reckoned, correctly, that Myrick had taken *Shoshone* some sixty miles, by the course of the river, above Reynolds' Landing. The place where they had been stopped was unsuitable for a terminal because of the high bluffs, but there was little doubt in the editor's mind that, with the aid of a line, boats could get through that troublesome rapid as easily as they did some like it in the Willamette and Columbia rivers.[31]

As usual, Joe Wasson of the *Avalanche* didn't agree. If ever the boat could make it above the Bruneau it would be now, when the Snake was running at high water. He said:

> That double-track railroad will have to be built to the mouth of the Bruneau to make navigable connection, instead of to Salmon Falls, as the ex-Governor [Lyon] and us calculated. This would require all the spare capital Gov. and us possess. We never strongly believed in the navigation of Snake, except by small Indian canoes and common-sized Salmon, but the Gov., being a very great man, we listened to his wily suggestions in this and some other matters, which have since proved the correctness of our first impressions. The firm of 'Gov. and us' is completely dissolved and our share of the railroad is for sale, to take place on the same day the Shoshone is auctioned. She is reported tied up, and her Commander gone to Boise City for an auctioneer.[32]

Not being able reach Salmon Falls was a great disappointment to the steamboat's owners—who had hoped to participate in the Salt Lake City trade—but they weren't quite ready to auction off their boat. They, however, made no further attempts to run above Reynolds' Landing. Instead, *Shoshone*

Advertisement in the Boise Statesman, June 5, 1866
(Author's Collection)

began making twice-weekly trips, between the landing and Olds' Ferry. Regular stops were also made near the mouth of the Payette River for the convenience of passengers and freight headed for the Boise Basin.

By July, a small town had sprung up at Farewell Bend, consisting of a warehouse, blacksmith shop, hotel, store and two dwellings. A cheerful report from Olds' Ferry said that, on her regular trips, *Shoshone* was causing "a mighty panic among the little fish as she puffs up and down the river."[33]

In June, Captain Myrick was called back to Portland, having been relieved of command of Idaho's little steamer by Captain Henry F. Gray. Based on Myrick's report, O.S.N. president Ainsworth wrote that *Shoshone* "had not and cannot pay expenses this season," but continuing to run her was warranted because it would help secure the Owyhee trade, as against Chico, and that next year she would "pay a direct profit."[34]

But, by mid-month, *Shoshone* was forced to stop running for a few weeks owing to a lack of fuel. High water had made it difficult for teamsters to transport wood from the mountains, and the plan to use coal had failed. The coal mine's entrance happened to be in close proximity to the bank of the Snake, and spring runoff had overflowed into the tunnel. Even the installation of a large pump wasn't enough to keep the mine dry. The energetic Captain Gray built a skiff and drifted down the Boise River to locate and contract with parties having wood for sale.

Twice weekly trips were resumed, but business was meager. In September, Captain R. R. Thompson, of the O.S.N. came up from Portland to see for himself what changes in the management of *Shoshone* the times demanded. He obviously saw the realities of the situation, because, with the coming of winter, all advertising ceased and, by March 1867, the enterprise had entirely failed.[35]

The inability to extend the run to Salmon Falls had helped kill it, but, of more significance, the overland routes through Oregon and Nevada had proven to be quicker and less expensive, by half, than the Columbia River route. And, Hill Beachy's "Railroad Stage Line" from Boise, through Silver City and Winnemucca to Hunter's Station, Nevada—a notable success— would soon connect with the new Central Pacific railroad. Another factor in the steamboat's demise was that the planned railroad from Wallula was likewise a flop, Gov. Lyon and the other directors having never even held a meeting.

And so, *Shoshone's* brief moment of glory was ended. For the rest of 1867 she was laid up at Fruit's Ferry, near Reynolds' Landing, with Captain George Molthrop her caretaker. Now the indignities began.

Since the coming of white men to the Owyhee country there had been vicious, unceasing conflict with the Indians of the area. This strife reached its peak in the year *Shoshone* was mothballed, as General George Crook and his forces fought Paiutes and Shoshoni all the way from southwestern Idaho to the border of California.

The road between the Snake River and the Owyhee mines was especially hazardous. On October 21, a dozen miles distant from where *Shoshone* lay idle, army Sergeant Denoille and his pregnant wife, along with a certain Sergeant Nichols, were traveling in a four-horse ambulance to Boise, from Camp Lyon on the Idaho-Oregon border. When about half way between the camp and Reynolds' Creek, they were ambushed by Indians.

Denoille was shot dead instantly, and fell from the ambulance. The horses bolted and ran about a half mile before being halted by their entangled harness. Nichols and the frantic Mrs. Denoille then leapt from the wagon, but Nichols could not persuade her to take shelter with him in the rocks. She ran back toward her fallen husband, and was never seen again. By firing and retreating, Nichols made it safely to a ranch on Reynolds' Creek.[36]

Even *Shoshone* at Fruits' Landing was not immune from the natives' wrath. Just nine days after the Denoille attack, a small raiding party appeared during the night and fired buckshot and bullets into the door of the cabin where caretaker Molthrop was sleeping. In writing of the incident, Molthrop said that the "devils knew well where to fire, thinking I would come out." Jim Reynolds of the *Statesman* wondered if these Shoshoni would "next attack the Overland House or post office"[37] in Boise City.

After this, poor *Shoshone* was moved to an island just down from Munday's Ferry, 30 miles below Boise. Here she sat until 1869, when the directors of the steamship company decided to try and recoup some of their enormous investment. Captain Cyrus Smith was sent with instructions to bring the steamer down to Lewiston where she could be put to beneficial use.

Smith made a good start down the Snake with *Shoshone*, but, upon reaching Lime Point, about five miles below the location of today's Oxbow Dam, he abandoned the project. Some two hundred yards downstream, plunging through a narrow bend of the river, lay the Copper Ledge Cascades, which Smith believed could not be navigated. He thought he might have been able to let the steamer down through these rapids using ropes, but did not have enough on hand for the job. So, leaving the boat in charge of two keepers, the captain went on to Portland to report the situation. With winter coming on, the O.S.N. decided to abandon the attempt for that year, and let *Shoshone* remain in the canyon.

The following spring, the company sent Captain Sebastian "Bas" Miller with orders to bring the boat through to Lewiston, even at the risk of losing her. Taking along Daniel E. "Buck" Buchanan,[38] a much-respected engineer, Miller left Portland on March 22, and headed up the Columbia. After landing at Umatilla, he and Buchanan traveled by buckboard, sled, wagon, horseback and on foot, to reach *Shoshone* at Lime Point about April 15.

The two men who had been tending the boat during the winter signed on as crew with Miller, one as mate and the other as fireman. After hiring another man as a deck hand, Miller and his crew set about putting *Shoshone* into good order for the voyage. Machinery was disconnected and overhauled, and the steamer's pine hull, which had shrunk in places, was wet down, using the deck pump, until the planking swelled and closed the gaps.

The river was rising rapidly with spring runoff. When Miller judged it to be at the proper stage, on April 20, 1870, he made his move. Lighted candles were placed in the hold, so that any leaks could be instantly detected and stopped.

The first challenge lay directly below—the Copper Ledge Cascades, which Captain Smith had reported could not be passed in safety. These rapids are now covered by Hell's Canyon Reservoir, but, in those days, running free, they had a fall of fifteen feet in a distance of two hundred.

Miller's plan of navigation for the trip down river was to drift with the engines backing. This is how he took *Shoshone* out into the river above the powerful rapids, where she began a silent and smooth acceleration that must have given those aboard a sense of being drawn into a maelstrom, over which they would have no control.

The little steamer conformed to the current, and, near a place where the river was divided by a small island, the whirling of a large eddy spun her around three times before she began her plunge down the steeply sloped cascades.

Once in the chute, *Shoshone* dipped and yawed broadly, causing her stern to come up until the paddle wheel was entirely out of the water. The engine raced wildly and when the paddlewheel took hold again all that part of it which had been so long exposed to the weather was destroyed, and was useless in checking the speed of the steamer.

At the foot of the cataract *Shoshone* hit some rocks, carrying away about eight feet of her bow above the waterline. So great was the shock that the weight flew off of the boiler safety valve, causing steam pressure to drop to zero.

Once out of the turbulence, Miller somehow beached the boat. He put the crew to work all day, repairing the paddle wheel and the smashed bow. Fortunately, the forward bulkhead had held, keeping water out of the rest of

Captain Sebastian Miller
(*Author's collection*)

the hull. But, unbeknownst to Miller and his crew, the jackstaff—a part of the bow that had been carried away—would drift far downstream to Umatilla, Oregon, long before *Shoshone* was heard from, and people in that region gave her up for lost.

The following morning, Miller started his battered boat plunging down through Hell's Canyon, with thundering rapids and whirlpools continually deluging the decks. Just before noon, a stop was made to cut up a small clump of trees, for fuel. Then the steamer was pushed off again for the wild ride through the heart of the canyon. Here, in quick succession, flows some of its worst water—the rapids at Brush Creek, Wild Sheep, Granite Creek, and Rush Creek. At the latter, the entire volume of the river is confined in a boulder-choked channel of solid rock, so narrow that the noise of the surging water overpowers all other sounds. And, high above this maelstrom soars the silent wall of Hat Point.

Through all these chutes, *Shoshone* bucked and pitched like an angry mustang, in several instances the wheel house distorting so much that the engine-order gong sounded of its own volition, deceiving the engineer. Water coming over the decks drove the fireman from the hold several times. Toward evening, the exhausted crew beached the steamer to patch up the paddle wheel once again. This work took until the morning of April 23, at which time the lines were cast off; but, before noon, Miller was compelled to tie her up because a strong wind interfered with steering.

On the twenty-fourth, only about ten miles were made, because Captain Miller was frequently required to disembark and walk ahead to examine the river before proceeding. That afternoon, he tied the boat up at the base of a mountain where fuel was plentiful. Here, poor Miller was badly bruised and abraded when a large tree, which was being rolled down the mountain, bounced over him.

Wisely, the captain took a day off to nurse his wounds before resuming the voyage. Starting again on the morning of April 26, the less-perilous water allowed backing the engines at only half-throttle. A stop was made at the mouth of the Salmon River for lunch, and to give the injured Miller a rest. By late afternoon the Grande Ronde was reached, and the steamer tied up for the night.

The next morning the boat whizzed through Captain Lewis Rapids, without incident, and arrived at Lewiston after a mere two hours travel. The local citizenry were startled to hear the sound of *Shoshone's* whistle as Miller brought her proudly down the river. While rounding to, in front of the town, he shouted down through the voice tube to engineer Buchanan, "I say, Buck, I expect if this company wanted a couple of men to take a steamboat through hell, they would send for you and me."[39]

On landing, the captain turned the boat over to an agent of the company, stating that, although she looked a little rough—what with a bruised stem and a few broken buckets on the paddle wheel—she didn't leak a drop.

Shoshone was taken downstream to Celilo, Oregon by someone else, while "Bas" Miller was sent to northern Idaho for another demanding task. In June he brought the steamboats *Missoula* and *Cabinet* over Cabinet Rapids into Lake Pend Oreille. According to reports, while going through Cabinet Canyon, the water was so rough that the steamers were totally buried from sight. Then, at the end of that month, Miller rejoined *Shoshone* and piloted both her and the steamer *Nez Perces Chief*, individually, on the perilous trip down through the dalles of the Columbia to the middle river.[40]

After being hauled out for extensive repairs, the much-abused steamboat ran as a cattle carrier until 1873, when Captain Ainsworth maneuvered her down through the Cascades to Portland. She worked on the Willamette River for another year, then struck a rock near Salem and sank. After every effort to raise her proved futile, the owners had all the machinery removed, and then left the hulk to the elements. It later floated down to Lincoln, where a parsimonious farmer hauled it out and made it into a chicken house—a most undignified end to the career of Idaho's sagebrush steamboat.[41]

Today, all that remains to remind us that little *Shoshone* ever existed are some dusty old newspaper accounts and her likeness as portrayed in an early territorial seal designed by Governor Lyon. In this depiction, the little boat can be seen, wending her way through the Idaho mountains, above a banner inscribed "Salve"—"Greetings."

Old Kale

Caleb Lyon, ca. 1852
(*Idaho State Historical Society*)

Those who have read the previous tale about Idaho's "Sagebrush Steamboat" will already have a nodding acquaintance with "Old Kale," the first of our scoundrels. Here is the rest of his story.

It is surprising that Idaho ever survived territorial status to become a state, given the corrupt impulses and ineptitude of some early political appointees.

Take Caleb Lyon, for example.

This vainglorious man—Idaho's second territorial governor—was surely the most eccentric and unfit politician ever seen in the West. One contemporary characterized him as a "revolving light upon the coast of scampdom."[1]

On the face of it, Caleb Lyon would seem to have been well qualified for any governmental position. He was born in 1822 to an upper-crust family of Lyonsdale, in upstate New York; and, after attending the best of schools, he traveled extensively in the Middle East and Europe.

In February, 1847, when Caleb was a mere 25 years of age, President James K. Polk accorded him the consulship in Shanghai, China. This appointment was due, in large part, to his father's influence with Secretary of State William Marcy. But young Lyon never saw China. Instead, he sent out a deputy, and then, within a year, resigned the post, displaying publicly for the first time his lifelong tendency to vacillate and avoid difficult tasks.

In 1849, the discovery of gold in California attracted his attention, and he sailed there, around Cape Horn, in the clipper ship *Tarolinta*. A fellow passenger would later vividly recall the day when the ship reached the warm Pacific waters off the Chilean coast, and Lyon appeared on deck with a Turkish rug over his arm, and a Turkish smoking cap atop his long, flowing locks. Plopping himself down cross-legged on the rug, Caleb puffed on his pipe and began regaling everyone in earshot with the tale of his appointment as minister, plenipotentiary and extraordinary, to Constantinople. He had been given no such commission, of course.

Arriving in California, Lyon toured the mining camps, and then wheedled himself a job as one of the two assistant secretaries of the constitutional convention that met during September and October in Monterey, in preparation for statehood.

With no other accommodations available, Lyon boarded in the home of an army couple, Captain and Mrs. George Westcott. The latter adjudged Caleb to be a "remarkably agreeable person & entertaining, but *very eccentric* & odd." Lyon loved to overwhelm anyone he could collar with stories of his consulship in China (even though he had never been there), and of his being a bearer of government dispatches to South American countries.[2]

Throughout his life, Lyon would boast of having designed the great seal of California, as authorized by the convention. But, according to J. Ross Browne—the official reporter of the conclave—the seal was actually created by Major Robert S. Garnett, an army officer stationed at Monterey, who was too modest to take credit for it. Garnett gave his drawing to Lyon, who submitted it after adding 31 stars around the bevel of the ring, which were meant to symbolize the number of states in the Union with the addition of California.

After the convention, Caleb traveled to San Francisco, where, in November, he happened to meet Jacob H. Bachman, a new arrival who was down on his luck. Years later, what Bachman would remember most about Lyon was an unfulfilled promise. In their conversations Lyon had spoken "very encouragingly," and offered to help Bachman find a job, but then made absolutely no effort to do so.[3]

After his brief dalliance in the Golden State, Lyon made another visit to Europe. Upon returning to New York, he was elected to the state assembly for the 1851 session, but took no meaningful part in its proceedings, being too busy seeking election to the U. S. Congress, as the representative of Herkimer, Lewis and Jefferson counties.

While on the "stump" he used every last trick in the politician's bag to appeal to popular tastes. He would appear at meetings with farmers and mechanics in a pair of huge, cowhide boots, and wearing a dirty woolen coat that might have just been fished out of the rag bag. Such artifice and his gift for gab won him the 1852 election.

Ever the dilettante, Lyon wrote several bits of ornate poetry during this period, which were published in newspapers at home and abroad. He even wrote a novel describing the adventures of an English traveler captured by Tasmanian natives. But, he was most renowned for reciting—to his circle of friends for hours at a time—an unbroken chain of poems, "with a melodious utterance, and a rich, full emphasis that would delight the most critical ear."[4]

It was this side of his character, as well as his hedonistic nature, that drew him, about this time, to the notorious and sensual dancer, Lola Montez, who was touring the Eastern seaboard. He acquired an oil painting of Lola and she presented him with an edition of the works of Pierre Jean de Bèranger, with a tender sentiment inscribed on the flyleaf. What else she may have given him is not known.

After serving one term in the House, Lyon was ousted by the voters. In 1856, his family's mansion at Lyonsdale was destroyed by fire, so he purchased a home on Staten Island, which he named "Lyonsmere." There, he amused himself by collecting fine books, ceramics, paintings, and bric-a-brac, and by delivering lectures describing his travels.

A grandiloquent and amusing speaker, he deliberately drew attention to himself by wearing flaming neckties and bizarre suits. And, though dressed in the finest linen, he would wear it for days, until it became dirty and worthless.

During one lecture, he greatly amused his audience by "jerking out a large quantity of dirty shirt sleeve every few moments in his excited gestures, and busily tucking it back again out of sight." Though the shirt sleeve kept coming out, it was soon forgotten in the eloquence of the orator.[5] Caleb's speech was always like the rush of a cataract, and, when interrupted by applause, he would bow repeatedly and profoundly, but would seize the first lull to push on again. The flexibility of his backbone, in all this bowing, was a wonder to his audiences.

Lyon dabbled in these trifling activities until his attention was drawn back to politics by the election of Abraham Lincoln as President in 1860. The eruption of America's Civil War found him in the nation's capital, foraging for governmental spoils.

Coincident with the onset of war, in early 1861, gold discoveries were made in the region that would become northern Idaho, and a great rush was made to the area. The town of Lewiston was established at the confluence of the Snake and Clearwater rivers, as a terminus for supplying the surrounding mining camps.

Most of the gold seekers who came to the district were southern Democrats, and many of these were fervent secessionists with an intense hatred of the federal government. In August, 1862, when A. S. Gould first raised the United States flag over the office of the Lewiston *Golden Age*—Idaho's first newspaper—twenty-one shots were fired into it by radical Democrats.

In March, 1863, the Territory of Idaho was created, which included all of today's Idaho, Montana and Wyoming. As first governor of this sparsely populated colossus, President Abraham Lincoln selected a westerner, William H. Wallace. Unfortunately, Wallace did little to organize and sustain a government. After choosing Lewiston as the temporary capital, he went there, had a census of voters taken for the purpose of apportionment, and set October 31 as the date for election of territorial legislators and a delegate to Congress.

Then, without any troubling sense of duty, the opportunistic Wallace resigned as governor, in order to run for office as the territory's congressional delegate. In the election, he was the sole Republican to be chosen, the Democrats sweeping every other post. Afterward, he quickly left for the East, under a cloud of suspicion that his victory was fraudulent, due to "late [forged] returns" from the Fort Laramie district.[6]

With Wallace's departure, the governorship temporarily devolved upon the territorial secretary, William B. Daniels. At Daniels' call, Idaho's first legislature met for sixty days at Lewiston, beginning on December 7, 1863. Its principal accomplishments were creation of the original seven counties, a system of courts, judicial districts, and a code of laws.[7] It also passed a strict and controversial "iron-clad" oath of office, meant to be taken by elected and appointed officials, that was patterned after the one required of federal officials.

For several years, including the time during which Idaho was being established, Caleb Lyon had been applying for consulships in exotic places, but all had been denied him, despite the efforts of influential friends such as John Palmer Usher, President Lincoln's Secretary of the Interior. Then, when it was learned in late January, 1864 that William Wallace had resigned, Usher asked Secretary of State William H. Seward to push Lyon's name for the vacant governorship.

The opposition was strong against Lyon. Western politicians, including Wallace, each had a favorite candidate, and Roscoe Conkling, a New York congressman, told Lincoln he had doubts about Lyon's moral character. As if that weren't enough, an Eastern newspaper correspondent wrote that Lyon had a reputation as a "poetaster [inferior poet] or something of that sort," and would not make much of a governor.[8] But Lincoln had apparently made an earlier promise to appoint Lyon, and he stood by it, signing his commission on February 26.

The newly-designated governor seemed in no hurry to reach Idaho. He dawdled for months at Lyonsmere, during which time he and his wife, Anna, and their son, Caleb, had as a houseguest 17-year old Arthur P. Usher, eldest son of the secretary of interior. Young Arthur had been given permission to accompany Lyon to Idaho as his private secretary.

Finally, on June 25, Lyon and his young companion took a steamer from New York, sailing around Cape Horn. The governor's arrival on the Pacific Coast spawned a cluster of glowing press notices in Western papers, containing marvelous, but bogus, tales about his life. Some of these even suggested that he had seen duty with General Winfield Scott in Mexico, and with General Irwin McDowell in several Civil War battles.

But Caleb had never smelt gun smoke. His only contribution to the ongoing war had come in its first year, when he had been sent to the Robert E. Lee house in Arlington, Virginia to take possession of the George Washington relics, and other priceless items, in the name of the United States. Presumably, Lyon had turned everything over to the Smithsonian Institution, although some who knew his reputation as a collector doubted that all of the items ever reached that repository.

In another distortion of Lyon's past, a friend living in Portland, who had known him in California fourteen years earlier, proclaimed him to be "a live governor," and an "old miner" who could "early learn, and promptly supply, all the wants of the miners among whom he is to govern." But, as events would prove, Lyon was a total misfit amongst Idaho's rough-cut sourdoughs.

While, at first, everything would be sweetness and light, ultimately his policies and dishonest nature would antagonize them.

And, Caleb's personal idiosyncrasies—amusing at first—would soon wear thin with Idahoans. He used fantastic sentences, literary quotations and high-flown expressions, but worse—as one of his acquaintances said—Lyon was "one of those irrepressible button-holers who seize on a victim and talk him dumb," while never seeming to "talk himself stupid in the operation."[9]

Another of Lyon's eccentricities was his snobbish habit of referring to, and signing himself as "Caleb Lyon of Lyonsdale." In explanation, he would say that there were half a dozen Calebs among the Lyons in his county of New York, and he used "of Lyonsdale" to distinguish himself from the others. This little conceit would furnish plenty of horselaughs for the hardy pioneers of Idaho, and it wasn't long before they were referring to the governor as "Cale of the Dale," or simply, "Old Kale."

Lyon was also too much the fop for a territory largely populated by two-fisted men. He always wore fancy (but dirty) linen, and expensive dress suits. He would be the first ever to appear at a social function in the territory in a swallow-tailed coat. And, according to one old-timer, "It was even hinted that he wore suspenders."[10]

After getting an earful from Oregon's governor, Addison C. Gibbs, regarding the current political instability in an Idaho full of southerners, Lyon left Portland for Lewiston, where he arrived on August 8, 1864.

The secretary, William Daniels, had done a good job looking after things, but he was one of those who had competed against Lyon for the governor's job, and so he left for Oregon, humiliated and disgusted, the day after Lyon's arrival. Lyon appointed Silas D. Cochran, Daniels' clerk, as acting secretary.[11]

In his first report to Secretary of State Seward, the new governor complained of the difficulties in starting operations without a U. S. marshal, and with only one judge in the territory. Even worse, debt stood at $40,000, and not a dime of the money appropriated to operate the territory for its first two years had yet reached the U. S. treasury's repository at Oregon City, Oregon. But, at least, Idaho was now smaller and more manageable. In May, all that part of it east of the Rocky Mountains had been used to create Montana Territory.[12]

Part of a territorial governor's job in those days was to act as ex-officio superintendent of Indian affairs. While there were many men who performed this function corruptly, no one would ever surpass Caleb Lyon in doing less for the benefit of the natives, while amply lining his own pockets. The governor's first bit of roguery involved the normally friendly Nez Perce tribe of northern Idaho, which, by the time of his arrival, had become very restless.

In the beginning, intercourse with whites had been beneficial to the Nez Perce. In 1836, at the invitation of the tribe, the Reverend Henry Harmon Spalding and his wife Eliza had established a mission on Lapwai Creek, about 12 miles east of the future site of Lewiston. The Presbyterian couple had labored there for eleven years, teaching farming methods and other practical arts. They had built and operated a school, a mission church, a blacksmith shop, Idaho's first flouring mill, and a sawmill. A year after their arrival, Eliza gave birth to a daughter, the first white child to be born in Idaho.

But the massacre of another missionary couple–Marcus and Eliza Whitman—by Cayuse Indians in 1847, at the Waiilatpu settlement in Washington, had caused a portion of the Nez Perce tribe to become hostile. As a consequence, the Spaldings abandoned their mission and fled to Oregon's Willamette Valley.

In 1855, Isaac I. Stevens, governor of Washington Territory, negotiated a treaty with the Nez Perce which the Senate took four years to ratify. Then, when northern Idaho's gold rush began in 1860, miners began violating the treaty by overspreading the reservation and building towns on it, including Lewiston.

A revised pact was deemed necessary, so a council was held in May 1863, at the army post which had been established the previous autumn at Lapwai. At this convocation, the tribe was pressured into reducing its reservation from 6,000 to 1,200 square miles. In return, the government agreed to pay $262,500 for specific improvements on the reservation, and to catch up on the overdue annuities required by the 1855 treaty.

This new covenant was made without the agreement of some of the Nez Perce chiefs—Joseph, White Bird and others—whose territory would be surrendered. A Christian chief, known to whites as The Lawyer, was mistakenly recognized by the commissioners as the leader of all the Nez Perce.

Henry Spalding returned to Lapwai at about the time this second treaty was made. Eliza having died in Oregon, he brought with him a second wife, and both were hired as teachers. That year, he and two friends located a mining claim a few miles east of Lewiston, on Hatwai Creek, but, since the claim lay within the limits of the revised reservation, Spalding and his friends were ejected from it by the commander at Fort Lapwai, who had their buildings dismantled and the logs thrown into the Clearwater.

More troubles for Spalding came from his dealings with the Indian agent to the Nez Perce, James O'Neill. Apparently the latter couldn't tolerate Spalding's rigid personality, so he and others at the agency petitioned Governor Lyon to remove him. A few weeks after arriving in Lewiston, Lyon made the short journey up the Clearwater to Lapwai to look into this and other matters at the agency.

While there, on August 21, 1864, he attended a church service for the Nez Perce, conducted by Spalding. The governor was introduced to Chief Lawyer at the service, and, afterward, Lawyer questioned Lyon sharply about the unfulfilled promises of the several treaties. Of most importance, only two annuity payments had ever been made—one of $6,000 and another of $10,0000—and nothing had been paid since 1862. Furthermore, the whites were now overrunning the new, smaller reservation. In presenting his complaints, Lawyer took pains to remind Lyon of all the past help the Nez Perce had given whites in subduing rebellious tribes.

Lyon replied convincingly, asking Indian forbearance, and promising that the annuities and the facilities pledged in the treaties would be provided. He also said he intended to make the whites abandon the reservation and all the improvements they had made thereon.

Having gotten a first-hand look at Henry Spalding during the church service, Lyon summarily rejected agent O'Neill's petition to remove the minister. Lyon came from the same county in New York as Eliza Spalding, so he was familiar with the good works the couple had performed when they had first come amongst the Nez Perce. According to Spalding, Lyon told O'Neill that he "wanted no instructions about Mr. Spalding, he knew him." And, turning to Spalding, he threw his arms around his neck and exclaimed, "You are the father of this country and the apostle of this people, and you shall have a place here for life if you wish."

The governor credited the "self-abnegating labors of this good old man" with benefiting the Nez Perce "more than...all the thousands of outlay by government." From the chiefs to the humblest, they obeyed and respected him "as a dutiful father."[13] Lyon then demanded that Spalding be given the best house at the agency for his home; that his former orchard be re-fenced, and the schoolhouse be restored.

The 1863 treaty had provided $2,500 for building two churches on the reservation, so—with great flourish—Lyon announced that a chapel would be erected at Lapwai, on the very site of the first meeting house that Spalding had built in 1843. Bypassing agent O'Neill, he personally contracted with a Nez Perce man named "Jonah" to erect such a building of stone and adobe, for a promised wage. The governor declared that he would inscribe over its portals the names of Spalding and the murdered Marcus Whitman.

One of the reasons for Lyon's warm support of Henry Spalding went unmentioned. Apparently, the former missionary told the governor about the promising mining claim on the Clearwater's north bank, from which he had been ejected in 1863, and which was now occupied by a Nez Perce named Wiaskus. Having learned of these diggings, Lyon hatched a scheme to enrich himself.

A provision of the 1863 treaty allowed Indians living on land that was to be relinquished to sell their "improvements" to any white man, with the consent of the agent or superintendent. The superintendent, Lyon, promised to pay Wiaskus $200.00 for the claim, but, since the tract which Lyon coveted lay within the boundaries of the new reservation, it was necessary that he get it excluded so that Wiaskus could sell him the rights.

This Lyon tried to do by writing Secretary Usher on August 31, asking that the reservation boundaries be moved:

> Do not fail when the [1863] treaty with the Nez Perces goes before the Senate again. Make the amendment instead of 'the mouth of the Hatwae creek' have it read 'to within one mile of the mouth of the Hatwae creek.' The reason is there are some 'good washings' that I wish to get hold of for our benefit that can not be done without this amendment is made for Arthur [Usher] & myself...I am buying through a 3rd party [Spalding?] the land from the Indian who owns it...right to the mouth and one mile above...Do see this is made straight...
>
> Arthur begins to work like a good boy and we get on very nicely. Do not forget about *Hatwae creek matter*. I should squat some where near it and would not miss it.[14]

To conceal his designs, Lyon put out an elaborate cover story, saying that he intended erecting a fine house on the land and would call the place "new Lyonsdale." He claimed to have coming to Lewiston, by express, 80 varieties of roses and 2,000 fruit trees. Lyon even made an arrangement with Rev. Spalding to have the minister's twenty-five year old son, Henry Hart Spalding, come forthwith to Idaho and manage this land he was purchasing.

Aside from setting afoot his devious scheme to get some "good washings," Lyon did nothing else during his visit to the agency, save gain the enmity of James O'Neill. Afterward, the governor fired off three letters to William Dole, Commissioner of Indian Affairs, complaining that everything at Lapwai was "out of kilter," and that most of its employees were guilty of "criminal negligence," and indifference to the treaty stipulations.

The Indians were discontented because no schoolhouse or church had been provided; they were being taught nothing; the agency sawmill had been used mostly for the benefit of white men; many trees on the reservation had been cut and sold for fuel in Lewiston, and so forth. Furthermore, there were some employees carried on the agency rolls who weren't actually working, and others who were holding second jobs at the fort. Agent O'Neill himself was listed as the agency tinsmith, yet he knew nothing about that occupation.

Lyon said stringent changes were necessary to make the agency self-supporting, but knew he could do it by "rigid economy" on his part, and "honesty on the part of the agent."

Before leaving the East, Lyon had been bonded for $50,000, and had asked Secretary Usher to get him $25,000 of Indian Department money, but it is not known how much he actually brought to Idaho. Some have said he came with $38,000 in greenbacks, most of which was intended for the Nez Perce.

But, while at the agency, Caleb Lyon did not disburse a dime to pay the overdue annuities, or redeem unpaid vouchers amounting to $13,207 for the years 1863 and 1864. So far as is known, the only Indian money he disbursed was a half-year's salary for James O'Neill and the agency employees, amounting to $6,660.[15]

Superintendent Lyon had been instructed by the Indian commissioner to make an extended tour of observation, forming any treaties required to keep the peace—but to get instructions beforehand. Shortly after visiting the Nez Perce, the governor traveled to Boise, in a party which included Major Sewell Truax, who had recently been relieved as commander of Fort Lapwai.

At the time, an Indian war was raging across southern Idaho, eastern Oregon and northern Nevada. The hostile natives were mostly Shoshoni, joined by a few renegade Bannocks and Paiutes. Within the previous nine months, at least 14 white civilians had been killed and as many more wounded in attacks within a 150-mile radius of Silver City. Added to these recent depredations, southern Idahoans still remembered the Ward party massacre of 1854, in which 17 people had been killed, and the butchery of 29 persons of the Van Orman party in 1860. Quite naturally, there was a great clamor for pacifying the natives.

Superintendent Lyon dealt with these concerns in his usual fashion, opting for a quick, contrived solution in preference to a real one. On October 10, he made a "treaty" with what he claimed was a band of 300 Shoshoni under chief "Tam Tomeco," whom Col. Reuben F. Maury, 1st Oregon Cavalry, had managed to gather together at Fort Boise. Lyon said he had

Caleb Lyon, ca. 1864. Photo by Matthew Brady.
(Library of Congress, LC-USZ62-13459).

purchased Indian title to all the land for 30 miles on each side of the Boise River, from its source to mouth, and had gotten the Shoshoni to agree to live upon any reservation the U.S. might provide.

Newspaper editors of the region were elated, having swallowed Lyon's buncombe hook, line and sinker. James Reynolds, editor of the *Boise Tri-Weekly Statesman* praised the new governor for accomplishing the work of months, in just a few days.

But one Idahoan, who observed it, called it a "pretended treaty," and one of the "greatest farces he ever witnessed." A mere twenty Indian men, and forty women had been present, and all "were in so destitute a condition that they would promise anything for a cup of flour."[16] And, indeed, the treaty was an egregious sham. Lyon never even bothered to submit it for ratification, and he didn't mention it until later, when it would become important for him to demonstrate how busy he had been.

It was reported that the governor had made an additional treaty in the Owyhee mining region, securing good behavior from the Shoshoni almost to

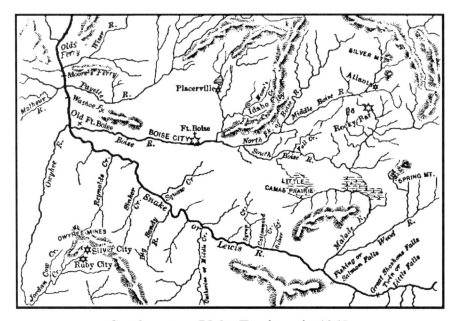

Southwestern Idaho Territory in 1865

the Utah line. But, in fact, Col. Maury hadn't been able to collect any more natives, and so Lyon made a tour of the region's mines, and then returned to Lewiston.

Once back in the capital, the governor issued a grandiloquent Thanksgiving Day proclamation, and, on November 16, addressed a joint session of Idaho's legislature. His long-winded speech was adorned with syrupy, patriotic phases and fawning gratulations to the lawmakers, most of whom were Democrats. Of substance, he recommended creation of a system of public schools, organization of a militia, and the dispatching of appeals to congress to build roads and establish a mint, mail routes and military posts. Again Reynolds of the *Statesman* praised Lyon, saying he had quickly comprehended the needs of the territory.

It would later be learned that the governor was also anxious, about this time, to initiate a movement for Idaho statehood, so that he might go to Washington, D. C. as one of its senators. He strenuously advocated the idea to many Idaho Republicans, and made a lot of promises of what he would do as a Senator. The scheme died aborning, however, because most Idahoans didn't want the higher taxes statehood would bring.[17]

The most contentious question facing this second legislature was where Idaho's permanent capital should be situated. Congress had given Idaho the power to make that decision, but the first legislature had been unable to agree upon a location.

When former governor Wallace had selected Lewiston, it was a logical choice for the capital. But, by now, placer mining in northern Idaho had declined substantially, causing the population in that part of the territory to shrink to 2,790 souls, of whom only 259 lived in the now-moribund Lewiston. In contrast, southern Idaho was booming, due to the promising new mining regions around Idaho City and Silver City. The population in the south by 1864 had grown to 18,997, of whom 1,658 lived in Boise.

In this second legislative session, Henry C. Riggs#—a wealthy man, and a close friend of Lyon—introduced a bill to remove the capital to Boise. Aggravated northerners, in turn, proposed that Congress be memorialized, asking for the territory to be split at latitude 44 degrees, 30 minutes north, and for the northern portion to be joined with Washington Territory. While the proposed memorial failed to pass, Riggs' bill for removal of the capital sailed through both houses and was signed into law by Lyon.

The second legislature adjourned December 23, 1864. The change of capital was to have taken effect the next day, when it was expected that Governor Lyon and his staff would leave for Boise. But, a group of northerners, led by a lawyer named Alonzo Leland, had filed a specious lawsuit to block the relocation. Leland alleged that the legislature which had just adjourned was an illegal body, the assembly having elected its officers prior to members taking their oath of office, and both houses having met prior to the expiration of the term of service of the previous set of legislators.

Aleck C. Smith, the hard-drinking judge assigned to the First Judicial District, had jurisdiction over the matter, but he remanded the case to the local probate judge, John G. Berry. This allowed Berry to temporarily enjoin Lyon and the acting state secretary, Silas Cochran, from removing the territorial seal, laws and archives to Boise.

Lyon engaged as his attorney 26-year old John Cummins, of Owyhee, late president of Idaho's legislative council (upper house). Cummins—who would later become an Idaho Supreme Court judge—requested that Judge Smith dismiss the lawsuit and dissolve the injunction. When the request was ignored, the highly wrought governor threatened to disregard the court and set out for Boise. But Leland's northern partisans, encouraged by the probate judge, threateningly dogged the steps of Lyon and Cochran everywhere they went, and ordered ferry owners not to take either official across the rivers.

Riggs was one of the founders of Boise; Ada County, in which the city is situated, was named after his eldest daughter.

Lyon waited patiently for six days while his friends devised a plan to sneak him out of town, and, on December 27, it was put into operation. How the governor escaped was later recounted by a northern Idaho legislator:

> The successful prosecution of our law suit...seemed to demand the arrest of the governor, but to arrest that dignitary meant, in the first place, to catch him. In the meantime, Caleb learned...what was in store for him; so, bright and early the next morning, taking with him Hon. Sol Hasbrouck of Owyhee County and his shotgun, [Lyon] embarked on a frail canoe, with the avowed purpose of shooting ducks on John Silcot's ranch, just across the Clearwater. When in mid-stream, the canoe became unmanageable and was borne away by the current down Snake River to White's Ferry, where a carriage was found in waiting...which took Caleb and his shotgun to Walla Walla...This was the last that was ever seen of Caleb Lyon, of Lyonsdale, governor of all Idaho, on our side of the Salmon River Mountains.[18]

Lyon's departure left acting-secretary Cochran holding the bag in Lewiston, as the only territorial officer. Enraged by Lyon's crafty exit, and determined to prevent any further bolting, the northerners served Cochran with a writ from the probate judge that very day, constraining him to remain within the court's jurisdiction, and not move a peg.

A few days later, certain Boiseans made an unsuccessful attempt to steal the archives and seal, during the wee hours of the morning. This led to even sterner actions by the probate judge. Cochran was given the choice of being clapped into jail or of putting up a $20,000 bond as security. When Cochran boldly refused to comply with either alternative, sheriff J. H. Fisk of Nez Perce County placed him under arrest and threw a continual guard of freshly-sworn citizen deputies around him, the seal and the archives.

One Boisean said that the arrest of Cochran was the "last resort of Lewiston bummers to get their regular free whiskey, since the departure of the legislature." These deputies—habitual idlers—were taking turns guarding him, six at a time, "marching him from one groggery to another to drink at his expense."[19]

Lewistonians held a public meeting on January 4, at which resolutions were passed demanding Lyon's removal, and the separation of the northern part of the territory. John Cummins presented the Boise reply and then, rather than "take part in so ridiculous a farce," he indignantly stalked out.[20]

As to Lyon's request to dismiss the lawsuit, district judge Smith—no doubt intimidated by the northerners—still refused to get involved, thus leaving the case locked up in Judge Barry's county court. Cummins represented Lyon at a January 9 hearing but, when Barry refused to dissolve the injunction, Cummins gave up and followed Lyon to Walla Walla.

The fugitive governor wrote Secretary of Interior Usher on January 16, telling him about the capital removal commotion. Lyon said his only fear was that his opponents might send "false and lying statements" to "Old Abe [Lincoln], God Bless him." Lyon called it a "tempest in a teapot affair," but thought he might have to call out federal troops to effect the removal. He appended a "testimonial" to his letter, for the president to see, showing how highly he, Lyon, had stood in the estimation of Idaho Republicans before the "capital farce"[21] had come along.

The frustrated Lyon failed to get any troops from the commander of Fort Walla Walla, so he appointed Major Sewell Truax as his agent and sent him to Lewiston to get the seal and archives. But, once there, Truax found the articles still under guard. And, although Cochran had been freed, he was now solidly in the Lewistonians' camp, and refused Truax's request for the items, with the excuse that he was awaiting instructions from authorities in Washington, D. C.

Believing that Lyon wouldn't return, Cochran had no doubt gone over to the enemy in the hope they would win, and that he might either become Lyon's successor, or governor of a new territory of northern Idaho. It is also possible that he was embittered by having recently lost a bid to become the permanent secretary of Idaho.

Trying another tactic, Truax returned briefly to Walla Walla, and then came back to Lewiston with a document from Lyon removing Cochran from office for not obeying his orders. But, Cochran argued that Lyon's directive was invalid, since it was issued from outside of the territory.

For awhile, Caleb Lyon continued to talk defiantly about taking the stage for Boise, but finally gave the idea up, and, with Cummins and young Arthur Usher in tow, traveled by mule train to The Dalles, Oregon, and thence by steamboat to Portland, reaching there about February 6.

Lyon's friend, Cummins, told the whole farcical story to the press, accusing the northern leaders of being disloyal Copperheads, and of threatening Lyon with physical harm if he dared sign the removal bill. Cummins said southern Idaho was sound in its support for the governor, and that those who had the division of Idaho on the brain, should have been satisfied after the memorial for that purpose was defeated in the legislature.

About the time Lyon was licking his wounds in Portland, the new, regularly-appointed territorial secretary, Clinton DeWitt Smith, arrived in San Francisco from the East. Smith had received his commission some months earlier, but Indian troubles had interfered with his attempt to travel the overland route, requiring him to backtrack and go via Panama.

At San Francisco, Smith first learned of the struggle over the capital, and of Lyon's undignified flight from Lewiston. Also, while there, he met a certain Horace C. Gilson, whom he hired to be his private secretary. Gilson was a bartender in a San Francisco gambling hall at the time Smith picked him up, and was known as a person of questionable morals. One of his acquaintances called him "a sweet scented band box kind of an apology for a man."[22]

Upon reaching Portland, on February 13, 1865, Smith found Lyon busying himself by delivering lectures to the local ladies about his travels in the Holy Land. The secretary urged the governor to return to Lewiston, but Lyon refused. Next, Smith tried to convince Lyon to go to Boise, while he, Smith, retrieved the items from Lewiston. But, the governor wanted no part of that either, and he tried to dissuade Smith from going there, because of the threats the northerners had made.

Finally, however, Lyon dumped the entire mess in the secretary's lap, saying he himself would go to Washington and see what could be done there. Before boarding a steamer for San Francisco, Lyon told the newspapers that he had arranged for the removal of the seal and archives, and would now go East to extol the prospects for Idaho and its mineral resources.

The *Boise Statesman's* James Reynolds had wanted Lyon to employ force to remove the capital. When it became clear that the governor would keep on running, the editor sadly declared that "the peacefully-natured, fine old country gentleman" had not been "made of stuff stern enough to deal with the...ruffianism of Lewiston."[23]

Thus DeWitt Smith became Idaho's acting governor. But, unlike Lyon, he was a man of action who would refuse to be intimidated.

At the Oregon City Treasury Department depository, Smith withdrew $18,000 of Idaho's money. Congress had finally appropriated funds for legislative and contingency expenses to run the territory for the two years ending June 30, 1865, but Treasury had only sent $20,000 of it to Oregon for Smith's use, because of the limits of his bond.

The secretary then traveled to Fort Vancouver to visit Brigadier-General Benjamin Alvord, commander of the Oregon Military District. From Alvord he obtained a general authorization—similar to those usually given to civil executives—ordering the commander at Fort Lapwai to provide him a military escort whenever he should need one.

After a stop in Walla Walla to leave Idaho's money in a Wells-Fargo safe, Smith arrived in Lewiston on March 2. Producing his credentials, he ordered

Clinton DeWitt Smith
(*Author's Collection*)

Cochran to give him the seal and archives. Cochran surrendered the coveted articles in a public ceremony, but not before yet another injunction had been issued by the probate judge, prohibiting their removal from Lewiston.

A strict watch was kept on Secretary Smith, but he pretended not to notice it, and did nothing that might antagonize his opponents. Also, he was taken ill and did very little over the next few weeks, save pay off a few of the longer-standing territorial debts, using his own money.

Meanwhile, north and south Idaho engaged in a war of words. On January 28, Alonzo Leland had started up the Lewiston, *North Idaho Radiator* as a voice for the north. From southern Idaho—to convey a sense of the pettiness of all things northern—Reynolds of the *Statesman* took to calling the *Radiator* the "lelander" or the "lewistonpaper." The town itself he dubbed the "Clearwater squaw ranch." Cochran was vilified for having betrayed Lyon, and the two sides argued over who was the greater drunk— Cochran or DeWitt Smith.[24]

Secretary Smith had told Leland that he would abide by the orders of the court, inasmuch as he had no preference whatever in the capital removal matter.[25] But, about March 20, when the secretary felt better, he went back to Walla Walla, accompanied by Horace Gilson and by the current publisher of the *Golden Age*, Frank Kenyon. Sensing that Lewiston's "golden age" was about over, Kenyon had suspended his paper, and was ready to try his luck in

Boise under Smith's tutelage.

At the Wells-Fargo office, in the presence of his two companions, Smith opened the sealed package containing Idaho's $18,000, out of which he took $8,000, and then put the rest back into the safe. This done, he returned to Lewiston to pay off Idaho's remaining debts in that area, and make preparations to leave for Boise with the seal and archives.

The secretary was still being watched closely by the Lewiston "vigilantes." When he announced his intention to leave, and was told that such a move would be firmly resisted, he contrived a plan for his escape that would oppose force with force.

Smith began riding horseback each day, saying it was for his health's sake. On March 29 he went riding in company with a lady and another couple. They had just started out of town when Smith suddenly turned back, leaving his female partner without an escort. The other man censured Smith for this ungentlemanly act, ordering the secretary never to speak again to either woman on pain of a cowhiding.

Smith went briefly to his office and then rode, in company with Gilson and Kenyon, up the Clearwater to Fort Lapwai—telling his clerk, Solomon R. Howlett, that he would be back in an hour. Smith and his friends, however, didn't return that day.

Next morning, Capt W. J. Mathews, the commander of Fort Lapwai gave Smith an escort of ten soldiers, under Lieutenant S. R. Hammer, to help him get out of Lewiston with the archives and seal. As they were preparing to leave the fort, one of the privates heard Smith say that if he were to be killed, he wanted the troops to burn the town and to inform Indian agent James O'Neill that he must expel all whites from the reservation.

When judge Aleck Smith saw DeWitt Smith and his escort arrive in Lewiston about ten A.M., he rushed to begin ringing a gong that had been selected to use as a signal for rallying the town's "vigilantes." But, the gong soon "caved in under the blows of the excited judge"—as did the Lewistonians, after a brief, comic showdown.

Amidst great public tumult, the soldiers brushed aside Special U. S. Marshal J. K. Vincent (Lewiston's auctioneer) who attempted to serve still another of the probate judge's injunctions. Smith, Gilson, and Kenyon, then strode boldly through the town and boarded the Clearwater ferry with the seal, archives and laws of the second legislative session—as much baggage as could conveniently be managed. The records of the first legislature were left behind, in the custody of clerk Howlett, boxed for shipment to Boise.

The Lewistonians might have been able to fool the old "Lyon of Lyonsdale," said one observer, but "the sly young fox was too smart to be caught in their trap."[26] The losers were exceedingly sore at Secretary Smith's departure. They wrote of "Skedaddle No. 2,"[27] and called him names like "buffoon" and "drunkard." Mass meetings were held to denounce the army's conduct and to compose a resolution to the President asking for the secretary's removal. Judge Aleck Smith issued another ruling declaring Lewiston the capital, and he ordered the few remaining archives to be seized from Howlett and locked up in the Lewiston jail.

Meanwhile, DeWitt Smith had gone to Walla Walla, retrieved his package of money in the presence of Gilson and Kenyon, and proceeded onward to Boise. On April 14–the same day Abraham Lincoln was assassinated in the nation's capital—Smith arrived to a hero's reception, complete with gun salutes fired in his honor at Fort Boise. A few days later, citizens passed a resolution praising him for his perseverance.

Thus Secretary Smith established the *de facto* government of Idaho at Boise, despite the continued howling of outraged Lewistonians. The legal duel to settle the capital question would drag on for months. In September, Solomon Howlett—with the help of U.S. Marshal James H. Alvord—would bring the remaining archives to Boise, and, finally, the Idaho Supreme Court, sitting at Boise in June 1866, would render a decision in favor of that city. But, so rancorous was the fight, that even today, there are those in north Idaho who believe the capital was stolen by Boiseans.[28]

Meanwhile, Caleb Lyon had lingered in San Francisco for several months. The only noteworthy thing he did while there, was deliver a bizarre lecture to the Union League, in which he proposed that newly-freed blacks be settled in Idaho, under government protection, to work the mines of the territory. Lyon thought the government-owned minerals might be used to pay off the Civil War debt. He was later accused of floating this scheme as a way to enlarge Idaho's population and accelerate the statehood process.

Although the runaway governor had recently told a newspaper editor that he would be returning immediately to Idaho, he instead boarded a steamer for New York, in late April, and a month later was in Washington. There he heard the bad tidings that the new president, Andrew Johnson, had dismissed him, based on the recommendations of the secretaries of state and interior.

Western congressmen pushed to give the governorship back to the first person to hold it, William Wallace, who was held in esteem as a man's man, who knew the territory, and wouldn't run off, as Lyon had done. Wallace's commission was made out and signed by Johnson on June 6, 1865. But the ambitious Lyon also knew some powerful men, and he immediately began wire-working to regain his position. Several senators, reacting to Caleb's pitiful appeals, convinced Secretary of State Seward to delay Wallace's appointment.

Back in Idaho, Secretary DeWitt Smith was doing a creditable job as Idaho's acting governor. But, as his letters to his father show, he was a very depressed and unhealthy young man. On August 19, while visiting the Rocky Bar diggings, he died suddenly of heart disease, leaving Idaho once again without any executive officer.

Word of his death was sent to Secretary of State Seward via the acting governor of Utah, Amos Reed, who urged appointment of a new secretary, or the hastening back to his post of Governor Lyon. Idaho contained "such a wild element in her population" that it was "hardly safe to leave her long without an executive."[29]

Horace Gilson, who had been acting secretary under Smith, now also became acting governor. Based on the recommendation of some prominent Boiseans, the president quickly appointed Gilson as regular secretary.

Inasmuch as DeWitt Smith had no relatives in the West, the county probate judge designated Gilson as administrator of the deceased's estate, and named District Judge Milton Kelly, and James Reynolds of the *Statesman* as appraisers of it.

Smith had left his valuables, and those of the territory, in the safe of a Boise merchant. About September 22, Gilson, Kelly and Reynolds went there and collected everything—a trunk, a sealed package and a collection of papers and vouchers. These items were examined behind locked doors, and, afterward, Kelly and Reynolds reported to the probate judge that the sealed package had contained no territorial funds—just $650 of Smith's private money, most of which they had used to settle his affairs.

Since Gilson said he believed that Smith still had in his possession upwards of $11,000 of government cash, and since none had been found, the implication was drawn that Smith had embezzled it. Perhaps Gilson let it be known that Smith had spent most of his own money, including an advance on his salary and loans from relatives, in getting to his post in Idaho.[30]

At length, Caleb Lyon's political cronies, led by Senator Edwin D. Morgan of New York, got him back his governorship. Lyon is said to have assured Morgan that he would continue to do everything in his power to secure statehood for Idaho. If he could accomplish this, so Lyon argued, he could return as one of its senators and support Morgan's political agenda. Lyon assured his friend that, in the event the legislature should fail to authorize a constitutional convention, he could easily whip up a public clamor calling on him to order one.

Supposedly, Morgan agreed to these plans, and persuaded New York's most influential politician, Thurlow Weed, to get William Wallace's commission withdrawn, then cover up Lyon's faults with President Johnson and win him reappointment.

First, however, Lyon had to explain his absence from Idaho to the president and secretary of state. On August 3, he gave them a copy of a telegram purportedly sent in March from his friend, Interior Secretary Usher, which granted him leave from Lincoln to "attend to official affairs connected with Idaho."[31] The surviving copy of this telegram looks suspiciously fake, but it did the trick and, by September 21, Caleb Lyon had been reappointed governor and superintendent of Indian affairs for Idaho.

The next day, President Johnson's new Secretary of the Interior, James Harlan, instructed Lyon to obtain peace treaties with the Shoshoni and other Indians of southern Idaho, which would provide them a permanent reservation embracing the fisheries on the Snake River. He was also told to go out personally and make treaties with the Spokanes, Coeur d'Alenes and Kootenais, and to negotiate a new pact with the Nez Perce—the 1863 treaty still not having been acted upon by the Senate.[32]

Before leaving Washington, Lyon said he would need $47,900 to pay Nez Perce expenses for the third and fourth quarters of 1865, and another $20,000 for "incidental" Indian expenses in Idaho. To enable him to begin carrying out his instructions, he asked that $50,000 be placed immediately in his hands, $10,000 of which he would use to buy Indian presents in New York or San Francisco.[33]

Lyon seems to have had no intention of making all the treaties asked of him, opting instead, in his fashion, for the easy way out. Before leaving Washington, he wrote Secretary Harlan that he had previously made an "extended tour of observation among the Indian Tribes of the Territory of Idaho." He claimed to have frequently talked with both the "heathen" and Christian factions of the Nez Perce, and said that, in September, 1864, he had gone north to the Coeur d'Alene Jesuit mission and held interviews with various tribes, including several from the Kootenai country.

These assertions were blatant lies, of course. Lyon had made no "extended tour," nor is there any record of his having spoken to any northern Indians, except the Nez Perce on that single visit to Lapwai.

The letter to Harlan also contains Lyon's first mention to his superiors of the "memoranda of a treaty" he had made in October, 1864 with that small group of Boise Shoshoni—his only contact with southern Idaho Indians. As noted above, Lyon said the tribe had ceded all the land thirty miles on each side of the Boise River and all the country drained by its tributaries. In exchange, the Indians were to get an amount—left blank on the treaty document—which the senate was to specify when it confirmed the pact. Lyon said these Indians were so poor that they would be entirely extinct in a few years, so he recommended establishing a temporary reservation for them on the Boise River.[34]

Idaho's resurrected governor traveled to Idaho his second time via the overland route, leaving the East about October 1. He took with him a new secretary, Newton Northam, and also William McCall, of New York, who had been assigned by the Interior Department as clerk for the Indian superintendency.[35]

Caleb Lyon probably had no idea that he was already in a peck of trouble for his mishandling of Indian affairs. He had scarcely left the nation's capital when Senator James W. Nesmith arrived back in that city from a tour of the Western agencies, as part of a committee looking into the condition of the tribes. Nesmith—who himself was a former Indian superintendent for Oregon and Washington—submitted a report, on October 23 to Secretary Harlan, that would be devastating to Lyon's ambitions.

Nesmith pointed out that Lyon hadn't shown himself in Idaho for more than six months, and accused the governor of conducting Indian affairs with an unparalleled ignorance, and a disregard of the rights and wants of the natives, and of the law.

Lyon's activities on the Nez Perce reservation were revealed in great detail. He had failed to pay the overdue annuities, and hadn't even given agent O'Neill—a cousin of Nesmith's—money for current expenses. The employees of the reservation hadn't been paid for nearly two years, and Lyon had never compensated the Indian, Jonah, for building the Lapwai church. This structure—which had been thrown up in a few weeks, using lava rocks—Nesmith said "resembled a Mexican corral or New England cattle pound,"[36] with its mud mortar all sloughed out, the walls settling, and no roof.

And, said the Senator, because of Lyon's promise to remove all whites from the reservation, the Nez Perce had begun parceling out amongst themselves all of the improvements made thereon by outsiders. The chiefs had unanimously denounced Lyon's conduct, and were threatening hostilities. The Reverend Spalding had also criticized Lyon for having reneged on his arrangement with Spalding's son for the management of "New Lyonsdale," and for not having even paid the boy's expenses in coming to Lewiston.

Nesmith hadn't been able to find any records in the Idaho Indian agency's Boise office, and the clerk there admitted that none had ever been kept.

There was nothing whatever to show where the treaty funds had gone. Nesmith concluded that the money disbursed by Lyon's order while he was "pretending to discharge" his Indian duties had been totally "squandered for objects which were neither authorized by the treaty or desired by the Indians."

The senator recommended that Lyon be severely rebuked, and that someone with "common sense and common honesty" be appointed governor and Indian superintendent for Idaho. Lyon was "an improper person to be permitted to run at large amongst the Indians or to be entrusted with public funds." Nesmith suggested sending future Nez Perce money directly to his cousin, agent O'Neill.[37]

O'Neill had been sending his reports to the Indian department in Washington, complaining that he didn't know whether Idaho had a superintendent of Indian affairs or not—he hadn't heard from Lyon since January 16, at the time when the governor was fleeing from the territory. O'Neill asked for $1,500 of the Nez Perce annuity so he could buy and distribute clothing before winter.[38]

While these damning reports were being digested by the administration, Caleb Lyon was bouncing unconcernedly across plain and mountain, politicking at every stage stop. At Camp Douglas, in Salt Lake City, he was the guest of Brigadier-General Patrick E. Connor, the noted Indian fighter, at a grand military ball. No doubt for the consumption of Connor and his men—as well as the folks in Idaho—Lyon assured the soldier editor of the *Daily Union Vedette* that he intended to make the Indians behave "by precept, if they would, and by power, if they wouldn't."[39]

And so, after being out of Idaho for over ten months, the rejuvenated governor appeared in Boise on November 9. At a reception held for him at May and Brown's Hall, on the evening of his arrival, he bragged at great length of the many hours he had spent in convincing Eastern capitalists to invest in Idaho mining. It had been for this reason, so Lyon claimed, he had been granted his "leave of absence." Some might have thought he had "quartz on the brain," he said, but he believed that, within Idaho, slept "the silver mountains of Mexico and the golden treasures of Peru."

Since he, himself, thrived on adulation, Lyon devoted much of each speech to soft-soaping the audience. So in this one, with flattering tongue, he expanded on the Spanish theme, calling his listeners "earnest pioneers" who possessed "the fearlessness of Cortez, without his crimes," and the "untiring perseverance of Pizzaro without his fanaticism or avarice."

One of Lyon's audience, James Reynolds of the *Statesman*, conceded that,

Ruby City, Idaho ca. 1865
(*Author's Collection*)

while Lyon's absence had been embarrassing, he was now "too-well pleased at his return" to remember he had been gone. Lyon had personally assured Reynolds he wouldn't be running off again.[40]

During that cold and snowy November, Lyon also went over to the Owyhee mines for an eight-day tour, taking along Albert D. Richardson, a correspondent of the New York *Tribune*, who was visiting Idaho. After scrutinizing silver ledges in the bitter weather, Richardson teased Lyon for having characterized Idaho, in one of his speeches, as "a land of Italian summers and Syrian winters." Richardson thought "Siberian winters" would have been more precise.[41]

At Magnolia Hall in Ruby City, one chilly evening, Lyon delivered another lengthy speech, this one to a crowd of rough-hewn Owyheans. After the usual smarmy flattery, he began:

> What the Pactolus was to the Greeks—what Ophir was to the Jews—
> what the Arno was to the Romans, the Choco to the Peruvians, and the

Examining The Ledges on War Eagle Mountain, Owyhee District
(Author's Collection)

Coast of Guinea to the English—the Jordan creek is to you—with this difference: the Old World's gold-bearing streams are nearly worked out, and the fruition of yours have just begun...here is found the home of that magnet to which men have been attracted...since the world was young. Confucius quotes in his works..."[42]

Then followed a seemingly-interminable history of the search for gold through the ages, until, finally, Lyon got down to what his audience really wanted to hear—how he intended handling the Indian problem.

By now, conditions had worsened in southern Idaho, and along the new roads leading to it across Nevada and Oregon. All summer long troops had been fighting on and near these roads to keep them safe. New military posts had been established over a large region, one of which was Camp Lyon—named after a Union army general, not his honor the governor—on Cow

Creek, some thirty miles west of Silver City. But, with the Civil War over, volunteer cavalry units were being mustered out, and there were only a few regulars to take their place.

These aggravated circumstances spurred the governor to speak fervently on the Indian question. He was also motivated by the sharp questions he had recently received from D. N. Cooley, the new Commissioner of Indian Affairs, concerning Senator Nesmith's report on the deplorable state of the Idaho superintendency. Lyon had been instructed to conduct all future transactions on a cash basis, and to make monthly reports on his accomplishments and finances.

The governor told the Owyheans that he had been absent for so long because he had been getting instructions regarding the many treaties that his superiors were *demanding* he make with the Indians of his superintendency. He spoke of the large amount he had with him to pay off treaty annuities. He said the frequent outrages "must cease," and that mounted regulars would soon take the place of the volunteers, and would pursue any natives guilty of depredations to their strongholds. Then they would be offered terms of "peace or death."

Lyon told his cheering audience that, "With sleepless vigilance," he would "watch their safety" and guard their thoroughfares, and within a year all these "offenses against law and order" would cease. He also made the absurd assertion that he had requested, with hope of success, two regiments of cavalry.

Several months earlier, Silver City and the surrounding mining region had gotten its first newspaper, the *Owyhee Avalanche*, published by the brothers Joe and John Wasson. Lyon's tough talk convinced John that Idaho now had a "live Governor," whose Indian policy was "just the thing."[43]

When, within days of Lyon's speech, word was received that two companies of regular soldiers were en route for the Boise district Wasson was sure this was the first installment of the troops asked for by the governor. But unfortunately, these were infantry units and, for the next few critical months, a twenty-two year old, Captain John H. Walker, would command the district from Fort Boise, with foot soldiers as his only assets.

Subsequent events would show that Lyon was conning Owyheans on the Indian question. But, for now, he had impressed them with his "honesty and unusual zeal" in trying to advance the interests of Idaho. He truly seemed to be the "right man in the right place."[44]

While in the Owyhee district, the governor set afoot another of his scams, which resulted in Idaho's one and only "diamond rush." It began when he showed John Wasson a pea-sized crystal, very brilliant, but off-color, with a spot of un-crystallized carbon in the center.

The governor claimed that, while going East on the steamer the previous May, he had met a certain Samuel Wilson, who had been prospecting for gold in the foothills south of Snake River, some fifteen miles from Silver City. Wilson showed Lyon a number of crystals he claimed to have found and kept as curiosities. Wilson didn't know what they were, but Lyon told him he thought they might be diamonds.

After arriving in New York—so Lyon said—he and Wilson went together to a jeweler's store where Wilson was offered $800 for his largest stone, but refused it. He then took the stone to a diamond dealer and sold it for $1,000. Wilson gave one of the crystals to Lyon, and promised to return to Idaho and show him where they had been found. But, unlike Lyon, Wilson had returned by sea, and had perished in the sinking of the steamer *Brother Jonathan*, on July 30, off Crescent City, California.

John Wasson was completely hoodwinked by Lyon's story, and printed it, unchallenged, in the next edition of the *Avalanche*. Not surprisingly, the article caused a major stampede. Off, pell-mell, went hundreds of men, headed for the foothills that Lyon had described, bordered on the north by the Snake River, on the east by Catherine Creek, and on the west by Reynolds' Creek.

Work at all the quartz mills stopped, because owners were unable to keep their employees on the job. Claims were staked off, and men could be seen crawling around on their stomachs over forty square miles of country, magnifying glasses in hand, searching for the fabulous crystals.

Knowledge on the subject of diamonds was scarce in Owyhee, but many stones were found which answered the general description. All were very brilliant, but considerably smaller than the one Lyon had displayed, the largest being about the size of a small grain of wheat. Viewed through a glass, they seemed to present the shape and face of diamonds.

Col. D. H. Fogus, J. C. Boone, and others subjected their crystals to rude tests. They scratched them with files, and rubbed them vigorously with a woolen cloth, having read in a book that, when thus stroked, a real diamond would create enough friction to raise a hair. In most cases, the men reported, the hair was lifted, "lode stone like, with ease."[45] But, for every man who pronounced the crystals genuine diamonds, another said they were not.

In December, two adjacent diamond mining districts were organized. The laws for the first district gave Caleb Lyon four 300-square foot claims, to be located by a committee headed by Col. Fogus. John Wasson, fully caught up in the excitement, took up two claims. He admitted that more quartz crystals were being brought in than diamonds, but this was due to a lack of knowledge and to highly wrought zeal. He thought the discovery was authentic, and was upset that some men were lampooning it.

But, it was his brother, Joe Wasson, who was doing most of the spoofing. In the same issue, Joe wrote:

> If the different bits of 'secret history' connected with the...diamond furore could be correctly put together, they would constitute...laughter for a month...To think how some of our most staid citizens rushed out of their blankets at 'midnight hour,' (mercury at zero) to...the inhospitable foothills of the Owyhee mountains; how they mistook each other for Snake Indians...how they charged each other with being in search of loose horses, etc...
>
> One fellow...who swears...that nothing *but* diamonds could have gotten *him* out, is of the opinion that the article is not of such stuff as diamonds are made, which he can mash in his teeth! Another says if *them* are diamonds, he's found a whole ledge of 'em! We understand that there is a divorce pending, because a snoozy old husband wouldn't rush out and pick up a 'set' for his better half. We expect society here will soon be rampant with diamond necklaces and shirt-buzzums done up in 'stud' (horse) style! We shall hereafter write with a diamond pointed pen.[46]

Joe kept poking fun. When a reader at Hog 'Em, on Grimes Creek, asked him how diamond mining could be made profitable, he replied:

> The only practical plan we have heard of...for working the Owyhee diamonds is by the 'Pismire [piss-ant] Process.' A friend of ours, who has spent some weeks in the Diamond District, says he has incorporated a number of the pismire nests that are running his mine very successfully. This process was suggested to him at the time of the 'first rush,' when most of the precious gems were obtained in the top of the ant-hills. By incorporating a large number of these nests, he expects to supply a large demand for diamonds...These insects are very industrious; show no disposition to strike for the eight-hour system or higher wages—in short, so far they have worked for nothing...They work shifts, and...are...better adapted naturally for searching the earth in diamond mining than man—it being necessary to prospect on all fours."[47]

Heavy snows hampered prospecting in December, but John Wasson remained optimistic. Samples had been sent for testing to New York City and, should they turn out to be genuine diamonds, John said, Owyhee could supply the world markets with them.

Governor Lyon didn't waste any time searching for "diamonds." He had some important politicking to do. In the fall elections, Democrats had won all the legislative seats, save one, and Lyon realized that if his plan for statehood was to be fulfilled, he must indulge the opposition. So, he continued his speechifying, spewing promises at every opportunity. At Idaho City—a Democrat stronghold—he even vowed to offer incentives that would induce more women to come to Idaho.

In one speech, Lyon's true feelings on the Indian question popped out. He called the race a dwindling, "short-lived" one, which required that whites—as Christians—"leave a stainless record" in their intercourse with the few that remained. The governor admitted this would be hard, but assured Idahoans that, within a few months, the natives would be put in a position where, by "treaty stipulations," their depredations would be punished.

Like most Idahoans, John Wasson was skeptical. While it was comforting to know that Indian crimes would be punished in a few months, it was news to him that only a few natives remained. These "short-lived" races were "heap" afraid of that popular Eastern remedy of "treaty stipulations," he wrote. But Wasson later relented; after talking to the "*live* Governor," he said he was satisfied that Lyon was sound on the Indian question.[48]

As 1865 drew to a close, Lyon was still fending off questions from Indian commissioner Cooley. The commissioner had gotten a statement from James O'Neill showing the indebtedness of the Nez Perce agency to be $27,992, most of that sum owed to employees.

When asked to explain, Lyon responded that O'Neill had recently come to Boise and had been given $18,000, which was enough to pay off his agency's debts accrued since Lyon had taken over in June, 1864, but not enough to pay those previously incurred under Governor Wallace. Lyon said he had no funds to liquidate Wallace's obligations, but that he would prepare a list of these liabilities for the Indian department.

Lyon accused O'Neill of hiring unnecessary and unauthorized employees, and he promised to personally examine the state of affairs at the Nez Perce agency, as soon as possible. He would also prepare a statement of funds he had received and disbursed, which he would send as soon as his "Legislative duties would permit." Lyon, of course, had no intention of ever again going near Lewiston, and the promised statement of his accounts would never be sent.[49]

When the third session of the territorial legislature met at Boise, on December 4, 1865, Lyon addressed its members with one of his highfalutin' speeches. He spoke at length of how "the temple of war" was now closed, and no more should its "brazen-throated cannon peal forth dread 'miseries' over half a thousand battle-fields." And, the governor's usual puffing of Idaho's mineral wealth now included mention of the discovery of that "most precious of gems, the diamond."[50] But the address said nothing of his promised plan to pacify the Indians.

During the legislative session, the governor continued to cozy up to the Democrat majority. He gave speeches and readings at the drop of a hat, and hosted two memorable dinner parties, entertaining both houses of the legislature, at separate *soirees*.

The affair he held for the council was called the grandest of the season. It was probably the first multi-course dinner held in the territory, and Lyon presided over it like a king. With the whiskey flowing freely, he paralyzed his guests with witty stories, jokes, speeches and toasts, such that they were awed into absolute silence. But his guests couldn't manage to "round up" Caleb—that is, figure him out. His stories of affiliation with great men, such as Henry Clay and John C. Calhoun, they hardly swallowed, but, nonetheless, they enjoyed the dinners, and talked about them for months afterward.

James W. Griffin, co-owner of the Idaho Hotel, catered these banquets. During the late war, he had been in command of the bark *Santos,* when it was captured and burned by the Confederate pirate, Raphael Semmes. After this, Griffin had crossed the plains, settled at Boise and drifted into the hotel business.[51]

Soon the governor was totally *en rapport* with the Democrats. A group of Owyheans, mostly of that political persuasion, and led by Edward C. Sterling, presented Lyon with a ten-inch long brick of silver, for his supposed promotion of Idaho's mineral resources. The brick was poured at the Morning Star mill, and cost $1,050. Sterling hosted a champagne and cigar party in Silver City to allow contributors to view the gift, and then it was presented to Lyon. The governor was ecstatic over this display of recognition, and Sterling was just as pleased—within a month Lyon appointed him territorial treasurer.

Since the governor was known as the creator of the California state seal, the legislative leadership commissioned him to design one for Idaho Territory, even though, in 1863, a design by Silas Cochran had been adopted and a seal fabricated. Perhaps the Democrats disliked the earlier version because it had the phrase, "The Union" in it.[52] In any case, Lyon produced a new one, which would be used, intermittently, from 1869 until statehood.

During the legislative session, not much was done of benefit, unless it was the act that prohibited hogs from running at large in Ada County. Also, in an attempt to smooth over the contention between north and south Idaho, a memorial was sent to the Congress, asking for creation of a new territory of

"Columbia," which, had it been approved, would have included eastern Washington, northern Idaho and western Montana.

Offensive to Republicans were all the franchises rushed through and signed by Lyon. Of these, James Reynolds groused that "every known mountain trail opened by the hardy pioneer would now have some licensed member of the [Democratic] 'faithful' to demand toll! toll! for every passing mule [and] jackass."[53]

For his cooperation, even Lyon got a piece of the franchise action from the grateful legislators. A bill was enacted allowing the governor and others to operate a railroad from Utah and Wallula, Washington Territory, to connect with a steamboat being built to run on the Snake River in southwestern Idaho. (The story of which has been told herein as "Sagebrush Steamboat.")

The legislature created the framework for a school system, but nothing could be implemented, inasmuch as Idaho was flat broke. Of the $18,000 DeWitt Smith had drawn of Idaho's legislative and contingency appropriation, an estimated $8,062 had remained unaccounted for since his death. Early in the session, the legislature appointed a committee to find out what had become of this money, and the governor told Secretary Horace Gilson to report the deficiency to the state and treasury departments.[54] More funds were now believed to be available at the Oregon City depository, but couldn't be drawn by Gilson until he was bonded.

The only cash thought to be immediately at hand was $14,000 in territorial taxes collected, in 1864, by Alfred Slocum, the treasurer of Boise County at Idaho City. But Slocum, a Democrat, had refused to turn the money over to territorial officials because Boise County was still owed for housing Idaho's prisoners in its jail. And, besides—so he professed—he did not know who should get the money because there were multiple claimants for the offices of treasurer and auditor, due to an ongoing Democrat-Republican conflict over whether the positions were appointive or elective. Slocum insisted on waiting until the courts told him what to do.

But, in fact, there was no money. Slocum had embezzled and invested it in mining stocks, for which he soon would go to prison.

In the name of "economy," a bill was passed which repealed the matching compensation being paid by the territory to the three federal judges (all Republicans), but which continued the extra money being paid to legislators, the governor, and the secretary.

Lyon's approval of these measures further incensed his fellow Republicans. Adding insult to injury in this matter, Lyon approved another bill which provided that the Slocum moneys—if and when surrendered—

would be used to pay the extra compensation, rather than being used for any of the many other territorial obligations.

All in all, Caleb Lyon's string of concessions to the Democrats thoroughly alienated his fellow Republicans. His greatest act of treachery, perhaps, was his handling of a controversial act written by Democrats which repealed the "iron-clad' oath passed by the first legislature. The new law simply required territorial officers and legislators to take the oath prescribed by the Organic Act, using the milder language in vogue before the war.

Lyon knew the dangers to his political career inherent in the bill—his approval of it would intensify the hatred Republicans now had for him; if he disapproved it, Democrats would override his veto and he would lose their support, which he had worked so hard to gain. So, the timid Lyon contrived to "lose" the statute, which allowed it to become law by lapse of time.[55]

Just before the close of the legislative session, a proclamation of praise was approved, thanking Lyon for his having cooperated so nicely. On the night of adjournment, January 12, 1866, exultant Democrats proceeded to the Idaho House and lustily serenaded their governor with patriotic songs.[56]

But, despite Lyon's coziness with the Democrat majority, he had been unable to realize his dream of starting Idaho on the path to statehood. He had floated the idea of a convention, and two separate bills calling for a popular vote on the question, had failed in the legislature. After adjournment, he had tried to generate interest in public meetings, which he hoped would ask him to call the election by proclamation.

But, all his efforts came to nothing. As Jim Reynolds noted, the people were not yet ready to double their taxes to gratify the personal ambitions of "kaleblyonoflyonsdalethegovernorofIdaho."[57]

Caleb Lyon's signature (*Author's Collection*)

In February, Reynolds began publishing venomous editorials about the traitorous governor, probably due, in part, to Lyon having vetoed a bill which would have continued the *Statesman's* territorial printing contract. Nearly every edition of the paper revealed more of the deceptions of the "old demagogue." Several contained letters from the East exposing Lyon's scheme for statehood, and his ambitions for senatorship.[58]

Reynolds claimed that, near the close of the legislative session, Lyon had written a note challenging him to a fight, but hadn't had the grit to send it; also that he had contemplated libel suits, a "cow-hiding" and other actions in which James Street, Democrat editor of the Idaho City *World*, was to have played a role. Street, in turn, took to calling the well-nourished Reynolds "Slim Jim," and accused him of having issued two editions of a recent *Statesman*, attacking Lyon in the one distributed outside of Boise.

With such a tenuous hold on his job, Lyon had taken pains ever since his return to Idaho to curry favor with Secretary of State Seward. He had recently told Seward that the "unpleasantness" over the removal of the capital had all ended, and that the government of Idaho was "running smoothly..."[59]

Now, with Reynolds on the attack, Lyon sent Seward a copy of the legislature's proclamation of praise, along with a "statement of confidence" in his policies, signed by his few friends and several subordinates. Another of his unctuous letters closed with a prayer that God might spare Seward's "valuable life for the sake of the Republic..."[60]

Further discord came with the issuance of the report of the legislative committee investigating the money missing from DeWitt Smith's accounts. Published several weeks after the legislature adjourned, the report confirmed that there was a deficit in Smith's accounts of not less than $8,062, but that someone had stolen the missing money subsequent to Smith's death. Editor Street of the *World* accused the "Black Republicans"—Reynolds, Milton Kelly, and Horace C. Gilson—of sacking the dead man's effects, "gobbling up" the money, and of keeping the results of their examination secret.[61]

Street had it only partly right; Secretary Gilson had stolen the money, shortly after his appointment as administrator of DeWitt Smith's estate, but Reynolds and Kelly had played no part in it.

Now that the legislative committee's report cast suspicion on Gilson, people recollected that he had been spending a lot of time in a Boise gambling house, "harnessed...up in gorgeous" jewelry, splurging on what was thought to be borrowed money.[62]

In short order, Gilson decided it was time to vamoose. By now, he had received his official bond, having found no less than ten bondsmen in Boise to back him for the unusually high limit of $40,000.

Several weeks earlier, he had sent the new territorial printer, Frank Kenyon, to San Francisco to arrange for the printing of the laws passed at the second and third sessions. Now, having decided to flee, Gilson dashed off letters to Secretary Seward, and the comptroller of the treasury, saying that, with the governor's consent, he was going to San Francisco to personally supervise the printing of the laws. He then quit Boise, leaving faithful old Solomon R. Howlett as acting secretary. Gilson told Howlett he would draw Idaho's funds for 1864-65 at Oregon City, and then join Kenyon in San Francisco.

Arriving in Oregon City on February 28, Gilson went immediately to the depository and withdrew the entire amount placed there to the credit of Idaho–$33,000 deposited just four days earlier, and $2,000 left from the previous year. A few days later, he sent a lying letter to Howlett, saying the funds hadn't yet arrived.

Gilson took a steamer to San Francisco, where he signed the printing contract. In late March he wrote Howlett saying he expected the $33,000 to arrive about April 15, at which time he would deposit most of it in a Portland bank, so that Howlett could draw on it. Meanwhile, he said, he and Frank Kenyon were rushing the printing job, which would be completed within 35 days. But, shortly after this, Gilson absconded to Hong Kong with all the money he had stolen, leaving Kenyon stranded at San Francisco, to explain to the printers why Idaho couldn't pay the $10,708 printing bill.[63]

What little good will Caleb Lyon could command after all his political missteps would soon evaporate because of his continued inept handling of the Indian problem.

During the early winter, depredations had continued only sporadically but, by mid-February, the settlers along Jordan Creek in the Owyhee region were being robbed repeatedly. In one midnight Indian raid on his livestock, rancher Andrew L. Hall took a bullet in the abdomen. Mounted infantry went out from nearby Camp Lyon and recovered some of the stock, but, as was usual, the soldiers proved to be of no help in preventing such attacks or punishing the raiders.

The ineffectiveness of the military prompted "war meetings" on February 14 and 15 at Bill Sommercamp's Challenge Saloon in Silver City, for the purpose of raising and equipping a 25-man volunteer force, to go "Indian hunting." Bounties were proposed for any scalps brought in—a male's hair would be worth $100; a woman's would bring $50, and $25 would be awarded for everything "in the shape of an Indian under ten years of age."

Within days, newspaper editors, far from the depredations, would censure the *Avalanche* for publishing the list of bounties. But the editor—probably Joe Wasson—said that such proceedings were "too rare to be consigned to fickle memory," and that he considered them "a curiosity," deserving of publicity. Perhaps, if outsiders learned the "pitch of feeling and madness wrought by continual outrages," it would bring some action.[64]

Subsequent to the Owyhee meetings, Ed Bohannan, a local legislator, was sent to Fort Boise to obtain assistance. All available troops, horses and rations had already left that place, under Captain Walker, on an expedition to the Malheur River. But, the acting commander offered to arm a volunteer force, and he sent a messenger after Walker to turn him toward the canyons along the Owyhee, where the marauding Indians were supposed to be.

Governor Lyon gave no help, confining his actions to informing Secretary of the Interior Harlan of the numerous instances of "horse stealing and plundering" by the Indians. Lyon stated, wrongly, that there had been only two whites killed within the previous eight months, when, in fact, there had been at least ten slain around Silver City, or on the roads leading to Owyhee.

Still smarting over Senator Nesmith's damming report on Idaho Indian affairs, Lyon groused to Harlan about the advice the senator had supposedly dispensed while in Idaho—"TO KILL ALL INDIANS WHEREVER THEY CAN BE FOUND." Lyon thought Nesmith's visit had damaged the moral and Christian controlling influence of the whites, and might result in a war. But he, Caleb Lyon, was "struggling against that kind of policy" as hard as he could, and hoped "God in his mercy" would give him strength to avert it.[65]

While Ed Bohannan was drumming up support in Boise, the raids continued, unabated, in Owyhee. On the night of February 17-18, as Chauncey D. Bacheler and "Yank" Blair were traveling in a horse-drawn sled from Camp Lyon to Silver City, they were surprised by several well-armed Indians, who succeeded in stealing their horses, and in wounding Bacheler severely in the arm. "Yank" Blair yanked off his old Union army overcoat to lighten up for a retreat, and, helping Bacheler through the deep snow, the two managed to escape. As they did, Blair looked back and saw a big native don his coat and walk off. Later Blair told his friends that he had "merely lent his coat to a man who was going across Jordan."[66]

In other attacks, on that same night, ten of Hill Beachy's horses were driven off from the stage station of Joseph Babbington and James C. Bernard, sixteen miles from Silver City on Reynolds Creek, and another two animals were stolen from the nearby Carson ranch. Beachy was trying to run a stage line between southern Idaho and Star City, Nevada.

Shortly after sunrise, the same raiders appeared at Cold Spring station, south of Carson's. Samuel P. Duzan, the station keeper, had just fed the four horses their morning grain, and then had gone down to the spring—some 40 yards from the stable—for a bucket of water. On his return, he was startled to hear the keen whistle of a ball, followed by the report of a rifle.

Looking up the road, not 50 yards away, Duzan saw two Indians on horse-

Staging in Reynolds Canyon, ca. 1866
(*Idaho Historical Society*)

back, one of whom had just fired at him. Another two were guarding some stock on a nearby hill. Duzan had left his only weapon, a revolver, back in the stable. He made a dash up the road for it, with the Indians galloping hard on his heels. After getting the gun, he cut loose the horses, saddled one of them, and got out of the stable with the Indians only a hundred yards behind.

The horses would not drive, and, with his pursuers gaining on him, Duzan abandoned all but the one he rode, and sprinted toward Babbington's, the Indians yelling and firing at him for half a mile or more. He managed to reach the station, clapped-out but unharmed, at which time his pursuers went back to Cold Spring and stole all his provisions, blankets and grain sacks, and made off with three of Beachy's horses. This brought the total number that Beachy had lost to Indians in the past nine months to eighty-eight.

During the same week that the aforementioned activities took place, Indian marauders were making nightly appearances at the ranch of Dr. G. W. Inskip on Cow Creek. Although they had been unable to do much damage, the doctor complained bitterly of the governor's inaction on the Indian problem. Said Inskip: "Could we have believed his speech in your city last

Fall, there would not have been an Indian track left in the mountains."[67]

Spurred on by Ed Bohannan and Hill Beachy, meetings were held at Riggs and Agnew's Hall in Boise on February 20 and 22 to see what could be done about the Indian threat. Despite his recent pacifistic letter to Secretary Harlan damning the killing of Indians by whites, Governor Lyon delivered several "violent war speeches" at these meetings in favor of raising a volunteer force, and he personally contributed $500 to that cause. But he told Beachy and others that his instructions prohibited him from using any Indian appropriations for such purposes.[68]

James Reynolds wrote a sharp editorial denouncing the governor for refusing to provide Indian money for a volunteer force. According to the editor, Lyon had claimed, at various times, that he was allotted $100,000 per year to distribute to the tribes, and he had been "blarneying all winter" about using it to establish reservations a few miles from Boise. Lyon responded by calling the *Statesman* a "venal and lying press," saying that he had never had but $26,000, of which $19,000 had been paid to the Nez Perce.[69]

Others piled on Caleb for his failure to finance an expedition. Sam Duzan—Hill Beachy's station keeper who had just been shot at and robbed of all his worldly possessions—wrote a lengthy card to Lyon. Duzan had been one of those northern Idahoans who had balked at removing the capital, so he hadn't liked Lyon to begin with. His carpenter shop had adjoined Lyon's Lewiston Indian office, and he had seen the governor sneaking out of town on that gray December, 1864 morning, to go "duck hunting."

Duzan cynically addressed Lyon as "Dear old Governor"—that "sweet old amalgam of French manners and Turkish voluptuousness"—and said:

> ...you and I differ as essentially in our views of the proper use to be made of a redskin devil, as we do in the proper use of a French waiter or Italian barber. You believe in making unmentionable uses of the two latter, while I believe in keeping the one to skip around a dining room...and employing the other in all the legitimate arts tonsorial. You believe in taming the 'fast expiring race' and making them a source of profit...I believe in making coyote feed of the whole breed...

Aside from this inference of homosexuality, Duzan charged Lyon with putting the money he claimed to have given to the Nez Perce, into mining speculations. He told Lyon that Jonah, the Nez Perce man who had built the Lapwai stone church, still periodically came to Lewiston, the "Ancient Capital of Idaho," looking for Lyon to pay him for his work. "Dear old Pelican," Duzan told Lyon, "send him a string of beads and a few dollars."

The man Wiaskus was also waiting for the first payment on the "new Lyonsdale" property, on Hatwae Creek. Duzan asked the governor to resign and ask Andrew Johnson to "send us a man."[70]

With depredations continuing, John Wasson of the *Avalanche* also voiced his dissatisfaction with Lyon's do-nothing Indian policy:

> The Governor assured us, last November, that he had made representations to the right sources, and would keep doing so until two regiments were obtained, but no troops have come...He said, 'with sleepless vigilance shall I watch your safety and guard your thoroughfares.' What the devil is the use 'to watch' unless you...act, and send a hail of leaden balls into this 'short lived race.' Governor, if you have the power to effect anything...do it now...If not...own up that your poppycock dream of a debut in the great Capitol of the Nation in the dazzling toggery of U. S. Senator from Idaho, incapacitates you for practical usefulness...You have the stand...shoot off your potato trap or goose quill.[71]

A small group of volunteers finally obtained some arms and provisions, and went out on foot beyond the forks of the Owyhee River, but found no Indians. Captain Walker's expedition, comprising 39 mounted infantry, however, had somewhat better fortune. On February 23, they stumbled upon a camp of Indians about twenty miles from Owyhee Ferry.

The soldiers charged the camp, killing eighteen native men and, "accidentally," six women and children. Three men escaped into some thick brush, from which they kept firing. Determined not to leave one man alive, several soldiers charged upon them, and a certain Corporal Burke—who had survived 23 Civil War battles—received a fatal shot through the breast.

At this, the contest was abandoned, and Walker's soldiers destroyed three lodges in which they found bunches of keys, soldiers' gloves, citizens' clothing, government saddles and some rifles. Walker and the detachment started back to Fort Boise the next morning, out of provisions.[72]

As Walker was returning, a group of Boise area volunteers was preparing to go out. Some $3,000 had finally been raised in Ada County, which had been enough to mount and equip thirty Indian hunters. A good number of these volunteers were some of the West's worst hoodlums, and they chose one of their own kind, thirty-six year old David C. Updyke, as their captain.

Updyke was a former New Yorker who had come to Boise, bought a livery stable, and then got himself elected Ada County's first sheriff in March, 1865. Like the infamous Henry Plummer, he was a lawman who used his job to conceal his outlawry. He set up his office in a saloon adjoining the livery stable, and surrounded himself with a gang of hooligans, who were thought to be responsible for a number of crimes, including stagecoach robberies near Boise and on the Portneuf River.

In September, 1865, the sheriff had been arrested by order of a local judge, charged with unlawfully dealing in county warrants, not turning over to the treasurer $1,000 in county taxes he had collected, and with negligence of duty in not arresting one of his friends, West Jenkins. When a grand jury indicted him upon the latter two of these charges, Updyke had resigned his position and pled not guilty. Then, unexpectedly, the prosecutor entered a *nolle prosequi* and the entire matter was dismissed. Many Boiseans suspected collusion.[73]

Updyke's volunteers chose Charles Ridgley, whose real name was James Archie, as their first lieutenant. He had been a member of Henry Plummer's gang, and, more recently, had shot and killed a man, while gambling, at Rocky Bar.[74]

On March 2, 1866, Updyke started his company and its pack train out of Boise. Before leaving, he informed the governor that he intended to march up the Snake River, and then up the Bruneau, killing all natives found. Many whites, especially a rancher named Isaac Jennings who lived on Catherine (Castle) Creek, thought the Bruneau Shoshoni were responsible for most of the Owyhee area depredations.

Although the fainthearted Lyon had made no objection to the plan when Updyke presented it, within a few hours after the ruffian and his volunteers left, he sent out his local Indian agent, Archie G. Turner, hot on their heels to head them off. After doing this, Turner was to arrange for a pow-wow with the Bruneaus, at which Lyon could treat with them.

Archie Turner had reportedly gone out with "his hair shingled [cut short]," and the program was, if he were compelled to fall back, "to have the Governor and several others naturally thin-haired in reserve." Arch's baggage consisted of "a bottle of cocktails, a carpet sack full of Mrs. Winslow's Soothing Syrup; a derringer with a blank cartridge, and a big John [Chinese] with a long pole over his shoulder."[75]

At the "Forest Grove" stage station, which sat a mile from the sagebrush-covered bank of the Snake, miles from any tree, Arch and his brother Sam were, reportedly, disputing over "the policy." Arch wanted to obey Lyon's order, but Sam was insisting on complying with the dictates of his conscience—"join the boys and kill everything Indian."[76] Thankfully, good judgment prevailed, and Turner got his message to the volunteers just as they were boarding the Snake River ferry.

Updyke took his men across the river and camped on Reynolds Creek. He said he would have continued on, but even Isaac Jennings was now asking that the Bruneaus not be molested. Although Jennings had been fighting these Indians, for allegedly stealing his stock, for over a year, he now thought they were innocent, and that they could be used to help locate the real marauders. But, despite the intercession of Jennings and the governor, Updyke kept his expedition in the field.

Lyon's interference with the expedition brought him further editorial abuse. The Wasson boys published a sardonic advertisement for a new Idaho stage line—"Lo and Co.'s Express"—with "His Excellency Gov. Lyon principal director and distributing agent." The company was said to be "making uninterrupted trips from the head office to Owyhee, Malheur and Bruneau rivers, thence to their employees on all the different routes to the Owyhee mines..."

Another ersatz ad was even more insulting:

> Wanted in Idaho—A Governor that is a man, not an old imbecile as we now have...We don't want any importation, but men of I. T.—not of any New York or eastern dale![77]

Lyon took solace in fraternizing a bit more with his friends, the Democrats, at a convention in Idaho City. A speech he delivered, endorsing President Johnson's recent veto of a proposal to enlarge the Freedman's Bureau, delighted the crowd, but they were gratified even more by his playing Cupid. In a territory virtually devoid of the gentler sex, he helped John Duvall and George Ainslie each find a woman to marry. Lyon took pains to inform Secretary Seward of his warm reception at the convention.[78]

While the governor was at Idaho City, tensions were increased by the killing, on March 11, of a number of Indians on nearby Mores Creek, by a party of whites. One man reported having seen "six bucks lying still on one stack..."[79] Some accounts said that no women had been killed, but others said there were two dead women and two boys. A large amount of arms and ammunition had supposedly been captured.

After sending Archie Turner to investigate the incident, Lyon wrote Indian commissioner Cooley, informing him of the slaughter of these "peaceable" natives. He said he had gathered the rest of the band—115 Shoshoni—at Fort Boise and placed them under military protection. The "cowardly deed" had been incited by James Reynolds, editor of the *Idaho Statesman*, "than whom a greater scoundrel never lived."[80] Lyon assured Cooley that things might "look stormy just now" but when the "road to the Indian country" became passable, he would "quiet the troubled waters."

Reynolds didn't learn of this accusation against him until later, but, at the time of the incident, the editor said that, even if these Indians were peaceable, they were providing ammunition to their brethren in Owyhee. "Let vengeance and extermination be visited upon all the hostile tribes," he trumpeted.[81]

The editor was also still annoyed about plans the governor had made to appropriate the Warm Springs Ranch and several others on the outskirts of Boise, in order to make a reservation for "a few renegade Snake Indians." "The garrulous old humbug and granny...known...as 'old Kale,'" he snarled, "should move them to an uninhabited valley." Reynolds expressed regret at having "blowed" enthusiastically about Lyon's pretended treaty with some Boise Shoshoni two years earlier.[82]

Lyon was reminded that he had promised to seek peace with the Indians as soon as the legislature adjourned. Reynolds reproached him for having done nothing of benefit in his two year tenure, for either the territory or the Indians, unless it was to "build that stone church" at Lapwai, which the rain had "thrown down." He urged Lyon to go make a treaty with the Bruneaus and give them a reservation from mouth of the Bruneau to Salmon Falls.[83]

Lyon might never have taken any such action had he not also been in receipt of a telegram from Commissioner Cooley to go out and settle the difficulties. Consequently, on March 28, he started for the Bruneau River, accompanied by a sizeable military escort under command of Major Louis H. Marshall, 14th U. S. Infantry, who had recently taken command of the Boise district.

On the very day the Lyon left to deal with the Bruneaus, news reached Boise by telegraph that he had been dismissed as governor and superintendent of Indian affairs. He was ordered to settle up his accounts and turn things over to a new man, Dr. David W. Ballard, of Oregon. President Johnson had removed Lyon based on the advice of Commissioner Cooley, the Secretaries of State and Interior, and Senator Nesmith. Johnson reportedly admitted that he never had thought Lyon was fit for the office, but left him where he found him, temporarily.

James Reynolds said the people of the territory were profoundly grateful to President Johnson for this news, and that no farewell parties would be held for Old Kale. Although Lyon must have received the news of his removal, he nonetheless remained in Owyhee to conclude the treaty with the Bruneaus.

Dave Updyke's Ada volunteers had returned to Boise on the day before Lyon left for the Bruneau. They had been out for three weeks, supposedly searching for the Indian marauders clear to the Forks of the

Owyhee. But, in fact, they had spent most of their time camped on the Snake, only 40 miles from Boise, shooting at a target and racing their horses.

Updyke's return sparked a brief season of vigilante terror in Boise. The troubles began when a certain Joseph Aden was arrested on Updyke's charge that Aden had stolen eleven of his horses. Aden had contracted with Updyke to provide transportation for the recent Indian expedition, and, according to him, Updyke had promised to give him the horses for his services.

A key witness testifying at Aden's hearing, on April 2, was a well-liked young man, named Reuben Raymond, who had volunteered for Updyke's expedition soon after his discharge from the army at Fort Boise. The charges against Aden were dropped, based solely on Raymond's testimony about the ponies in question, which ran counter to the statements given by some of Updyke's gang.

On the morning following the hearing, some of Updyke's men cornered Raymond in Updyke's stable and accused him of having sworn falsely. During the heated quarrel that ensued, a gambler and former volunteer, John C. Clark, stepped in front of Raymond and began cursing him. Clark tried to strike Raymond, but Raymond dodged and backed against a wall, and drew his pistol.

At this, Clark also drew his revolver and shouted "Shoot, damn you, shoot," to which Raymond replied that he didn't want to do that, but didn't intend letting anyone beat him up. Someone tried to take Clark's pistol, but he refused to give it up, taking deliberate aim and shooting young Raymond through the gut. As Raymond died, he gasped, "I hate to be shot down like a dog for telling the truth."[84]

A surgeon, Ephraim Smith, who had witnessed the shooting, made a hasty examination of the boy and, finding him mortally wounded, turned to the crowd and said "Gentlemen, this is a damned outrage." Whereupon, Dave Updyke stepped up to the doctor and said, "That affair grew out of the law suit yesterday, and there will be many more like it."[85]

Clark was arrested for murder. At a preliminary hearing, held that same evening, most of the witnesses—all confederates of Updyke—testified that Clark had shot in self defense. The whole tenor of this inquiry convinced James Reynolds and other prominent Boiseans, that the means used so often before to defeat justice would be used once again to prevent Clark's conviction.

There had been at least 60 deaths by violence in the region without a single conviction of murder in the first degree. Most notable had been the acquittal, a year earlier, of the vicious murderer, Ferd Patterson, on charges of killing a former Boise County sheriff. Law-abiding people had come to believe that the courts were "but a farce to enable criminals to escape."[86]

Accordingly, Reynolds and the others met secretly that night and formed a vigilance committee, patterned after a similar group which had recently operated effectively at nearby Payette.

Because Ada County had no jail of its own, and there was no territorial prison, John Clark had been placed in the stone guardhouse, located on the square at Fort Boise. At the time, many of the soldiers were out on the Bruneau River, protecting the governor, and there were no officers present at the fort.

In the early morning hours of April 7, perhaps with the acquiescence of the sergeant of the guard, some twenty disguised men "overpowered" the guardhouse sentries, and dragged Clark away. No search was made and, when daylight came, Clark's body was found hanging from a makeshift, three-pole gibbet, just outside of town, on the prairie toward the bluff. Pinned to one of the poles was the following notice:

> NO. 1. Justice has now commenced her righteous work. This suffering community, which has already lain too long under the ban of ruffianism shall now be renovated of its THIEVES and ASSASSINS...an outraged community has most solemnly resolved on SELF PROTECTION.
> Let this man's fate be a terrible warning to all his kind...
> This fatal example has no terror for the innocent, but let the guilty beware, and not delay too long, and take warning. XXX.[87]

Sheriff Duvall buried the body, and a coroner's jury conducted a brief investigation. There were some threats made by Updyke partisans about burning the town, and the like, but nothing transpired. Said Reynolds:

> There can be no doubt but there is a most effective and determined organization of "vigilantes" in the community. All agree that Clark was guilty of a cold blooded murder...[88]

Most of Updyke's confederates, frightened by Clark's hanging and the establishment of nightly patrols of citizens, hurriedly left Boise. Updyke himself bolted on April 12, in company with one of his ruffians, Jacob Dixon. Before leaving, he made threats against several men, whom he charged with having had a hand in Clark's hanging, and he announced his intention of returning to Boise, one last time, to get even.

But, Updyke would get no revenge. Within days, his body was discovered by travelers at B. M. Durell's Syrup Creek Ranch, on the road from Boise to Rocky Bar. The corpse was suspended by the neck in a shed between two vacant houses, and on it was pinned a card saying: "Dave Updyke, the aider of Murderers and Horse Thieves. XXX." Jacob Dixon's body was found hanging from a tree a few miles down the creek.

Several days later, another card was posted at Updyke's stable on Boise's Main Street, written in the same hand as the one previously found pinned on Clark's gibbet. It recited the crimes of the latest men strangled, and served notice on others:

> DAVE UPDYKE, Accessory after the fact to the Port Neuf stage robbery. Accessory and accomplice to the robbery of the stage near Boise in 1864. Chief conspirator in burning property on the Overland Stage line. Guilty of aiding West Jenkins, the murderer, and other criminals to escape, while you were Sheriff of Ada County; Accessory and accomplice to the murder of Raymond, Threatening the lives and property of an already outraged and suffering community, Justice has overtaken you. XXX.
>
> JAKE DIXON, Horse thief, counterfeiter, and road agent generally. A dupe and tool of Dave Updyke. XXX.
>
> All of the living accomplices in the above crimes are known through Updyke's confession and will duly be attended to. The roll is being called. XXX.[89]

H. C. Street of the *Idaho World* hotly accused Reynolds and the Republicans of having gotten up the vigilance committee, claiming that Updyke had been hung for his money, and "to get a powerful political foe out of the way."[90] Reynolds didn't confirm or deny being a vigilante, but he offered this explanation for the hangings:

> For something more than two years this Territory has been...ruled by...bands of men, who have made...robbery, burglary and murder...their profession. Juries and officers of the courts have been terrified by their threats from a discharge of their duties, and in some instances [these criminals] have succeeded in being elected to offices of trust, only to betray the too-confiding public into the hands of their bloody confederates...The express and stage companies have been obliged to conduct their operations with the utmost secrecy to avoid robbery by villains whom they knew to be daily in their offices and on their stages watching for opportunities of plunder...[91]

Now, said Reynolds, good citizens could go about their business in comparative safety; and only criminals had cause for fear. When the grand jury that was in session finished its work, its members could disperse without danger of being assassinated.

Indeed, when that grand jury next met, the judge seemed strengthened as he reminded the jurors of their responsibility:

> You are the servants who are to...cleanse this cess-pool into which the outlaws of Utah, Nevada, California, Kansas and Oregon have emptied themselves...You and I are the Vigilance committee, not self constituted, but legally appointed...Stand firm in the discharge of that duty. But go away from here with the crimes unpunished and, they will meet you at your own door.[92]

During the period of vigilante action, Governor Lyon and his party had been dealing with the Bruneau Shoshoni, or, as Joe Wasson put it, they were "slumbering with their red brethren and cultivating friendly feelings."

Eventually 250 impoverished natives from scattered bands had been gathered, and a "treaty" was concluded on April 12. Lyon reported to Secretary of the Interior Harlan that he had dealt with 150 chiefs, headmen and women, who represented nearly 1,000 natives. The pact—concluded "in the heart of hostile Indian country"[93]—had extinguished the Owyhee war, quieted all the Indians of Idaho, and procured for the United States all the rich mineral lands known as the Owyhee mines.

In exchange for the lands ceded, the Bruneaus were to get a reservation, and $80,000 beginning one year after ratification. Lyon complained once again to Secretary Harlan of having "to labor against a public sentiment viciously in favor of exterminating the Red men at all hazards, backed by a press throwing ridicule upon all efforts towards tranquilizing the wronged and much-abused class." Ever the sycophant, Lyon recommended creating the Indian reservation in "Harlan Valley" on the Bruneau River.[94] Reynolds was contemptuous of Lyon's report of the treaty:

> People who know Old Kale's habit of lying will recognize [this] as a description of his trip up the Bruneau, where there are not over a hundred and fifty poor, half-starved miserable wretches...who have nothing to do with those who are continually engaged in acts of violence...As to the "lands and minerals ceded"...that is ridiculous.[95]

The editor noted that no overall chief had been found—merely headmen for bands of ten to twenty persons—and that, after witnessing the agreement, Archie Turner had been so disgusted he resigned his job as Indian agent.

As events would prove, Lyon's latest treaty did nothing to diminish the Indian war, and none of his sloppy pacts would ever be acted upon because, by now, no one in the federal government trusted his judgement.[96]

Treaty with the Shoshone Indians in 1866. Charles C. Nahl painted this imaginative scene of Lyon's council with the Bruneau bands. The man on Lyon's left is Rev. Hiram Hamilton. (*From the Collection of the Gilcrease Museum, Tulsa*).

The deposed governor was evidently terrified by the recent vigilantism and, after returning from the treaty site, he wasted no time in leaving Idaho. After paying McCall his salary, Lyon and Newton Northam fled during the night of April 20-21. The "weak old granny," said Reynolds, kept his departure time from Boise a secret and hadn't even the courage to shake hands with his few friends. Some of them "felt badly sold" after finding that "Caleb of the Dale" had sneaked away. Just before leaving, he had obtained signatures on a paper, endorsing his actions. Reynolds called it a "pass," which he thought Lyon would use to offset Senator Nesmith's letter.[97]

The Wasson brothers likewise expressed their disgust. Twice the "shrewd humbug" and "schemer" had been generously received in Idaho with the "tooting of horns." His first reception was given because of his position; the second because a governor was needed, "and to encourage him to BE-ONE, overlooking his former failure and disgrace." Now he had sneaked away again, before the arrival of a successor, amid "a big cloud of unparalleled disgust."

He had always "piteously pleaded"—for popular applause. He had meanly denounced the papers that would not blindly endorse his decisions and excuse "his vanity, idleness, incapacity and roguery." He had tried to buy, directly or indirectly, first, their good words, and later, their silence. "Never did...people swallow a rotten bait thrown at them, so easily..."[98]

John Wasson was probably mad because he had made a fool of himself over Lyon's "diamond" story. At the time of Lyon's departure Wasson was about the only person still touting the shiny stones—perhaps hoping to find a buyer for his claims. But, a man who had been to New York, and looked into the truth of the story, had found it to be totally false. There it was being treated as a good joke, and was known to be one of "Lyon's big lies."[99] The truth had already been suggested in an *Avalanche* editorial:

> Our readers will remember our story of the Wilson-Governor Lyon discovery: How Wilson was returning on the unfortunate Brother Jonathan... to reap some benefit from his discovery...[and an] All-wise Providence ordained that Wilson should go down and the Governor be spared to us...
>
> No one seems to know the birthplace of Samuel Wilson—our hero. But let Owyhee establish a new era in diamond mining and...every one-stop crossroads in the land will have its Sam Wilson of Owyhee memory.[100]

Indeed, Sam Wilson did not exist. His name cannot be found on any listing of *Brother Jonathan* passengers. Most likely Caleb Lyon made up the story, thinking that by "booming" diamond fields he could speed up statehood. The so-called "diamonds," were probably common chalcedony—a form of translucent, crystalline quartz.

After his dismissal, Caleb Lyon, in company with Newton Northam, lingered for awhile in Walla Walla, awaiting, as he claimed, the arrival of his successor. Then he went to Portland, where several Boiseans saw him, but were avoided by the disgraced former governor.

By June Lyon was in San Francisco, where a fellow named A. S. Downer, caught up with him. Lyon had hired Downer in March as a special Indian agent, to go north and report on the condition of the Nez Perce. When Downer learned of Lyon's removal from office, he sent his reports on the Nez Perce to McCall in Boise and to Commissioner Cooley, and then had followed after Lyon to get his salary and expenses.

Lyon told Downer he didn't have any government money with him, but that he was going East immediately, and would see to it that Downer was promptly paid.[101] Lyon, of course, had plenty of Indian money with him; and, he would remain in San Francisco for another five months.

At about the same time that Caleb Lyon was enjoying San Francisco, Horace Gilson was comfortably settled aboard a steamer bound for Hong Kong, counting his stolen money. Frank Kenyon had returned to Boise from San Francisco with the news of Gilson's disappearance and, at the time, it was generally thought that Gilson had absconded with some of the territory's money, but that he hadn't been able to get his hands on the funds in the Oregon depository. Not until January, 1867 would Idahoans learn for sure that he had plundered everything in the territorial till.

And, Gilson got away clean. One of his Idaho bondsmen, Morris B. Baer, would later find the thief in Paris, living the high life under an assumed name. But, before he could be extradited, Gilson flew the coop. In 1869, it was rumored that the former secretary was in New York City, but the Secret Service failed to locate him.

With both Lyon and Gilson having bolted Idaho, Solomon Howlett was left to act both as territorial secretary and governor. When Ballard, the new governor, arrived on June 13, 1866 he found the territory dead broke, and everything connected with the executive department perfectly demoralized.

The San Francisco printers were threatening to sue the government for breech of contract, territorial indebtedness amounted to at least $65,000, and credit was so poor that Howlett had been required to buy essential supplies using his personal funds. Upon investigation, it was found that less than $10,000 had been disbursed for the benefit of the territory since its creation, despite $58,000 having been made available to the several secretaries.[102]

Indian affairs were in a similar shambles. Lyon's clerk, William McCall, who was still minding the store, stated that the only property held by the agency was some blank government forms—even the furniture had been borrowed. There were no proper records of Lyon's expenditures, but it would soon be discovered that, of the more than $70,000 in Indian money he had been given for his superintendency, all that he had disbursed was a few hundred dollars to the Bruneaus and the $18,000 he had given to James O'Neill in November, 1865 for the Nez Perce.

Learning of the shortage, on July 14, Commissioner Cooley addressed a letter to Lyon at his New York address, directing him to give an immediate accounting, lest he be reported to the Treasury Department. Meanwhile, "the lecherous old bag of infamy"—as the *Statesman* was now calling the former governor—was still in San Francisco, "luxuriating at a private residence," and stood accused of speculating with the missing money.[103]

On August 6, Lyon's son wrote Cooley that he had just discovered the July 14 letter to his father, and had sent it to San Francisco, where the elder

Lyon had been detained "on pressing business." The son begged Cooley not to initiate any proceeding compromising Old Kale's "integrity as a public officer" until dad could learn what was wanted of him, and attend to it.

By this time, Governor Ballard was so desperate for funds that he asked Cooley to allow him to go San Francisco and get the money directly from Lyon. But Cooley refused, and, instead, in early October, the Secretary of Interior started legal proceedings to recover from Lyon or his sureties, the public money remaining in the former governor's hands.[104]

Ballard, no doubt referring to Lyon and Gilson, would later say:

> The first two years after the settlement of our Territory, Idaho was considered but a grand field of speculation; a place only for a temporary residence where large fortunes might be extracted from Government appropriations; and this having been done, they could return to the Atlantic States, or perchance to China.[105]

At length, Lyon decided he must return and face the music. But, in typical fashion, the devious man set afoot one last ruse in hopes of evading responsibility. He and his former assistant, McCall, arrived in New York in November and, once there, McCall obtained the necessary forms from the Indian Office to make an accounting for the entire period of Lyon's superintendency. These papers were drawn up, and Lyon boarded an overnight train to Washington, D. C. on December 13, 1866.

Upon arrival in the capital, he claimed to have been robbed on the train of $46,418, comprising all of the unspent Indian money which he had held. In telling his story to the Washington police, Lyon said he was on his way to return the currency to the treasury department, but that a thief had taken it out of his money belt, which he had put under his head as a pillow while sleeping. During the night, the belt had become uncomfortable and he had pushed it to one side.[106]

Thus, all Lyon had to turn over to his superiors was the trumped-up paperwork. It seemed very strange to most people that he should have carried such a large amount of cash upon his person over the past months, when he could have put it for safekeeping in any government depository. Idahoans, in particular, didn't swallow his incredible story. "That is a new thing, green-backs uncomfortable to old Kale" said Jim Reynolds. "Did any one ever hear such a fool's story to cover up clear defalcations?"[107]

The government agreed. Lyon's accounts were immediately sent to the auditors, and an investigation was begun by government detectives. Meanwhile, Old Kale retired to his home on Staten Island, and dropped from public view, under a cloud of suspicion.

After threatening Lyon with legal action, the secretary of the interior asked the attorney general in December, 1866, if there weren't a federal law under which Lyon could be arrested. The attorney general replied that he could not be certain what law, if any, had been violated, but he cited some sections of an act of August 6, 1846 that he supposed might apply.

But, at that point, the matter was dropped and no further effort was made to prosecute Lyon. The treasury department informed him in February, 1867 that his property account from June 27, 1864 to April 22, 1866 had "been adjusted" and stood "balanced and closed on the books."[108] His bondsman evidently had to reimburse the treasury for what he had stolen.

Caleb Lyon died on September 7, 1875, at age 53. At the time, he was writing a book concerning the ceramics of the Revolutionary period. Later, after the death of his wife, Lyon's two sisters sold his valuable collections of rare books, ceramics, historical plates, antique furniture, weapons, theatrical costumes and fine works of art.

His death went un-mourned in Idaho. Judge Milton Kelly, who was by then editor and publisher of the Boise *Statesman*, certainly shed no tears. Had the deceased suffered the penalty of law for his theft, Kelly said, his funeral services "would have been announced from the doors of Sing Sing or some other penitentiary."[109]

And, Idaho's most infamous governor left little of lasting value as a heritage. One could posit that he tried to soften the harsh attitudes of Idaho's pioneers toward Native Americans, and to temper the strained relationship between the races with Christian morality and love. But, while this may have been partly true, Lyon's actions spoke louder than his ever-busy mouth. No truly moral man would have made empty treaties, nor would he have stolen money pledged to the natives by the government. And certainly, such a man would not try to enrich himself in land or mining schemes at their expense.

Until about 1930 one could still see a pile of rocks at Lapwai, known as "Lyon's Folly"—the residue of the unfinished church he had promised the Nez Perce. But even this reminder of the rogue has now vanished, and Caleb Lyon's only legacy to Idahoans is the few good chuckles the memory of his antics will always provide.

Oh yes, and there is that gold mine today at the mouth of Hatwai Creek, on the same spot where Old Kale told folks he wanted to build a "New Lyonsdale." Except that this mine is in the form of an upscale Nez Perce gambling casino, mining wealth at full blast from its patrons.

A Hard Road To Jordan

Here is another story about the hazards of getting to Idaho Territory. But, in a larger context, this tale concerns the sad state of relations with Native Americans that existed during the early years of Western settlement. Politicians like Old Kale often planted the bad seed; men like Charles McDermit were often the harvest.

Nearly lost to historical memory is a soldier who played a considerable role in sustaining the fledgling state of Nevada, during the dark days of our Civil War. Today, there is little to remind us of the flesh and blood Charles McDermit. His name is remembered only by its assignment to a creek and an Indian reservation in northern Nevada, and to a nearby beer stop along Highway 95. But, sadly, even these small remembrances of McDermit have been marred by some careless cartographer, or bureaucrat, who tacked an extra "t" onto the end of his name.

As if this weren't enough, the labels on certain other northern Nevada landmarks associated with the man have likewise been botched, or forgotten —Quinn River should rightfully be Queen's River; a rocky eminence called Big Butte should be Godfrey's Mountain, and a stream nearby it, called Willow Creek, should be named Otter Creek or "Wells' Run."

Charles McDermit was one of those daring young men who came to California in the Gold Rush of 1849. A Pennsylvanian, he served in the Mexican War as a second lieutenant, and then traipsed overland in search of his fortune. He earned a grubstake by supervising construction of the original army barracks at Benicia, and then began prospecting in the spring of 1850 in the Trinity wilderness of northern California. A bit later, he packed supplies to miners, and operated a ferry across the Klamath River.

This adventurous man was one of the first to arrive in the valley where Yreka, California subsequently sprang up and, when Siskiyou County was created in March 1852, he was elected as its first sheriff. In August of 1854, he was a member of the first party to climb Mount Shasta, and led his companions in three cheers for the "Stars and Stripes" as the flag was planted at the summit. About this time, he married Hannah Jane Davidson, the sister of William Davidson, his business partner in lumber and flouring mills.

During these early years, McDermit had several ugly encounters with California's Indians. In one episode, four companions traveling with him to Trinidad were murdered; in another, his ferry was burned. And, later, when the natives began harassing Happy Camp, which he had helped establish, McDermit led a force which fought them in the "Battle of Lowden's Ferry."

One summer, McDermit raised a company of forty volunteers to escort emigrant companies through a dangerous part of the Applegate Road near Goose Lake. On this outing, four of his men were killed by Modoc Indians. In another incident that season, McDermit and two others were ambushed by Modocs while driving a large pack train across the Siskiyou Mountains; one of his companions was killed, but McDermit and the third man survived by abandoning most of their mules and fleeing down the mountain.

An active Douglas Democrat, McDermit represented Siskiyou in the state assembly during the period 1859-60. At that time, he was described as a man of sound judgment, who had experienced many reverses, but who had held fast to his integrity.

At the outbreak of the Civil War, when Governor John Downey called for volunteers, McDermit left the legislature to enlist in Company M of the Second California Volunteer Cavalry. During the organization of this "Siskiyou Cavalry" at Fort Jones, near Yreka, he was unanimously elected as its captain. In November, 1861, he was promoted to the rank of major and crossed the Sierra Nevada Mountains on horseback, with his wife and three children, to take command of Fort Churchill, Nevada.[1]

This lonely desert outpost had been built at the conclusion of the "Paiute War" of 1860, a short, bloody conflict between the natives living around Pyramid Lake and the miners who had come in such a flood to the Washoe

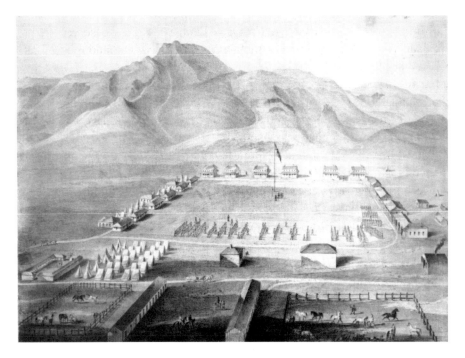

Fort Churchill, Nevada, in 1862
(*Bancroft Library*)

region of western Nevada. The "fort"—the crumbled remains of which can still be seen—sat on the big bend of Carson River, and had no defensive wall. Twenty-one adobe buildings, and two of wood, formed a square enclosure of about 400 yards around a central parade ground.

By the standards of the day, it was a comfortable post. Its buildings were roomy, with 20-inch thick walls, high ceilings and wide porticos. The adobes were painted a gleaming white and—set against the green cottonwoods along the river—were a welcome sight to travelers arriving from the desert. It is, however, a stark locale, and life there in the 1860s was harsh, what with gnats, four-inch scorpions, agonizing heat, and blowing sand.

Much of Charles McDermit's time was spent in dealing with deserters, gamblers, secessionists and over-zealous politicians. Of more importance, beginning in 1863, he oversaw the raising and training of Nevada's volunteer infantry and cavalry companies. His performance was such that Brigadier-General George Wright, commander of the Pacific military region, called him an officer "of great merit, irreproachable in his habits, industrious and careful of the interests of the government."[2]

Major McDermit also came to be *de facto* Indian agent to the Paiute Indians. Most of the regularly appointed agents and superintendents had proven to be notoriously corrupt or lazy, and had done little for either the Paiute or Shoshoni tribes of Nevada.

The state's first governor and *ex-officio* Indian Superintendent, James W. Nye, had squandered $25,000 of Indian money on a dam and sawmill on the Truckee River, near present-day Wadsworth. Begun in 1863, but never finished, the mill had been meant to make lumber for Indian needs, and its outflow was intended for irrigating the bottomlands. But Nye, his agents and a few favored contractors were the only ones to benefit from the scheme. As one newspaperman said of Nye, "he built a dam by a mill-site, but didn't build a mill by a d___n sight."[3]

In contrast, Major McDermit always tried to be fair and helpful to the natives. Such a man as he, said one admirer, was "worth all the Indian Agents ever upon the [Pacific] coast." Thanks to his "enlarged sense of the duties of man to man," he had done more than anyone "to harmonize the conflicts between the white and the red races."[4]

But, unhappily, none of Charles McDermit's good faith efforts could stay the dreadful events that began to unfold in early 1865.

As America's Civil War drew to a close, Indians from the Missouri River to the Sierra Nevada Mountains went on a rampage. There had always been conflict as Americans moved westward, but, at war's end, emigrants were coming in large numbers, and pressing hard on the natives. As a result, freighters, settlers and road builders everywhere were at risk of being bushwhacked for their goods and their lives. The strife was particularly fierce in the region with which our story is concerned—northern Nevada, eastern Oregon, and southwestern Idaho.

As we have seen in a previous story, the mines in the Owyhee Mountains and Boise Basin of southern Idaho were attracting large numbers of men, and, to support them, an immense freight was being carried, mostly from California. But, getting people and goods to Idaho was difficult. For the first few years of the boom, the usual route had been by sea to Portland, then up the Columbia River by steamer to Umatilla or Wallula, and thence overland by pack train. An alternate road passed over the Sierra Nevada Mountains, followed up the Humboldt River to Star City, Nevada, and thence veered northward to Jordan Creek and Boise.

But, by 1865, a number of energetic men were trying make things easier. To improve the Columbia River route, the Oregon Steam Navigation Company was building a steamboat to run on the Snake River. And, on the

Humboldt route, an Idahoan, William C. "Hill" Beachy, had begun a tri-weekly stage line between Boise and Star City, where connections were made with an existing line to Sacramento.⁵

Also, E. D. Pierce and J. B. Francis—both well-known to Idaho—had launched the more formidable project of opening a direct road from the head of navigation on the Sacramento River at Chico, California. It would go to Boise via Susanville and Surprise Valley, California; Puebla, Oregon and Ruby City in Idaho's Owyhee mining region. In January, work was begun on the California end of this route. The partners planned to begin with a weekly passenger saddle train, and put on a line of stages later.

One reason Pierce and Francis picked Chico as their California terminus was the willingness of John Bidwell, of that place, to back their enterprise. Bidwell, a U. S. congressman-elect, had already built, mostly at his own expense, a fine wagon road from Chico to Susanville, where it connected with the Noble emigrant road running across the desert to the Humboldt River and the mines around Star City, Nevada.⁶

In addition to the increased mining activity and new transportation projects to support them, white settlers were beginning to take up every spot with any promise of cultivation. One such place was Paradise Valley, to the north of Dun Glen, Nevada. It had first been settled and cultivated in 1864, and was now filling up with stockmen and farmers. Well-watered by a number of mountain streams, the valley had long been a favorite hunting and gathering place for the Indians of the area.

Early in 1865, Major McDermit was given command of a new military sub-district, embracing all of Nevada and part of eastern California. His immediate superior was still Brigadier Wright, who, having been relieved of the Pacific region by Maj. Gen. Irvin McDowell, was now in command of the California and Nevada district.

That turbulent year began with attacks by Paiute Indians in the desolate Black Rock region, and on the route from Star City to Idaho—all within McDermit's vast new area of responsibility.

In response, Gen. McDowell arranged to send companies of California cavalry from Camp Bidwell (at Chico), to Surprise Valley and to Smoke Creek Station, Nevada. These movements, however, were delayed by deep snow in the Sierra Nevada.

Then, in early March, two prospectors, Isaac Stewart and Robert Rebe, were murdered by Paiutes at Walker Lake, south of Fort Churchill. Farther north, near Susanville, Smoke Creek Paiutes stole a large number of mules, horses and cattle. In Paradise Valley, two men were killed and some horses and cattle run off by Shoshones and Paiutes.

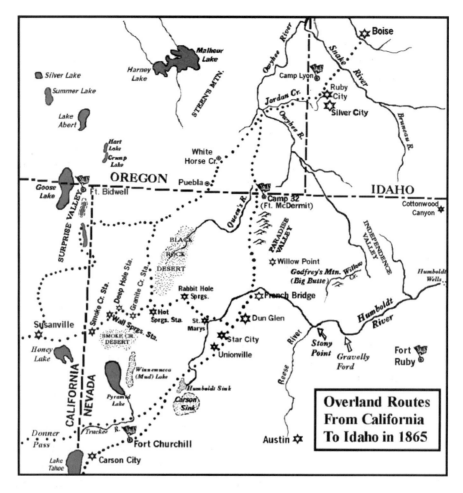

About the same time, the shot-riddled body of Lucius Arcularius was found near Wall Springs Station, on the Noble emigrant road. Arcularius was a part owner of Granite Creek Station, and had been out searching for stolen stock. During the same week, and on the same road, George Thayer, an express rider, was killed.[7]

The only troops McDermit had at his disposal to deal with the troubles were Companies D and E of the First Nevada Volunteer Cavalry, at Camp Nye, near Carson City; Companies A and C of the First Nevada Volunteer Infantry in garrison at Fort Churchill, and infantry Company B at Fort Ruby, Nevada.

The major met with Azapokah, the war chief of the Walker River Paiutes, and, with the chief's acquiescence, on March 12, dispatched Capt. William Wallace to Walker Lake, with a force of ninety infantry and cavalry, to arrest the alleged murderers of the two prospectors. On that same day he sent out

23-year old Captain Almond B. Wells and fifty of his Company D, Nevada Cavalry, on a scout to the north of Fort Churchill.

Wells and his troop arrived at Pyramid Lake in the evening of March 14. There, he learned that about thirty Paiutes were camped nearby at Mud (Winnemucca) Lake, and were thought to be the Smoke Creek group that had been stealing cattle near Susanville. According to Wells, he placed a guard over those Paiutes who were camped at Pyramid Lake, so that none could warn the suspect band of his presence. Then, at 3 A.M., he left for Mud Lake with 29 soldiers and two civilian guides.

At daylight, when approaching the camp of the Smoke Creek band, its occupants were seen to be packing up stolen beef, and preparing to leave. The captain divided his command into three squads, and closed on the Indians, intending to make arrests. But, when within about 150 yards, his men were fired upon. One shot slightly wounded Corporal John Dolan in the shoulder and another passed through the cape of Wells' overcoat.

Wells then ordered a charge with sabers, causing the natives to retreat into the bushes on both sides of the slough. A lengthy engagement ensued, which left 29 dead Indians scattered over a ten mile swath. In his report, Wells praised his men for their valor and coolness under fire, and for their bravery in the fierce hand-to-hand fighting. Although he had no immediate casualties, one private would die ten days later, supposedly as a result of being beaten with a clubbed gun during the fight.

The expeditions of Captains Wallace and Wells arrived back at Churchill on March 17 and 18, respectively. Major McDermit told his superiors that Wells had "whipped those Indians badly."[8] He expressed an equal pride in Wallace, who—with help from friendly Walker Lake Paiutes—had managed to capture the alleged murderers of the two prospectors, without bloodshed.

But, while the two captains had been out, the depredations hadn't abated—a Susanville-Surprise Valley express rider had narrowly escaped being killed near Smoke Creek Station, and all of the station keepers between Hot Springs and the Humboldt River had been driven into Star City. Indian raiders had even made attacks near St. Mary's, a mere 20 miles from Star City. Added to all this, a gathering of some 200 Shoshoni and Paiutes had stolen a lot of livestock in the region northeast of Unionville, driving many frightened whites down to Centerville (Metcalf's), near the "French Bridge" across the Humboldt.

After a series of "war meetings," the people of Paradise Valley, Dun Glen, Star City and Unionville sent telegraphic pleas for military help to Governor H. G. Blasdel at Carson City. Blasdel immediately wired the request to General McDowell, who ordered McDermit to provide protection.

Old Winnemucca
(*Nevada Historical Society*)

Accordingly, Captain Wallace and Wells' companies were sent to Camp Nye to outfit themselves and prepare for a march up the Humboldt.

Meanwhile, a heated controversy had erupted concerning Wells' action at Mud Lake. Based on Indian reports, the Virginia City *Daily Union* alleged that innocent Paiutes had been killed, including a few children and 16 women, two of the latter the wives of old Chief Winnemucca. Also known as Poito, this chief was the head medicine man of the Paiutes, and his influence stretched from Walker Lake clear into northern California and southern Oregon. The *Union* editor was undoubtedly aware of a directive, recently issued by General Wright, ordering expedition commanders not to allow the indiscriminate slaughter of friendly Indians.

Another paper had reported that Wells' men had taken some fourteen scalps—including that of a notorious chief called "Smoke Creek Sam"—despite orders forbidding the practice. Of this charge, the *Union* said Wells "might have unintentionally attacked and killed a number of friendly Indians...and been excused of the error. But if he suffered his men...to take the scalps...no Court Martial...that ever convened in a civilized country... would acquit him."

The *Union* also pointed out that, if the Indians had fired first, as Wells had reported, there should have been more soldiers wounded. And, there was no "desperate hand-to-hand fight,"[9] as Wells had claimed, since other witnesses had said that, if any women had been killed, it was because they been indistinguishable as to sex when shot at the range of half a mile or more.

By McDermit approving Wells' actions, the *Union* charged, he was covering up the murder of innocent people. The editor demanded that he and the governor investigate the incident.

But, unlike the *Union* editor, most settlers in the region were delighted with what Wells had done, and preferred the Indian policy expressed by the *Gold Hill News*:

> We have no hope for the savages, and long since came to the conclusion that their extermination is a 'military necessity,' and that the...slaughter might as well be on our heads as on the heads of our children...This story...amounts to just this: Capt. Wells with his twenty-nine men killed exactly twenty-nine Indians, not one of the bold cavaliers having received a scratch (except Corporal Dolan, who, for thus marring the symmetry of the story, should be drummed out of the service). The number of Indians killed...[allowed] precisely one Indian for breakfast to each of the dragoons; not counting the Captain, who, of course, messes by himself.[10]

To justify his actions, Wells stated that, after the fight, Poito came to him and expressed pleasure with the result. The chief had supposedly been urging the band that Wells had attacked not to steal white men's cattle, and he thought that "the punishment they had received would teach them a lesson."

John Gilson, the Indian agent at Pyramid Lake, said that the reservation Paiutes were also pleased at the result; that only two women had been killed, and that half of the band had been from Smoke Creek.[11]

While Wells was flayed by the one side for being too hard on Indians, Wallace was criticized by the other for not punishing the Walker Lake band for its previous crimes. J. D. Fairchild of the Austin *Reese River Reveille* said Wells was "not such a strategical cuss,"[12] as Wallace, but he had made no mistake in his actions.

The Paiutes having become inflamed by the Mud Lake incident, Governor Blasdel felt the need to calm them. At his request, McDermit invited all of the principal chiefs and "captains" to a meeting on March 24 at Fort Churchill.

The governor arrived at the post on the evening before the council, escorted there by the Virginia City provost guard. An honor guard of garrison infantry, "their bayonets glistening in the evening sun," greeted his party, and then took them to Major McDermit's headquarters.

The publisher of the *Union*, John Church, who had been invited along, later wrote that McDermit displayed "that easy graceful courtesy which distinguishes the polished gentleman and soldier." Paiute and soldier, alike, fondly respected him.

After dinner, McDermit invited in some of the chiefs who had already arrived. Among these was Numaga, also known as "Young" Winnemucca, who spoke for the bands that lived most of the time around Pyramid and Mud Lakes. He was not related to "Old" Winnemucca (Poito).

The chiefs seated themselves with *sang froid*, not a bit awed by the presence of the tall governor and the officers. Blasdel passed out cigars and some of the chiefs lit up, smoking them "energetically...their sharp black eyes alone expressing their enjoyment of the weed." But Numaga seemed upset and sullen, and had his "face painted, as though he was bound on the war path."[13]

Richard A. Washington, a young Paiute man employed by the government, acted as interpreter. After a brief general talk, the chiefs all departed except Numaga, whom Blasdel and McDermit wanted to question regarding Captain Wells' attack.

Numaga told them that the natives who had been stealing cattle were young men belonging to his bands, and whom he had frequently warned not to take the white man's property. These thieves had carried their beef into the camp that had been attacked, but, having learned of the approach of the troops, they escaped before Wells arrived—leaving only three or four men, and a number of women and children to face the soldiers.

The chief said that Wells had killed some 16 or 18 women and children, and one or two men. Only one male had escaped. Some of the women had jumped into the river, and were shot or drowned. Old Winnemucca's two wives were killed, but the chief and his daughters had not been present at the time of the attack. Numaga also said that, if Wells had only asked him, he would have helped in identifying the cattle thieves. But he thought his people were also somewhat to blame, for firing upon the soldiers.

By the next morning, when the formal council was held, Numaga had taken off his war paint and seemed somewhat mollified. He and 65 other head men, representing the several Paiute bands of the surrounding region

Numaga
(*Nevada Historical Society*)

were assembled in a large hall. The Indians sat down in a semi-circle, the most distinguished chiefs in front, facing the governor and the officers of the fort. McDermit presented Blasdel to the chiefs, who gravely shook hands with him. Then, interpreter Washington read a letter to the governor, composed by the chiefs, in which they praised the way the Walker Lake difficulty had been handled, and said they had come to Blasdel's meeting to discuss the other problems in the area, and get a clear understanding of the whites' intentions.

Blasdel then spoke, saying he wanted peace, and that the Paiutes should state their grievances. This triggered the recital of a few complaints—white men refusing to pay Indians for their labor, the stealing of some horses, failure to pay back a loan, and the seizure of a legally-owned pistol.

"Joaquin Ben," from Walker River, also complained that a man of his band had been killed by a white man some time ago, and the murderer had never been punished for the crime. He wanted to know why it was that Indians must be killed for such offenses while white men escaped.

McDermit arose and spoke to the case Ben had brought up. He said that, as always, he had acted in good faith in that instance. The accused man had been arrested and brought to the post for examination both by white and Indian witnesses. From this testimony, it had been learned that he and others had gone to a settler's house, and, in the absence of other members of the family, tried to take undue liberties with a 12-year old girl—and that the girl had torn herself away from him, jumped upon a horse and sought help from two white men in the vicinity.

These whites went to the house, and when the Indians saw them approaching, one drew a knife and advanced toward them in a threatening manner, at which a white man shot him dead. McDermit had turned the shooter over to civil authorities for trial, and he had been acquitted for reasons of self-defense.

McDermit was said to have spoken the explanation in a convincing manner, his face "an index of sincerity." But, after hearing it, Joaquin Ben still thought the incident was an unprovoked murder by the white man, but said he didn't wish to call up old grievances—he wanted peace.

Blasdel assured Ben and the other Paiutes of continued friendship and protection from their enemies if they behaved themselves. In conclusion, Numaga spoke at length, saying he desired to be at peace with the whites as heretofore; that he didn't wish to molest any one and didn't want to be molested. The chief's voice "was full and strong," wrote John Church, and he looked like "a man to command."[14]

After the council, generous amounts of calicoes, blankets, flour, and money were divided among the chiefs. McDermit also called together those who had helped capture the accused Walker Lake murderers and rewarded them with the same items.

After the pow-wow, Captain Wells' second lieutenant, Joel Wolverton, and 47 Nevada cavalrymen of Company D left to establish a temporary cavalry post in Paradise Valley for the protection of settlers and travelers. The *Union* publisher said the troops were a "splendid looking body of men," and Wolverton was "just the man to trust with such an enterprise,"[15] prudent enough to avoid hostilities, if possible, but dependable if a fight came.

Wolverton was sent because Captain Wells had to remain at the fort and face a court of inquiry, convened by Major McDermit, to investigate the Mud Lake affair. The inquiry seems to have been a *pro forma* affair, since, after having heard Numaga's story, McDermit told his superiors that Wells' attack "was the right stroke in the right place."[16] In any case, the probe was a short one, the court finding no grounds to bring charges against Wells, because the natives had fired first.

The voice of northern Nevada was William J. Forbes, editor of the Unionville, *Humboldt Register*. He was one of several astute and witty journalists then resident on the Western frontier. Forbes had faults common to many pioneer men of the era—he drank too much, jumped to quick judgements, and was always restlessly seeking the next bonanza. His longest stay in any one place may well have been as editor of the *Register*.

But, to Forbes' credit, he was tough as nails and always manly in the face of adversity—no colored ribbons ever adorned his office, nor dangled from the sagebrush out in front. Were he alive today, he would likely be widely shunned, and labeled as being bigoted and chauvinistic. But, lovable or not to today's critics, Forbes was immensely popular with his contemporaries, most of whom, like him, were of the unflinching type that opened the West.

The editor was also blessed with a wry and self-denigrating humor, and an erudition without which a man could have gone mad in a place like Unionville. By the time Forbes arrived there, in early 1863, he was fairly well known in the West. He had first learned the printer's trade in Columbus Ohio, and had come to California in 1852, to work in succession for the *Coloma Argus, Marysville Herald*, and Downieville *Sierra Democrat.*

The arrival of the editor and his press at Unionville, in an ox-drawn wagon, had triggered a gay celebration. A 30-gun salute had been "fired" on an anvil, followed by nine cheers, and then everyone had paraded noisily through town behind the Unionville Cornet Band (a single horn). The festivities continued at the new printing office with the consumption of a case of champagne, which had been donated for the occasion by the Magnolia Saloon in Carson City.

With Forbes as editor, the *Humboldt Register* was begun on May 2, 1863, flying at its masthead a motto appropriate for an allegiant Union man in the Civil War years—"Patriotism is not Sectional—it embraces, in its sympathies and Purposes, the cause of Loyal Citizens Everywhere."[17]

From the outset, Forbes, who used the *nom de plume* of "Semblins," had great fun chiding his readership. In one case, he expressed fears of the setback mining would receive if a stormy season should suddenly begin—most of the miners had only been in Unionville a few years, and hadn't yet "got their tunnels in far enough to protect themselves from the rain." Another time he said he was cheered to see the "large number of miners congregated about the saloons day and night, evidently waiting for the blacksmiths to get their picks and drills sharpened."[18]

Unionville owed its existence to a certain Louis Barbeau. He was the Frenchman, and long time trader on the Humboldt, who, in the spring of 1860, ran the gauntlet of rampaging Paiutes, to discover gold in the region just southwest of what is now Winnemucca, Nevada. His discovery motivated a party of thirteen men in Silver City, Nevada to make the same dangerous journey and establish "Humboldt City" in a large ravine on the northwest shoulder of the Humboldt Mountains.

In May of the following year, 1861, "Captain" Hugo Pfersdorff and J. C.

Unionville, Nevada, ca. 1865. (*Humboldt County Library*)

Hannan, guided by four Paiutes and leading a couple of donkeys, came eastward over the mountain from Humboldt City and discovered some good ledges in a canyon they named "Buena Vista." It was there that Unionville was established. Star City and Dun Glen soon sprang up in the same district.

One of the early arrivals at Unionville had been Samuel Clemens—better known as Mark Twain—who traveled there from Carson City, for a brief stay, in company with two friends who had been appointed officers of Humboldt County. Twain described the new town as being "eleven cabins and a liberty pole," the rude structures strung out along each side of a deep canyon. He and his friends built themselves a small hut and roofed it with canvas, leaving a corner open to serve as chimney, "through which cattle used to tumble occasionally." Fires were fueled with sagebrush purchased from Paiutes, who carried it to the town on their backs.[19]

By the time Nevada's new Indian troubles began in 1865, Unionville had grown to over 1,000 persons, and could boast ten stores, nine saloons and six hotels—but not a single church. It was really two towns; the lower was only one-quarter of a mile or so from the valley, and the upper, about a mile farther up the canyon.

The nethermost—nicknamed "Dixie"—contained some 70-80 structures, including the jail and county buildings, grouped together. And, situated there on the stream that flows through the canyon, was John C. Fall's water-powered "Pioneer" quartz mill, built in 1862, the first in the district.

The upper town contained about the same number of buildings. The post office was located there and also Freeman's Hotel, the best in the place. And it was there that Forbes located the office of his *Humboldt Register*, in a comfortable one-story adobe building, with a clay floor. It contained the fine "power press," three cases of type and the other paraphernalia of the printer, while Forbes' "sanctum" was in an adjoining building, which served as his editorial room, bedroom, dressing room and "boudoir."

In the space between the two towns were many gardens, a few scattered residences and the schoolhouse. The buildings of Unionville were made chiefly of stone and adobe, many of them with thatched roofs. Forbes once remarked that the adobe didn't endure well, and that half of the lumber, imported at great expense, was "just what it was cracked up to be," and the other half was "knot."[20]

Fearful Humboldters were greatly relieved by the arrival of Lieutenant Wolverton's cavalry on March 30. During his trek up the river, conditions had worsened in Paradise Valley, and the Shoshoni were now brazenly stealing stock and ransacking cabins when owners were away.

The soldiers brought with them, for distribution to civilians, some 100 muskets, which had been gathered from three companies of Virginia City home guards. Forbes was grateful for the freshly-arrived protection, but assured persons who had friends in Humboldt County, "or acquaintances who owe them coin," that quiet reigned in all the towns, and people felt "secure under their scalps."[21] Only in the remote areas was there any cause for fear.

One of those perilous remote locales was Granite Creek Station. After the killing of Lucius Arcularius, his partner, Andrew Leech, had become sole owner of that station, but had left it temporarily in the care of A. J. Curry, Cyrus Creele, and Albert Simmons, whom he furnished with plenty of guns and ammunition.

On April 1 the station was assaulted by Indians, but no whites became aware of the attack until Leech returned there more than a week later, traveling in company with a large party of prospectors. The scene of death and destruction that greeted Leech and his companions upon arrival at the station was hair-raising.

From the splattering of lead bullets, it could be seen that the attack on the station house had been made from a stone corral about 30 paces off. The three whites besieged within the house had chiseled rifle loopholes through its thick sod walls. It seemed the Indians must have exhausted their ammunition during the fight, since they fired several inch-long missiles, crudely made from wagon bolts. One of these was found in a bellows near the house, and another sunk two inches deep in some wood.

Curry's body—its lower legs removed—was discovered inside the house. He had apparently been killed by a chance bullet coming through a loop-hole. To get at the remaining two men—Cyrus Creele and Albert Simmons—the Indians had torn out a wall of the storehouse adjoining the dwelling. This enabled them to reach the roof and set it on fire, causing the whites to flee.

Footprints in the wet alkali showed how Creele had run out across the flat toward Hot Springs, chased by three Indians on horseback; how he had been captured, then brought back near the house and burned to death. Only a part of his skull, his jawbone, and some small pieces of bone were found, lying in the ashes. His arms had been weighted down by piles of rocks, and then a large stack of sawed lumber built up over him and set on fire.

Albert Simmons' skeleton, minus arms, was found a short distance down the road leading toward Deep Hole Station. A nearby pool of dried blood showed that he had died there, and thus avoided torture. But the body had been dragged off a short distance and severely mutilated. It was recognized as Simmons' only by the teeth.

Even the dog belonging to the station—a savage animal that disliked Indians—had been killed and its skin tanned. A wagon, reaper, hay press and other equipment had been demolished.

Andrew Leech and his friends buried the bodies in a common grave and then went on ten miles to Deep Hole Station. Its occupants, the three Partridge brothers, were entirely ignorant of the calamity at Granite Creek. Leech's party helped them cache such goods as they could not bring away, and a note was posted on the station door warning travelers of the danger. Then everyone, including some other nearby settlers, started with their stock, back through Granite Creek toward the settlements.[22]

Lieutenant Wolverton had no knowledge of the Granite Creek attack, but it wouldn't have mattered, since he had to deal with problems closer at hand. His men barely had time to treat the saddle sores from their trip when, on April 2, Indians raided a grazing camp belonging to John Bryden and a certain Cunningham, located in the East Range, about 20 miles southeast of Unionville. The herders were burned out of their shack, but escaped, despite one of them being wounded.

Wolverton went in pursuit on April 4, following a clear trail made by the sixty head of stolen cattle, leading eastward toward Gravelly Ford. Upon reaching the Austin road, the lieutenant found a house belonging to Gay and Evans on fire. A mile beyond it, he surprised twenty-three warriors, who fled to the mountains, leaving behind a saddled horse and a pair of holsters, identified as being the property of M. J. Ragan.

Ragan was a salt freighter who, at last report, had been returning home to Dun Glen from a trip to Austin. Later, a search party would find his body—pierced by rifle balls and arrows—some eight miles from the Gay and Evans ranch. It appeared that Ragan had been wounded and had taken refuge in the vacant Gay and Evans house. When the Indians had set fire to that, Ragan remained until his whiskers began to scorch, whereupon he got his horse and led them on the chase that ended in his death.

"The Indians we fear move too fast for [Wolverton]," wrote Forbes, expressing the hope that the lieutenant would have the "good sense to slay them first" if he came upon them, "and let John Church [of the Virginia City *Daily Union*] come out at his leisure, and hold postmortems."[23]

Wolverton's cavalry was indeed being outrun. Another attack was made during the night of April 4-5, by about 20 Paiutes, upon the grazing camp of J. R. Withington, southeast of Unionville. Withington, an Austin butcher, was absent, having left matters in the hands of J. D. Page, three other men and a ten-year old Indian boy from California.

Page took a bullet in his right shoulder as the men abandoned their tent and fled southeasterly to the Fish Creek ranch, 15 miles distant. Having dashed off shoeless and unprepared for a foot race, they reached safety, but with their feet bruised and torn to a pulp, and with the wounded Page nearly dead from loss of blood. Later, Withington's camp was found to have been destroyed and the Indian boy killed and scalped. The raiders had driven off twelve horses and a few head of cattle in a southerly direction.[24]

While Wolverton was occupied in the direction of Gravelly Ford, Mark W. Haviland, the justice of the peace of Paradise Valley, left that place carrying letters for Major McDermit, urging creation of a permanent military post. But, the very day he left, April 4, serious Indian troubles began in the valley.

Aaron Denio, who lived with his family on the east side of Martin Creek, was warned by two friendly Shoshoni that a band of warriors was about to kill all the settlers and run off their livestock. Denio sped these words to his neighbors and everyone prepared to flee to the Willow Point stage station for safety. A man named Chris Fearbourne was sent with a wagon up the valley to the Packard ranch, to warn the two herders there—Barber and Collins—and to help get them and their belongings to Willow Point. Packard's place was on Cottonwood Creek, about 20 miles north of the station.

Early on April 5, Denio and his neighbors set out with as many of their possessions as they could transport. Denio had converted part of a wagon into a handcart to carry his four smallest children, along with old T. J. Fine, who had been laid up for weeks with rheumatism. Others in Denio's party were his wife and a 12-year old son; Thomas Byrnes, Waldron Foster, John Lackey, J. T. and A. Bryant, Mr. Rembreaux, and Mrs. Stockham.

The fugitives had to cross Martin and Cottonwood creeks—which were swollen from heavy rains—and a two-mile wide muddy swamp that lay between the streams. Mr. Fine, the women and children had to be carried most of the way, which made for slow going.

After crossing the watery obstacles, Denio and Rembreaux manned the cart and set a course for Hamblin's sod corral, some three miles distant. Mrs. Denio and Mrs. Stockham followed on foot, but the rest of the party remained at Cottonwood Creek to get more provisions and goods across it. Denio and those with the cart were met by Jacob Hufford and his wife, and, by using Hufford's horse, soon had the cart and its cargo safely in Hamblin's corral. They waited there for the others to catch up before continuing on to Willow Point.

Denio expected that, by this time, Chris Fearbourne, Barber and Collins would have joined them from the Packard ranch. But, as it happened, the Shoshoni had other plans for these men.

Fearbourne had spent the night at Packard's ranch house, and, upon awakening that morning, the three men discovered a large group of natives, led by a certain "Captain George," surrounding the house. When Barber cautiously opened the door, four of the Indians sprang to their feet and pointed their guns at him, thumbs upon the hammers. Keeping cool, Barber returned to the house to discuss options with his two companions.

Barber would later say it was agreed that he should take his horse and get help from the settlers farther down in the valley, while the other two stalled the Shoshoni until aid arrived. But, more likely, Barber saw the situation was hopeless and decided to save his skin, if he could, by coolness and daring.

 In any case, he walked nonchalantly out to the corral and began saddling his horse, with a few of the natives following him, their guns at the ready. When they asked Barber where he was bound, he casually replied that he was going to drive in some stock. For some unaccountable reason he was allowed to proceed until he had mounted, when quick as lighting, he drew his revolver and, pointing it at them, put spurs to his horse and escaped without their having fired a shot.

Barber fled down the valley to where the last of the settlers were just finishing getting their goods across Cottonwood Creek. He enlisted the help of Thomas Byrnes and John Lackey and started back to relieve his two companions. The other settlers high-tailed it for Hamblin's corral.

When Barber, Byrnes and Lackey got within sight of the Packard sod house, they saw its rye-grass roof in flames and, on riding closer, two dozen mounted Indians charged upon them. The three whites retreated to Hamblin's with all the speed they could get out of their horses, the Indians close on their heels. They arrived at the corral just as the last of the other settlers, on foot and with every nerve strained, also gained that place of refuge.

Within moments, about seventy-five Shoshoni had the sod corral surrounded. The total weaponry in the hands of the settlers consisted of three rifles, a musket, two double-barreled shotguns, one navy and five small Colt's revolvers. Aaron Denio assumed command of the besieged little garrison, and his first order was to burn Hamblin's house, which stood about 50 yards distant, to prevent its being used as cover for Indian sharp-shooters. J. T. Bryant and Waldron Foster dashed over, under fire, to apply a match.

Though the Shoshoni made charges to within 200 yards, they seemed to have no desire to come inside the effective range of the whites' rifles, so a standoff developed. At length, Thomas Byrnes decided to run the gauntlet to get help, and, on a swift horse, he was able to dash through the circle of Indians, and reach Willow Point Station at about 3 P.M.

Thirteen men were there, all eager to help, but only twelve horses were available, so an old man named Givens snatched up a rifle in one hand, and grabbed the pommel of a saddle with the other, and told his companions to "heave ahead."[25] In this fashion, he kept pace with the relief party over the twelve miles back to the besieged settlers at the corral. The rescuers arrived at dark, to find that, after three hours of firing, the Indians had just departed, without having killed any one. The rescued settlers marched for Willow Point, reaching there at 3 A.M. on April 6.

The initial reports of the Paradise Valley troubles reaching Star City and Unionville that day were greatly exaggerated, and led to a series of frantic telegrams to Major McDermit. He was informed that a massacre of six women and two men had occurred and that 1,000 Indians were on the warpath, murdering people from Granite Creek to the head of the Humboldt.

The people of Star City and Unionville thought that Wolverton was still after Indians to the east of them, toward Gravelly Ford, so they began gathering horses and arms for a citizens' expedition. But, in fact, the lieutenant had reached Willow Point in the early hours of that day, just after the survivors arrived there.

Later in the day he learned that ten Shoshoni had fortified themselves in a corral at the Frenchman's store on the Humboldt, south of Willow Point. That evening the lieutenant's cavalry and a few citizens went there to learn what the Indians' intentions were. As they approached the corral, they were fired upon, badly wounding two men.[26] In the resulting engagement, all of the Shoshoni men—five in number—were killed, and five women and children taken prisoners. Supposedly, among the dead was Captain George, the leader in the murders of the previous day.

Wolverton remained on the river that night, but sent a message to Unionville reporting this fight, and asking that Major McDermit be telegraphed for additional forces. The next morning, April 7, having heard that more Shoshoni had collected in the Martin Creek gap, at head of the valley, he sent 20 men to engage them, while he and some civilians went to see what had happened at Packard's ranch.

The ghastly scene there showed that Collins and Fearbourne had remained in the burning house until the last possible moment. Collins was found at the door, his body horribly mutilated and burned, a fire of poles having been built over it. Chris Fearbourne had apparently remained inside, holding a pan over his head to protect himself from the burning roof, until his hair was burned off and his hands and arms were cooked. He then rushed out and was shot in the back. His corpse was found still clutching the pan.

Around 10 P.M. that night, thirty civilians from the Star City area arrived at Willow Point, and, after a few hours rest, followed on after the soldiers who had gone up Martin Creek. When they learned that the troops were reconnoitering the gap, and had killed two natives, but that the remainder had escaped into the mountains, the civilians returned home.[27]

By this time, editor Forbes had correctly surmised that no women or children had been killed at Paradise Valley, but he reckoned that the different bands of Indians had swept the valley of about 1,000 head of cattle and horses, including 500 belonging to Packard and Hamblin. As before, it appeared that the stolen animals had been driven toward Gravelly Ford.

Now, riding into the fray, came the brave hero of Mud Lake, Captain Almond B. Wells, leading 103 men of Companies D and E, Nevada Cavalry. Wells left Fort Churchill on April 9, 1865, with instructions to proceed to Paradise Valley, and take command of Wolverton's forces. This would give him a total force of 150, with which he could "whip all the Indians that may oppose him."[28] Or so said Major McDermit, in a bit of flawed prediction.

By now the decision had been made to build a permanent camp in Paradise Valley and garrison it with a company of infantry. Wells was instructed to use soldier labor to build it, at a site that Mark Haviland would help him select. The camp would also serve as a temporary depot for Wells' cavalry, which he was authorized to use beyond Nevada's borders, if necessary.

En route to join Wolverton at Willow Point, Wells and his soldiers had laid over for a day at Unionville, where they made a fine impression on Forbes of the *Register*. They behaved well, and, before cooking their supper, nearly every man took a bath in the creek. "Cleanliness is akin to godliness" said the editor, "and we don't believe these fellows would disturb any godly sort of Indian."

As to Wells, the Forbes found the captain to be "a clever fellow, seeming quite civilized." He had "...no Indian scalps at his belt...didn't give any savage war whoop as he landed; but put his boys through a bit of circus performance, by talking square English to them, and then...took a smile [drink] with sundry civilians, much the same as a bloodless militia Captain in the States would have done." Forbes thought the *Virginia City Union* had been mistaken about Wells. He, Forbes, "wouldn't be afraid to go on a fishing excursion in his neighborhood."[29]

Now that more soldiers were available for an all-out war, settlers took steps to clear the area of the band of Paiutes, called Sidocaws, that normally ranged between Winnemucca Mountain and the Humboldt Meadows (near today's Lovelock, Nevada). Though apparently friendly, the Sidocaws were mistrusted by the local whites, and it was thought that some men of the band were abroad with the marauding natives. With the Sidocaws out of the region where depredations were occurring, any Indians found therein could be regarded as hostile.

The band consisted of some 800 persons, whose chief was "Captain Sou," or Moguannoga. Sou had formerly been an avowed enemy of the white intruders, but, in recent years had worked closely with them to maintain peace, often delivering up Indians guilty of crimes.

On April 16, A. P. K. Safford, M. S. Bonnifield, and others obtained approval for the removal scheme from Governor Blasdel. But there was some doubt as to how the Indians would subsist, since there were no funds to feed them. It was well known that the appropriations for Paiutes made by Congress in past years had been squandered or misappropriated by former Governor Nye and his friends. Blasdel offered, however, if the emergency required it, to let Safford draw on him personally, and he would attempt to recover the money from the government.[30]

Accordingly, a contract was signed with Captain Sou and his brother, Captain John, which stipulated that any Indians found in the Humboldt region, after a week had passed, would be killed. Sou's people packed up and left the Meadows to meet Gov. Blasdel's agent, who selected the Carson River sink as a "safe place" for them, far removed from the coming conflict. Sou's people had kept their part of the contract, said Forbes, and now it was "the duty of white men to kill any Indian found in this country..."[31]

Despite the erupting troubles, operations had begun on the new northern overland route from California to Idaho. Captain Pierce's first saddle train had left Chico on April 3 with about 40 hardy "passengers." For $50, each traveler was supplied with two animals—one to ride and another to carry provisions and blankets.

After traveling through Susanville and Smoke Creek, Pierce arrived at Surprise Valley only to learn that a party he had sent ahead to find the shortest route had been defeated by Indians, and one man killed. But, the captain took his train through on a slightly different route, and safely reached the Owyhee mines at Ruby City on April 24.

John Bidwell pestered the military relentlessly to ensure the success of the Chico road. He was working to get stages running on it, and had arranged for a new Susanville to Boise postal route. Responding to the wishes of Bidwell and the settlers, General McDowell sent his chief engineer, Maj. Robert S. Williamson, to choose a site for an army post in Surprise Valley.

Bidwell and Honey Lake area residents also asked McDowell for a cavalry force to be stationed at Smoke Creek—30 miles from Susanville—to protect the road to Surprise Valley as well as the one to the Humboldt. The station had been used before by soldier detachments, and its owner was anxious to lease it again. There were companies of California volunteer cavalry available to man it, but the roads over the Sierras were still closed by snow.[32]

McDermit, who had just been promoted to Lieutenant Colonel, had no men to send to Smoke Creek. His only asset, Captain William Wallace's infantry company, had been chosen to garrison the post in Paradise Valley, but had just been sent once again to Walker Lake to recapture the two Paiute murderers of Rebe and Stewart, who had broken out of jail.

Several other problems were consuming McDermit's time. The removal of Captain Sou's Paiutes from the Humboldt had led the Carson Lake band to think that whites were bent on war against them. They had begun sending away their women and children and burning their lodges, and this, in turn had alarmed the whites. McDermit went to Carson Lake and had a talk with both sides, calming them and saying he would protect all concerned. He allowed

Sou's people to return to the Big Meadows where food was more plentiful.

The colonel had also been to Reservation House, on the Truckee River, to listen to the complaints of the Pyramid Lake bands. He learned that their agent had leased reservation land to whites for grazing, pocketed the money, and then had left the state. The agent had also failed to provide his charges with any subsistence or clothing, telling them that if they gave any trouble he would send for troops and clean them out.

McDermit was surprised that the Paiutes had borne these impositions. He ordered the whites to remove their livestock, and he told the Paiutes to be peaceful and, now that the Civil War was over, the government would do something for them. In the meantime, if whites abused them, they should let him know and he would investigate and punish any guilty persons. A report he wrote on the subject was endorsed by General Wright, recommending that a copy be furnished to a Congressional committee looking into Indian affairs on the Pacific coast.[33]

Meanwhile, Captain Wells had established and settled in at what he called "Camp McDermit," at Willow Point, and seemed content to wait for trouble to come to him. And, it soon did.

To the north, on the road from Star City to Boise, an attack was made at Canyon Station, Oregon (35 miles beyond the Nevada border) on the night of April 26. Hill Beachy's station keeper, Abijah Ives, and a traveler named Mitchell had to flee for their lives from the burning station house. Poor Mitchell was shot in the back as he emerged, but was able to catch one of the express horses and escape. Ives had to bolt on foot, clad only in his birthday suit. Though closely pursued, by leaving the road, he reached the camp of some packers five miles away. There, he found the badly wounded Mitchell, who would later die while being taken in a wagon to Queen's River Station.[34]

Wells made no attempt to go after those guilty of the Canyon Station attack, but, finally, on May 3, he marched his cavalry toward Gravelly Ford, looking for the band of Indians responsible for the raids made to the east of Unionville.

In that area, on that very day, Cunningham and Bryden's ranch was assaulted for a second time. Several dozen Indians surrounded the stone house and fired a volley of bullets through the open door. To prevent the straw thatch roof from being set afire, three of the five inhabitants charged the Indians and kept them at bay while the other two men tore off the roof. While this was being done, one man was hit with a rifle ball in his leg.

The white men all had guns, and the house was a virtual fort, but ammunition was in short supply. Seeing that help was required, Cunningham caught a horse and headed for Star City. He escaped without difficulty, but, when three miles from the house, he was fired upon by several Indians stationed there to prevent escape. Two balls hit his horse, but the animal could still run, and "for ten miles it was a race for life or death."[35]

The rancher arrived in Star City at 4 A.M. and, within a few hours, 30 men from there and Unionville—everyone who could find a horse—were on their way to the rescue. On arriving at the scene it was learned that the Indians had left, taking with them most of the cattle and horses. A few of the men went to see if other settlers in the area were safe, and the rest followed the trail of the stolen livestock until late that night.

Before dawn of May 5, John Bryden and fifteen men—all of the tracking party that still had good horses—started following the trail again, northeastwardly, and struck the Humboldt River about 15 miles below Stony Point. A short distance up river, the stolen cattle were seen on the opposite bank, surrounded by a band of arrogant and taunting Indians, on foot and horseback, who dared the ranchers to cross.

As Nevadans know, the Humboldt is ordinarily pretty easy to ford. After seeing it, Mark Twain wrote that one of the most pleasant and invigorating exercises one could contrive, was "to run and jump across the Humboldt river till he is overheated, and then drink it dry."[36]

But, this particular spring, the Humboldt was swollen and surrounded by sloughs, so it took some time for the whites to find a place to lead their horses across. Seeing that they were coming, the Indians rounded up as many cattle as possible and escaped with them. The ranchers eventually recovered about 90 head.

In the opinion of the tracking party, there was a large collection of natives in the vicinity of Gravelly Ford and Stony Point, whence raiding parties were being sent forth. This section of the California Trail was notorious for the many attacks on emigrants that had taken place there over the years.

While the ranchers were tracking their cattle and confronting the Indians, Captain Wells had been moving his men slowly up the Humboldt toward Gravelly Ford, traveling only at night. On the fourth day out, May 7, when about fifteen miles downstream of Stony Point, Indians were seen at a distance—perhaps the same bunch that had just escaped from John Bryden's party. Wells took 45 men to follow them up river, and ordered 1st Lieutenant John Littlefield, with 68 men, to circle through the head of Clover Valley and meet him in the vicinity of Stony Point.

As a civilian, "Big John" Littlefield—also known as "Little" Littlefield—had been a bartender in Marysville and Carson City, and had also driven stagecoaches across the Sierra Nevada. The former "Jehu" was a huge, amiable man, who tipped the scales at about 250 pounds.

After traveling most of the night, Littleton's command camped in the upper part of Clover Valley. Then, just before dawn, Indian campfires were seen burning about fifteen miles distant. Horses were saddled without delay; and the cavalry galloped their horses across sloughs and bottoms to get at what proved to be about 75 Shoshoni. In a quick skirmish, during which one soldier was wounded, the Indians were driven into a canyon, where they took shelter behind piled-up rocks on its rim.

Lt. Littlefield thought it would have required a siege to capture the Shoshoni in such a place, which the soldiers dubbed "Fort Redskin." Consequently, he sent his guide, Thomas C. Gregg, to Stony Point to get Wells. The captain and his men arrived at Fort Redskin that evening, but, by then the Indians had fled. So, being short of provisions, the entire command returned to Paradise Valley, arriving on 12 May.[37]

That day, a sergeant of Wells' command came down to Unionville, and, in recounting the story of the expedition around town, accused Lt. Littlefield of cowardice for allegedly ordering a retreat when the Indians had ridden out to fight. The troops had asked permission to fight—so this sergeant said—and had even fired a number of shots at the jeering natives, but Littlefield had put a stop to this, and the command retreated fifteen miles before halting and sending the guide, Gregg, to Capt Wells.

Gregg was quick to refute the sergeant's charges in a letter to the *Register*, but Forbes withheld publishing it, at Wells' request. It would be October, long after Littlefield had proven his courage, and Wells had failed to prove his, before Forbes published the letter. Gregg also said that Wells had done all he could to get a fight, and "if he ever gets in with them he will lose his last man or take the last scalp."[38] Like McDermit, Gregg would prove to be a poor judge of Wells' true character.

While Wells had been out, another Indian attack had taken place. A group of ten prospectors from Humboldt City, led by Joe Voshay, had gone toward the Black Rock country to work on some promising ledges. While at Dunshee's Spring, northwest of St. Mary's, on May 6, two of the party were jumped by Indians and wounded just at daylight, while looking for their horses.

In the ensuing fight, the whites got flat on their bellies and were able to use their Henry repeating rifles to great effect. Five Indians were killed and two others, who were wounded, mounted and rode off. The prospectors took scalps, and then returned to the Humboldt, where one of the wounded men, James Emory, was treated by Dr. C. W. Shaug to remove a ball that had traversed six inches through his bowels.

Joe Voshay reported that the new, highly accurate, lever-action .44/40 caliber Henry rifles "tore holes in the heads of their victims that you could put your fist in," and he recommended that every man in the region get one.[39]

Captain Wells left Camp McDermit once again on May 16, with seventy troopers, in search of the band of marauders previously encountered in Clover Valley. Lt. Littlefield and ten men had been sent out to scout in advance. A few days later, Wells' command laid over at "Fort Redskin" while a detachment was sent to find the route the natives had taken. A fresh trail having been discovered leading northwest, the squadron was underway again on May 20, traveling over rolling hills and across a number of small streams of clear and beautiful water.

At noon, the scouts reported having seen Shoshoni to the northeast and, by late afternoon, the command had pushed these Indians into an exceedingly narrow, rocky canyon. As it was not practicable to take horses any farther, Wells left the animals in the care of a few men, and ordered an advance up the canyon on foot.

Once through the deepest part of this gorge, it was seen that the Indians had retreated to the summit of a high table rock at the head of it. This flat-topped bluff was in the shape of a peninsula, with perpendicular sides, 3/4 of a mile long and 1/4 mile wide, a full 300 feet above all of the hills adjoining it. The troopers continued up toward the foot of the bluff but, by then, there was not an Indian to be seen.

A halt was called, and the command was split into three squads—the captain with most of the men remained in front of the bluff; Sgt. Sherman, with a squad was sent around to the left, and Corporal Dolan with another to the right.

Soon after setting out again, Dolan's men were subjected to a rain of rifle balls and arrows fired by natives concealed in the rocks. Because the Indians failed to compensate for firing downward, the bullets passed harmlessly over the soldiers' heads and they were able to take shelter behind rocks, whence they returned fire whenever a head or puff of rifle smoke could be seen.

Once the fight began, Wells ordered a ten-man guard to take the pack train and the men's horses into the protection of a nearby ravine. Lt. Littlefield and his advance scouts had now arrived on the scene, having just engaged in a running fight with some 200 mounted Indians.

About the time Littlefield joined up, Captain Wells' squad was fired upon for the first time from the hilltop. No one was hit, but the startled men took to the rocks, and Wells—said one of his men—"sought his mother earth, and embraced a huge boulder for protection." And, as soon as the firing ceased for a moment, and he deemed it safe, "the 'skipper' skedaddled, being in great haste to find a camping place, and leaving his men behind to their fate."

Before leaving, Wells reportedly told his men that they must hold certain points at all hazards, and that, at 2 o'clock on the following morning, "at the sound of the bugle, they must charge the hill, and not let an Indian escape; he said he expected to lose many of his men, but the Indians must be routed."[40]

Once abandoned by their leader, the men lost heart. Behind every crevice and pile of rocks there seemed to be an Indian firing a good quality rifle. The soldiers were completely surrounded and whenever any one of them showed part of his body, it drew fire from a multitude of guns. The men on the left took the worst of it. Isaac W. Godfrey of Company D was shot through the head while firing his piece, and two other privates were severely wounded.

As darkness descended, the troops decided to retreat in order to save themselves. During the confusion of this withdrawal another man, Private James Monroe, of Company D, was lost. Monroe—"a popular young man of good morals"—had been taking cartridges to the men fighting on the hill, and while on his way in the darkness he apparently failed to see his comrades retreating. Only after everyone had returned to camp, was he reported as missing.

With his men unwilling to fight, Captain Wells fed them and then ordered a general retreat, using darkness as an excuse. The body of Godfrey and the missing James Monroe were left to the Indians and—as one soldier said—"all hands, 'pell mell,' shook the dust from their feet, mounted, and got out of the way as soon as possible."[41] Littlefield brought up the rear with the pack train and, after traveling west about three miles, a halt was called.

Wells would later report that his command was completely surrounded during that long night, the enemy's campfires ablaze on every side. And, when morning came, Indians were seen in great numbers on top of the mountain where they had been the previous day. So, Wells said, he decided to make for the safety of Paradise Valley. Ten men were sent in advance to see if the route had been blocked, and, after burying most of the ammunition, the main body retired at a gallop. In the afternoon, the command overtook the advance party, and found them to be surrounded by about 100 warriors. But, when the Indians saw more soldiers coming up, they retreated.

The expedition reached Camp McDermit on May 25. On the twenty-sixth, Wells told Lt. Colonel McDermit by telegraph that he had fought 500 Indians who were strongly fortified, and "had failed to rout them."[42] Then, the gallant captain boarded the stagecoach for Fort Churchill to get reinforcements and a howitzer.

In his journal of the expedition Wells wrote that only a few volleys were exchanged during the fight, killing several Indians. The account he gave to several newspapers, however, was much more expansive. He purported to have killed 25 of the 500 Bannocks, Paiutes, and Shoshones he had faced, all of whom had been armed with repeating rifles, and were in a strongly fortified position, inaccessible from the place he was compelled by the nature of the ground to occupy.

The captain also claimed to have charged the Indian "works" repeatedly during a four-hour fight, only to be repulsed, and that privates Godfrey and Monroe had fallen within 30 feet of those works. To his credit, however, Wells repudiated the previous charge of cowardice against Lt. Littlefield, and described his lieutenant's conduct in the fight as cool, brave and daring.

Forbes of the *Register* said: "A few more retreats, and Indian hunting will conducted with white people in the lead—Indians pursuing...We pray [Wells' defeat] may not prove a calamity—to our people."[43] While Wells had been out, more muskets had arrived from Silver City for the defense of isolated camps. Forbes thought every man felt safer with one, "though he may not know how to load or fire it."[44]

During Wells' absence at Fort Churchill his soldiers in Paradise Valley began to desert at a rate of about two a day, most of them heading for the Boise and Owyhee mines. Because of the low pay and hard duty, desertion rates had always been high in the Nevada volunteer companies, but Wells' Company D would hold the record at war's end, reaching 37.5 percent, or 57 out of 152 men serving.

Three of Wells' men wrote complaining letters to the papers. One soldier said, "I will not make comment about our officers, but will say that the men did all that was asked of them." Another said Wells had led them right into the Indians' trap, and that none of the soldiers "ever expected to see the sun rise again."[45] And, there were several other grievances—the only transport for food was deserters' horses, and not enough of those to carry ten days worth; and the men had been ordered out looking for an Indian fight without a surgeon, or even a bandage.

The raids occurring to the east and south of Unionville had greatly alarmed the citizenry around Austin, Nevada. In response to their appeals for troops, Captain George A. Thurston, the commander of Fort Ruby, agreed to send a detachment of Nevada Infantry. Also, a volunteer company, the Lander Guard, had been organized, for which Governor Blasdel had promised to provide arms and ammunition.[46]

Seeking a solution to the problems, George Washington "Wash" Jacobs, the Indian agent for Reese River country, telegraphed McDermit asking for a few cattle to feed the natives. The colonel sent the request on to General Wright, remarking that if the agents "had taken an interest in the Indians...all present...troubles could have been avoided." Wright denied Jacobs' request, saying the Indian department, with its "liberal appropriations," could take care of the natives or transfer responsibility for them to the Army.[47]

Troops from Fort Ruby arrived in Austin on May 25 in the form of 1stLt. William G. Seamonds, with forty hand picked men of Company B, 1st Nevada Volunteer Infantry. The soldiers were armed with Springfield muskets and a six-pound howitzer, and had rations for 40 days carried on pack mules.

With the soldiers, as interpreter, was the Ruby Valley Indian agent, Henry Butterfield; also ten native scouts under Captain Frank, "Chief of all the Shoshones." After the newcomers paraded through town, the Indian scouts visited Jesse Beene's drug store and bought up all the vermilion with which to fix themselves up "pretty for the...purpose of taking Bannock scalps." Seamonds then marched his men to a point just north of Austin and camped, intending to leave shortly on an expedition toward Gravelly Ford.[48]

Those around Austin thought Seamonds's force was too small to face the several hundred Indians said to be near the ford. Capt. D. W. Welty telegraphed Gov. Blasdel asking that the Lander Guard be allowed to go along, saying they had 125 stand of arms, but needed a team and provisions, which would cost about $1,500. The *Reveille* was sure the state would gladly "reimburse the boys for their time," were it not for Blasdel—an "excessively economical and timid sort," Indeed, Blasdel wired back that the regulars should suffice and that the state couldn't afford such expense.[49]

But Blasdel was worried. He sent General McDowell a grim letter noting that Indians all over the state were restless and desperate. In the previous two months, hundreds of cattle and horses had been killed or stolen, and many whites had been murdered. Since all the state militia's arms had been distributed, and all troops were engaged, Blasdel asked McDowell to provide troops from California.

In response to this request, and to the Wells debacle, McDowell ordered Company B, 2nd California Volunteer Cavalry, under its interim commander, 1st Lt. Richard A. Osmer, to march from Camp Union, at Sacramento, to Fort Churchill. A few weeks earlier Capt. James C. Doughty's Company I, of the same regiment, had been sent to occupy the station at Smoke Creek. Now, the general ordered Doughty to take his men to Ft. Churchill, whence they could be sent up the Humboldt, if McDermit thought it necessary. That same day, May 27, General Wright ordered

McDermit to take the field personally and to go after the hostiles.

Meanwhile the depredations continued. Three men traveling from Unionville to Idaho were bushwhacked near Summit Springs, on the divide between Paradise Valley and Queen's River. One of the men, Henry Floder, was killed and was later buried by members of the Ryland Circus, en route to Ruby City. All stations north and south of Summit Springs had been destroyed, or were deserted.

About the same time, the little settlement at Puebla was abandoned after attackers killed a certain Mr. Brooks and severely wounded another man. A Boise-bound traveler was killed while helping retrieve Brooks' body. A few days later, two Surprise Valley ranchers were ambushed and killed for their animals and goods while returning from Susanville.[50]

Although McDermit had been ordered to take the field, Gov. Blasdel insisted that the colonel come with him to Austin, to investigate the troubles in that area. After this, he could take personal command of an expedition to the upper Humboldt.

McDermit dutifully made his arrangements to accommodate his honor, the governor. He wired Lt. Seamonds at Austin to wait there for him to arrive. On May 28, he sent a messenger to intercept Capt. Doughty and have him proceed with his company direct to the junction of the Humboldt and Little Humboldt rivers, and wait there for further orders. He also hired a pack train, which 1st Lt. W. H. Clark, was to load and bring out when it was ready.

On May 31, General McDowell ordered two companies of the Sixth Volunteer California Infantry, then at Benicia Barracks, to Fort Churchill. At the same time, Captain Starr's cavalry company of the 2nd was told to proceed to Surprise Valley and build a new post, Fort Bidwell.[51] These dispositions left just two cavalry companies at Camp *Union*, both unhorsed and without adequate arms.

Capt. Wallace, who had been recalled from Walker Lake, was sent on his way to Paradise Valley on May 30. He took with him 73 infantrymen and an old 12-pound howitzer obtained from Silver City, which the cocky editor of the *Virginia Union* thought would surely drive the Humboldt Indians from their fortress. They had "never yet smelt rotten shot," he said, and if they would just "maintain their 'posish'" until Wallace got there, they would "likely be slightly astonished."[52]

Just a few hours after Wallace's departure, McDermit and Blasdel left for Austin with a 13-man cavalry escort, comprising the balance of Captain Robert C. Payne's Company E. Only 21 soldiers remained behind at Fort Churchill and Camp Nye.

Upon arrival at Austin, on June 2, the governor sent forth word that the

Indians of the region should come "into the settlements and separate from the hostiles, be peaceable, and they would be protected."[53] On the evening of June 6, he held a grand pow-wow with some 266 Shoshoni men, women and children at Jacobsville, in the open valley at the rear of Jacobs' residence, not far from the big spring. Quite a number of Austin dignitaries and their ladies were there, and, acting as secretary was J. Ross Browne, the peripatetic author, U. S. Treasury agent and mining commissioner, who was on a tour of mining regions of the West.

With his audience sitting in a semi-circle, Blasdel—wearing a red sash as an insignia of office—spoke through interpreter Samuel H. Gilson, brother of John Gilson. Now that the Civil War was ending, the governor said, the "Great Father at Washington" would pay the Shoshoni more attention. Some provision would be made for them during the coming winter, but they must not rely upon the government for a living.

The "Great Father was grieved" about the bad Humboldts and Bannocks, with whom Blasdel warned the Shoshoni not to have any dealings. Though he preferred to treat his "red children" kindly, his soldiers—"numerous as the sage bushes"—would deal severely with all bad ones.

Reportedly, the natives liked the speech. A pipe was filled, and there was an amicable smoke all around the circle. Then, at the request of the ladies, came "some amusing trials of skill with the bow and arrow." The whites provided coins the Shoshoni could win if they hit them. The Indians all missed the mark, and when the whites tried their hand at it, they missed by even greater distances. One man shot so far from the mark that he alarmed the ladies, who were seated on a bench at a 45-degree angle from the target.

Then followed "races and scrambles and other amusing games, which afforded much satisfaction." The evening concluded with the Governor and his Austin friends partaking of a sumptuous collation at Jacobs' house.[54]

Forbes chided Blasdel for going so far from the scene of real troubles to have his "pretty" talk, and asked, sardonically, why he hadn't had "a (powder) smoke with the murdering sons of guns on the Upper Humboldt?"[55]

While in Austin, Colonel McDermit obtained more information concerning his enemies' whereabouts. On Sam Gilson's recommendation, Indian scouts had been sent out to gather information, and, a few days earlier one of them had brought a letter from a man at Cortez camp, saying that the natives from the Humboldt to Austin were friendly, and should not be molested, but that the hostiles were camped in large numbers about 80 miles northeast of Gravelly Ford. The raiders comprised a half-dozen allied bands of Paiutes, Bannocks, and the Shoshoni known as White Knives. They had a young, white female, and her infant, both probably captured from an emigrant train in earlier days. A man at Cortez had seen her but had not been able to talk to her.[56]

McDermit took a handful of cavalrymen and left his civilian master in Austin on the morning of June 4, headed out to join his other troops and prosecute a campaign. On reaching Lt. Seamonds' camp north of town, he sent half of the 40 infantrymen back to Fort Ruby. Seamonds and the other twenty would join his expedition, along with interpreter Butterfield, Captain Frank, eight of the Shoshoni scouts and the howitzer from Fort Ruby. The designated infantrymen were all mounted, many having just bought horses, at their own expense, at Austin.

McDermit, with Seamonds' men, rode northward, past a number of burned-out and abandoned ranches, to a point on the Humboldt near present day Golconda, and then proceeded down river to the French Bridge, where camp was made on June 8. Nearby, on the south side of Winnemucca Mountain, a new mining district was beginning to boom.

At the bridge, the column was further augmented by Captain Wallace's company, which had arrived a few days earlier from Fort Churchill. McDermit wrote Gen. Wright that evening, saying he planned to move upon the hostiles reported to be north of Gravelly Ford. And, if he could catch them he would "give them a whipping" they would remember.[57]

Lt. Charles C. Warner had come along on the expedition as a supernumerary. A vain and smarmy man, he had failed to fill the roster of his infantry company before recruiting had been stopped in April. While at the bridge, Warner dashed off a letter to the *Virginia Union*, stating that "his command" had traveled 330 miles in just eight days, through a region that had been "laid waste," by Indians from the north, and that, after Doughty's cavalry company joined up in a few days, a "bloody fight" would ensue.

Warner said all of the Reese River difficulties had been caused by a rancher who sent an Indian to find a missing pony and promised him ten dollars if he brought it in. The Indian had found the horse but, instead of a reward, he received a sound beating with a club, for some slight provocation. This had caused the starving Indians to drive off about a dozen of the rancher's cattle.[58]

The *Reese River Reveille* berated the "quill-driving" Warner for his "ridiculous stories of terribly wronged Indians and white man's treachery." Even if a beating had occurred, the editor said, it could not have caused any depredations, as the natives employed in the region were peaceable, and had no dealings with the hostiles.[59]

On June 10, McDermit sent a message to Fort Churchill asking for another company of cavalry and one of infantry. He then took his command

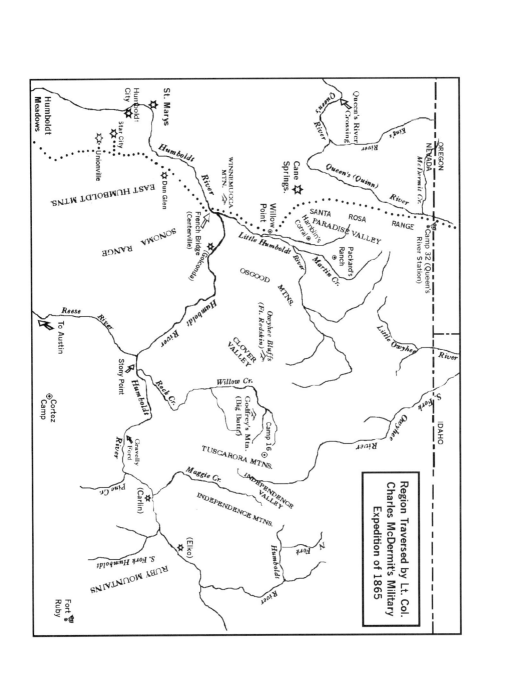

across French Bridge, marched eight miles up the Little Humboldt, and crossed it with the aid of a boat procured at Dun Glen. The following day, Captain Wells and his 124 cavalrymen arrived from Camp McDermit, giving the colonel a grand total of 240 troops.

The column moved fourteen miles eastward on June 12, and encamped on the Humboldt near some hot springs. Intending to examine the places where Littlefield and Wells had encountered the Indians, McDermit left on June 13 with 50 cavalry, Captain Wells and other officers, interpreter Butterfield, and four native scouts. The balance of the command was left behind to build a supply road over the Osgood mountains, through what would come to be known as Soldier's Pass.

The colonel's group traveled some 39 miles northeastward through level sagebrush country and arrived June 14 in "Wells' (Clover) Valley" opposite "Fort Redskin (Owyhee Bluffs)," where Littlefield had had his May 7 scrap. Here Camp 14 was made near "Soldiers' Spring" (probably today's Sawtooth Springs). A visit to the deep canyon and ledge where the Indians had been posted convinced the officers that Littlefield had been wise not to send his 35 men against the large number of natives posted there in "ingeniously constructed" rifle pits.

On the fifteenth, McDermit's group traveled northeast again about 26 miles to encamp at the foot of the table mountain where Wells had been defeated on May 20. An ambulance was sent out to locate and retrieve the remains of Godfrey and Monroe. The former was found where he had fallen in the rocks, shot through the head. Monroe's body was discovered only 200 yards from where the troops had eaten their supper after the fight. He had been wounded and then captured by the Indians, who built a fire on his stomach—probably before his death, as his tongue was nearly bitten off. His chest and bowels were burned to a crisp, his scalp taken off, skull smashed in and nose cut off.

After seeing the brutalized corpses that had been abandoned by Captain Wells, a cynical correspondent of the Virginia City *Territorial Enterprise* dubbed the creek that runs around the foot of the mountain, "Wells' Run" (today's Willow Creek).

Seamonds and others went up onto the table mountain, which they named after Godfrey, but which is now called Big Butte. They saw where the Indians had built walls of stone, behind which they could lay and shoot downward.[60]

McDermit's native scouts found that the hostiles had retired to the northeast leaving a plain trail toward a large valley at the headwaters of the Owyhee, 25 miles distant. On June 18, McDermit followed in this direction,

Godfrey's Mountain (Big Butte)
(Author's Collection)

and made Camp 16 along what he called Otter Creek. This was at the farthest point toward the Owyhee River that could be reached with wagons, and at the western base of what are now called the Tuscarora Mountains.

Here the remains of Godfrey and Monroe were placed on a scaffold to undergo a drying process, preparatory to their removal to Fort Churchill for burial.[61]

While Lt. Col. McDermit was making his leisurely tour to the northeast of Unionville, Major Michael O'Brien had been marching from Fort Churchill up the Humboldt with the additional forces McDermit had requested—Company B, 2nd California Cavalry under Lt. Richard Osmer, and Company D of the 6th California Infantry under Captain John T. Hill. Another infantry unit, Captain Hahn's Company I, was being posted at Dun Glen, and Captain W. L. Knight and his company of California cavalry had been ordered to establish the depot at Smoke Creek, from which task Captain Doughty had been diverted.

In the Owyhee mining region, Oregon volunteer cavalry had created Camp Lyon on upper Cow Creek, 30 miles southwest of Ruby City. The new camp was meant to guard the Idaho end of the two roads coming to Owyhee Cone from Chico-Red Bluff, and the other from Unionville, Nevada. Other Oregon cavalry units were patrolling the trails of southeastern Oregon and southern Idaho.

But, despite so much military activity, Hill Beachy's Humboldt Express, running between Unionville and Boise, had been discontinued because most of its livestock had been stolen and its messengers imperiled. Beachy had abandoned all of his stations, and most of the settlers had left the surrounding country.

The cross-country route from Chico had seen increasing use by freight and passenger saddle trains, the latter making the trip in as little as 13 days. Working parties under E. D. Pierce had gone out to improve the road and establish stage stations along a more direct route, which bypassed Surprise Valley, and instead went via Smoke Creek, Granite Creek and Puebla.

Captain John Mullan, a former army officer and noted road builder, had just purchased an interest in the Chico saddle train, and he, Pierce and Francis were working to start a stage line in its stead. Mullan had traveled with a train to Boise, to make arrangements for the eastern end of the stage line. On the twentieth, when near Puebla, his train had found the survivors of the Burson party of seven men, which had just been attacked by Indians.

Burson and another man had been killed, and three others wounded. One of the dead had been burned at a stake, and the Indians had cut the head from the other body, driven a stake through its mouth, cut off the legs and arms and cut the torso to shreds, including the testicles. All of the severed parts had been hung on nearby sagebrush.[62]

Colonel McDermit dawdled two weeks at Camp 16. Captain Doughty and his cavalry company had arrived on June 23, but, the pack train for carrying the command's baggage into the mountains hadn't come up. And so, there the troops sat in the wilderness, occupying their time with a required inspection of the cavalry, a muster and a payday.

From this camp, a disgruntled soldier wrote a letter to a friend, which a newspaper published under the pseudonym "Recruit." The man complained that McDermit knew the Indians' location—at "Owyhee Lake," 60 miles distant—but was doing nothing get at them. The expedition, he said, was nothing but a "get-up" to keep the officers in the service. There was no danger of a fight, since the Indians were given every chance to keep clear. "If I had fifty dollars in my pocket," groused Recruit, "I would not be here."[63]

Finally, on June 28, the pack outfit arrived and McDermit prepared to restart his expedition. He moved his supply base back to Fort Redskin, and set up stations from there to Dun Glen for the protection of trains. A message was sent ordering Major O'Brien to join up, bringing Hahn's infantry company, and take charge of the new post to be established, the site of which McDermit would select on the coming march. Orders were sent to Osmer to use his cavalry to scour the country between Unionville and Reese River and to "punish the predatory bands"[64] which had tormented settlers in that region. Capt. Hill was ordered to march his infantry company from Dun Glen to the Queen's River region to protect settlers and travelers there.

McDermit himself would lead a two-pronged advance toward Gravelly Ford—Captain Doughty was told to take a mounted force directly there and search the region; McDermit would lead the main body across the Tuscarora range, and then meet Doughty at the ford.

The colonel moved on July 2 with the 20-mule pack train, a disassembled 12-pound mountain howitzer, a force of 100 cavalry under Wells and Littlefield, and 50 infantrymen under Wallace. Also with him were Lt. Warner, a surgeon and Indian agent Henry Butterfield with three Ruby Valley native guides.

Doughty left the following day with his company, Lt. Seamonds' twenty mounted infantry, Surgeon Z. N. Spaulding of Susanville, six native guides and the other 12-pound howitzer.

As related by McDermit, his force, guided by Hank Butterfield's scouts, followed the trail of the hostile Indians, passing over the Tuscaroras. On July 3 they arrived in a beautiful valley at the eastern foot of these mountains. On July 4, in honor of the day, they called the place Independence Valley, which name it still bears.[65]

It was seen that the hostiles had separated into two parties—the larger one traveling to the northwest down the south fork of the Owyhee River, and the other heading east for the Humboldt. Having previously ordered his supplies sent up the Humboldt—so McDermit reported—he followed the Indians traveling in that direction, and arrived on the river, thirty miles above Gravelly Ford (between present-day Carlin and Elko), on July 8. He found Captain Doughty and Lt. Seamonds waiting there with the news that an Indian trail had been found, leading downstream.

Upon following this trail, an Indian camp was discovered, whose occupants were seen to be hurriedly crossing to the south side of the river. According to McDermit, his Indian scouts convinced about 25 of them—mostly old men, women and children—to come into his camp. But the chief and some 20 other men escaped, leaving behind their guns, provisions, rabbit nets, and other possessions. The colonel ordered Lt. Seamonds and his mounted infantry, and Lt. Littlefield with 25 cavalry, in pursuit.

But McDermit, in his report, may have omitted some embarrassing details of his march from Camp 16. If Lieutenant Warner is to be believed, on July 6 McDermit had divided his force, sending Wallace's infantry directly to Gravelly Ford, while he and the mounted troops made an excursion northward. Warner said that, while crossing some mountains, the pack train lagged in the rear, allowing a band of Shoshoni to capture the whole kit and caboodle, leaving the command destitute of provisions. Some 48 hours later, the advance scout discovered 150 Indians at the Gravelly Ford hot springs, with the stolen baggage and mules in their possession. The soldiers made a charge and recaptured the stores and animals, and took 40 prisoners. The balance, including a chief named Zelauwick, beat a hasty retreat, pursued by squads under Seamonds and Littlefield.

Several years later, Lt. Seamonds would say that the Indians had been overhauled as they were fording the Humboldt, at the place where the South Fork empties into it—not at Gravelly Ford—and in the ensuing fight, three Indians were killed and 24 captured, who were turned over to McDermit at his temporary headquarters on Maggie Creek.

From a letter Seamonds wrote at the time of the incident, we learn that he and Littlefield ended their chase after the escapees on July 12 at Fort Ruby. They had killed one Indian 30 miles south of Gravelly Ford, and captured two more, identified by friendly Shoshoni as having been at Godfrey's Mountain. They also brought in a Shoshoni woman who said she had been forced to carry the wood used to burn Private Monroe's body.

Littlefield left Fort Ruby on July 14 for Gravelly Ford with the two male prisoners, but apparently McDermit had released Seamonds and his company, and they remained at the fort. Seamonds claimed that he and the Shoshoni chief, Captain Frank, subsequently went to a friendly Indian camp where they found and killed one of Littlefield's prisoners, who had escaped, and another man said to have been at Godfrey's Mountain.

Regardless of whose story of the march from Camp 16 to the Humboldt is correct, McDermit wound up with a handful of prisoners. He reported having made a compact, on July 12, with those who were known not to have participated in any hostilities. The natives entering into the agreement were released, after promising friendship, and delivering up four men whom Butterfield's Shoshoni scouts alleged had taken part in the fights at Fort Redskin and Godfrey Mountain, and who also had been with the band stealing cattle in Humboldt County. McDermit decided to send the four prisoners to Fort Churchill where they were to be delivered to civil authorities for trial.[66]

While McDermit had been making his ineffectual march, Lt. Richard Osmer and his cavalry had done no better in searching the country, as ordered, between Humboldt and Reese rivers. They had arrived at Dun Glen on the same day Hill's infantry company reached that place, June 27, and then had gone to Fairbanks' "milk ranch," located near the French Bridge. Fairbanks led the troopers on a futile trek to a deserted Indian camp in the Sonoma Range, in search of supposed hostiles. Subsequent expeditions had likewise produced no results.[67]

By this time, John Mullan had concluded his arrangements in Idaho for the eastern end of the stage line. To see him safely back to California, Lt. Col. John M. Drake, the commanding officer of Fort Boise, gave him a cavalry escort. When Mullan reached Camp Lyon to join these troops, he learned that Lt. Charles Hobart and his Company B of Oregon cavalry, operating out of Camp Lyon in search of stolen horses, had recently been involved in a fight with some 150 Shoshoni, who had brazenly attacked their camp on the Malheur River. Two soldiers had been wounded.

Mullan, and others, wrote letters complaining about the Indian situation to the Boise *Statesman*, and to the acting governor of Idaho. These letters mentioned Wells' defeat, the murderous attacks near Puebla, the huge loss of livestock, and the destruction of Hill Beachy's stage stations. Mullan, who believed the Indians were being driven northward from the Humboldt and southward from the Canyon City, Oregon region, asked that a military post be established at Puebla.

Captain Mullan was not aware of another brutal attack that had taken place, on July 3, about 12 miles north of the abandoned Queen's River Station. A party of eighteen men had been traveling to Boise, most of them riding in three wagons. About a mile and a half in the van were three on horseback—P. W. Jackson of Virginia City, Thomas Rule of Paradise Valley, and Thomas Ewing of Unionville. At high noon, as the travelers crossed a sagebrush-covered ridge, about thirty Indians suddenly came riding out of a nearby ravine and began firing on the men in the lead. One of the first balls hit Ewing near his backbone, and Rule received slugs in a lung, both thighs and his left arm. Almost instantly another volley was fired, dropping Jackson and his horse—the rider dead without a groan.

Though wounded, Ewing and Rule wheeled their horses and started back for the wagons, with a handful of screeching natives hot on their heels. Rule was faint from his injuries, and scarcely able to sit his horse. Bullets whistling around him, Ewing stopped to steady his flagging comrade and encourage him to keep up. Looking back, he saw some Indians firing into Jackson's body.

The two men managed to reach the wagons of the main party ahead of their pursuers. They were helped down and placed on some blankets, while the wagons were unhitched and preparations made for a fight. But, to their dismay, the whites realized that only five of their number had brought rifles. The others were armed only with Colt revolvers, which were fairly useless with the attackers firing from a long distance. Thomas J. Butler had a good Springfield gun, and used it well, but the enemy was hidden in the sage and only raising up long enough to fire. Ewing was unable to use his Henry rifle because, on account of loss of blood, he couldn't see the forward sight.

In the late afternoon, another 150 natives appeared, riding fine horses and wearing war paint. With this development, the beleaguered travelers decided that they must abandon Jackson's body and hightail it for safety. Under continual fire, the teams were hitched up and the whites fought their way through the circle of Indians back toward Queen's River Station.

While crossing a ravine, the attack intensified for a few minutes, and another man was shot through the breast by an iron bolt, 3/4 inches long. This rude missile cut through the upper portion of the right lung, and lodged in his back.

But the whites pushed on, their pursuers staying out of gun range. Finally, two hours later, at dark, the natives abandoned the chase. The survivors arrived at Queen's River Station about one A.M. on July 4. They rested there until nine, when, fearing that the wounded would die, they moved on without stopping, except for an hour to allow the teams to graze enough to survive the trip. At Buffalo Creek, Thomas Butler and another man went ahead to the military camp at Willow Point in Paradise Valley, which they reached at 2 P.M. on July 5. Not a soldier could be found.

A messenger was hired to carry a request for a doctor to A. P. K. Safford at Unionville. The balance of the party, with the wounded, reached Willow Point at 7 P.M., completely worn out, the wagons, and all their contents, saturated with blood.[68]

When the courier reached Safford at dawn, a doctor left immediately for Willow Point in a wagon carrying refreshments, mattresses and blankets. After resting a day or two, Butler went to Unionville in search of arms, or a military escort to go back with his party so they could bury Jackson's body.

Forbes of the *Humboldt Register* had harsh words for McDermit because of his inability to provide security against the Indians. "If he didn't clear the road soon," Forbes said, "we must conclude he is incompetent."[69] In his next edition, Forbes aptly summarized the sorry state of things:

> A lion is in the path of...enterprise which ought to be now building up

settlements on the Upper Humboldt, and in the Queen's River and Owyhee valleys...The Indians are there, fat on American beef, swaggering in their blankets, and bestriding the horses of murdered American citizens, and sporting as fine muskets and rifles as the best of us. The Indian is in his element—his glory—it his Summer, and the harvest is golden.[70]

Colonel McDermit and his expedition arrived back at French Bridge about July 17, and he marched the next day northward on the Idaho road, taking 128 of Doughty's cavalrymen, and fifty Nevada troopers under Capt. R. C. Payne of Company E.

Captain Wallace and his infantry were sent home to Fort Churchill, taking with them the four recently captured Shoshoni men. Lieutenant Osmer's Company B was dispatched to patrol the Gravelly Ford region, and Captain Wells was given command of small detachments to man the temporary camps at Paradise Valley and Dun Glen, guarding livestock and other government property.

The correspondent of the *Virginia Union* didn't know why Wells was left behind, but thought, perhaps, "it was the Godfrey Mountain affair," where it was "now generally conceded, Wells was well whipped, though his men fought bravely enough." Since that affair, however, the soldiers had been "slightly averse" to going into a fight with an officer who preferred "sipping his coffee at his ease to leading his men in a charge."[71]

Upon reaching the Little Humboldt River, McDermit learned of the July 3 attack on the Jackson party. Upon getting that news, he sent an express to the survivors at Queen's River Station asking them to wait for him, and then he pushed on that day. He overtook Hill's Company D, California Sixth Infantry, who had preceded him from Paradise Valley, and marched with them to Queen's River Station, arriving July 23. He found the survivors waiting for him and, together, they went to the scene of the attack, a dozen miles farther on, near what is now called Jackson Creek.

Jackson's body was found in the middle of the road, his breast cut open and the heart taken out. The right knee had been un-jointed and put into the cavity in the breast, so that the foot stood up in his face. All the skin was taken from his head, all the sinews from his legs and arms, and a "stick sharpened at both ends was run through the gristle of his nose, and he was otherwise mangled so horribly that it [was] not proper to describe..."[72]

McDermit was convinced that the natives responsible for this horrible atrocity were the same who had gone north after defeating Captain Wells, and whom he had been following for so many miles.

From the scene of the murder, the colonel sent Lt. Charles Tagge with some of Doughty's cavalry to escort the survivors, and other civilians, through to the Owyhee mines. Then, he and the rest of his soldiers returned to Queen's River Station to make the 32nd camp of his expedition.

The attack on the Jackson party, coming in the wake of so many other depredations, led the people of Unionville to seek retribution. When Wallace's infantry passed through town on July 21, on its way to Fort Churchill, the captain was asked to surrender his four prisoners to them. Wallace refused, so A. P. K. Safford and McKaskia S. Bonnifield—"fearing harsh treatment of the red men if left with the soldiers"[73]—procured a warrant from Judge E. F. Dunne, of the 6th Judicial District, which deputized Bonnifield to arrest the Indians and bring them before the court.

Bonnifield and Safford overtook the soldiers that evening at Buffalo Springs Station, 15 miles beyond Unionville. Bonnifield's blackly-humorous report of his actions tells us what happened next:

> Humboldt county, state of Nevada, ss.—I hereby certify, that I executed the warrant of arrest on 22d July, A.D. 1865, by taking into custody the within named: John Doe, Richard Roe, Richard Doe, and John Roe—being four Shoshone warriors, found in the custody of Capt. William Wallace, of the U.S. Army, Buffalo Station, in said county.
>
> A.P.K. Safford, Esq....and myself succeeded in bringing said defendants about three miles and a-half on the road, when, after repeated attempts to escape, said defendants made a preconcerted effort to release themselves from the civil authorities. It became necessary to disable them. A fire with Henry rifles was ordered for that purpose—but our guns ranged high, and instead of breaking a leg to retard their flight, the several balls...took effect in their several bodies and heads, and proved almost instantly fatal. Having no means of conveyance, we were compelled to leave their bodies in the several places in which they fell. M.S. Bonnifield, Special Constable.

Said Forbes: For a first act in office, "it strikes us the performance on this warrant was thorough...Bonnifield and Safford can not be charged with 'nursing' their first case, with the purpose of making a large bill against the county." The editor of the *Reese River Reveille* thought McDermit should have killed the prisoners himself, and criticized him for merely driving the bands out of the state, instead of fighting them.[74]

From Camp 32 at Queen's River Station, on July 27, McDermit ordered a cavalry escort to go through to the Owyhee mines with six freight teams and a drove of cattle from Chico. Then he, Capt. Payne and ten men followed the trail of a party of mounted Indians leading toward Steen's Mountain in Oregon. A detachment under Sgt. Van Nostrand was sent to scout in another direction. In the next few days, the troops had two skirmishes with small bands of natives. Seventeen Indians were reported to have been killed, at the cost of one cavalryman wounded. By August 1, both expeditions were back at Camp 32.

Upon return, D. McGowan, a soldier who had been with McDermit since leaving Fort Churchill, wrote to a friend about the most recent excursion. They had fought some fine-looking Bannock Indians in a canyon of the Owyhee River, whose sides were 500 feet high. In the canyon's center, at various points, arose "Spiral Mountains of towering rock which might resemble the mausoleum of dead heroes." "They say the road to Jordan is hard to travel," said McGowan, "and I believe it my boy." He praised his officers—Doughty and Payne—for their bravery, but he spoke most proudly of McDermit, who was "himself a host,"[75] and would assure their success.

That day Lt. Littlefield arrived with 20 more cavalrymen and the news of a victory over an Indian band in Paradise Valley. On the afternoon of July 26, some 30 braves had come down out of the mountains to a place, about fifteen miles above Willow Point, where six men of cavalry company I, under Sgt. James F. Stevens, were tending stock. The Indians were naked and painted for a fight, armed with bows and guns. Expecting trouble, Stevens sent a soldier to inform Sgt. Thomas, who was camped with nine men of Company D about four miles down the Little Humboldt.

The Indians raised a white flag, and asked for a parley, whereupon Stevens bantered with them across the creek, doing everything in his power to retain them, while keeping an eye out for Thomas. At length, Thomas and his men, who had crossed the river, were seen riding hurriedly for a point at which they could cut off the natives from retreating to the mountains. A reporter of the event wrote:

> What a thrill ran through that little band, at the sight of the comers!...the thought was with them of their friends butchered; the women and children pitilessly brained and inhumanly mutilated; the dwelling places of the...pioneers laid in ashes...and now, here was vengeance within gun-shot!
>
> They gave one shout, and turned loose their guns on the miscreant dogs! Thomas charged, bidding every man to go in for all there was in him!...The Indians tried to gain the mountain. Thomas arrested them at every turn. They fought bravely, desperately but 'Blood will tell!' They...divided into squads, of five and six to scatter the hunt. The boys singly engaged these squads, often fighting them hand-to-hand with their sabers. The Indians would fight

this way till one of a squad fell—then the others would scamper for the swamps. Mounted men could not pursue them into the swamps. Some dismounted and followed on foot; others brought down their game with long-range rifles.

No prisoners were taken. Five natives were driven into two unoccupied houses, whose roofs were set afire, and the fugitives killed as they emerged. Not until the last Indian disappeared into the Santa Rosa Mountains after sunset, did "the boys" examine their afternoon's work, finding some nineteen warriors lying dead in the brush.

In all, 20 whites had been involved in Sgt. Thomas' victory, including several civilians of Paradise Valley. Private Herford of Company I was killed by an arrow through the heart, Private Joshua C. Murphy and Sgt Thomas J. Riehl were both wounded, and Joseph Warfield, a civilian, was killed.

Forbes jubilated over the soldiers' work, while, at the same time criticizing McDermit and the other officers who "should act upon the example of the valiant Thomas and his brave men."[76]

The news of the fight increased McDermit's disappointment at having had no opportunity to personally lead his troops in such a glorious defeat of the enemy. He groused in a letter to Gov. Blasdel of the natives' refusal to meet him in battle. Since leaving Fort Churchill, he said, he had traveled 1,200 miles, following the same bands into Idaho and Utah Territories, then back into Nevada and finally now into Idaho's Owyhee region. But, he intended remaining in the field until he succeeded in fully punishing the marauders. As soon as he rested his horses and had some shoeing done, he would follow them to Oregon's Snowy (Steen's) Mountain.

McDermit also wrote to Hill Beachy that military posts were being established on the most dangerous part of the road, one of them at his present location, Queen's River Station. Based on this, Beachy thought he might soon have stages running again on the route to Humboldt. But, to make sure, he left Boise on August 7 to have a personal look at the road, and to talk to McDermit.[77]

Although Col. McDermit would never learn of it, another of his subordinates, Lt. William Seamonds, had also just gained a victory. Shortly after returning to Fort Ruby, Seamonds had sent out two Indian scouts who learned that Zelauwick—the chieftain who was supposed to have fought Wells at Godfrey's Mountain, and who later had escaped across the Humboldt—was camped in the mountains 50 miles north of the Humboldt Wells.

Accordingly, the lieutenant left Ruby on July 25 with fifteen mounted infantry, Henry Butterfield and the Shoshoni chief named Captain Frank. At dawn on July 31, Zelauwick and some thirty of his band were surprised and overwhelmed at a place the soldiers called Cottonwood Canyon. According to report, the troops circled around the chieftain, wounded but refusing to die, firing their carbines until he collapsed, riddled with bullets. Butterfield then finished him off and took the scalp as a trophy. It was claimed that twelve other natives were also killed in the struggle, with only one white soldier wounded. The Shoshoni scout, Frank, was praised for his great bravery and skill, and for having saved Seamonds' life at the risk of his own. As proof of Zelauwick's guilt, the soldiers said they found, in his lodge, a portion of the saber taken from the body of private Godfrey.[78]

In retrospect, Charles McDermit—feckless commander that he was—should have settled for the small victories won by his men, and ended his expedition, as one senses he wanted to do. Instead he made the fateful decision to do a bit more scouting.

On August 2, two small parties set out westward from Camp 32. One consisted of Capt John T. Hill and part of his infantry company. The other was led by McDermit, and comprised twelve cavalrymen, Captain Payne, 2nd Lt. William G. Overend of Osmer's company, and a Mexican mule-skinner with a few pack mules carrying supplies. Most of the information we have about McDermit's trek comes from the telling of it by Lt. Overend.

On the first day's march, the colonel's party found abundant Indian signs—fresh tracks, bundles of grass stacked and ready to harvest for its seeds, and dams and weirs in the streams for trapping fish. The colonel taught Overend how to discern Indian trails, and advised him as to tactics for attacking the foe. Camped that night, without a fire, McDermit mentioned that he had written to tell his wife that she must have one of her fattest turkeys in readiness for dinner about the end of August. His conversation was cheerful and animated, and he expressed his certainty of capturing some Indians on this trip.

On August 3, the party continued westward, discovering more Indian signs and abandoned camps. At lunchtime, McDermit and Overend rested in the shade of a cottonwood tree and the colonel spoke frankly to the lieutenant. He said he was "sorry to say that he had officers under his command he could not trust," especially two who had failed to capture an old Indian chief who had been within pistol shot of them. One of the officers, he said, boasted of the qualities he had attained by having been in the regular army for nine years. The identity of these two troublesome officers is uncertain, but Seamonds and Wells are likely suspects.

Charles McDermit and family, ca. 1863
(Nevada Historical Society)

After lunch, three enlisted men, who had been sent to scout in a different direction, returned with an Indian scalp, the "trophy that is taken as a usual thing..." and Overend said that he and McDermit were "were well pleased to be in possession of it."

The march was continued on foot along a trail which led over a mountain some seven hundred feet high. During a rest stop on the climb, Overend sat down and began to sing "Who Will Care For Mother Now?" McDermit said it was a beautiful song, that he would like to learn. The lieutenant then said that they had ascended so high that he felt the next place they would march, if they followed this trail, would be the firmament. And then, he continued singing:

> Soon with angels I'll be marching
> With bright laurels on my brow
> I have for my country fallen,
> Who will care for Mother now?

McDermit remarked that, sooner or later, they both would, "with the help of Almighty God, wear those bright laurels that never fade in a world of immortality," and that it would be infinite pleasure "to join with a band of angels in heaven, where wealth or rank would not divide us, in Unity of worship to the Giver of Life who had put us here on earth to love one another and to do justice to all men."

The colonel missed his family. Eighteen months earlier he and Hanna had buried their youngest child, a babe of three months, but since then another child, Elizabeth Maude, had been born. He told Overend that, despite being deprived of the society of those they loved, God had been good to them so far on the expedition. Even in this remote area He had supplied them with little luxuries such as wild currants and trout.[79]

But McDermit knew that his long trek had proven fruitless, save for the handful of natives killed here and there. He revealed to Overend that he had decided to return to Fort Churchill, leaving his captains to establish the required posts. He thought the hostile bands had gone farther into Idaho and Oregon than it could be expected the Nevada troops should follow them. What went unsaid, perhaps, was his grim realization that he had been found wanting as a leader in fighting Indians.

On the way back to Camp 32, the party took a nearly direct course. On August 7, they ascended a mountain, and came to the head of a deep, dark, rocky canyon. McDermit ordered six men to keep on the ridge until they arrived at the valley beyond, then to proceed to the mouth of the canyon and await his command. He, with the rest of the men, started down the canyon, through which flows what is today called McDermit Creek.

Lt. Overend was with the group on the ridge, and, at about noon, upon reaching a rocky point near the mouth of the canyon, they saw some Indians hiding behind rocks. The soldiers opened fire, but without effect, and the Indians retreated into some willows, keeping up a constant fire. In this skirmish, two cavalrymen received minor wounds. Overend, believing that the Indians were in large force in the willows, and that they were trying to draw him into ambush, continued on down the ridge.

Shortly after noon, Captain Payne was slightly ahead of McDermit and the others, coming down through the rough, steep part of the canyon, on foot and leading their horses. From above, on the hillside, an Indian hiding in the rocks let Payne pass, then fired and hit McDermit in the breast, the ball passing clear through his body and coming out near the right thigh. None of the colonel's comrades ever saw the man who fired the shot.

The shooting took place within two miles of Camp 32. When news of it reached there, about 4 P.M., Major O'Brien, in command at the camp, rushed with a detachment of cavalry to the scene. Upon arrival at the mouth of the canyon they learned that the colonel had expired a few moments before, under the shade of a few willows raised over him.

A messenger with news of the 45-year old leader's death reached the Humboldt on the morning of August 9, where it was forwarded by telegraph to the outside world. Hill Beachy got the sad tidings on August 11, and he continued on to San Francisco to talk to General McDowell about getting more protection.

Despite his failures as a leader in the field, McDermit was widely praised as a candid, straightforward, kind-hearted gentleman and soldier, whose men were devoted to him. Word of his death "caused tears to well from many a manly eye."[80]

But there was a general feeling that he had been too kind to Indians. Rather than kill them, he took them prisoner, and some were fed at camp as long as they chose to remain. Because of this kindness and familiarity, it was believed that the Indians guilty of killing him had known who he was. If not, the trappings on his horse would have called particular attention to him.

The colonel's corpse arrived at Dun Glen on August 10 in the custody of Captain Payne. Based on letter written by Captain Wells, the body was initially expected in Virginia City by August 16. The militia companies there made elaborate plans for an escort procession through Silver City and Gold Hill to Virginia City, where, at Armory Hall, a *catafalque* had been erected on which the remains would lie in state.

But, by August 17, the body had not yet arrived. Hannah McDermit—who was planning to bury her husband in Scott Valley, California, where they had lived for so many years—was reported to be "crazed with grief." Little wonder, if she knew the circumstances, said Forbes at Unionville. Her husband had been shot on the seventh, and, as of noon of the fifteenth, his remains lay "in the brush in Spring Canyon—emitting a stench that assails at a quarter-of-a-mile distant." With such "red tape and military circumlocution," Forbes asked, "Is it any wonder that...Indian depredators escape punishment?"[81]

Finally, on August 19, Captain Wells and his company arrived at Fort Churchill bringing in the decomposing fruit of the Indian expedition—the corpses of McDermit, Godfrey and Monroe. A decision was made to quickly bury all of them at the fort. The Virginia City militiamen were by now in high dudgeon, blaming Major O'Brien, who had assumed command of forces in the field, for the delay in getting the colonel's corpse to the settlements, where his friends might have prepared it properly for burial.

Lt. Col. Ambrose E. Hooker, of the 6th California Infantry, had arrived with his staff a few days earlier and taken command of the Nevada district. He obtained a metallic coffin, and Charles McDermit was buried with military honors on, August 20. Godfrey and Monroe were interred in separate rites about an hour later.[82]

After McDermit's burial, Hooker wrote a windy letter to General McDowell, claiming that the entire country surrounding Queen's River Station had been thoroughly searched for Indians, without result. Officers and men, alike, were eager to avenge the death of the late much-beloved McDermit. Hooker also spoke of the grief expressed by some of the principal Paiute headmen—Captains Charlie, Big George and Ben—upon hearing of the killing. The three had volunteered to lead 200 warriors against the hostiles to avenge it.

By late August, the companies of captains Doughty and Hill were at Camp 32 building a permanent post, which was named Camp McDermit. Payne's Company E was at Paradise Valley manning "Camp Black." Osmer had returned from Gravelly Ford to take station at Dun Glen, where soldiers were making adobes to improve that camp. Three companies from Camp Lyon were scattered along the new Chico road from Smoke Creek to Ruby City and escorts were being provided, as needed, for travelers.[83]

Certain soldiers returning to Washoe after the campaign proudly displayed the Indian scalps they had taken. While at Moore and Parker's Theater Saloon in Carson City, a private of Wells' company flaunted one he had "amputated"[84] from a Shoshoni. Henry Butterfield distributed segments of Zelauwick's scalp—reported to be nearly as thick as sole leather—to his friends.

General McDowell, the Pacific Commander, had, of course forbidden barbarities such as scalping, and the indiscriminate killing of women and children. But, of the several Nevada and California soldiers who committed uncivilized acts, only Captain John T. Hill, of the Sixth Infantry, California Volunteers would ever be called to task.

Hill, it will be recalled, had left Camp 32 at the head of an expedition on August 2, the same day that McDermit had left with his party. On the second day of his scout, Hill's men had found the putrefying corpse of an Indian woman, partially covered with stones, with a living child upon its breast. The child had evidently been abandoned, in the Indian manner, when its mother had died.

Hill ordered his men to kill the baby by throwing it over a precipice and mashing its brains out with stones, which was done. He also ordered the men to scalp the dead woman, even though the hair pulled out of her rotting head as attempts were made to do so. Hill then had the two bodies burned.

Just who brought charges against Hill is not known, but a general court-martial was convened in October, at Benicia, California to try him on four counts—murder of the child; conduct unbecoming an officer and gentleman (for scalping the dead woman); neglect of duty, for delay in acting on orders to proceed from Dun Glen to Queen's river; and conduct prejudicial to good order and discipline for saying, about July 3, in the presence of his men that he intended disobeying written orders from McDermit, and for referring to the colonel as "a damned old fool."[85]

In November, Hill was found guilty of the three lesser counts, but, as to the murder charge, the court found only for manslaughter. Hill's punishment was to have been dismissal from the service and imprisonment for one month at Alcatraz, and forfeiture of all pay and allowances. General McDowell, however, only approved that part of the sentence that cashiered Hill for conduct unbecoming an officer. He adjudged the child's killing to have been murder, and he rebuked the court, regretting that a new trial for that crime could not be ordered. McDowell wrote:

> There have been many atrocities committed in this land, by both the white and red man, with...and...without provocation...but...this is the only occasion where a person holding the honorable position of Captain in the military service...has been a party to the cold and deliberate killing of a child...and it will stand alone as the most atrocious act on record committed by an officer...for which, to the reproach of the military service, he was not punished.[86]

One of Hill's fellow soldiers argued that men on the warpath out in the wilderness could not well take care of and nurse an infant. And, that when Hill had ordered the child killed he had, perhaps, been thinking of Andrew Jackson's order to the soldiers in Florida when they were fighting the Seminoles, that "by killing the nits thereafter there would be no lice."[87]

After McDermit's death, the volunteer soldiers serving in Nevada got better results in quashing the natives, due largely to help from the friendly Paiute chieftain, "Captain Sou." Over the next six months Sou kept the soldiers informed of the presence of hostiles, and he vigorously helped eradicate them.

In September, the chief led Lt. Osmer and his men to a small Paiute camp southeast of Unionville, and in a surprise attack, at dawn, nine Paiute men and ten women were killed—the women "accidently." Not a soldier received a scratch.[88]

Soon afterward, Sou led the cavalry under Captain Robert Payne and Lieutenant Littlefield from Camp Black to an Indian camp on the west side of Queen's River valley, where they annihilated thirty natives, with only one soldier being wounded. A saddle was found that allegedly had belonged to Jackson, the man killed in July on the road to Idaho.

This fight caused editor Forbes to admit that he had been wrong about Littlefield's alleged lack of courage. He noted that the lieutenant and Payne hadn't followed "Wells' system of fighting, as exemplified at...Godfrey Mountain...by taking refuge behind large rocks...and leaving the boys to fight the battle...as best they might, nor by starting off from the scene of conflict to hunt up a new camping ground, as it is said the gallant Wells did."[89]

In mid-November, the murder of a teamster, J. W. Bellows, by Paiutes near Rabbit Hole Station, led to yet another successful reprisal. With help from Sou and his brother Bob, Lt. Osmer tracked the killers to a camp located in the Black Rock Mountains, on a stream now named Battle Creek. Here they fought a band led by a Paiute called "Black Rock Tom," and killed an estimated 60 natives, with the loss of only Private David W. O'Connell. Tom Rule, who had been so dangerously wounded on his way to Idaho with the Jackson party that summer, was in thickest of the fight, and "made a good beginning in getting even."

Forbes' appreciation of Captain Sou grew stronger with each victory. Sou's "fidelity to the whites and zeal in their cause," said Semblins, "entitle him to the gratitude of our people."[90]

Within a month, "Black Rock Tom," who was thought to be responsible for many of the recent depredations, was himself was captured with Sou's help, at the Big Meadows on the Humboldt, and was shot "while trying to escape."[91]

Sou piloted a final punitive expedition in January, 1866, led by Captain George D. Conrad, who had by then taken command of Company B of the California cavalry from Osmer. Conrad was an old hand at killing Indians, having been with General Connor in a fight on the Bear River in Idaho three years earlier, which had dealt a severe blow to the Shoshoni.

Conrad's expedition—comprising about 80 cavalrymen, civilians and Paiute scouts—went out in snowy, intensely cold weather, and made a midnight march to surround and charge into a camp of Paiutes at daylight, horses at a gallop. The location of the hostile camp was at Duke Hot Springs, about 40 miles west of Cane Springs. In a fight lasting several hours, 35 natives were killed, one of whom, Captain John, was said to be the murderer of McDermit. Seven whites, and one friendly Indian, Jim Dunne, were wounded, mostly by arrows.[92]

Only one "coach and four" of John Mullan's Chico and Idaho Stage Line ever ran to Idaho in 1865. With a government escort, carrying only four passengers and a Wells-Fargo messenger, and never changing horses, the stage reached Boise on September 1. But, at the end of that month, the company's property was attached by Isaac Roop of Susanville, for debt.[93]

In 1866, Mullan would finally get his line running, with the help of new Eastern money and the powerful John Bidwell. And, as the result of the pleas of Mullan, Bidwell, Hill Beachy and the many settlers affected by the Indian troubles, a number of military posts would be established in Idaho, Oregon and Nevada.[94]

Neither the victories gained during the fall and winter after McDermit's death, nor the establishment of the many camps in 1866 totally ended hostilities in northern Nevada, but the preponderance of the Indian problems would henceforth be seen in southeastern Oregon and southwestern Idaho.

The war might have been won by the whites in 1866 had not the volunteer soldiers been relieved and sent home during the fall and winter of 1865-66, just as they were beginning to get the hang of Indian fighting. Their replacements were few in number, and consisted mostly of regular infantry, fresh from the Civil War in the East, and useless in chasing after the natives.

The vicious Indian war would continue in the region until 1867, when General George Crook took command, massed the available forces, and doggedly stayed in the field until all organized opposition was crushed.[95]

We cannot leave this story without revealing what became of the old typo, William Forbes, and the "savage," Captain Sou. No two characters in Nevada's history better typify the early conflict of cultures.

In 1866, Sou and his band continued helping the soldiers and civilians round up and dispose of renegade Paiutes. To honor him for his help over the previous several years, a document was prepared by Humboldt County officers resolving that he be chosen chief of the friendly Paiutes, be given the title of "Winnemucca and...have supreme command of the Piute Nation," an "exalted position" which he was "by nature so well-fitted to adorn."

The "Whereas" of this remarkable document said there was proof plenty that Old Winnemucca, the "late Chief of the Piutes," had "turned traitor to his tribe, deserted the Country and joined the hostile Indians of the North," and was now "inciting said Indians to continue the war." Sou, on the other hand, had "often attested his fidelity to his white brethren on the battlefield," and had always been "a devoted friend to peace and progress."[96]

Shortly after Sou received this praise, he and John had an argument with their brother Bob, in which the later drew his gun and severely wounded Sou with two shots, and John with one. The injured men were treated by a doctor, who hurried to the scene from Unionville.

While Bob swore that the shootings were an accident, many whites supposed he had done it in order to gain Sou's position. It was thought, at the time, mistakenly, that Sou would not recover, and this worried community leaders, because the chief was the glue that held the peace together with the local Paiutes.[97]

With Unionville beginning to decline, and unable to survive financially, William Forbes sold the *Register* to H. H. Bonnifield and Charles L. Perkins, in February, 1867. He would try another field, Forbes lamented, "while our mines are developing," because the "young ravens must be fed."[98] The journalist took his family to Virginia City where he bought the *Daily Union*, and changed its name to *Trespass*.

While Forbes was running the *Trespass*, Captain Sou became seriously ill. He had been in poor health ever since being shot by Bob. An Indian medicine man at Pyramid Lake was sent for and, after preparing remedies for Sou and another sick man, he departed that night. In the morning, the other native was dead and Sou was showing symptoms of poisoning. Also, one of Sou's horses was missing. A number of Sou's braves set out after the medicine man and overtook him, finding the stolen horse in his possession. They "lost no time in sending him by the lightning train to the happy hunting grounds." The tribesmen then returned in time to see Sou die on January 20, 1868. He was about 35 years of age.[99]

The people in Humboldt realized they had lost a true friend. Elegizing Sou in the *Trespass*, Forbes described him as a remarkable man, of medium size, square built, with a high, intellectual forehead and large, flashing eyes. He was an eloquent orator, who never failed to have a powerful influence over his tribe in maintaining friendly relations with the whites.

Forbes told of an incident in Sou's life, during the early days of the emigration across the plains, when there were only a few traders located along the Humboldt. Sou, then a young man, was arrested and held as a prisoner by one of the traders, on account of the loss of some stock, which the trader believed Sou, through his influence, could restore. Sou chafed under this restraint, and, seizing a revolver, made good his escape; not, however, without receiving a severe wound in the shoulder. Still, he did not shoot, though pointing the gun at the trader to prevent him from coming too near. Sou then went to a trading camp a few miles distant, and gave up the weapon, with a request that it be returned to the owner, saying he could have killed him, but had not done so.

In his praise of Sou, Forbes again mentioned the chief's help in dealing with hostile Indians, and noted his personal bravery in the engagements. Normally, a pleasant smile had been seen upon his countenance; but, when in battle, the spirit of the devil seemed to possess him, so changed was his demeanor. Where the battle raged fiercest there was Sou, always dealing out heavy blows, neither sex nor age staying his hand.

D. Fairchild, the editor of the *Reese River Reveille* at Austin, chided Forbes for having lost some of his former journalistic flair, saying, "Forbes, when we used to eat bread and butter with you, a long time ago, you would have got off something to grace a rude head-board over the grave of the 'dusky warrior' after this style:

> Beneath this mound lies Captain Sou,
> Of Whites an ally brave and true.
> When Gabriel's trump at last shall sound,
> His lot be—happy hunting ground."[100]

"Semblins" had indeed lost his exuberance, and, before long, the *Trespass* failed under his management. Disappointed with journalism, he went to Treasure City (later named Hamilton), Nevada and, in December, 1868, started a wholesale liquor business and a saloon called the Sans Souci, declaring that, "of twenty men, nineteen patronized the saloon and one the newspaper, and he was going for the crowd."[101]

But, the old profession still tugged at Forbes and, before long, he bought a share of the *White Pine News* from W. H. Pitchford. The salutatory of the May 10, 1869 edition proclaimed that he once again was making "that old bow," and setting about the "old time drudgery." "Not much need be said between us on the occasion," he wrote blandly, "for we are all acquainted ...[and] pretty promises...in these columns, would not be worth the uttering."

Tired of losing money, Forbes also said the paper would "be conducted on business principles, true to whoever or whatever is honest and manly, without regard to antecedents or belongings." He had "friends to reward," but hadn't "the means to reward them now." He had "enemies to punish," but mostly they were "too mean for the resources of the world," and he would "leave them to take it all out in the last scorching."[102]

Within a few years, business at Hamilton was declining, but in the nearby Schell Creek range a new boom was beginning. In April 1872, after visiting the new town of Schelbourne, Nevada, Forbes and Pitchford shipped a press and type from Hamilton, and, for just a few months, published the *Schell Creek Prospect*. By early November, the failing *White Pine News* came out in reduced size, due to the general retrenchment of business.

William J. Forbes
(*Author's Collection*)

Forbes took the press and materials of the *White Pine News* to Salt Lake City where, in February 1873, he began publishing *The New Endowment*, a first-class daily paper. But, in a field crowded with competitors, this paper also was a total financial failure. In the last issue, Forbes said he was stopping publication because "we did not bring enough money with us."[103]

After the failure in Utah, Forbes was attracted by a big mining boom at Tuscarora, Nevada. He received encouragement from the citizens of nearby Battle Mountain, so he went there, and in December, 1873, started a weekly sheet he named *Measure For Measure,* using dilapidated equipment formerly used in publishing the *Reese River Reveille,* the *Silver Bend Reporter*, and the *White Pine News.*[104]

Forbes also bought some mining property, which he named "Measure For Measure," but these new endeavors were no more profitable than the others. Soon after settling in Battle Mountain, his wife, Mary died, and he sent his ten-year-old son, Sheridan, to live with the boy's maternal grandparents in Coloma, California.

Impoverished and alone, Forbes succumbed to heart disease, at age 46 in October, 1875, and was buried in Coloma, alongside his wife. Ten years earlier, he had written what could have been his own epitaph:

'Semblins' says death cannot be a matter of much moment to an editor—no thirty days notice required by law—it is the local incident of a moment, a few days as advertised on the fourth page, a few calls by subscribers not in arrears. A short, quick breath—then *the subscription paper for burial expenses.*[105]

Slaughter at Bear River

Comes the message to the Colonel:
"Indian warriors dare your guns.
Camp'd for murder and for battle
where Bear River's channel runs."[1]

Old Fort Douglas, Utah was recently closed as an economy measure, and the military reservation land given to the University of Utah and others. Here is the story of its beginnings, and of a fierce battle fought by the men who built it.

The slaughter was greater than at Sand Creek; the fighting was far more savage than at Wounded Knee. Some recent historians have called it a ruthless massacre, and labeled the architect of the episode a scoundrel for his actions which, at the time, earned him praise as a hero.

Today, few people are aware of the furious clash that took place so long ago, between Shoshoni Indians and volunteer soldiers from California. This little-remembered battle was fought on the banks of the slow-flowing Bear

River in southeastern Idaho, a short distance north of today's Preston. An historical marker near the site provides the only hint that the surrounding farmland was once a killing ground.

During America's Civil War, the Third Regiment of California Volunteer Infantry was chosen to protect the Overland Trail and the newly-completed transcontinental telegraph in Utah and parts of Nevada and Wyoming. These two vital lifelines were thought to be at risk from Secessionists, Indian marauders and from the Mormon (Latter-day Saints) Church, led by the strong-willed Brigham Young.

The commander of the Third was the fiery, Irish-born Patrick Edward Connor, a successful Stockton businessman who had previously served with valor while leading a company of Texas volunteers during the Mexican War. He had been in California since 1850, seeking his fortune in a variety of exciting ventures, but was best-known for having been second in command of the ranger company that had captured and lopped off the head of a man supposed to be the notorious bandit, Joaquín Murrieta.

Colonel Connor and his infantry regiment, augmented by several companies of California cavalry, made the long march across the Sierra Nevada Mountains, and over the hot, alkaline desert to Utah in the late summer of 1862.

Once in Salt Lake, the tempestuous colonel turned vehemently anti-Mormon, after witnessing widespread disregard of a new federal law prohibiting polygamy. As a consequence, rather than re-occupy a former army post to the west of the Mormon capital, he built his major garrison—Camp Douglas—on a sloping plateau to the east of it. This location commanded the city from a point, he said, where "one thousand troops would be more efficient than three thousand"[2] in the former location.

A four square mile reserve was declared, which was later expanded when a few saloons "and another institution forbidden by Moses"[3] threatened to grow outside the original boundaries. With the cold Utah winter close at hand, the first quarters erected at the new post were of necessity crude ones. Known as "Connor tents," they were simply holes dug in the ground, covered with canvas, and equipped with fireplaces.

From the beginning, Connor used his cavalry under its ruthless commander, Major Edward McGarry, to engage the surrounding Indian tribes in small skirmishes, provoked by depredations, both real and imaginary. On one expedition, prompted by reports of a massacre in Nevada, McGarry and his men executed, or shot while they were "trying to escape," 24 Western Shoshoni and Goshiutes.

In late January of 1863 Colonel Connor found an opportunity to deal a

Drill with mountain howitzers, Camp Douglas, Utah Territory
(Fort Douglas Museum)

major blow to the natives of the region, and make an impression upon them strong enough to stop attacks like those of the past few years against emigrants, miners and settlers. He was visited in November, 1862 by Zachias Van Orman, who sought help in recovering his young nephew, Reuben, from the Shoshoni. The little boy and his three sisters had been captured in a savage 1860 attack on the Utter-Van Orman emigrant party on the Oregon Trail, west of the Salmon Falls of Snake River.

By the time Reuben's uncle, Zachias, appealed to Connor for help, he had been searching for the missing children for many months. That spring he had received information at his home in Oregon that the children had been seen living with the Shoshoni in the Cache Valley of northern Utah. His informant had tried to ransom the captives but could not raise the high price demanded by the Indians. Subsequently, that summer, Zachias had tried, unsuccessfully, to obtain help from an army expedition sent out along the emigrant road from Fort Walla Walla.

Undaunted, Zachias made his way to the Cache Valley, and found young Reuben near Smithfield in the hands of a Shoshoni chief called Bear Hunter. Zachias had been able to talk to Reuben, and had even seen an opportunity to steal him away, but thought it unwise. He also learned that the boy's three

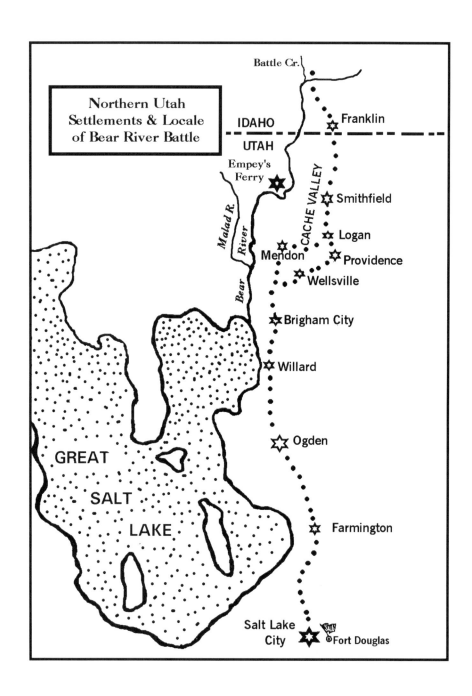

little sisters had died of starvation in the Goose Creek Mountains, to the northwest of Cache Valley. Before leaving Smithfield, the frustrated uncle threatened the Indians with forceful measures, but this totally failed to impress them.[4]

After hearing Zachias' story, Colonel Connor dispatched Major McGarry and a troop of sixty cavalrymen to Cache Valley. The major was told to encircle Bear Hunter's camp, capture the Indians and demand that they surrender Reuben. If the boy was not given up, McGarry was to bring three of the principal Indian men to Camp Douglas as hostages. He was to find out if Bear Hunter's band had been involved in the massacres west of Fort Hall that summer, and arrest any natives he thought to be guilty. McGarry was also told to search nearby for a large herd of livestock supposedly stolen the previous summer from murdered emigrants and Cache Valley settlers.

Colonization of Cache Valley had begun in April of 1859, with the founding of the hamlets of Logan, Providence, Mendon, and Smithfield. These were followed in 1860 by other villages, including Franklin—the first settlement in what would later become Idaho.

An ever-present fear of Indian depredations caused the settlers to build these towns in the form of a square fort, about 200 yards on a side. Stock was generally driven into stables and corrals within the fort each night. Adjoining ground was laid out in little patches of a few acres each, for the cultivation of garden vegetables. Still farther off were larger fields.

Although the Indians took no concerted action against the Mormon pioneers of Cache Valley, they did harass them constantly by the theft of horses and cattle and by frequent intimidation of individuals for food and gifts. Any settlement beyond the fort area had been impossible. In the summer of 1860, the "Cache Valley Militia" had been formed, with Ezra T. Benson as its colonel, to deal with emergencies.

A hard night's journey of seventy miles brought McGarry and his detachment to Providence just before midnight of November 22. Here, an eager Zachias Van Orman was ready to lead them to where Bear Hunter and his tribe were encamped several miles away. McGarry left his horses in charge of a guard, walked his men to the Indian camp, and had his men surround it. But, with the coming of daylight, it was found it to be deserted, save for two old women. Fires still burned in many of the shelters, indicating that the remainder had just flown the coop. An irate McGarry marched his men back to Providence to retrieve their horses.

At about 8 A.M., forty mounted Indians came out of a canyon and onto the bench between Providence and the hills and "made a war-like display, such as shouting, riding in a circle, and all sorts of antics." McGarry had his men mount up and divided them into three groups. Captain Samuel Smith was sent to the right, Lieutenant George D. Conrad to the left, and McGarry himself took the center to begin driving the Indians into the canyon. At its mouth, when Conrad's party came under attack, McGarry unhesitatingly ordered his men to commence firing, and to "kill every Indian they could see."[5]

The major soon concluded that it would be impossible to enter the canyon without exposing his men to fire from the hills on each side. Accordingly, he reinforced Lieutenant Conrad and gave orders to take the hill on the left of the canyon at all costs. After three braves had been killed, and about the time the reinforcements reported to Conrad, Bear Hunter appeared on one of the hills with a white flag.

McGarry ordered a cease fire while a local Mormon man arranged a truce. Bear Hunter came to McGarry with some of his warriors, and the major questioned them, through an interpreter, as to the whereabouts of young Reuben. Finding that the boy had been sent away several days earlier, Bear Hunter and four others were held hostage while Indian messengers were sent out to bring Reuben back. The next day the lad was brought in and McGarry released his prisoners. Before leaving, Bear Hunter told the major that he had been warned of the soldiers' approach by an Indian known as "Weber Tom."

The California cavalrymen suffered no injuries in the hour-long affray with Bear Hunter's warriors, and the command soon arrived safely back in Salt Lake City. The mission had not been a complete success, since no trace had been found of the missing livestock.

Newspaper accounts of Reuben's recovery gave conflicting stories regarding his race. According to one report, some of the whites in Cache Valley had seen the boy with the Indians, and, although the latter had painted his face like a native, his light hair and blue eyes betrayed his background. These Mormon settlers had tried to get the boy, but the Shoshoni refused to let him be ransomed and began keeping him hidden.[6]

Another article spoke of Shoshoni claims that he was a half-breed, whose father was French, and whose mother was a sister of Washakie, the well-known chief of the Eastern Shoshoni. Still other story claimed the ten-year old could still remember the massacre of his parents by the Indians who had taken him and his sisters captive. It was said he could speak both English and the Shoshone dialect fluently, and that, when he was delivered up, he was "dressed and bedaubed with paint...and acted like a regular little savage...fighting, kicking and scratching when the paint was washed from him to determine his white descent."[7]

It is not known what ultimately became of Reuben, but Uncle Zachias

Reuben Van Orman and Zachias Van Orman (at the boy's right) with Zachias' Indian fighters. (*Courtesy of Edith Farmer Elliot, granddaughter of Zachias Van Orman*)

stayed on for a time in Utah and served as one of Colonel Connor's scouts. As for Bear Hunter, he quickly resumed his harassing of the Mormon settlers. Just a day after the troops left Providence, he and his band reappeared, accused the Mormons of sheltering and feeding McGarry's troops, and began making warlike demonstrations near the village.

Finally, seventy settlers were sent from nearby Logan to assist, and when the Shoshoni saw them they sued for peace, asking that they be given two beeves and a large quantity of flour as a gesture of goodwill. Colonel Ezra T. Benson and the local bishop, Peter Maugham, concluded that this might be the best solution, so the supplies were produced forthwith from the bishop's stores.

Still wanting to recover the stolen livestock, Colonel Connor sent Major McGarry on another expedition against the Shoshoni on December 4. The major and 100 cavalrymen left secretly and traveled northward for two nights to Empey's Ferry on Bear River, eighty miles distant, near present-day Colliston, Utah. But the deception failed, the Indians having been forewarned once again of his approach.

From the ferry, McGarry could see the Indian camp on a hill, several miles distant, beyond the Malad River crossing. The Bear was full of ice and the ferry scows had been disassembled for the winter. To further complicate matters, the rope had been cut on the opposite bank by the Indians. But, despite these difficulties, some troops got across and, by the next morning, four Indians had been captured.

McGarry then sent an Indian boy "belonging" to a certain Jacob Meek to the Shoshoni to inform them that must they deliver up the livestock by noon the next day or he would kill the prisoners. Upon receiving McGarry's threat, the Shoshoni broke camp, crossed to the east side of the Malad, and then proceeded up into the Bear River canyon.

Having received no word by the deadline at noon on the eighth, McGarry had the four prisoners executed. The Indians were tied by their hands to the ferry rope and shot, after which the cords by which they were fastened were cut and the bodies tumbled into the river. It was said that fifty-one shots were fired before life in all of them became extinct.

In its first reports of the encounter the *Deseret News* chided the Volunteers for not making a real fight of it, saying that the "bold and saucy" warriors were anxious for one and that "a better chance for giving them a brush could not well have been had."[8] Later however, the newspaper expressed fear that the killings would make the Indians even more vindictive.

Indeed, major thefts of horses and cattle continued through late December and early January in Box Elder and Cache Counties, requiring that herds be moved closer to the settlements to ensure their safety. Rumors were received that the natives near the northern settlements had become more hostile, that they were determined to have "blood for blood,"[9] and that nothing but the killing of some of the whites would satisfy them.

Colonel Connor would soon afford them the opportunity.

The years 1860 through 1862 had seen the beginnings of significant mining activity in the regions surrounding Salt Lake City. Discoveries were made in the area near present-day Austin, Nevada; on the Humboldt River at Unionville, Nevada; in what is now central and northern Idaho, and—of most importance to this story—in southwestern Montana at Bannack City.

The diggings at Bannack on Grasshopper Creek—"Gras," as it was affectionately known—were 430 miles from Salt Lake City, the nearest town of any size. All during November and December 1862, freighters and express riders were busy shuttling between Salt Lake City and the new bonanza.

The route to Montana not only passed through Shoshoni-Bannock territory but, in November, the road was altered a bit such that it passed near a large Shoshoni winter encampment, about twelve miles north of the tiny community of Franklin. Here, at the point where the new road crossed Bear River, the declivity provided by the river's course, and some nearby hot springs, had provided the Indians winter protection for many years.

About January 12, 1863, express rider A. H. Conover arrived in Salt Lake from Bannack and reported to authorities that two men, George Clayton and Henry Bean, who had left Bannack with an express on November 25, had been killed by Shoshoni near the head of Marsh Valley, Idaho. Conover, Clayton and others had recently been given an exclusive charter by the miners at Bannack to run an express company between there and Salt Lake, because of their bravery in getting the express through in previous months.

Conover had learned of the fate of Clayton and Bean from some Indians he had met near the Portneuf River. The murders were said to have been committed to avenge the blood that had been spilled by Major McGarry's men, and that Bear Hunter's intention was to kill every white found on the north side of the Bear River until the score was evened.[10]

Following this, on January 19, a miner named William Blevins swore in an affidavit to Utah's chief justice that, on the eighth, while on his way from Bannack to Salt Lake City, he and seven others had been attacked in Cache Valley. One of Blevins' party had been killed, and some gold dust, animals and other property been stolen by the Indians. Blevins further stated that another ten men from the mines had been murdered by Indians only three days before the attack on his party.

The chief justice issued a warrant for the arrest of several of the chiefs—Bear Hunter, Sanpitch and Sagwitch—thought to be leading bands presently in the Cache Valley, and gave the warrant to Marshall Isaac L. Gibbs for execution. Gibbs—no one's fool—went promptly to Colonel Connor for assistance in its execution. Connor, however, had already commenced his own preparations for a move against the Indians, being fully convinced that they were "part of the same band who had been murdering emigrants on the overland mail route for the past fifteen years, and the principal actors and leaders in the horrid massacres of the past summer."[11] The colonel informed Gibbs that he was welcome to join the expedition, but that no prisoners would be taken.

Having seen the Indians alerted to McGarry's recent forays against them, Connor resolved to prevent any recurrence by use of a well-planned deception. By moving a single company of infantry northward in broad daylight, he would lead the chiefs to believe that only this ineffective Indian-fighting force was to oppose them. But meanwhile, a large troop of cavalry

Patrick E. Connor
(*Utah State Historical Society*)

would march at night, undetected, to the Shoshoni winter encampment.

So it was that on the cold, clear morning of Friday, January 23, Company K of the 3rd Infantry, under the command of Captain Samuel N. Hoyt, left Camp Douglas and headed north. Traveling in company were Lieutenant Francis Honeyman with a battery of two small mountain howitzers, and a train of fifteen wagons with supplies for twenty days, and a large quantity of ammunition, all guarded by twelve cavalrymen. Judging from subsequent events, it seems certain that early intelligence was gained by the Indians on the make-up of this slow moving force.

Two days later, on the evening of the twenty-fifth, Colonel Connor followed with detachments from Companies A, H, K and M of the Second California Cavalry, under the command of Major McGarry. With Connor and the 220 cavalrymen were Marshall Gibbs and two supernumerary officers—Major Patrick Gallagher, the commander at Fort Ruby, Nevada, and Captain David J. Berry of cavalry Company A. Both officers were at Fort Douglas

Orin Porter Rockwell
(*Utah State Historical Society*)

attending a court-martial, and volunteered to come along, eager to serve as aides to Connor, just to get into the fight. For Berry, it was a bad decision.

Five or six "irregulars" also went along, either for the thrill of it, or to settle old scores with the Indians. One of them was Zachias Van Orman. Also joining the expedition, strange as it might seem, was Orin Porter Rockwell, the notorious Mormon mountaineer and alleged assassin of various enemies of the church. Three days earlier he had signed on as a guide for $5.00 per day and keep.

Rockwell, with his balding forehead and long, flowing hair, plaited and gathered at the neck, and his ever-present revolvers, looked every bit the part he was said to have played in the Mormon saga—bodyguard to Joseph Smith; supposed unsuccessful hit man on Governor Boggs of Missouri; pioneer mail carrier; and soldier in the Utah War a few years earlier against federal troops. He was reputed to be a deadly shot with either pistol or rifle and to know the country better than anyone in the area.

The fifty-year old Rockwell was quiet and shy, except around friends. Sir Richard Burton, who had met him in 1860, said he had the manner of a jovial, reckless, devil-may-care English ruffian. Army officers who knew Rockwell called him "Porter," and preferred his company to that of "the slimy villains" who would "drink with a man and then murder him." When drinking, Rockwell, would raise his glass to his lips—little finger cocked—and, with a twinkle in his eye, exclaim "Wheat!"—that is to say, "good"—and then drain the tumbler to the bottom.[12]

In addition to using him as a guide, Colonel Connor must have taken Rockwell along so as to have someone who could effectively deal with the Mormons. Unfortunately, there is some evidence to suggest that Rockwell may have sought the job in order to spy on Connor's activities on behalf of Brigham Young.

It had begun snowing in the region on December 17, abruptly ending the Indian summer that had prevailed up until that time. Thereafter, every few days, a new storm would sweep through the area. By the time the Volunteers left the relative comfort of their "Connor tents" at Douglas to move on the Indians, conditions were deplorable. The march of the cavalry was described thus:

> Those who were there at that time...how can they ever forget? that fearful night march. Clear and brilliant out shone the stars upon the dreary earth mantled with deep snow, but bitter and intense was the cold. The shrill north wind swept over the lake and down the mountain sides, freezing with its cold breath every rivulet and stream. The moistened breath freezing as it left the lips, hung in miniature icicles from beards of brave men.
>
> The men's feet froze in the stirrups while on the trot; hands became powerless to hold the rein; ears and nose were made lifeless, whiskers and moustache were so chained together by ice that opening the mouth became most difficult...
>
> All that long night the men rode on facing the savage wind...hour after hour passed on...with not a word save that of command at intervals to break upon the monotonous clamp, clamp of the steeds and the clatter of sabres as they rattled in their gleaming sheaths. As morning [January 26] dawned the troops, stiff with cold, entered the little town of Box Elder [Brigham City]... Many were frozen and necessarily left behind, but the troops after a halt by day, again faced the severity of winter in the mountains and pressed on: the Infantry by day and the Cavalry by night, in order to deceive the wily foe.[13]

Early on the morning of Tuesday the twenty-seventh, Connor's cavalry overtook the infantry and artillery at the town of Mendon. The infantry marched again that night at eleven P.M. followed by Connor's group at four A.M. Wednesday morning. A dozen more men with frostbitten feet were left behind.

Bear Hunter and some of his braves came to Franklin on the twenty-seventh to demand wheat of Bishop Preston Thomas. Not getting all they wished, the Indians treated the bishop to an impromptu war dance around his house. Thomas capitulated and, the next day, three of the Shoshoni returned to Franklin, to collect nine bushels of the grain from the community granary.

These braves didn't seem terribly worried when they saw the infantry approaching the town about four in the afternoon, and they chose to leave only when the soldiers came quite close. An inhabitant of Franklin is supposed to have said to them, "Here come the soldiers. You may get killed," to which they replied, "Maybe so soldiers get killed too."[14] But, once out of town, on the road back to their village on Bear River, the natives quickened the pace, and dumped the wheat to lighten their load.

Hoyt's men went into camp in Franklin that afternoon, as though intending to stay a week, and, at midnight, Connor's force joined them. The colonel had planned for the infantry to start toward the Indian camp at one A.M., and for his cavalry to follow several hours later. There were difficulties, however, in obtaining a local guide to lead them across the unfamiliar terrain toward the river, and this caused a delay in the infantry's march until 3 A.M. An hour later the cavalry set out and overtook Hoyt about four miles south of the Indian village.

The approach of dawn caused Connor to push rapidly on ahead of Hoyt, and, after a short ride, the cavalry reached a point on the bluffs above the river, in full view of the large Indian encampment, about a mile away to the northwest.

All along the march, Connor had been told by the local citizenry that the Shoshoni had abandoned their camp and dispersed into the hills, and, for a moment he feared that was, indeed, the case. Scanning with his glass, the colonel saw steam rising from hot springs just to the south, but not the least sign of life was visible in the village. Then he detected a faint smoke, then presently another, and finally the glare of a morning fire, just being kindled.

The Shoshoni camp lay in a deep ravine, dense with willows, through which flows the stream now known as Battle Creek. At the site of the encampment, near where Battle Creek then joined the river, the ravine was from thirty to forty feet wide and about six to twelve feet deep. It began in the steep, cedar-covered foothills to the north, about three-fourths of a mile from the river, and emptied into a flat about 300 yards wide, which bordered on the river. The Bear, at this place, flows nearly westward, and the ravine runs generally toward the south. About seventy wickiups had been built amongst the willows with their lower parts protected by banked-up earth and rocks. Some two hundred ponies were tied to the willows in the ravine.

Although the Shoshoni knew of the infantry movement, they had chosen not to stir from their camp. It had been fortified skillfully, particularly on the east side, where they had cut fire steps, and had woven willows with loopholes through which to fire across the open tableland—covered with two feet of snow—that extended to the ford of the river about three-fourths of a mile away. To approach the ravine from the east, the troops would have to pass over ground which would expose them to the fire of the Indians before the defensive position in the ravine could even be seen.

Connor was apprehensive that the Shoshoni would discover the strength of his force and make their escape. Immediately upon arriving—despite the infantry still being some distance behind—the colonel ordered Major McGarry to advance and surround the camp, without attacking, while he remained in the rear for a few minutes to give the infantry and artillery their orders as they came up.

The four cavalry companies loaded their weapons, and then were led by McGarry, accompanied by Major Gallagher, into the river. The crossing was difficult, the Bear at this point being from four to six feet deep and choked with floating ice. Private John S. Lee of Company K recalled in later years that several troopers were thrown by their horses, the animals being reluctant to enter the half-frozen, swift stream.

Once across, everyone knew the fight would be a hard one. Lee had never seen so many Indians in his life, all "screaming, dancing, yelling." "Reminded me of a hornet's nest,"[15] he said. Lieutenant Darwin Chase, with Company K and Captain George Price, with Company M, were first to reach the north bank. After a short gallop, they reached the base of the foothills to the east of the Indian camp to form a line of battle. Captain Daniel McLean with Company H and Lieutenant John Quinn with Company A soon joined them.

As the troops formed their line, about fifty of the Indians came riding out onto the plain in an attempt to decoy McGarry's cavalrymen into a charge, which would allow those in the ravine to easily pick them off. A chief brandished his spear, from which dangled the scalps of his previous victims, as the warriors behind him taunted brazenly: "Fours right, fours left; come on you California sons of bitches!"[16]

Thus invited, McGarry advanced his men on foot frontally against the ravine, having either forgotten about his instructions to surround the site, or deciding such a course to be impractical. The Shoshoni warriors all retreated into the ravine and, when McGarry's men got to within fifty paces of the upper end of it, began to pour a deadly fire into the oncoming cavalrymen. When the firing commenced, Connor hurried across to the battle, leaving instructions for Hoyt to ford the river as soon as his infantry arrived.

Nothing could be seen of the Shoshoni but the tops of their heads, but the effect of their fire was devastating. A good number of soldiers fell dead and wounded in this opening sally but, with the good sense of Western mountaineers, which most of them were, they soon threw themselves to the ground and began fighting cautiously, even before being told to do so.

Private Lee was shot in the arm by an Indian woman, and later also received a hip wound. In the advance, First Lieutenant Darwin Chase was wounded, first in the wrist and, moments later, in the lung, but he fought on for another twenty minutes before reporting himself mortally wounded to Connor and asking permission to retire. It is thought that he drew heavy fire because of his richly caparisoned horse, the Indians mistaking him for Connor. Captain McLean was wounded in the hand, but kept advancing until stopped by a bad injury in the groin.

Regimental Surgeon Robert K. Reid won praise for his bravery. Instead of smoking his pipe in the rear and contemplating the polish of his saws—behavior the soldiers expected from their surgeons—he acted as an aide to the colonel, until the wounded began to appear, when he improvised a field hospital in the rear. Sleeves rolled up, Reid soon was awash in the blood of his comrades.

After thirty minutes of this intense duel, Connor decided he must try something else. He ordered McGarry and twenty dismounted men to try and turn the left flank of the Shoshoni, up where the ravine entered the foothills.

About this time, Hoyt and the infantry arrived at the ford and eagerly attempted to cross and join in the battle, but after several men tried it, only to be swept downstream, Hoyt sent word to Connor that it was impossible to cross the river on foot. The colonel ordered a detachment of cavalry, leading additional horses, to bring the infantry across. This being done, Hoyt's men, some wet and freezing, were sent to support McGarry's flanking movement.

With the main body of cavalry still bearing the brunt, McGarry's detachment finally succeeded in scrambling up the hill, skirmishing as they went. Hoyt got to the west side of the ravine, and, while a portion of his men kept up their fire directly in the rear of the Indians, McGarry's troops stretched out in a cordon over the north end of the ravine, forming, with the cavalry in front, about three quarters of a circle. Thus, by enfilading fire from three points, the Shoshoni were gradually driven to the center and southward.

Major McGarry sat astride his large white horse, unconcernedly walloping his shoulders to keep his fingers warm, while the snakish whistle of bullets masked the commands that he issued. Major Gallagher, near McGarry, also remained upon his horse, at times acting as an aide, and at others fighting on his own hook.

Despite their untenable position, the Shoshoni fought doggedly and made no attempt to run. To cut off the only remaining escape route, Connor next ordered a detachment of cavalry under Lieutenant Conrad to ride around to the west side of the ravine, near its mouth along the river's edge. He posted portions of Companies K and M on the east side. As expected, the Indians ultimately broke and hurried toward the river, and the slaughter began. One contemporary account said they fought bravely:

> ...but now, away from their lodges and places of natural and artificial defense, it was their turn to feel the weakness of exposure. The Indians therefore fell in heaps; some attempted to escape into the river, but the keen eye of the Volunteer in avenging the helpless emigrants, the women and children whose blood had been unatoned, and the fresh flowing blood of his comrade lying at his feet, was in a moment, upon the fleeing form of the savage, and the deadly rifle did its work, and few escaped.
>
> Other Indians sought refuge in the thick willows of the ravine, and on the border of the river; but the order to 'scour the brushes' dislodged the sneaking foe. Some of them, counting no doubt, on the fate that surely awaited them, revealed the places of their concealment by the deadly fire they kept up from the willows, and one by one, they were dislodged, and the silence of grim death began to reign where before the hills had reverberated with the incessant crack of the rifle.[17]

In the final few minutes of this bloody melee, one concealed but determined Shoshoni put a ball through Major Gallagher's left arm and into his side, and then was able to reload and shoot a trooper close by Colonel Connor before a volley into the brush stilled his gun. Captain Berry was also wounded near the end of the fight—shot through the shoulder and lung.

Scores of Indians were killed. Probably only twenty or thirty braves escaped, including Chief Sagwitch, who was reported to have been killed, but who, in fact, had made his way across the river holding on to the tail of a horse another man was riding.

Another survivor was Ray Diamond, the nephew of Sagwitch, who ran toward the river with several soldiers hot on his heels. When he reached the river he fell into the water, feigning death, and then floated under the ice and made for an air hole where he clung with his head just far enough out of the water to allow him to breathe. The soldiers spotted him and fired again, wounding him in the thumb. After the troopers gave up their attempts to kill him, Diamond swam to some willows, and lay hidden for several hours in the intense cold. He would later settle on the Washakie reservation and live to be a hundred years old.[18]

One warrior told how he swam away with his buffalo robe upon his back. The soldiers shot at him, but their balls didn't penetrate the robe. Sagwitch's oldest son, Soquitch, escaped on a horse with his girl friend behind him. She was killed, but he survived to sit at a distance and watch the rest of the battle in safety.

One Indian woman, being chased by soldiers, threw her small baby into the river where the child drowned and floated down the river with the other dead bodies and the bloody red ice. She then jumped into the river herself and escaped by hiding under an overhanging bank.

Yeager, the twelve-year old son of Sagwitch, kept running around until he came upon a small grass lodge that was so full of people that it was actually moving along the ground. Inside the shelter, Yeager found his grandmother. At her urging, the two of them went outside to lie among the dead before the soldiers could set the teepee on fire.

Near the end of the battle, as the soldiers were searching among the dead Indians, one of the Volunteers came across the inquisitive youngster, who was looking around to see what was happening. The soldier stood over Yeager, pointing his gun at the boy. The two stared at each other; the gun was lowered, then raised a second time before finally the soldier lowered it and walked away.

While Lieutenant Quinn was passing among the Indian dead, he noticed a large warrior without any marks of injury. Quinn gave him a dig with his spur, which caused the body to shrug its shoulders. Quinn put his revolver to the warrior's ear, pulled the trigger and, when the gun did not fire, the "dead" Indian leaped up and seized the gun, as well its owner. The much smaller Quinn was only saved by the quick action of another soldier whose weapon functioned properly.

The Californians experienced many another close call during the fight. Captain George Price of Company M was hit in the left side by a ball, but it was stopped by a package of pistol cartridges he was carrying in his pocket. Price was startled to find that he didn't fall and wasn't bleeding, and he fought on, "much relieved in his feelings."[19] Lieutenant Conrad had a ball tear through his coat; two men of Price's company had skin cut close from their scalps without any further injury; other men had balls flatten against buttons, belt buckles and miniature portraits carried in their jacket pockets.

The battle lasted from six to ten o'clock in the morning. When it was ended, the troops began the grim task of collecting their dead and destroying the Indian camp. Seventy lodges were burned, some of them covered with canvas taken from wagons, and still bearing the names of their former white owners. When the surviving women and children saw that the soldiers did not want to kill them, they came out of hiding and walked to the rear of the troops where they sat down in the snow like a "lot of sage hens."[20]

Huge quantities of provisions and emigrant plunder were found, including powder, lead, bullets, modern cooking utensils, fine guns and a thousand bushels of wheat. The soldiers helped themselves freely to Indian souvenirs such as tomahawks, arrows and buffalo robes. Then, after leaving enough provisions to subsist the 160 women and children reported to have survived the battle, the Volunteers burned much of the remaining property.

There is a great disparity among observers and historians with regard to the number of Indians who died at Battle Creek. Connor's report puts the number at 224, but he admits that his concern over his wounded prevented a close personal examination of the battlefield. The historian, Edward Tullidge, quotes two sources, one of whom put the number at 200, and the other—William Hull of Franklin—who pegged it at 368, including about 90 women and children.[21]

Nearly all accounts agree that in places on the field the slaughter was intense. At one place near the river, 48 Indian bodies were counted. Chiefs Lehi and Bear Hunter were both killed; Bear Hunter's severely burned body was found lying in a fire near the mouth of the ravine, where he had been making bullets.

According to William Hull's account, on the morning after the battle, the bishop at Franklin dispatched William Head, captain of the local militia, along with Hull and another man to go to the scene of the battle to learn whether any Indians were still alive. The men found bodies everywhere—in several places, three to five deep. Two Indian women whose thighs had been broken by bullets were found alive, as well as two boys and one girl about three years of age. The little girl had eight flesh wounds in her body. Hull and the others took them back to Franklin for care.[22]

Most eyewitness accounts of the battle state that there were women and children killed, but say the deaths were unavoidable. It seems unlikely that Connor's men deliberately killed women and children. Had such been the case, with so many men at the scene, and with the event so well reported, the truth would certainly have emerged, as it did a few years later at Sand Creek.

Mae T. Parry's "Massacre at Bia Ogoi" is the only document which tells the story of the battle from the Indian point of view. Parry, the great- granddaughter of Chief Sagwitch, based her story on oral history. In her work, the entire blame for the confrontation is laid to the white man, except for "a few Indian troublemakers."[23]

According to Parry, Connor's attack on the Shoshoni camp was precipitated by three minor incidents. In the first, three men of Bear Hunter's band stole some cattle from a nearby farmer, drove them north and ate them. In the second instance, some of the infamous Chief Pocatello's band killed several miners near old Fort Hall, but none of the bands on Bear River were said to have had anything to do with this affair. In the third instance, a fight occurred between white and Indian boys in which two of each race were killed. These Indians were also said not to be from the bands at Bear River.

Parry makes no mention of who might have been killing whites at such a fierce pace on the Oregon and California trails the previous few seasons, and she fails to mention that a nephew of Sagwitch later stated that the Indians had planned to raid the white settlements as soon as spring arrived.[24]

Although Pocatello's group is blamed for two of the three incidents that she says led to Bear River, and although she tends to disassociate the Northwestern Shoshones from Pocatello, Parry admits that only a few weeks before the battle, thousands of Shoshones, including Pocatello's people, had gathered at the Bear River site to hold the annual "Warm Dance," which was supposed to speed the onset of spring. It is perhaps fortunate for General Connor that his attack did not take place earlier in the month.

Parry's version of the battle credits Sagwitch and his people as having only a few old guns. Sagwitch is supposed to have told his warriors not to shoot first, expecting Connor to simply ask for the guilty men and, as soon as Sagwitch turned them over, that would be that. The soldiers, however, are supposed to have fired first without asking questions, and the ensuing massacre was such as one might expect wherein bows and arrows were pitted against muskets. And, according to Parry, the rifle pits and dugouts used by the Indians from which to fight the Volunteers, were in actuality the make-believe fox holes dug by Indian children, playing at war.

Bear Hunter, it is claimed, was shot, then whipped, kicked and tortured by the soldiers. One of the soldiers purportedly took his rifle, stepped to a burning campfire and heated his bayonet until it was a glowing red, and then ran the burning hot metal through the chief's ears.

Although several histories state that Bannock Indians were encamped with the Shoshoni at Battle Creek, there is no evidence that such was the case, and certainly there were no Bannock chieftains present. Sanpitch and Pocatello were reported by Connor to still be at large after the battle.

Of Connor's 303 men in the expedition, only about two hundred engaged the enemy. Seventy-nine had to be left behind on the road, suffering from severe frostbite, and some of them became crippled for life. Others who didn't get into the fight included those men guarding the train and those with the howitzers, which weapons Connor was never able to bring into the battle.

A total of twenty-six Volunteers died either on the field, or later as a result of their wounds. At least forty-five more men were wounded, mostly in the upper part of their bodies, bearing witness to the closeness of the fighting. One soldier, who had been a nine-month volunteer in the East, and had fought at the first battle of Bull Run, thought the Bear River affair was "infinitely more interesting and warm" than the one in Virginia.[25]

Connor, as he had in the Mexican War, exhibited great personal bravery. Mounted on a large mottled racer, he was reported to be continually in the thickest part of the fight, and seldom out of the range of the Indian rifles, showing no fear of exposing himself. He and the other officers remained mounted throughout the fray, resulting in a high proportion of casualties. He took a bullet through his hat, but remained uninjured.

It was early evening before Connor was able to take his men back to the south side of the river, where they loaded the dead into wagons and then spent a cold and miserable night nursing the wounded and frost-bitten. Only one officer and twenty-five men could be found who were fit for duty. One soldier, Corporal Hiram Tuttle, never forgot those hours:

> The night of January 29th, 1863 I never shal far get (how can I) there we camped on the Bank of Bear River with our dead dieing wounded and frozen 2 feet of snow on the ground nothing for fire but green Willows which would burn about as well as the snow oh! the groans of the frozen it seems to ring in my ears yet the poor fellows some lost their toes some a portion of their feet I worked all night bringing water from the river to wett cloths to draw frost from their frozen limbs I had not sleep any for two nights befor it was a dreadful night to me but managed to get through the night while some never saw the morning.[26]

After the soldiers quit the battleground, Sagwitch, and some others who had escaped, returned to the terrible scene of death and destruction. All the wickiups except Sagwitch's had been destroyed. Inside it he found his dead wife with his infant daughter at her side, still alive. Sagwitch had the baby put into her cradleboard and hung from a nearby tree in the hope that someone would find the girl and raise her.

That night Porter Rockwell spurred the citizens of nearby Franklin to provide sheets and other comforts for the wounded soldiers. He also obtained eighteen sleighs, and the next morning Doctor Reid loaded his charges in them and started toward Camp Douglas. Private Lee, a ball in his leg, was one of those transported in this manner. When he would awake from time to time, he wondered which he would do first—freeze or bleed to death.

Surgeon Williamson of the 2nd Nevada Cavalry and Dr. Walcott Steel of Dayton, Nevada met the wounded at Ogden, along with regimental Chaplain John A. Anderson. Mrs. McLean, alarmed at reports of her husband's death, rode day and night to reach him and render him her "kind offices," sitting in the ambulance "like an angel of goodness."[27] The correspondent of the *Sacramento Daily Union* expressed the wish that the other brave fellows had the same ministering spirits around them.

The wounded stayed the night at Ogden, where the Mormon bishop showed them every attention and provided for their needs. Two apostles of the church, John Taylor and George A. Smith, happened to be in Ogden at the time and both were observed to be visiting with, and encouraging, both the soldiers and surgeons.

A hot meal was provided at Farmington, twenty miles from Salt Lake City for the party of wounded soldiers. Governor Stephen S. Harding was there and asked the *Union* correspondent to thank the people of the northern settlements, in his name, for their attention to the troops. At Farmington, a shift was made from the sleighs to eighteen wagons, and the wounded were carried onward to arrive at Camp Douglas the night of February 2-3. The wounds of Lieutenant Darwin Chase necessitated leaving him behind in Farmington, where he expired on the fourth

The officer who had been left in charge at Douglas had made every provision possible for the care of the wounded, considering the uncompleted state of the post. After receiving an express from Connor, he had equipped the theater and the chaplain's big meeting house tent as hospitals, heating them as best they could be. Wives of the regiment offered their help in caring for the men.

The balance of the command was detained by snows on the pass between Wellsville and Brigham City, and didn't arrive until the evening of February 4. They entered camp driving about l00 of the 175 Indian horses they had captured, the balance being ridden by Hoyt's weary infantrymen, now known as the "light cavalry." Colonel Connor and Porter Rockwell rode together in a buggy, leading the procession.

Although Connor later reported that no assistance was offered him by Mormons on his march to the battlefield, this was not the case on the victorious return journey. Aside from the teams, food and sleighs which were provided for the wounded, the bishop at Wellsville assisted the command in getting over the snow-drifted pass to Brigham City.[28] It was Porter Rockwell however, who was of the greatest help to Connor, and their experience at Bear River engendered an enduring mutual respect and friendship.

While Connor expressed pride in all of his soldiers, he specifically cited

Bear River Memorial at Camp Douglas
(*Author's Collection*)

Majors McGarry and Gallagher, the company officers, and Surgeon Reid for their skill and bravery. His report included, however, a swipe at the Mormons by giving credence to rumors that the Indians at Battle Creek had received their rifles and ammunition from the inhabitants of the territory, in exchange for the property of massacred emigrants.[29]

On February 5, fifteen of the dead Californians were buried with full honors in the military cemetery located to the southeast of Camp Douglas, which had been laid out only a month earlier. In spite of it being a cold, raw day, a large number of persons from Salt Lake attended to pay their respects. One historian reported that, up until this time, scarcely any of the locals had set foot within the encampment but, now there were "quite a number of carriages from the city, many equestrians and a large concourse of people on foot, and had it been generally known, thousands from the city would have paid reverent tribute to the slain, for it was duly appreciated that they had fallen in the service of Utah."[30]

The coffins lay in a row in the quartermaster's storeroom until one P.M., when they were taken to the cemetery, accompanied by the whole command in procession. The band went in advance, playing a mournful air, then came the escort, with arms reversed and regimental colors at a trail. Just in the rear of the escort came the coffins, borne on litters by pallbearers, the stars and stripes spread over each one. Then came the remaining troops in procession and, in their rear, the citizenry.

At the cemetery the coffins were lowered, Chaplain Anderson read the burial service, and three volleys were fired tribute to the dead. After this, the band struck up a gay tune and the Volunteers marched back to camp to resume the duties of the living.

A day later, Lieutenant Darwin Chase was buried in an impressive Masonic and military ceremony, led by a group of about twenty prominent Masons from the area. Chase had been a Royal Arch Mason and, in his youth, was a Mormon elder of great promise, having served as member of the noted Mormon Battalion during the Mexican War.

Three more Volunteers, who had died since the return to Camp Douglas were buried on Saturday the seventh, and two more on Sunday—all with the same military honors. Another trooper, wounded in the neck, would hold on until November. The last to die of his wounds would be Captain David J. Berry, of cavalry Company A, who expired at Camp Union, near Sacramento, California on May 9, 1865 of "inflammation of the bowels, liver and lungs"—all Bear River complications.

Observers all seemed to agree that Connor's victory completely broke the spirit and power of the Shoshoni people in the region, and allowed uninterrupted expansion of Mormon settlements, as well as the development of mines, railroads and other commercial interests in the region, without interference. It also led directly to several significant treaties with an estimated 8,650 Shoshoni, Goshiutes and Bannocks.

Even the Mormons, whose policy toward the natives was a peaceful one, were ecstatic over the results of the battle, and were impressed with the bravery of the Volunteers, both in the battle and in the frigid march of 140 miles. The people of Logan stated that they looked upon the coming of Colonel Connor to relieve them of their Indian problem as "a providence of the Almighty,"[31] since the Indians had caused them to stand guard over their stock and other property most of the time since their first settlement.

Connor executed the battle perfectly as regards the use of surprise and the selection of the time of day and year. He seems to have underestimated the strength of the Indian position, but after the initial shock of this discovery, he did a superb job of directing the fight. The campaign established Connor as the foremost Indian fighter of his time and, for years thereafter, army commanders used his example by striking at the Indians during winter or early spring, when they could be surprised in a fixed location.

After his Indian troubles around Salt Lake were largely settled, Patrick Connor, by then a Brigadier-General, set about to "regenerate" Utah by luring to it a large non-Mormon population. He encouraged off-duty soldiers—many of whom were former miners—to prospect over a wide region. As a result, the volunteers discovered the first rich silver and copper deposits in Utah, as well as many in Nevada and Idaho. Connor and his men also published Utah's first daily newspaper, and gave help to a group of dissident Mormons in establishing Soda Springs, Idaho.

In 1865, General Connor was appointed commander of the Department of the Plains, and led a large expedition deep into the Powder River region. Near what is today Ranchester, Wyoming, he fought some 700 Arapaho and burned their camp before his expedition was recalled during the period of post Civil War retrenchment.

At war's end, Pat Connor left the service and spent the remainder of his life involved in mining and railroad ventures in Utah and Nevada. In 1869, he was instrumental in establishing a new boom town, Corinne, north of Salt Lake City. He built and ran steamboats and schooners on the lake, smelters at Rush Valley and a devised many other expansive schemes, but died in relative penury at Salt Lake in 1891 at age 71. He is buried in the Fort Douglas cemetery, near where he first camped with his Californians in 1862.

The Last Battle

The dreadful carnage wrought by General Patrick Connor at Bear River on that bitterly-cold day in 1863 seems to have been the mainspring for still more slaughter. For from that event—so it was reported—hate became imbedded in the heart of a young Indian boy, which, after quietly festering for some forty-eight years, led to what has been called the "last Indian battle" in the United States.

He used the surname Daggett, but just how, or when, he came by it no one knows. Perhaps it was given to him by friendly Mormon folk, since he is thought to have been born in northern Utah or southern Idaho.

About 1891, the man commonly known as "Rock Creek Mike," or "Shoshone Mike," removed his family from the Indian reservation at Fort Hall, Idaho, and traveled westward to establish a semi-permanent camp on Rock Creek, just upstream of the old stage station, and near what would become Twin Falls. Once there, he and his family seemed content. Unrestricted by artificial boundaries, the little band used the Rock Creek encampment as its headquarters, but lived the greater part of the year across the state border, in northeastern Nevada.

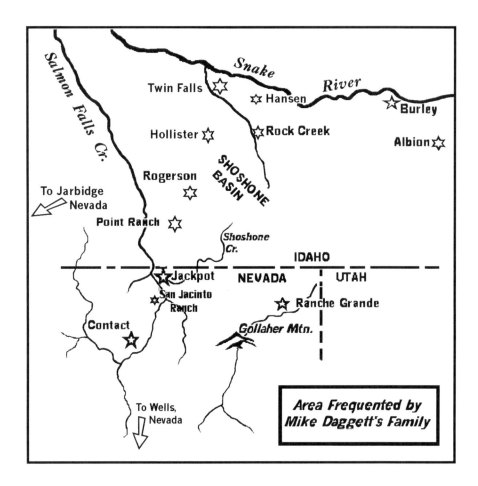

For many years, the huge cattle companies had maintained a series of pastures, corrals and ranches in southern Idaho and northern Nevada. Thousands of fat, sleek Herefords and Shorthorns grazed in the hills from early spring until roundup time in the fall, when animals to be marketed were gathered at the various ranches, then driven south to the Southern Pacific Railroad siding at Tecoma, Nevada.

In season, Mike and his sons worked for the cattle outfits, haying and handling horses. Family members were respected by the local ranchers and cowboys. They always paid their bills, and were considered to be honest and industrious. Mike, however, usually remained somewhat withdrawn and aloof. Rumor had it that, a few years earlier, he had murdered two local Indians, one of them the father of a certain Willie Gibson.[1]

Beginning in 1903, living in such a free manner became much more

THE LAST BATTLE

difficult for Mike and his family. For, in that year, the desert region to the north of Rock Creek began being developed as a consequence of the passage of the Carey Land Act. Over the next few years, the desolate plain bloomed, as huge tracts of the rich, fertile soil were grubbed free of sagebrush and made arable by the diversion of water from the Snake River into extensive canal systems. Towns sprang up, and, every day, hopeful new families arrived. Before long, the district was being called "Magic Valley," because of the wondrous, transmuting effect of the water.

By mid-1909, the regional boom had extended southward into the territory over which Mike Daggett's people roamed. Gold seekers were busy in nearby Jarbidge, Nevada; Salmon Falls Creek was being dammed-up to irrigate a new tract of land surrounding the freshly-surveyed town of Hollister; track was being laid for a Twin Falls to Wells, Nevada railroad, and the Twin Falls-Shoshone Land and Water Company was building canals in Shoshone Basin, where it hoped to irrigate 10,000 acres.[2]

At this time, according to the statement of Jim Mosho—a Shoshoni relative from Fort Hall who visited them in the summer—Mike's family consisted of his Ute wife Jennie; four sons, ranging in age from seventeen to forty; three fully-grown daughters, and three small children. Whites called the sons Jack, Jim, Jake and Charlie—the latter two being the youngest.

The Daggetts spent the entire winter of 1909-10 in Nevada, just across the border from Rock Creek. The family traded at the Vineyard Stock and Cattle Company general store at the San Jacinto ranch, which is situated about seven miles south of today's little gambling town of Jackpot. The old Vineyard store still stands at the ranch—its tall windows and huge doors still rigged with the iron shutters installed in the early days to defend against Indian attack—but its white sandstone walls are severely eroded and marred by names scratched in it by hundreds of residents and visitors over the years.

Mike's family had owned about 35 horses in the fall of 1909, but the ensuing winter had been a hard one, and, with no hay available, a few of the horses died. The remaining animals—about 30—were observed by local cowboys to be in very poor condition. So poor, in fact, that on April 16, 1910, four of Mike's band were seen, several miles east of San Jacinto, walking to the store for food. This was shortly after branding had been completed, and the cattle outfits had turned out their huge herds for summer grazing on the vast plateaus and hills of southern Idaho and northern Nevada.

James Buchanan Rice was a tough and colorful old bachelor cowboy, who owned a ranch on Cottonwood Creek, south of Twin Falls. Known affectionately as "Buck," he was one of those pioneer wranglers who had

Store at San Jacinto Ranch as it looks today
(Author's Collection)

ridden in the first trail drive from Rock Creek to the railhead in Nevada.[3]

Sometime in April, 1910, Rice hired 33-year old William Gay Tranmer to look in Nevada for some of his horses that were missing that spring. Gay Tranmer was a popular "master of the saddle and rope"[4] who often worked for the big cattle outfits. He owned a ranch along Soldier Creek, on the west side of Shoshone Basin—not far from Rice's place—on which he raised alfalfa and grain.

Tranmer convinced a friend, Gordon G. Girdner, to join him in the horse-gathering enterprise. In December, Gordon had quit his job at a Twin Falls grocery store, and had resigned his position as a volunteer firefighter, in order to devote all of his time to his "Nevada ranch interests."

Next, Tranmer recruited two other young men—F. Edward Diffendarfer and Nimrod R. Urie—who were working in Bliss, Idaho, as a blacksmith's helper and teamster, respectively. Tranmer told the others that he had built a corral at a good place to catch horses, and that he intended rounding up Buck Rice's animals, along with some of his own that were missing, and some of the many unbranded ones in the region. He thought that he and his friends could make good money.

Tranmer's party outfitted at his ranch. Gordon Girdner's wife, Hattie, who had an infant child, joined the group as its cook, and Tranmer's sixteen-year old nephew, Frankie Dopp went along as camp tender. Young Frankie's stepfather was Gay's brother, 43-year old John Franklin Tranmer, who lived at Rock Creek, and who, at the time, was off prospecting at Jarbidge, Nevada with three other men.[5]

The would-be horse gatherers proceeded south to the Vineyard Company's "Point Ranch," just beyond Rogerson, Idaho, where they arrived on April 17. After remaining there for nearly a week, Tranmer took his group into Nevada and encamped on Cow Creek, where he had his horse corral. The campsite was located just west of the summit of Gollaher Mountain, about ten miles east of the San Jacinto ranch.[6]

Just exactly what happened next depends upon whose story is to be believed. The following is the sequence of events as related by the cowboys.

Camp was made in a quaking aspen grove not far from Tranmer's horse corral, on the morning of April 25. The four men then left Mrs. Girdner, her baby, and Frankie Dopp in the camp, and went on foot up the canyon to the place where Gay Tranmer planned to build a fence for catching the horses. Tranmer took along his rifle, and Girdner a six-shooter, but Urie and Diffendarfer went unarmed.

After climbing out of the canyon, and making a short walk, the cowboys reached the rim rock above the designated place. Much to their surprise, below them, they saw Mike Daggett's family camped along the creek, and, nearby, a corral in which the Indian men were branding horses. The whites said they didn't expect any trouble, since they had frequently worked amicably alongside of these men, running horses for various ranchers.

There were another thirty or so horses in a quaking aspen grove just upstream of the Indian camp. The buckaroos came down the hill and, as they began examining these animals, one of Mike's sons, Charlie, rode up and asked what they wanted, and whether Tranmer had noticed any of his own horses in the bunch. Tranmer took a close look at the animals, and saw that many of them had brands belonging to stockmen in Nevada and Idaho, or fresh brands, that were disfigured and hard to make out.

While Tranmer continued examining the horses, Charlie went back to his camp. When leaving, he gave the impression that Tranmer's missing horses were down in the Indian corral, and that the whites were to come there. According to the Idaho buckaroos, they had only gotten about halfway to the corral when Charlie rode up and confronted them again. He fired a Winchester rifle into the dirt at Tranmer's feet, and then pointed the gun directly at him and said he was going to kill him. Gay asked why he would do that, since the two of them had always been friends, and Charlie replied that he was "like a wild horse," he "had no friends," and would "kill all whites who came to this place."[7]

Then, another of Mike's boys, Jim, rode up. After accusing Tranmer of stealing a buckskin colt, Jim pointed his six-shooter deliberately at each of the cowboys, repeating "Me killum you—me killum you—me killum you."[8] Tranmer thought Mike's sons were so agitated because the cowboys had just caught them in the act of altering brands on stolen horses.

After Gay denied having stolen the colt, Jim said that the whites could come back again in a few days. But, when Gay mentioned his intention to build a fence across the canyon, close to the Indian corral, the Daggetts' anger flared again, and they once more threatened to kill the cowboys. Gay said he and his friends would leave, and they started down the creek toward their camp. Jim rode off into the brush, but Charlie headed the whites off with his gun and pointed them up the hill the way they had come down it.

The cowboys started climbing, with Charlie following. When about 500 yards up, they saw Charlie point his rifle in their direction, so they dashed behind a cluster of large boulders, just as Charlie began shooting.

Tranmer returned fire with his Winchester and, in the brief skirmish that ensued, thought he had managed to badly wound or, perhaps, even kill Charlie. After this, the cowboys dashed for their camp, using the cover of a grove of trees to get to the top of the hill and out of sight. With Girdner considerably in the lead, they continued down, only to discover that two Indians had gotten ahead of them. One could be seen on the ridge to the east of the cowboy's camp, and the other was riding to head them off. Several shots were heard, supposed to have been fired at Girdner.

Tranmer, Urie and Diffendarfer got safely down the hill, but came under fire from the Indian on the ridge as they were crossing the flat to the creek. Once they reached the screening cover of the brush along the stream, they were able to get safely to their camp. Girdner came in about the same time.

When Hattie Girdner was asked where Frankie Dopp was, she said he had gone out just a few minutes earlier to round up the saddle horses and wash out some saddle blankets. When he left he had not been aware of the trouble with Mike's family.

The two Daggetts now began to shoot down into the whites' camp from the ridge to the east. One with a pistol, thought to be Jim, remained on the ridge, but his companion was seen going down toward Tranmer's horse corral, about a quarter mile distant, and then back up the ridge to rejoin the other. Finally, about 1:30 P.M., the Indians disappeared, and this allowed Ed Diffendarfer to start for the little mining town of Contact, Nevada, some 21 miles distant, to report the attack and Frankie's disappearance to a deputy sheriff of Elko County.

About 2 P.M. the saddle horses that Frankie Dopp had gone out to round up came down the hill, and Tranmer began putting them in his corral. At this, the two Indians reappeared on a high point north of camp and once again began shooting. Gay galloped hurriedly for his camp and its sheltering grove of trees, dodging bullets as Nimrod Urie gave him covering fire with a rifle.

The two Indians moved from ridge to ridge, firing intermittently into the camp until about 7 P.M., when they disappeared. The last round to be fired missed Tranmer's head by only a few inches. Urie and Tranmer waited for 30 minutes, and then went down to the corral and got the saddle horses. The two men took Girdner, his wife and child down the creek to a safer place, and then came back up to keep watch that night over their animals and equipage.

Thus was told the cowboy side of the story.

The next morning, April 26, Gay and Urie rode down to check on Girdner and his wife and, as they were starting back, Ed Diffendarfer arrived from Contact with Deputy Sheriff George B. Grimm and a black cowboy, "Nigger Henry" Harris.[9] After assessing the situation, Grimm went back for more men and Winchester rifles, returning the following day, April 27, with three newly-sworn deputies.

A search was begun for Frankie Dopp and the Daggett family. The sheriff's posse went up the canyon to the large corral, which the Indians allegedly had used in branding stolen horses. Near the place Charlie had been when the firing started, it was seen where he had dismounted from his horse to get behind the rocks. Blood stains were discovered nearby, as was a Dutch oven, pieces of overalls, and some empty cartridges. That night, the searchers reached the Vineyard Company's Rancho Grande, on Goose Creek, a dozen or more miles east of the Indian camp.

The first news accounts of the encounter on Cow Creek stated that the search continued for a week, and that, finally, Frank Dopp's body was found by Deputy Sheriff Grimm and his men. But, in fact, April 28 was the last day of the search. Grimm and his men went to the San Jacinto ranch that evening to disband, and Tranmer's bunch went back to their Cow Creek camp. No trace of Mike's people or Frank Dopp had been found, although evidence had been seen that the natives had hastily disappeared in a westerly direction.

According to Tranmer and Urie's testimony, it was May 4, a full nine days after the skirmish with the Indians, before Dopp's body was finally discovered. Tranmer and Girdner were building an addition to the corral, and while dragging poles over from the quaking aspen grove, Tranmer noticed Dopp's body laying by a bush on the side of the hill, within 75 paces of the corral. The lad had been shot through the head and the heart, as supposed, by

Henry Harris came with John Sparks from Texas to Nevada as a house boy, and later became a skilled cowboy. (*Northeastern Nevada Museum, Elko*)

Mike Daggett's sons.

But, Joe Stewart, one of the men Grimm had deputized, later said he couldn't understand why it had taken so long to find the body, which must have been easily visible from the corral.

Tranmer apparently informed Grimm of the discovery and asked him to get up a posse to go after the Indians. Then he and his group headed for the Twin Falls area, supposedly to summon a posse of their own, return and join up with Grimm.

The story appearing in the Twin Falls newspaper describing the incident was badly distorted, both as to date and fact. It even reported J. Frank Tranmer, Gay's older brother—not Frankie Dopp—as the person who had been killed.

A few weeks earlier, so said the paper, the sheriff at Elko, Nevada—I. G. Clark—had received many appeals for help. Upon investigating, he had learned that Indians had stolen some 80 horses, collected them in Shoshone Basin, and had run them over the Nevada line. The sheriff had supposedly sent word to citizens to "kill all the Indians"[10] that might be found roaming

THE LAST BATTLE   223

the region, and it was in response to this appeal that Gay Tranmer's party had originally gone out.

Now, on hearing news of Frank Tranmer's death—mistaken though it was—some sixty ranchmen and cowboys were said to have gathered all the rifles they could find, formed a posse, and left Rock Creek early on May 7, headed south. People thought that this Idaho posse strictly intended to obey the instructions of the Elko County officer.

If, indeed, such a contingent went out, nothing came of it, nor were any men sent out from Elko. What actually happened was that Deputy Grimm, after learning of the discovery of Dopp's body, rode from his post at Contact over the summit to Wells, Nevada, arriving on May 5 in time to board a passenger train for the county seat at Elko. There, he conferred with Sheriff Clark and District Attorney E. J. L. Taber, about the trouble on Cow Creek.

One man would later say that Grimm suspected it had been the cowboys who had done the rustling and murdering, and that he had been so insistent on this point that the sheriff had fired him.[11] But such was not the case. Grimm swore out a complaint that very night before Judge Morgan, charging Mike Daggett and his people with the murder of the boy, and the judge issued a warrant for their arrest. Grimm then left immediately to apprehend the Indians at Fort Hall, Idaho, where he believed they had gone. But, finding no trace of them there, he was soon back in Contact.[12]

Shortly, there were fresh discoveries which only added to the mystery surrounding the killing of the white boy, and the disappearance of Mike's people. About May 25, a buckaroo named Jack Haden came to Rancho Grande and reported having found a large pit, containing a number of horse carcasses. The pit was located six miles south of Little Goose Creek corral, at the south end of April Fool Point, which would put it at least eight miles southeast of where the Tranmer party had encountered Mike's family.

On the following day, Haden took the Rancho Grande ramrod, Frank Dale, and another cowboy, Dell Hardy, to the place for a more detailed look. They found the pit to be thirty feet long, eight wide and four to six feet deep, and it appeared to have been made with pick and shovel. The ranchers only dug a short distance down and found four horses, but could not see the brands. The horses had been piled in the pit very compactly, with feet doubled under.[13]

Dale and his men went to Contact that day and informed Deputy Grimm of their discovery. Grimm also went to the pit and looked, but said the stench from the rotting horses was so great that he couldn't get near enough to make a thorough investigation. He wrote Sheriff Clark stating his opinion that, after the Indians had killed Frank Dopp, they had driven the stolen horses to

Elko County Sheriff I. G. Clark (at right)
(*Northeastern Nevada Museum, Elko, Nevada*)

what Grimm called a ravine—not a pit—shot them, and covered them with a shallow layer of dirt. Grimm also suspected that if Charlie Daggett had been killed by Gay Tranmer's return fire, he also probably had been buried with the horses.

A few days later, about May 30, the local cowboys found another smaller pit, from which four horses were pulled, about one-quarter mile northeast of the first one. Nearby was an abandoned Indian camp and corral, thought to have been made that spring and used only a few days. Also discovered was an old Indian wagon, containing a bow and arrows, empty cartridge casings, powder in a small sack and other Indian belongings.

Perhaps as a result of Deputy Grimm's visit to Fort Hall, the Indian Office in Washington, D. C. learned of the Dopp murder. The commissioner instructed the Fort Hall agency police to be on the lookout for Mike's people, and he tasked C. H. Asbury, the superintendent of the Carson Indian School at Stewart, Nevada, to look into the affair. Asbury sent two inquiring letters to Sheriff Clark but, not until late July did Clark reluctantly admit that he hadn't learned anything yet, but was working on the case, and that he was "in doubt whether the Indians done it or not."[14]

Probably at Clark's request, on September 20, 1910, Gay Tranmer, Ed Diffendarfer, Nimrod Urie and Gay's brother, J. Frank Tranmer, came to Elko, where Gay and Nimrod made statements in the presence of District Attorney Taber. They told the story of the fight on Cow Creek much as they had told it before, except that the date of the fight was given wrongly as May 6, not April 25, as one can correctly deduce from contemporary newspaper accounts. This erroneous date would be repeated later by Tranmer's group.

Tranmer and Urie gave details of the appearance, dress and temperaments of old Mike and his sons, Jim, Jake and Charlie, and even described how their horses were caparisoned. Mike's son, Jack, was not mentioned; instead Gay Tranmer said the fourth boy was called "Sagebrush," but that little was known about him, because the boy didn't associate with whites very much.

Tranmer said Frankie Dopp had played with Mike's sons as a child and, at the time he was killed, he had no weapon with him and had been entirely unaware of the trouble. Tranmer thought that the Indian responsible for Frankie's death had gone right up to him and shot him in cold blood.[15]

Gay and his friends loafed around an Elko saloon for three days, then left for Winnemucca. District Attorney Taber sent Gay's statement in a circular to over 100 sheriffs in Utah, Idaho, Wyoming and Montana asking for their help in capturing the Indians. He said the murder was so atrocious that it called for vengeance, and if Mike's people had been caught right afterward, "the law would never have had a chance to deal with them, as the people in the vicinity were worked up to a high pitch."[16] In sending the circular to the Office of Indian Affairs, Taber said he had only heard of the Cow Creek affair about September 4—a plain lie, since he had, after all, given details of it to the *Elko Independent* for a story appearing in the May 13 edition.

It was late October before the Indian Office forwarded Taber's circular to a number of agencies and schools in Nevada and Idaho, asking them to inform Taber if they should get any information regarding Mike's people. The only agency to respond was that of John B. Hoover at Fort McDermit, in northernmost Nevada. In early November, he informed Taber and the Indian Office that, in July, some Indians from his agency had seen Mike's band traveling westward through Cedarville, California. Mike reportedly had about 20 horses, and anyone approaching near enough to discern their brands had been told go away or they would be killed.

Hoover also sent this news to the Indian school at Fort Bidwell, California, the nearest activity to Cedarville, hoping they might be able to obtain more information. But, unfortunately, neither Taber nor the people at Fort Bidwell took any action on Hoover's report.[17]

And now, information came to light which would cast Shoshone Mike's people as victims, rather than murderers. On November 24, Jim Mosho and two other Indian men arrived at Albion, Idaho to see T. Bailey Lee, the district attorney of Cassia County, which encompassed some of the territory used by Mike Daggett's family. Mosho and his companions lived on the Fort Hall Reservation, and claimed to be relatives of Mike. One of them said his wife and three of their children had gone with the Daggetts over into Nevada.

They said Mike and his people had been missing all summer. The last time any of them had been seen—except as related by Gay Tranmer and his party—was at the San Jacinto store, during the last week of April. Before calling on Lee, Mosho's group had been over to Mike's camp on Rock Creek, but had gotten no trace of them there except a story that they had been killed by white men, by order of a Nevada sheriff, and their remains burned or concealed. Mosho had also tried, in vain, to get the Nevada officers to take some action.

T. Bailey Lee recalled that he had heard of the Cow Creek affair back in July. Some strangers he had encountered on the streets of Twin Falls told him that they thought the cowboys—who were tough, unsavory men—had gone on a drunken spree and, after having killed one of their number, concocted the Indian story. Having also heard of the discovery of the horse pits, Lee readily subscribed to the theory that the family had all been killed.

Lee dashed off a muddled report of this alleged massacre to the United States attorney-general. He said, mistakenly, that Frank Tranmer, not Gay, was the man who had told the story of the fight on Cow Creek, and that he had disappeared not long afterward. As soon as he had departed, his wife—Frankie Dopp's mother—had accused him and others of having killed Frankie, because the boy had caught them stealing cattle, and they were afraid of exposure. From the beginning, Lee, and subsequently the Washington authorities, confused Frank Tranmer for his brother Gay.

In his letter, Lee also criticized the Elko County authorities for having done nothing to investigate the matter. They hadn't even examined the trenches, at the bottom of which Lee was confident the bodies of Mike and his people could be found. Lee wasn't aware that, in October, the horse pits had been thoroughly excavated by men sent out by some ranchers around Rock Creek, who were also concerned about the absence of Mike Daggett's people. In all, sixteen horses had been pulled out of the first hole, and nine from the second, but no human remains had been found.

Lee said he couldn't interfere in a Nevada crime investigation, but he asked the attorney-general to have some "Secret Service" men placed in his area to "ferret" the thing to a conclusion. Some of the murderers were, doubtless, still "lurking" along the border, and the others could be traced.[18]

The authorities in Washington seemed quick to believe Lee's allegations. The attorney-general passed the letter to the Interior Department, which, in turn, gave it to the Indian Office. Lee was asked if there were not some feature of the case which might bring it under federal cognizance.

The Washington, D. C. *Star* broke Lee's story on December 7. Spurred on by the national interest the article generated, the Indian Office ordered its Denver, Colorado office to conduct an investigation. G. A. Gutches, the District Forester at the Fort Hall agency, was appointed to do the job.

The Indian Office also sent Lee's letter to District Attorney Taber in Elko, asking him to investigate and inform them whether Mike's people had actually been murdered, and if not, whether their disappearance could be otherwise be accounted for. Taber was asked to look at the trenches, and "leave no stone unturned in bringing to justice" those who had murdered "these apparently defenseless Indians, including women and children."[19]

But this request fell upon deaf ears. After reading the national news story a few days earlier, Taber had told a local paper that there was "hardly any foundation" for Lee's report. The previous May, a party gathering horses for a Rock Creek, Idaho stockman had run across "Indian Mike" and his four grown sons who were holding 30 horses belonging to Idaho and Nevada stockmen. The Indians, without warning, had opened fire and killed Frankie Dopp; the whites had returned fire from shelter behind a rock, and the Indians had fled.

Then, Taber went on to say, falsely, that the authorities of Elko County had "never let up in their chase of the Indians until they crossed the state line into southern California with the band of horses a short time ago," and that California authorities were "now after the Indians" and hoped to "capture the entire band."[20]

The new year of 1911 brought a second murderous escapade, involving some of the same Idaho cowboys who had taken part in the Cow Creek affair. But, this next crime would only further deepen the mystery surrounding the disappearance of Mike Daggett and his family.

In those days, young Eugene Quilici and his wife, Maria, ran a saloon about a mile west of Imlay, Nevada—a remote little whistle stop, west of Winnemucca, on the railroad's main line. The couple were recent immigrants from Italy, who spoke very little English.

At about 10:00 P.M. on Friday, January 6, 1911, two men, wearing masks made out of flour sacks, entered the Quilicis' barroom. It was shortly before closing time, and the owners, husband and wife, were sitting at a table talking. Mrs. Quilici, who was pregnant, had been to Winnemucca that day where she had drawn $300 from a bank to pay off a debt.

The intruders commanded Eugene Quilici to get his hands up, but he hesitated a moment and then grabbed the pistol of one of the men and pushed him against the bar. Seeing this, the other masked man shot Quilici, hitting him in the shoulder. When Quilici tried to reach the swinging doors in the back of the place, the man shot a second time, and poor Quilici fell through the doors, dead, with a bullet in his back. His wife also ran for the door, screaming, and was gunned down, mortally wounded.

The man with whom Quilici had wrestled went into the back room where the Quilici's four-year old son, and an older boy—Mrs. Quilici's brother, Alesandro Lammori—had been sleeping. When the man pointed his pistol at Alesandro's head, the four-year old stood up in his bed, pleading with the robbers, "you killed Poppa, don't kill Uncle."[21]

Keeping an eye on the boys, the two intruders hurriedly ransacked the house. They found the $300 hidden under a pillow but, in searching Eugene Quilici's body on the floor, they overlooked about $400 he had in a trouser pocket. One of the men emptied the cash register of some small change, raising the floursack mask from his face as he worked. Then, having completed their foul work, the murderers took flight.

When word of the crime reached Winnemucca by telegraph, the Humboldt County Sheriff, Selah G. Lamb, left immediately for the scene, taking with him a Paiute Indian, named "Skinny" Pascal, who had the reputation of being one of the best trackers in the country. The sheriff had to release Pascal from jail, where he had been confined for a misdemeanor.

By the time Lamb and Pascal arrived at Imlay siding, the wounded Mrs. Quilici had been taken to the hospital at Winnemucca. Lamb and Constable Rich of Imlay formed a posse and, with "Skinny Pascal" leading, took the trail of the bandits, which led toward the Blakeslee ranch on the Humboldt River, a few miles away.

Cartridges and a mask were found along the trail and, shortly after this, a man was seen coming toward the posse, evidently looking for something he had dropped. The man freely identified himself as Nimrod R. Urie of Twin Falls, Idaho, and said that he and his partner were living at the Blakeslee place. Lamb arrested and handcuffed Urie, and took him along to the ranch. Here, Lamb ordered the prisoner to call his partner out, and, when this second man appeared, he was also arrested.

A search of the cabin produced the stolen money, weapons, and other evidence of the crime. The man arrested at the ranch refused to give his name, but, from a paper found on him, he was identified as J. Frank Tranmer, brother of Gay Tranmer, and stepfather of Frankie Dopp.

Citizens at Imlay told Lamb that Urie, the two Tranmer brothers, and Edward Diffendarfer had been camped at the Blakeslee ranch—ostensibly gathering wild horses in the region—since late September, shortly after they had been in Elko to give testimony regarding the Cow Creek encounter. In November, however, Gay had returned home to Idaho and, of late, Urie had been working in Winnemucca on the sewer system, and had been in that town on the day before the Quilicis were killed.

Mrs. Quilici had died soon after reaching Winnemucca, but not before giving a graphic description of the crime and the men involved. Based her testimony and on information gleaned from Lammori and other witnesses, Nimrod Urie was positively identified as the robber who had raised his mask while he was looting the cash register. Sheriff Lamb thought that a third bandit had remained outside while the robbery was in progress and, for a few days he jailed as a suspect, a certain Duncan, a hanger-on at May Slaughter's whorehouse at Imlay.

After Urie had been in the Humboldt County jail a short time, Lamb and the local district attorney confronted him with the stolen money, the mask found along the trail, the murder weapons and other articles found at the ranch. At this, the overwrought Urie broke down and told his story.

He admitted taking part in the crime, but said Frank Tranmer had planned it and had done all of the killing. He also claimed that Tranmer had threatened to kill him if he, Urie, didn't take part, and had gone so far as to tie his hands to the saddle on the way into Imlay to keep him from bolting.

Urie said that he had first gotten acquainted with Frank Tranmer the previous spring while running horses in Idaho, and next met him at Imlay when they all came there to catch wild horses. But, he didn't like the way Tranmer and Diffendarfer were acting, so he went to Winnemucca to get work on the sewer. Urie said that Ed Diffendarfer had not been involved in the crime.

Diffendarfer gave testimony at the preliminary hearing of Tranmer and Urie. He identified the guns found in the bandits' camp as a .30-40 caliber rifle belonging to Urie, and a .41 revolver of Tranmer's—these being the guns used in the murders according to Urie's confession. Diffendarfer admitted being in partnership with the other two in gathering horses and having been with them at their camp near Imlay up until a few weeks before the murders, when he had left to go to Dutch Flat, north of Winnemucca, to do assessment work on his mining claims.[22]

The arrest of Urie and Frank Tranmer, combined with the prompting of the Indian Office, resulted in the Elko County authorities making a more determined effort to get at the bottom of the Cow Creek mystery.

With the new year had come some changes in personnel. The former district attorney, E. J. L. Taber, had been elected district judge. James Dysart was the new district attorney; Joseph C. Harris was the new sheriff, who, after superceding Clark, had dismissed George Grimm, the deputy at Contact.

Judge Taber told the Indian Office that, until Lee's allegations appeared in the press, he hadn't been aware that many Idaho people thought white men might have killed Frank Dopp, as well as Mike Daggett and his entire family, or that the Nevada officers were being criticized for doing nothing. Taber said he had been relying on the story given in September by Gay Tranmer and the version reported to him by George Grimm, which was substantially as related by Tranmer and the men in his party.

The judge correctly pointed out that J. Frank Tranmer, who had been arrested with Nimrod Urie for the Imlay murders, was not the same person as Gay Tranmer, who had been involved in the Cow Creek affair. Frank was merely the stepfather of the boy, Dopp, who had been killed. Taber had heard a rumor that Gay had owed this boy two hundred dollars or more.

Taber promised that the new sheriff and district attorney would cooperate in solving "this business." The sheriff was going out to look at those trenches again and see if Mike Daggett's people were buried below the horse carcasses. He, like Lee, was apparently unaware that the pits had already been thoroughly excavated. C. H. Asbury, of the Carson Indian School—who obviously didn't trust the Elko authorities—suggested to his superiors that some special officer accompany the sheriff in looking at the trenches.[23]

On January 12, Judge Taber, District Attorney Dysart, along with G. A. Gutches—the investigator from Fort Hall—went to Winnemucca and interviewed Nimrod Urie, but were unable to get the prisoner to change the story he had been telling since May. He firmly reiterated that Gay Tranmer's party of buckaroos had been the ones attacked, and that they had neither stolen any horses nor killed any Indians.[24]

When T. Bailey Lee learned from Taber of the involvement of Frank Tranmer and Nimrod Urie in the Imlay murders, he was ecstatic. This prosecuting attorney, who liked to shoot from the hip, was now positive that both Frank and Gay Tranmer, Urie and:

> ...possibly Walter Sparks (nephew of former governor Sparks, and supposed to be the third man connected with the Imlay murder) and others were out stealing horses, and, coming upon Mike's people either tried to steal their horses, or feared exposure and killed the entire band along with...Dopp.

Gay Tranmer, who was reported to have left the area, was "as deep in it as anyone," and was "the kind of scoundrel that would turn state's evidence to save his neck."[25] Indeed, Gay had been absent in Nevada for a few months, but had by now returned to his ranch, as noted above.

Just a day after writing this letter, Lee was at the Twin Falls hospital, where he ran into Sarah P. Tranmer, the mother of Frank and Gay. The widow Tranmer, who was there nursing a sick man, "jumped" Lee for having slandered Gay, and assured him that her son and the others had been the ones attacked at Cow Creek.

Lee, of course, by then had learned of the Imlay murders, from Judge Taber, but he didn't tell Mrs. Tranmer that her son, Frank, had been jailed for them. The next day, after the news of the murders had appeared in the local papers, Lee went once again to the hospital where he eavesdropped on a conversation, in an adjoining room, between Mrs. Tranmer and two men. He overheard them speculating about possible court dates in Winnemucca, and that afternoon they all left the hospital, turning the sick man over to another nurse. There was a gathering of relatives at the house where Mrs. Tranmer was staying, and then she disappeared.

In his next letter on the subject, the cocky Lee wrote that Nimrod Urie would confess the whole "miserable business" with the Indians, if pressed, and that no time should be lost in apprehending Gay Tranmer. And, if the Elko officers would only dig in those horse pits, they would find the dead Indians, because only an "imbecile" would "suppose that a band of Indians could make such an attack as these men claim, kill one of their number and get away without some one knowing where they went."[26]

Amazingly, Lee also said that the black cowboy, Henry Harris, had been present at the gunfight with Mike's sons, and that one of the young women now missing was in love with Henry, and she would never have left the country without letting Henry know of it.

The next to offer an opinion on the Indian disappearance was the investigator from Fort Hall, G. A. Gutches. He had failed to locate Mike's family, but submitted a report of his findings on February 6, 1911.

Gutches accused Gay Tranmer and Urie of having made false statements at Elko. He said the "general opinion" was that "the Indians caught Tranmer's outfit stealing horses and [Tranmer and others] killed the Indians; later they killed the boy [Dopp], fearing he would give the crime away." It was "hardly possible that the Indians would remain in hiding so long."[27]

The new Elko sheriff had told Gutches that there was no record of Deputy Grimm having reported the affair to the officials of Elko County, or of anything having been done by the sheriff and district attorney at the time, or of their having had any knowledge of the affair until months later. The new sheriff and district attorney had said they didn't know of the pits until December 8.

Gutches complained that, although the alleged murder had taken place on public land, prosecution of the case belonged to the foot-dragging Nevada authorities. Being an innovative man, however, he suggested that the federal government might become involved by claiming that Mike's family, though not enrolled at the Fort Hall agency, were still wards of the government.

Gutches recommended trying to find evidence that would lead to the discovery of the Indians, or to the conviction of Gay's "gang" for their murder. This would include a thorough search in the vicinity of the alleged crime, after the snow melted in the spring. Also, the Girdners, who had moved to Washington state, should be interrogated to help solve the mystery.

Gutches had obviously talked at length with District Attorney Lee, and had heard his low opinion of the white cowboys. He said they had the reputation of being all-around bad men and horse thieves. Frank Tranmer and Urie were in jail at Winnemucca on murder charges; Gay Tranmer was under bond to appear before the district court at Twin Falls in February, for his having refused to pay Frankie Dopp's mother $150 due him in wages at the time of his death. Girdner was wanted for selling mortgaged property.

But, all of these accusations made by Lee, Gutches and the Indian Department would soon be discredited by the startling discovery that the missing Indians were still very much alive.

The next bloody chapter in the lamentable history of "Rock Creek Mike" Daggett opened a mere eleven days after the Quilici murders, when three prominent livestock operators—Peter Erramouspe, John B. Laxague and Harry Cambron—started together from Eagleville, California to check on their respective flocks and herds. Erramouspe and Laxague were Basque immigrants who had fulfilled the American dream, rising from humble beginnings as sheepherders to men of independent means. Cambron was the partner of Herbert Humphrey of Reno in the Humphrey-Cambron Cattle Company.

All three men, like others around Eagleville and in Surprise Valley, ran their livestock during the winter near High Rock Lake, on the verge of the Black Rock Desert. This area, in northern Washoe County, Nevada, was—and still is—one of the most isolated places in the West.

There had already been a series of blizzards that winter that had blanked the area with nearly three feet of snow. Breaking a trail on the ride into Nevada was slow going, but, on January 17, 1911, the stockmen arrived at

William Denio's sheep station, about 50 miles east of Eagleville. Here they met Bertrand "Dominic" Indiano, head camp tender for Erramouspe and Laxague, who had just come in from a sheep camp at Soldier Meadow, some nine miles distant. Indiano informed his employers of having seen the carcasses of three freshly skinned beeves while passing through Little High Rock Canyon, and of also seeing two horsemen near that place.

After spending a day with Denio and his wife in their small house, the three stockmen and Indiano set out on the morning of January 19, in fine weather, for the sheep camp at Soldier Meadow. They intended to investigate the cattle killings on the way. But, after leaving Denio's, the four were not heard from again, seemingly swallowed up by the desolate Nevada terrain.

Erramouspe and Laxague were married men, and Cambron had set a date to wed Laura Murphy of Surprise Valley, but, nonetheless, considerable time elapsed before any of their loved ones, associates or employees became alarmed enough to investigate their disappearance. Finally, the camp tenders at High Rock Lake sent men to search the trail to Denio's. These herders found no trace of the men, so Will Denio dispatched a rider bearing this ominous news to the wives. The messenger arrived at Eagleville on February 7, and, the next day, ten heavily armed riders set out in a snowstorm to seek the missing men.

There were theories that the stockmen might have perished in the cold, or from eating bad canned meat, or that, perhaps, outlaws operating along the Oregon border had killed them for their horses and equipment. But there were a few persons around Eagleville who thought Indians might be involved. A party of about nine, known to be "desperate characters," had recently been seen, camped in the same country which had absorbed the four stockmen. These Indians had placed signs on piled-up stones warning people not to follow them on penalty of death. It was also said that they had killed a boy some time ago.

After a hard ride, the searchers from Eagleville reached Denio's on February 10. They headed immediately for Little High Rock Canyon and, about a mile below the head of the canyon, they found where some cattle had been slain. Close by lay the carcasses of two emaciated Indian ponies that had been led into the brush and shot. Higher up the side of the canyon, under an overhang of rim rock, the searchers discovered several abandoned Indian wickiups made of willows. In a nearby cave, was found a small quantity of beef, cut into strips and jerked about ten days earlier.

No trace could be found of the missing men's horses, their outfit, or anything else of value, but the bodies of the men were finally discovered in the bed of the creek that runs through the canyon. It was a gruesome scene.

Cave and abandoned Indian camp in Little High Rock Canyon
(*Humboldt County Library, Winnemucca, Nevada*)

Frozen arms were extended above the bullet-ridden torsos, and fingers, noses and wounds had all been gnawed by mice. Some clothing had been removed from the bodies after death.

Nearby, it could be seen where the men had come down off the north rim of the canyon. The general opinion was that they must have suspected that something was wrong because, instead of entering the canyon on the normal trail, they had remained on its northern rim for some distance, and then descended to the bottom on a footpath which passed about a hundred yards west of the Indian camp.

Eight of the search party remained with the bodies, while Ben F. Cambron—the forty-year old manager of a Costantia, California ranch, and brother of the murdered Harry Cambron—hastened with another man back to Eagleville carrying the terrible news. From there, messages were sent to the Nevada state police in Carson City, and to the sheriffs of Washoe County, Nevada and Modoc County, California. The Washoe sheriff, Charles P. Ferrell, telegraphed Sheriff Lamb at Winnemucca, asking him to guard possible avenues of escape in his direction.

THE LAST BATTLE

Little High Rock Canyon, showing where the cattlemen's bodies were found. (*Humboldt County Library*)

A special train was chartered which carried authorities northward from Reno to Alturas, California, the railhead nearest the crime scene. Its passengers were the Washoe County coroner, Dr. Sydney K. Morrison; Sheriff Ferrell; Captain J. P. Donnelly, the newly-appointed superintendent of the Nevada State Police; and three of Donnelly's officers.

From Alturas, these Nevadans—now joined by Sheriff A. Elsy Smith of Modoc County—proceeded on horseback to Eagleville. Here a sled was obtained to take them to Little High Rock Canyon. So intense was the feeling against the murderers around Eagleville, according to a news report, that they might "never reach a jail if taken alive."[28]

Upon arrival at Little High Rock Canyon on February 15, Coroner Morrison had the frozen bodies separated, after which they were carried on stretchers for two miles through the rugged canyon, and then were taken by sleigh to Denio's camp. There, the coroner held his inquest and autopsy by candle light, in the snow, and with the temperature standing at five degrees below zero.

Morrison found that the men had received multiple gunshot wounds from

The cattlemen's bodies on stretchers
(*Humboldt County Library*)

a .30-30 rifle, and that two of them had also been shot in the head with a .32 caliber pistol, apparently to finish them off. Harry Cambron had been carrying such a pistol, the only weapon available to the four murdered men.

Pete Erramouspe's heavy black mustache had been removed with a knife, and his gold teeth had been knocked out. Indiano's left eye was gouged out, his upper lip and lower eyelids were gone, his cheek had been shot away and there was a gaping hole in the back of his head.

Both Captain Donnelly and Coroner Morrison agreed that the murders had been committed by a small band of Indians, whose tracks had been plainly seen going in the direction of the Black Rock Desert. These Indians had apparently ridden away on the fine horses of the ranchers, after shooting their own half-starved mounts. Other identifiable possessions taken by the Shoshoni included Cambron's pistol, an open-faced watch and a silver hunting-cased pocket watch.

A fellow named Otto D. Van Norman, who lived nearby in the canyon on a small ranch, was able to identify, in detail, the Indian band involved. He said there had been one old man, about 65 years old; three younger men; two adult women; a 17-year old girl, and three children ranging from ten to thirteen years of age. Van Norman said they had holed up in the canyon for the winter, and had been living by killing cattle belonging to outfits that had been unable to get them out before the storms. In late November, they had stolen some ammunition from Van Norman's house.

The accused Indians were, of course, Mike Daggett and family. The incident on Cow Creek, whatever its true nature might have been, had caused them to take flight and travel through Nevada, subsisting on stolen cattle and provisions. As best can be ascertained, they had first headed south to a point east of Ely, near the Utah border. Here they were involved in a fight with some whites during which one white man was shot, and some of Mike's band were hit with shotguns.

They had then journeyed westward, past Ely, Mount Hamilton, and Austin, to Wadsworth, near which place they stole a rifle from an employee of Cowle's Ranch. In July they had stopped at Albert Lay's ranch in the Jackson Mountains, and traded for some old harness. Later, an Indian man who was out hunting saw them running a band of horses in the western part of Humboldt County. The hunter had tried to ride up to them but one of Mike's sons, brandishing a rifle, had warned the man to keep his distance.

After this Mike may have taken his band as far west as Goose Lake, for it would later be remembered that they were seen in September coming from that direction through Surprise Valley, California. Some of the cowboys in the rescue party recalled that such a band of natives had stopped at Eagleville that month to buy supplies and had then headed east, toward Nevada.

It would also subsequently be learned that the Daggetts had spotted Indiano coming up the canyon on the day before the murders, and, seeing him return the next day with three more men, Mike and his older sons thought he was bringing law officers to arrest them. Accordingly, the Indian men had concealed themselves in the rocks and gunned the stockmen down as they passed. Then Mike's people had killed their own malnourished horses, and, taking the four belonging to their victims, they had left that night, packing what meat they could.[29]

Having completed his grisly work, Coroner Morrison took the bodies by sled to Eagleville. In a dispatch from there on the seventeenth, he gave the nation the first authentic news of the tragedy. Based on his report, Nevada's governor, T. L. Oddie, asked Senator George S. Nixon to see the President and obtain a cavalry troop to assist in the Indians' capture.[30]

State police superintendent Donnelly, and several of his troopers, remained at Denio's camp and organized a posse of 22 mounted men, most of them cowboy volunteers from around Eagleville and Denio's, recruited by Ben Cambron. But, these wranglers preferred to retain their independence, and refused to be deputized. Sheriffs Ferrell of Washoe County, and Smith of Modoc County also joined the group.

On the night before the posse left, only a few men could be accommodated in Denio's small three-room house, and in its adjoining small shed. The others slept outside in the cold, huddled close to blazing sagebrush fires. Then, early on February 16, they arose, chilled and stiff, to take up the trail. Still plainly marked in the snow, it would lead them down the canyon, across the dried-up High Rock Lake and onto the Black Rock desert, one of the roughest and most desolate regions in the West.

That first day the posse only traveled as far as Soldier Meadow where they laid over to shoe some horses, obtain supplies and organize a pack train. Then, on February 18, the men rode out, fully prepared for the cold of a northern Nevada winter.

The fugitives' track went eastward through the southern end of the Pine Forest Range and then to Paiute Meadows, on the east side of the Black Rock Range. Here, the posse stayed at one of the ranches of the huge Pacific Livestock Company owned by Henry Miller and Charles Lux. Nearby, a place was seen where Mike's band had butchered a beef and camped for about a week.

On February 20, Donnelly divided the posse. Frank Perry and others followed the Indian spoor—fording Quinn River and getting wet in the bitter cold—while the pack train and most of the men went north to spend the night at Miller and Lux's home ranch, at Quinn River Crossing. Donnelly wanted to obtain fresh horses and cross the river there.

That day, a messenger sent by Donnelly arrived at Amos (Cane Springs), north of Winnemucca, the telephone exchange nearest to the posse. From there, the messenger contacted Sheriff Lamb in Winnemucca, saying that the Indians had crossed the Black Rock Desert well below Quinn River Crossing and were believed to be in the southern end of the Jackson Mountains.

Lamb arranged with the Western Pacific Railroad for a special car to take him, his brother "Kise" Lamb and the trailer, "Skinny" Pascal, along with their horses, to Sulphur siding, the nearest railroad point to the Jackson Mountains. Before leaving Winnemucca in the early morning of February 21, Lamb said he didn't intend making an independent effort to capture the fugitives, but he would simply act as a pilot for the Donnelly posse, as he and Pascal were familiar with every foot of that region.

Arriving at Sulphur that same morning, Lamb and his two men left immediately for Lay's Willow Creek ranch, about 25 miles northeast of

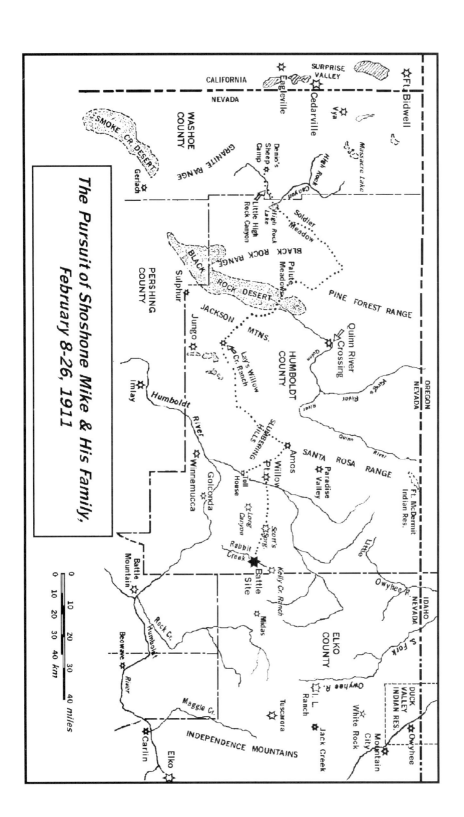

Sulphur, where the posse was waiting for him. At Lay's, Lamb found Donnelly with all his men, the superintendents's party having rejoined those who had kept on the trail. A few of the Eagleville cowboys had gone home, unhappy with Captain Donnelly's leadership. Donnelly told Lamb that the fugitives were probably headed for the Duck Valley Indian Reservation, but were making slow progress because of worn-out horses.

None of their nightly camps had been more than twelve miles apart. All had been situated in natural depressions, and rocks had been thrown up around them to make rude forts. At several, remnants were found of the murdered men's clothing, indicating that the Indian women were altering the garments to fit their men. Near one camp, a sheepherder told the posse of having seen a saddled horse, running loose, that matched the description of the one Harry Cambron had been riding.

On February 22, Sheriff Ferrell of Washoe County, and state policeman Frank F. Buck left the posse and rode to Jungo, Nevada, to catch a train into Winnemucca. Ferrell intended raising a second posse and riding north from Elko to intercept the fugitives before they could reach Duck Valley.

That same day, Donnelly divided the men into two parties, and each made separate sweeps eastward, through the sand-laden Slumbering Hills. A campsite was found where the Indians had killed a horse and a dog. In late afternoon, after a ride of about 60 miles, the two parties rejoined and camped at Amos. The trail was followed again on February 23, as it led southward past Willow Point, until, some twelve miles north of Winnemucca, all trace of it was lost.

Most of the posse men camped nearby at Toll House, while a few went into Winnemucca for supplies or to have their horses re-shod. Sheriff Lamb also came in, and learned that Sheriff Ferrell and Sgt. Buck had just left by train for Elko to get up their posse.

Before leaving that day, Ferrell had questioned Nimrod Urie and Frank Tranmer at the county jail, where they were awaiting trial for the Quilici murders. From them he had gotten detailed descriptions of Mike Daggett and his people that conformed to those of the group the posse had been following. Tranmer said he had known old Mike for at least 15 years and that Mike's advanced age had caused his somewhat heavy-set frame—generally clothed in ragged overalls—to become stooped, his legs slightly bowed and his face wrinkled.[31]

By Friday, February 24, the net was beginning to close around Mike's people. In response to reports that some of them had been seen near the I. L. ranch, about 30 miles northwest of Tuscarora, Constable Young of the latter place left that morning with six miners and cowboys. Also, the Bureau of Indian Affairs had ordered out a mounted squad of native police from Duck Valley to scour the country to the southwest of that reservation.

That same day, Sheriff Lamb was notified by telephone that a prospector had discovered the trail of the fugitive Indians in Clover Valley, northeast of Winnemucca. Lamb at once notified Captain Donnelly at the Toll House, and Donnelly, with part of the posse, hurried to Golconda, a little village nearest the reported location.

The prospector's report would prove false, but Lamb got a telephone call in the afternoon from Willow Point that would put the posse back on the right trail. Another miner had seen some Indians camped in Long Canyon, about 25 miles north of Winnemucca, whose horses resembled those of the murdered stockmen.

On Saturday morning, February 25, Lamb sent Deputy Sheriff Nofsinger by train to convey this latest intelligence to Donnelly, who had spent the night at Golconda with his men. Donnelly set out in a wagon with a small force to investigate. Arriving at the campsite, they found Constable Charlie Byrnes, of Paradise Valley, and his deputy, Merl Prussia, who had also come there at Lamb's request. A smoldering fire indicated that the Indians had left only a few hours earlier, and, in the camp was found a pair of *chaparreras* that had belonged to Harry Cambron.

The trail led east, but, since it was too late to follow it that night, Donnelly took his party back to Willow Point, and recalled the rest of his men from Golconda. That evening the posse men camped at the S. Stewart Ranch, four miles east of Willow Point, while Donnelly remained at the latter place. In a phone call to Sheriff Lamb, designed to deceive Lamb and ensure that he didn't get any reward money, Donnelly said the camp in Long Canyon had not been that of Mike's Indians.

Meanwhile, Constable Young's group had found only one Indian to the northwest of Tuscarora, whom they ridden down upon, brandishing their weapons. The frightened man—no fool—surrendered first, and then identified himself as a Duck Valley policeman.

Sheriff Ferrell and Sgt. Buck had organized their posse at Elko, comprised of themselves and three county lawmen. They had gone to Tuscarora and, on February 25, had ridden about 50 miles north to Jack Creek in a blinding snowstorm, without having found any evidence of the Daggett band. But Ferrell planned to go out on the following day and head them off in the White Rock Country. A bit of a braggart, he telegraphed back, "I want to add one Indian scalp to my collection and I am going to get it."[32]

Everyone following the unfolding story sensed that a showdown would soon occur, what with four groups of lawmen within an 80-mile radius of the fugitives. With prescient accuracy, one newsman guessed that, because the Eagleville men had refused to be deputized, there would likely be "a disposition on the part of many of them to wreak summary justice on the Indians."[33]

Sunday, February 26, was the eighteenth day of the pursuit, for those who had started from Eagleville. At daylight, most of the posse left the Stewart ranch, under command of Sgt. P.M. Newgard of the state police. With Newgard were Sgt. Charles H. Stone; Sheriff Smith; Ben Cambron; Otto Van Norman; the Indian trailer, Skinny Pascal; Eagleville buckaroos Edward Hogle, Warren Fruit, William Parsons, Henry Hughes, Mort West, and Jack Ferguson; an Eagleville carpenter, George Holmes; an Eagleville teamster, Frank Perry; a Gerlach, Nevada miner, Joseph Reeder; and Merl W. Prussia, deputy sheriff and butcher from Paradise Valley, who had joined up at the Stewart ranch, as requested by Captain Donnelly.

Donnelly started a bit later from Willow Point, accompanied by Constable Charles T. Byrnes of Paradise Valley, whom Donnelly had also asked to come along with the posse.

On the previous day, the fugitives' trail had been traced to the summit of the mountains, about ten miles to the northeast of Willow Point. Now, Newgard's group picked up that track again near Scott's Springs, whence it was followed southeasterly. Along the way a dead horse was found with the brand "B"—the same as had been on several of the horses found dead in the camp at Little High Rock Canyon.

At mid-day, after a 20-mile ride, and not long after crossing the summit of the mountains, the posse was about eight miles west of the Bliss Kelly Creek ranch. The riders had just rounded a little butte on their left into more open country, when several horses were seen ahead. Within minutes, rising smoke was also noted. Then the posse came in full view of Mike's band, some 500 yards distant.

The Indians were just making camp in the small ravine formed by Rabbit Creek. A pot of water was on a fire, around which sagebrush, saddles and blankets had been piled up as a windbreak. Some of the men were dozing around the fire and the horses had been turned out to graze. The site was on a rolling slope, rising to the north, bare and rocky except for sagebrush and an occasional scrubby juniper. There was very little cover for making a stand.

One of the earliest reports of the ensuing confrontation would state that, as soon as the Indians were sighted, Captain Donnelly peremptorily ordered a volley that felled two Indians, and caused the rest to seek concealment. But, in fact, Donnelly had not yet arrived on the scene. Sheriff Ferrell—who was also absent—later said it was Ben Cambron who first jumped off his horse and began pumping lead. Still others blamed the Indians for starting the shooting, at long range. But, in later sworn testimony, posse members would tell the story of the fight as follows.

A woman ran down the ravine toward the camp, raising the alarm. Four Indian men ran out to have a look, and then turned and scurried back. A cowboy shouted, "Hurry up, hurry up, they have got their guns."[34] Sergeant Newgard galloped his men to within 300 yards, and then had them dismount and form a skirmish line abreast. As the whites strode toward the camp and took up positions, the Indian men ran northeastwardly about 200 yards, onto a hill, as though they were looking for a place from which to make a fight.

The Indian trailer, Skinny Pascal, was on the extreme northern end of the skirmish line. Newgard passed the word to him to act as interpreter and ask the Indians to surrender. Most of the posse would later insist that Pascal did this, speaking both in English and Shoshoni, before any firing began.

According to Pascal, as he rode out to comply, Mike's three adult sons dashed toward their camp, while Mike ran in an opposite direction and hid himself in the brush. Pascal started after Mike, and when he got closer to where the old man had been lost to view, Mike suddenly arose and fired a shot at him with a rifle, but, having missed, dropped to the ground again. The tracker slipped from his horse and, when Mike exposed himself again, Pascal fired twice, thinking that one of the bullets had struck home. By now, Newgard had ordered the posse to start shooting and, within moments, another Indian man was struck down by a hail of bullets.

Meanwhile, the two unharmed Indian men, and the rest of Mike's family had abandoned their camp and were sneaking eastwardly down the draw. One of the Indian women ran toward the horses, and tried to drive them in the same direction, but the order was given to the posse to shoot the animals. After several were killed, the woman fled to join the rest of her family.

In response to Ben Cambron's request for some men to head off the fleeing survivors, Ferguson, Hughes, Pascal, Ed Hogle, West and Holmes crossed over the wash and followed them down the ridge—under fire all the time, so they said. They cornered the remnants of the family in the bed of another little wash off Rabbit Creek, about a mile below the camp, As the Indians took cover in the brush, the six cowboys positioned themselves around the wash to hold them there.

By now, Captain Donnelly and Constable Charlie Byrnes had arrived at the Indian campsite. Donnelly apparently took charge but, uncertain as to whether Mike and his son were dead or merely wounded, he was content to let his men sit and watch the area. After a time, Byrnes, Merl Prussia, Warren

Fruit, and Frank Perry advanced cautiously toward the camp, on its south side. As they got near, Mike showed himself and took a pot shot, which allowed Byrnes and his men to pepper the brush where he lay with gunfire.

Everyone stayed put for another ten minutes and then finally closed in on the camp. The body of Mike's oldest son, Jim, was found several dozen yards from the campfire. After being shot, Mike had crawled through the brush, trailing blood, and was discovered, dying, about a hundred yards to the north. His .40-82 caliber Winchester rifle was close at hand.

With considerable difficulty, Ben Cambron restrained the impulse to finish Mike off, and avenge his brother's death. Instead, he merely removed the cartridge from the old man's gun, and laid the weapon out of reach. According to Joe Reeder, as Mike gasped his last words—"Me Shoshone Indian"—Frank Perry took from his pockets a knife and $26 in cash.

By this time, the fight had gone on for about two hours. The men surrounding the remainder of Mike's family, about a mile down slope, sent a request to Donnelly, at the camp, asking for more men. Accordingly, Donnelly ordered Sgt. Newgard to go down and lend a hand, taking everyone except Constable Byrnes, William Parsons, Ben Cambron and Sheriff Smith. Cambron stayed behind because his horse had run off, and in Smith's case, he insisted that he was not under Donnelly's command. Donnelly, himself, also remained at the camp, ostensibly to take care of such important details as having the Indian horses rounded up.

On the chase down the wash, one of Mike's boys—probably Jake—had dropped his shotgun in the brush, having been severely wounded in the arm. Thus, as would later be learned, the surviving natives only had one gun—the .32 caliber Savage pistol taken from Harry Cambron's body at Little High Rock. Although several of the posse would claim that one of the Indian women used this weapon, Charlie seems to have been the only one to fire it.

Ever since being surrounded, the two Indian men had kept hidden in the sagebrush, while the women and young boys taunted the whites and shot arrows at them. But the cowboys hadn't taken the bait, and kept their stations surrounding the wash. They took pains to "holler" from one to another not to shoot the women, whom they thought understood what was being said, and that was why they were taking no precautions to protect themselves.

When the reinforcements finally arrived from the camp above, Sergeant Newgard took command and decided to force the issue. He started the men toward the wash and, as they advanced in a semicircle, some of them told the Indians to come out and they wouldn't be hurt. The only response was from a woman who answered, contemptuously, "Go back you sons of bitches."[35]

The women launched even more arrows as the men approached. Mike's wife, Jennie, was directly in front of Ed Hogle of Eagleville. A short distance away, to attract attention, a teen-age girl kept running back and forth out of the wash toward the posse, brandishing a crude spear made of sheep shears fastened to a wooden handle. Believing that the girl was advising her brothers of their whereabouts as they approached, some of the cowboys tried, unsuccessfully, to catch her.

As Ed Hogle advanced in a crouch, dodging arrows, he fired several rifle shots into the brush where the Indian men lay hidden. In his eagerness, he got about ten feet ahead of his comrades, almost to the edge of the wash. Perhaps he had been deceived by the women's actions into believing that the men were out of ammunition, or that both of them were dead.

But Hogle had made a deadly mistake. Suddenly, Charlie arose from the wash and fired at the young cowboy. As Hogle's hand flew to his breast he cried, "My God boys, I have been shot."[36] Taking a few steps back, he fell to the ground and expired. The men nearest to Hogle fired a volley into the brush, causing Charlie to jump up and start running down the wash. Another volley lifted him off his feet and slammed him face down, dead. Mike's wife Jennie was also fatally wounded by those volleys, and Jake was killed.

One news account asserted that, at the time of Hogle's death only three of the natives had fallen, but, after he was killed, "volley after volley was fired, and it was with difficulty that the leaders restrained the men from exterminating the whole band."[37] Whatever the truth may have been, the shot that killed Hogle was the last one fired by the natives.

And so, after three hours, the fight was over. Scattered about in the bottom of the wash lay six Indians, dead or dying, all riddled with bullets. Jake and Charlie had fallen close together; fifteen feet farther down from them were two dead boys, about 10 and 12 years old, and, still farther on were two adult women—Jennie and one of Mike's daughters. Counting Mike and Jim, who had been killed earlier near the camp, a total of eight natives had been struck down.

Aside from Hogle's death, the only damage done to any of the posse was a steel-headed arrow that had struck George Holmes in the chest, merely puncturing his coat lapel. He had reportedly smiled, pulled it out and said he would keep it as a souvenir.

The Indian survivors were huddled nearby, trying to hide in the brush. There were four of them—the teen-aged girl who had shown such grit with her spear, a boy, aged about six, and two girls, ages four and eighteen months, the latter having been carried across Nevada in a basket on the backs of the two older women.

As the cowboys approached, the youngsters threw rocks at them. The teen-aged girl still had the spear in her hand, and when anyone went toward her she pointed the weapon at them in a threatening manner. But the cowboys soon disarmed her, after which she took the infant girl in her arms, sat down on the ground next to Jennie, who was about to die, and, hugging the old woman, began wailing a kind of death song.

Still defiant, the six-year old boy ran down the wash, followed closely by Jack Ferguson on his horse. Ferguson caught and restrained the boy—but only after being hit with numerous rocks and getting kicked in the shins. The cowboy threw his young captive over the saddle and jumped on, but, while he was reaching for the reins, the boy whacked him fiercely on the wrists. And, in a final venting of his frustration, the youngster tried to beat his own head violently against the pommel of the saddle.

A look around the campsite and the locale of the final stand revealed plenty of evidence to prove that the Indians had murdered the stockmen. Harry Cambron's Waltham watch and his boots were found, as well as the checkbooks of Cambron and Pete Erramouspe. Of the half-dozen horses recovered—all in poor condition—three had belonged to the stockmen.

It isn't clear just how many guns the Indians possessed. In addition to Cambron's .32 Savage pistol, there was a shotgun and Mike's .40-82 Winchester rifle. And, according to the statements of the various posse members, there may have been two other rifles—a .38-55 caliber Winchester and a .30-30, but, if these weapons ever existed, both later vanished.

The cowboys also collected bows and arrows, several war drums, tomahawks and a feathered headdress that had belonged to Mike. The tomahawks were two feet long, with heads made of sheep shears. The yellow and green designs painted on the tomahawks, drums and weapons, indicated to the whites that the Indians had been on the warpath.

A plentiful supply of cartridges was discovered in the Indian camp, but there was very little food. And, Mike's people—both the quick and the dead—wore clothing that was in rags. The children had on outfits made over from the clothing taken from the murdered stockmen.

After coming down to the scene of the final stand and taking a look, Donnelly sent a messenger to the Kelly Creek ranch, six miles away, asking for a team and wagon. When it arrived, about dark, the Indians' possessions, Ed Hogle's body and the young prisoners were placed in it and everyone went to the ranch for the night. The Indian bodies were left where they lay.

For the Eagleville cowboys, it was a mournful thing to be riding alongside a wagon in which their dead comrade lay, and to listen to the young Indians wailing a monotonous lament as they sat in the box next to his corpse.

Perhaps the wranglers remembered how eagerly Hogle had joined the posse after seeing the barbarities that Mike's people had inflicted on the dead stockmen. And, realizing that the deceased was to have married a young woman of Eagleville within a few weeks no doubt added to the general melancholy.

Frank Perry recalled an incident that had occurred that morning, just after setting out. Hogle's saddle had turned and skinned him up a bit, prompting him to remark, "I guess I'll get mine today; I'm getting a damned good start."[38] Hogle had been a close friend of Henry Cambron, and it was thought to be a bitter irony that he had been killed by a bullet from Cambron's gun.

At the Kelly Creek ranch, Hogle's body was laid out in a back room. In a larger room, bedding was placed on the floor by the fireplace for the children. A man was sent to North's ranch, thirteen miles away, to telephone Golconda and summon Sheriff Lamb and James Buckley, the county coroner. But the Golconda telephone office was closed for night, so word of the day's events didn't reach Winnemucca until early the following morning.

While at the Kelly Creek ranch that evening, Donnelly asked a Shoshoni cowboy to try and get the young Indian woman to tell her story. But the girl refused, berating the buckaroo for not having come to the aid of her people, so that they might have killed more of the white men. She terminated the interview by removing her moccasins and throwing them in the man's face.

The next morning, February 27, efforts to induce the girl to talk were renewed and, finally, she spoke of the crimes that had been attributed to her family. In the coming weeks, she would be interrogated a number of times, giving the Indian side of the story. These various interrogations contained disparities, some of which were likely attributable to the interpreters used.

In this first interview, the girl confirmed that Mike was her father, and the other dead adults her brothers and sister. She admitted that Mike and his sons had killed the four stockmen, and provided details of how they were ambushed. The young woman also conceded that her family had killed Frankie Dopp in Elko County the previous May, and then had buried the horses to make people think that white men had committed the crime.

The girl went on to reveal other crimes about which nothing had previously been known. She said they had killed a Chinese man for his money, somewhere near the California border, before they killed the stockmen, but they found only four dollars on him. This murder had been partly verified by the discovery of a queue among the effects of the Indians in their camp. The girl also told of killing three white men at various places, but she didn't know just where.

About noon, Sheriff Lamb arrived at Kelly Creek, having been on a wild

Stacked bodies of Mike and his family
(*Humboldt County Library*)

goose chase in another direction, thanks to Donnelly's deceitful telephone call. Now, he and the posse left for the scene of the battle to gather up the Indian bodies and take them to Golconda for an inquest. They had just started out when they met the county coroner, James Buckley.

The coroner decided that the Indian remains should be buried on the spot, and said he expected the posse to do it. But Sheriff Lamb said no, those boys had done more than their share. So, the remains of Mike and his family were piled in a heap near the place where the last stand had been made, and Buckley returned to Golconda, where he arranged for two men to come out and dig a large grave. The ground being frozen to a considerable depth, the men used dynamite to blast a hole. All of the bodies were thrown into it and a tall pole was erected so that the grave might be located, if needed.

While the rest of the lawmen and posse remained at the Kelly Creek Ranch for another night, Skinny Pascal returned to Winnemucca. There, he became the center of attention for being the first posse man to give an "authentic" account of the battle. He was also called a hero for having been the first to go under fire, and for having killed Mike. The local paper that day

Posse members at Golconda
(*Humboldt County Library*)

was exultant about the results of the fight, proclaiming that, "Fittingly and fearfully was the fiendish crime of the Indian renegades avenged."[39]

The posse left Kelly Creek ranch early on February 28 with the four captives and Hogle's body. The young Indian woman, a "demon," fought the guards in the wagon along the way. When they arrived that afternoon in Golconda, the little village was crowded with throngs of the curious, its population augmented by people from Winnemucca and other places. Some in the crowd were disappointed that the dead Indians hadn't been brought in for them to gawk at.

Hogle's body—wrapped in canvas, clothed as when he fell, chaps and all—was removed from the spring wagon and, within the hour, two coroner's inquests were begun—one over his remains, and another to inquire into the deaths of the eight Indians.

While the posse members gave their testimony, the prisoners were placed in the village's little box-like jail. The teenaged girl, dressed in a coarse cloth dress of shapeless design, shrank into a corner, where she kept her long hair and a blanket in front of her face to evade the gaze of the curious crowd. The little ones followed suit by covering up their heads with blankets.

Local Shoshoni women were permitted to enter the jail to give clothes, food and other items for the care for the prisoners. The teen-aged girl asked one of them for a pair of scissors so that she might cut off her long hair, as a sign of mourning for her dead family. Her request was refused for fear that she might try to kill herself, and the little ones in her care. She told most of her story to one of the women, who concluded that she was a Bannock, and couldn't speak the Shoshoni tongue.

After their testimony was taken in the two inquests, the men of the posse were allowed to go about their business, and they evidently spent the remainder of their time at Golconda unwinding in the saloons and swapping stories of the chase and fight.

And in mutual backbiting.

The Eagleville boys expressed complaints about the delays Donnelly and his state police had caused during the pursuit across Nevada, by their insistence on staying at the Miller and Lux ranches, well off the trail, when their pack train had adequate bedding and food for both men and horses. They also said that Skinny Pascal had been of little use, and that talk of his native trailing skill was a fairy tale. Ben Cambron was given credit for keeping the posse on the trail, and being its *de facto* leader. Pascal was even accused of retreating soon after the fight started.

Sheriff Smith of Modoc said his Eagleville boys were always in the forefront of the fight. But Smith himself was accused of using a loose saddle as an excuse to lag behind as soon as the posse came within sight of the Indian camp, and of not having reappeared until the battle was nearly ended.

There were also attempts to lionize poor dead Ed Hogle. One fanciful report said that, "On the first hail," the Eagleville cowboys "gave a warlike yell and spurred their horses on to the charge, accompanied by Donnelly's men, who could not restrain them." Hogle had ridden "on far ahead, firing his rifle repeatedly and dropping the nearest buck." The Indians replied with a scattering fire and, as Hogle fell from the saddle, "the Shoshoni became maddened with the craze of battle." With Hogle dead, this report said, Donnelly managed to persuade the cowboys to open out in a skirmish line and take it easier. "Then followed such exhibitions of sharpshooting as have not been seen since the Boers cut down the British on the Modder river."[40]

Even Sheriff Ferrell—who was, at the time of the battle, far to the north—glamorized Hogle, crediting him with having shot old Mike from a distance of 150 yards. Then, Ferrell claimed, Hogle had run forward gleefully, only to have Mike rise up on one elbow and shoot him.

There were other stories told about the fight. In the wash, at the final stand, it was said, the fugitives did a war dance to the staccato sound of a

THE LAST BATTLE

sheepskin drum being beaten by one of the women, the men's faces decorated with war paint. Then, when they were surrounded, the Indians, men and women alike, put up a terrific battle to the death, even the youngest children helping in the struggle by handling the cartridges.

Although Captain Donnelly hadn't been present at the final stand, he would later say that the women were shot down with as little compunction as the males, since they had fought no less fiercely. And, the killing of the two young boys couldn't have been avoided, since they had gotten into the thick of the fight. At one time, Donnelly said, the Indians placed the boys' bodies in front of them as protection against the bullets of the posse.

The reports of both inquests that were begun in Golconda would be published a few days later. The one concerning Hogle concluded that he had died from a gunshot wound at the hand of a member of Old Mike's band, and that the teen-aged girl had been instrumental in the death, since she had induced Hogle to come within range of the Indian man's pistol.[41]

In the case of the death of Mike and his family, the jury concluded that Captain J. P. Donnelly and his posse had been "justified in their actions,"[42] and that the women and children had been accidentally killed when they got into the line of fire. In their statements to the jury, the state policemen had taken great pains to mention that the Indians had frequently been asked to surrender, and had responded each time with shots.

This latter inquest report doesn't give the names of the two dead young boys, and it assigns Mike's other dead offspring names that seem to have been concocted out of thin air. The young woman it calls Mary, and gives her age as 17. The men—Charlie, Jim and Jake—are dubbed "Big Cupena," "Disenda," and "Kinnan," ages 25, 33 and 23 respectively.

Most of those who had taken part in the bloody showdown at Rabbit Creek left Golconda on Number 3, the evening passenger train for Winnemucca and Reno. While waiting in the depot before boarding, the defiant little Indian boy, who had been so hard to catch, made one last attempt to fight his captors. Sheriff Ferrell had leaned his rifle, empty of ammunition, against a counter. The boy eyed the gun intently, then, fancying himself unobserved, crept stealthily toward it. When the sheriff picked up the rifle, the little would-be warrior jumped back and played possum again.

Hogle's body also left on this same train, in the care of undertakers. At Reno, it would be taken charge of by his brother, to be buried in his mother's hometown of Anderson, California. Business associates of the murdered Cambron, paid all expenses.

Coroner Buckley collared Frank Perry and several other cowboys, before letting them board Number 3, and made them produce fifty dollars they had taken from the bodies of the Indians. The wranglers had spent the money for drinks in Golconda, but they somehow managed to scrounge enough cash from their friends to pay the coroner. Buckley intended using the money to defray the Indian burial expenses—the dynamite bill, one supposes.

As the train pulled out of Golconda, and again during the stop at Winnemucca, the men of the posse received tremendous ovations from crowds of citizens that had gathered to see them. All of the men were later paid a share of the rewards that had been offered for the capture of Mike's "gang." In June, Captain Donnelly distributed $3,143 given by the Humphrey-Cambron Cattle Company and the widows of Peter Erramouspe and John B. Laxague. And, in July, California authorities paid $75 apiece to Ed Hogle's mother, the three state police officers, Sheriff Smith, Merl Prussia, Skinny Pascal, and the several cowboys from California. It is unlikely that the $5,000 offered by the state of Nevada was ever paid.[43]

The men of the posse also kept, as souvenirs of the fight, all of the artifacts gathered up at the Indian camp—two drums, bows and arrows, tomahawks, and the spear the girl had used. Mike's brilliantly fashioned war bonnet was taken home by Sheriff Smith. Reportedly, he refused an offer of $100 for the headdress, saying he would display it at the California state fair, and perhaps also at the upcoming world's fair in San Francisco.

Crowds of inquisitive citizens were at the station when the train bearing the Shoshoni survivors arrived at Reno. Sheriff Ferrell took his prisoners in a closed carriage to the county jail, where he placed them in a basement cell. Although warm, the tiny cubicle's only comforts were some bench-like hammocks, strapped to the walls.

At first, getting the captives to talk proved fruitless; none of them paid the slightest attention to questions. When no whites were visible to them, they could be overheard chattering animatedly, the young woman laughing and playing with the children. But, when any visitor came down the stairs and peered through the bars at them, the four became silent and almost motionless. After having been caged up for a few days, they were reported to be "restless as a group of eaglets."

When one reporter saw them, the infant was asleep, swaddled in layers of garments on a hammock. Nearest the bars, the nine-year old girl sat silently, like an image of Buddha, a brown rag thrown over her head and shoulders. The teen-aged girl sat with a blank expression on her face, and an old gray blanket thrown around her, which she regulated so as to make a curtain to protect the six-year old boy. The boy, however, brazenly exposed his head and stared, round-eyed, at visitors.

Sheriff Ferrell with three of the surviving children
(Nevada Historical Society)

When the Washoe County district attorney decided not to prosecute the young woman for murder, the county probation officer began looking for someone to take charge of the survivors. C. H. Asbury, superintendent of the nearby Stewart Indian School, was reluctant to take them without Indian Office authority. And, because of the young woman's vengeful anger, Captain Donnelly thought it would not be safe to place her in a school.

One newspaper editor thought the "entire covey" should be sent to the Indian college in Pennsylvania. It was a reproach on American civilization, he said, "that these young Indians should be in the condition of close cousins to savage wildcats." Why hadn't they been educated at that expensive school on the Duck Valley Indian Reservation, which had seven teachers for only 80 pupils? The government had appropriated enough money to board every one of them "at a swell hotel and give them an auto drive daily."[44]

While waiting for a solution, Sheriff Ferrell treated his charges well, giving them good food, with plenty of milk for the baby. He and visitors also brought them candy and fresh fruit. Clean clothes were provided by local mothers, both Paiute and white, and Ferrell hired a woman who could speak

Shoshoni to scrub the prisoners up. The baths prompted a local newsman to comment that Mike's children were not only being restrained in their freedom for the first time in their lives, but also had received another novelty at the hands of the white man—"the ignominy of a modern ablution."[45]

After a week, the young woman had begun to thaw out a bit, so Ferrell arranged for a certain Colonel J. W. Reddington to interview her. The colonel had been an army scout and claimed to know a "smattering" of Indian languages. He said the girl used both Bannock and Shoshone words, and he understood her to say her name was O-luk, which meant Snake. The old scout said she was a fatalist, and didn't care what happened to her, except for the sake of the infant girl, for whom she showed wild affection.

A few days later, "Captain Dave," chief of the Paiutes, also interrogated Snake. He used doughnuts, candy and apples to loosen her tongue, and learn a few more details of her family's history. Dave said that she spoke a jumbled mixture of the Shoshoni and Ute languages, and that she had expressed neither sorrow, nor justification for the killings.

Meanwhile, the story of the fight with Mike Daggett's family was being hailed by newspapers all across the country as having been "the last of the Indian wars." Several urgent inquiries were received asking on what terms and conditions the four captives might be secured to play parts in a moving picture, or perhaps in a vaudeville show, depicting the chase by the posse and the battle at Rabbit Creek.[46]

At this time it was believed that the children had two aunts living on the Fort Hall reservation, and an uncle, "Salmon River Jim"—a "known outlaw" who was still "at large in the Contact [Nevada] country."[47] Sheriff Ferrell expressed fears that Jim might incite the Shoshoni to go on the warpath to revenge Mike's death, but old Jim was reported to be peacefully working in the hay fields for the O'Neill-Capell Cattle Company north of Wells, and was vouched for by James P. O'Neill. Furthermore, Jim was quoted as saying that Mike had been an all-around bad man who had gotten what he deserved. Jim, a Shoshoni, said he was not even of the same tribe as Mike, a Bannock.

Harry Preacher, the leader of the Shoshoni around Wells, Nevada also stated that Mike was a Bannock, and that the Shoshoni were pleased to know that he was dead, as they thought he had murdered several of their tribesmen some time ago.

There was another brief "Salmon River Jim" scare on May 30 when John B. Hoover, superintendent of the Fort McDermit Indian School, reported that Jim and a party of six other men and women had been seen, armed and painted for the war path, seeking to avenge the death of Mike's family. This story was greatly overdone by the newspapers, but was soon discredited, the natives in question having been identified as a hunting party.

Hoover was chastised for the false report, but he reminded his superiors—as he had in February—that if the Indian field force and local authorities had taken action on his November report of the sighting of Mike's people at Cedarville, the murder of the four Basque stockmen and a Chinese man might have been prevented.[48]

On April 25, C. H. Asbury, of the Carson Indian School, interviewed the girl Snake at length, in company with Mary Austin, a young Shoshone woman and former student at the school. Asbury thought Snake to be hardly more than 15-years old, and he saw no reason for the fear expressed by the state officers that she might commit some crime. It was natural, he said, that she should have been wild after having seen eight members of her family killed, including her father and mother.

The girl was now smiling, but remained somewhat stoic. She spoke in detail of her people's movements from the time they had killed Frank Dopp. But first, she set the record straight about her identity. Her name, she said, was Henie, not Snake. Snake was her older sister who had been killed in the fight. The six-year old boy was named Cleve, while the younger girl was called Hattie. The baby, about 18 months old, hadn't yet been named.

Henie recited a version of the previous year's skirmish in Elko County that differed from her earlier interviews. She claimed all the trouble had started when one of her brothers, Jack, was driving their horses to camp. The boy was shot by a white man, unknown to them, and his leg was broken so badly that the wound resulted in his death shortly afterward.

Under the anger caused by this unwarranted attack, her other brothers went out, shot Frank Dopp and buried his body. That same night her people stole some horses and left the area. But Henie insisted that they had not killed and buried any horses.

The fugitives had worked their way gradually westward, avoiding other people, stealing beef and taking food as needed from sheep or cattle camps. In this way, they traveled all the way to California's Sacramento River, where they found abundant fruit in the orchards and melons in the fields, to which they helped themselves. In late autumn, when they came back across the Sierra Nevada Mountains to Nevada, most of their horses weakened and died in bucking the deep snows. Finally, they reached Little High Rock canyon, where they camped for the winter and later killed the four stockmen.

Henie also said that, a day or two before her people committed those murders, they had stolen several articles from the nearby camp of a Chinese man. This Chinese was on his way to Mike's camp when he met one of Henie's brothers. When he explained that he was going over to kill Mike's whole bunch, the brother killed him "in his tracks,"[49] and covered the body with earth. This was probably the same Chinese man that Henie had mentioned in an earlier interrogation as having been killed.

And, it was Henie, in this interview, who said her father, Mike, had a grudge against whites dating back to the battle of Bear River, at which his father and two uncles had been killed. Mike and his brother were then just young boys, and were among the few survivors of the battle.

Henie described Mike and Jennie's family as comprising sons and daughters as follows: a grown, married daughter whose husband had not been with them; three grown sons—Jim, Charlie and Pete [not Jake]; Henie; two boys, 10 and 13; Cleve, the 6-year old boy in jail; Hattie, the girl in jail, about four years old; and the baby girl about 18 months old. Asbury said he thought that the baby was the child of Mike's married daughter.

Henie also said that her only known relatives were an aunt and uncle who lived and worked at Tecoma, the small railroad siding for shipping cattle in northeastern Nevada. Henie said she would like to join them, if allowed to return to her people, but that she did not want to be separated from the three younger children.

Asbury found the young prisoners to be so ragged and pathetic that he felt he must care for them until permanent arrangements could be made. And so, after getting agreement from the matron of the school and the county officials, Asbury took custody of them on April 27. He later obtained permission for Henie and Cleve to remain on the rolls of the Carson School until satisfactory arrangements were made for the other children. He also made an effort to learn something of the aunt's fitness to care for the youngsters.[50]

Soon the little orphans were prospering at the school, and seemed to fast be forgetting the awful events of the winter. Henie gradually left the youngsters more to the care of others, and associated herself with the older girls at the school. And then, in mid-September, 1911, just when she was beginning to be thought of as a model inmate, she and another girl ran away.

Henie returned, or was apprehended, and on November 16, she and the three younger children were taken to the Shoshoni-Bannock reservation at Fort Hall, Idaho, where they could live with relatives that had been located. The superintendent of that place, Evan W. Estep, came personally to get the children, and they were placed on the tribal rolls as nieces and nephews of Jim Mosho—the same man who had come to Rock Creek and Albion the previous year, searching for the missing family.

Tragically, over the next few years, death would carry away all but one of the remaining children. Hattie died of spinal meningitis, and Cleve and

Henie (later called Louise) of tuberculosis.

Only the baby remained. She had been named Mary Josephine Mosho, and, when Jim Mosho died in 1913 at age 77, she was taken care of by the family of another uncle, Jack Mosho.

In 1920, when Mary Jo was about to be removed from the reservation because she had contracted tuberculosis, Superintendent Estep and his wife Rita took her into their home, where she recovered. Mary Jo was then adopted by the Esteps, and later moved with them to the Indian agency at Toppenish, Washington.

A 1934 graduate of Ellensburg Normal School, she became an elementary school teacher and an accomplished pianist. Mary Jo led an active, Christian life, but never married. On December 19, 1992, this last survivor of the Rabbit Creek fight died at age 82 in Yakima, Washington.[51]

And what of the white men who had played a part in the Mike Daggett saga? Of Gordon Girdner, nothing is known. Ed Diffendarfer and Gay Tranmer both returned to the Twin Falls area and led normal lives, Gay continuing to work in the cattle business, Diffendarfer as a teamster. Gay died in July 1952 at age 75, and is buried in Twin Falls.[52]

Nimrod Urie was tried, convicted and sentenced to hang in April, 1911 for murdering the two Quilicis, but an appeal to the Nevada Supreme Court caused a lengthy delay. When the appeal was denied, a date for his execution, by hanging, was set for March 7, 1913. The Board of Pardons deliberated late into the night of March 6, and, after a visit with Urie in his cell, and a talk with his mother, who had come from Twin Falls, its members commuted his sentence to life in prison. They accepted his version of the murder—that he had been forced by Frank Tranmer to take part in the robbery, and that Tranmer had fired the shots that had killed the two Quilicis. The differences in age and mental capacity of the two participants also helped convince them that Urie's story was true.

In early 1915, Urie invented and patented a new automobile transmission. In August he applied for a pardon, but was denied. In January, 1916, he attempted suicide by ingesting a solution of mercury and hydrochloric acid, but a doctor was able to save him.

After this brush with death, Urie was a model prisoner, acting as a trusty, and even as the warden's chauffeur. In 1922, his sentence was commuted to 25 years, and, on November 26, 1923, he was pardoned and discharged from prison. The rest of his days were spent, quietly, as a sheepherder in the Twin Falls area. In 1927 he married Agnes Hollingshead in Twin Falls.

Frank Tranmer, who had been indicted for the murder of Eugene Quilici,

Nimrod R. Urie at the Nevada State Prison
(Author's collection)

was granted a change of venue to Washoe County, because feelings against him ran so high in Humboldt County. A jury at Reno found him guilty and he was sentenced to life in the Nevada penitentiary.

But, since Urie was supposed to have been under Tranmer's command, and, since Urie had been given a death sentence for the killing of *both* Quilicis, the citizens of Humboldt County thought Tranmer should also have to stand trial for the murder of Mrs. Quilici. As ordered by the county grand jury, the district attorney attempted to prosecute Tranmer on that charge. He was brought back to Winnemucca in October, 1911, but once again got a change of venue back to Reno. Meanwhile, the Tranmer ranch on Soldier Creek had been sold to finance Frank's defense.

Tranmer's clever attorney managed to delay the trial for over a year by arguing that to try him before his life sentence was served—that is, before he was dead—would be contrary to law. A writ of *habeas corpus* went clear to the Nevada Supreme Court before being denied in September, 1912.

So, finally, Tranmer was tried for the murder of Mrs. Quilici, in January of 1913. Sheriff Lamb, Ed Diffendarfer, and Alesandro Lammori, the brother of Mrs. Quilici, all testified on behalf of Washoe County, as did Nimrod Urie, who was brought from the state prison to relate how the crime had been committed.

Tranmer was found guilty and, when sentenced to die, he chose a firing

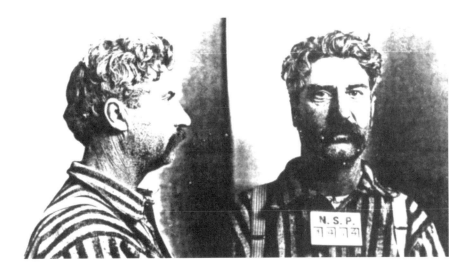

Prison photographs of J. Frank Tranmer (*Author's collection*)

squad, rather than the gallows. But, his attorney appealed, arguing that the prosecution had not introduced any evidence that Mrs. Quilici was actually dead. Despite the absurdity of this thesis, an indefinite stay of execution was ordered and Tranmer was removed from death row on April 18.

The State Board of Pardons reduced Tranmer's sentence to life imprisonment in November 1916. In March of 1918, he asked to be paroled to work as a *vaquero* on some Carson Valley ranch, offering to give half his wages to his widowed mother in Twin Falls, and the rest to an orphanage. In his parole application he claimed to still be married. The appeal was denied and, on September 16 of that year, the captain of the guard at the prison found Tranmer dead in his cell, ostensibly of natural causes.[53]

It is difficult at this distance to determine what might have caused Mike Daggett and his previously peaceful family to turn bitter and vengeful. We shall never know, for sure, which side was rustling cattle and who fired the first shot on Cow Creek that began the whole tragic chain of events.

As has been shown, there were inconsistencies in both the white and Indian versions of the initial trouble. Henie admitted in two different interviews that her people had killed Frankie Dopp, and said they had buried his body. However, the cowboy version has the body being found, unburied, in a place where it should have been seen much earlier. And, for some reason, the cowboys seem to have falsified the date of the encounter on Cow Creek.

In her first interview, the young woman conceded that her family had killed and buried the horses to make people think that white men had committed the crime. Later, she denied this, but did admit that they had stolen several horses.

One factor giving some credence to the theory that the Daggett men had been stealing and re-branding horses, as alleged by Gay Tranmer, is that their own animals were observed by other cowboys to be in bad condition, and, just nine days before the Cow Creek fight, some of the Daggetts were seen walking to the San Jacinto store.

Another area of confusion lies in the identity of Mike's son Jack. Henie said he was shot by an unknown white man at Cow Creek, and she called him "Dugan" in an earlier interview. Gay Tranmer, who knew the family well, said the fourth brother was called "Sagebrush," and of course, Tranmer didn't admit to killing anyone at Cow Creek; merely that he may have hit Charlie in their exchange of rifle fire.

There is a possibility that Mike's oldest daughter, who was killed at Rabbit Creek, may have been the widow of a certain "Indian John" who died of pneumonia in March 1910—not long before the Cow Creek fight At the time, John and his wife were working for a Rock Creek rancher, Lawrence Hansen. After John's demise, his wife burned her possessions, to get rid of the evil spirit of death. Then she and her children were cared for by Hansen until "the father" sent for them. Perhaps that father was Mike Daggett.

This woman was also the mother of the baby, Mary Jo, and perhaps of several of the other children. And, it may have been that her dead husband, John, was the brother of Jim Mosho who had told T. Bailey Lee that she had gone with three children to join Mike Daggett in Nevada.[54]

One historian, at least, has painted old Mike Daggett as the "last free man," and has blamed the whole mess on Frank Tranmer (not Gay) and his associates. But, there are enough omissions and errors in this account to render its conclusions suspect. There seems to have been enough violence and barbarism exhibited on both sides of the affair to make it a toss-up as where the blame for starting it might rest. In any case, one prays that the souls of Mike Daggett and his family are at peace.

Their bodies no longer lie in that dynamite-dug grave on the Nevada desert. In 1919, a Kelly Creek rancher exhumed the partial remains of three adult males; two adult females, two adolescent males and three children—two more persons than previously reported to have been killed—and sent them to the Smithsonian Institution. The remains were "repatriated" to the Shoshone-Bannock tribe in 1994.

First Family

This story is chock full of scoundrels—a whole clan of them, in fact. Yet, in the end, two of these rogues find redemption by a rediscovery of their religious faith.

The first white family to make a home in northern Nevada was of rough stock—a hardy, but unscrupulous, collection of pioneers, whose patriarch was a Canadian named Peter Haws. In the fall of 1837, when Peter was age 41, he and his family were converted and baptized into Joseph Smith Jr.'s Church of Jesus Christ of Latter-day Saints.

The young, charismatic Smith had founded his "Mormon" church seven years earlier at Fayette, New York. Within two years he had moved his followers westward into frontier colonies at Kirtland, Ohio, and Independence, Missouri. But, everywhere the new religionists settled they met with hostility. Coming in large numbers, and tending to be clannish, they inevitably raised economic and political fears in the minds of the older settlers. Added to this, their friendship for the Indians was seen as a threat to the general security.

The "Saints" were threatened, mobbed, and ultimately driven from their various communities into a region surrounding a village called Far West, in Caldwell County, Missouri. But, when harassment began there in 1838—and they struck back at their tormenters—the governor called out the militia.

Confronted by an overwhelming force—and after certain church leaders, including Joseph Smith, were charged with treason and thrown into jail—the Mormons agreed to leave the state. During the winter of 1838-39, over 10,000 of them left Missouri. Traveling eastward, they crossed the Mississippi River, and, despite an immense loss of property, and some loss of life, by springtime, most were safely in the more congenial state of Illinois.

Land was purchased for a new gathering place on the east bank of the Mississippi, north of Quincy. There, the little town of Commerce was occupied and renamed "Nauvoo," which meant "the beautiful" to the faithful. After six months of incarceration, Joseph Smith rejoined his flock of refugees, with fresh hope.

In an attempt to win Mormon votes, the politicians of both parties in the Illinois legislature voted to grant a liberal charter to Nauvoo, which made it an almost independent municipality. And, as a protection against further mob violence, the Mormons were permitted to organize a militia, which, though part of the state organization, was also virtually independent. This "Nauvoo Legion" had as its commander Lieutenant-general Joseph Smith.

Peter Haws and his family missed all of the early tribulations of the church. They had come to Ohio from Canada in the fall of 1838, then moved to Knox County, Illinois, and, in the spring of 1840, had joined the settlement at Nauvoo.

The new community prospered, with Peter Haws as one of its most dynamic citizens. From the beginning, the eager disciple placed his talents totally at the command of the prophet, Smith. There were many families who had lost everything in the exodus from Missouri, and Haws, who arrived with considerable property, converted much of it into meat, flour and other necessities to feed the less unfortunate.

Peter's initial business venture, as a Saint, was raising hogs, but he soon became involved in bigger things. On September 10, 1840, he bought, at a government surplus auction, the steamboat *Des Moines*. Lieutenant Robert E. Lee, of the U. S. Army Corps of Engineers, who had just completed a two-year survey and river-clearing expedition on the upper Mississippi, acted as the government's agent in the sale.

Haws signed a note for $4866.38, payable within eight months. His sureties for the obligation were the brothers George and Henry Miller, and Joseph and Hyrum Smith, all of whom were partners in the project. Haws and the others had their steamer remodeled a bit, and renamed it *Nauvoo*. They hired two steamboat pilots to run it, and placed the boat in the upper Mississippi River trade, mainly hauling lead ore to St. Louis from the mines at Galena.

But, that autumn, the boat was run onto some rocks and wrecked. Haws and his partners brought a civil action against the steamboat pilots and had them arrested, but the two men jumped bail and fled. Thus, when the note Haws and his partners had given the government came due in May 1841, and was not paid, a succession of lawsuits was commenced against all of them, which dragged on for several years. By timely disappearances, feigned insolvency, and concealment of property that might be subject to execution, Peter Haws was able to successfully avoid any payment of the liens against him in the matter.[1]

A capable miller and sawyer, Haws responded readily when he was named by the prophet Joseph Smith, in an 1841 revelation, to help build both the Nauvoo temple and Smith's boarding hotel, the Nauvoo House. Over the next few years he worked relentlessly to complete these two projects. He organized and ran the Wisconsin Black River Lumber Company, which cut timber in a Wisconsin pinery and floated it down the Mississippi to Nauvoo, where Haws prepared it using his steam sawmill. Joseph also sent him and Bishop George Miller to Mississippi and Alabama, briefly, to solicit funds for the temple project.

By this time, Peter had fathered at least five children with his wife Charlotte—a seventeen-year old married son, Alpheus Peter; a twelve-year old, Albert; a fourteen-year old, Abigail; a nine-year old, Lola; and a four-year old, Catherine. Peter and his entire family were totally devoted to Joseph Smith, and were well satisfied that he was a prophet of God. In 1842, their faith was strengthened when young Albert was stricken with a fever. After the boy had been unconscious for days, and lay near death, Smith came and prayed for him, and he recovered.[2]

In March, 1844 Smith began secretly choosing a council of 50 "princes" to form what one of them described as the "highest court on earth." This Council of Fifty, to which Peter Haws was named, comprised Smith's most

The Mormon temple at Nauvoo
(*LDS Historical Department*)

trusted men, and its purpose was to control the civil and political affairs of the church. Smith chose men for this ghost government who were trained in a variety of useful crafts, all of whom were willing to place the needs of the church ahead of their personal interests. One of the council's first acts was to ordain Joseph as ruler of the Kingdom of God.[3]

By this time, the Mormons in Nauvoo had created a thriving community that numbered nearly 12,000, and rivaled Chicago as the largest city in Illinois. But, they were beginning to feel pressure from their "Gentile" neighbors, who were afraid of the religion's growing influence in politics and business, and of its large Nauvoo Legion. When none of the presidential candidates in the 1844 national election seemed willing to defend Mormon rights, Joseph Smith launched his own presidential campaign, and Haws was one of many men sent out to various cities, in March, to preach and campaign for Smith's election.

Dissension was also growing within the church over the emerging practice of polygamy, which had been established a year earlier by one of Smith's revelations. Smith's second counselor, William Law, broke off, formed a separate church and began an opposition newspaper called the *Nauvoo Expositor*. After only one issue, in June 1844, Smith ordered a midnight raid by a gang of his legionnaires—including Peter Haws—in which Law's press was destroyed and his type pied.[4]

This act inflamed the surrounding Gentiles, and led that month to the arrest of Joseph and his brother Hyrum Smith. The two were jailed at Carthage but, before they could be tried, were assassinated by a mob of disbanded Illinois militiamen.

After the prophet's death, Brigham Young and the Quorum of Twelve Apostles took charge of church affairs. But Nauvoo had become totally untenable for the Saints, so plans were made to abandon the city and flee to the Rocky Mountains, where a new Zion would be established.

By September 1845, mobs were burning Mormon homes and property around Nauvoo, and the town was humming with activity in preparation for yet another exodus. Peter Haws was in the thick of it, helping move families and their goods into town for safety, negotiating for time with the mob leaders, and helping to build hundreds of wagons for the contemplated movement in the spring.

Peter and other high officials met December 9, 1845 with Brigham Young to plan the westward journey, and to organize its participants into manageable units of fifty and one hundred families. Peter was appointed captain of the fourth fifty.

Spiritual preparations were also made. There had been no temple ceremonies since the Saints had left Kirtland, seven years earlier, so Young ordered rooms in the attic of the uncompleted Nauvoo temple to be dedicated and, in them, the endowments and "sealings" were administered to worthy members before going out into the wilderness. The faithful came around the clock, day after day, in December and January to partake of these ceremonies, held to be so important to their salvation.

Peter Haws seized the opportunity to be sealed to his first wife, Charlotte Harrington, as well as to three others he had acquired since arriving in Nauvoo—Betsy Harrington (age 56); Mary Quard (age 40) and Sarah Morris (age 36). The available records are silent as to whether these were wives in fact, or only in spirit. All of Peter's children were sealed to their parents except Alpheus, who was sealed to his sixteen-year old wife, Adeline (née Dunn).[5]

Because of increasing harassment by the Gentiles, and the fear of government intervention, in February of 1846 the Saints began their exodus earlier than expected. Peter and his family were members of the first "Camp of Israel" companies to take a hurried departure. They crossed the partially frozen Mississippi and assembled at Sugar Creek Camp, seven miles into Iowa Territory.

Thus began a five-month, 300-mile trek to the Missouri River. Peter was involved in all of the planning meetings, and frequently rode out with Young to help scout the road ahead. Short of cash, the Mormon men were sent into the surrounding country to find employment at any task. Since he was good at it, Peter was frequently used to scrounge money, both in camp and from homesteads along the route.

Not too far into the westward trek, disreputable activities by certain men in his flock began to irritate Brigham Young. For some time, Haws, along with Thomas S. Williams, and others, had been involved in passing counterfeit money. On April 5, Young heard from Bishop George Miller that Williams had bought a yoke of oxen, part of the payment for which was bogus. When Miller asked Brigham to make the counterfeit amount good with the wronged party, Brigham refused, and became angry at the implication that he knew about, or was an "accessory to the game played" by the "thieves, bogus men and makers" of Miller's camp that were always doing something to "bring distress upon the saints."

Brigham ordered Williams to return the oxen and settle the matter forthwith. "Brother P. Haws," Brigham declared, "will attend to this matter; there is some one that knows about it and it will all come out." A week later, Young again noted that there were men in camp who had been passing bogus money ever since leaving Nauvoo, and there were also some who stole, pleading suffering from persecution at the hands of Gentiles as an excuse.[6]

Peter's children seemed to have inherited his lack of scruples. The two boys, Alpheus P. and Albert, had been so troublesome three years earlier that Joseph Smith had cautioned Peter that, "if he did not curtail them in their wickedness, they would eventually go to prison."[7] Now, on the trail in Iowa, 17-year old daughter Abigail displayed the flaws in her temperament.

On a night in early May, some of the boys in camp discovered Abigail inside a wagon, frolicking in bed with a beaux named Erastus Derby. The spirited boys upset the wagon, putting the girl and her paramour in "an uncommon nonplus and disappointment."

Next morning, while at breakfast, Abigail threw a cup of boiling coffee in the face and eyes of Benjamin Denton—one of Peter Haw's young teamsters—whom she suspected had taken part in the prank. The doctor who treated Denton's scalded eyes thought for a time he might lose his sight.

"The Lord reward her," said one observer of the incident.[8] The midnight lover, Derby, was rewarded with banishment from the Mormon encampment.

Peter himself was in trouble again a few days later, at the temporary settlement of Garden Grove. Hearing an outcry from Haws' camp, Brigham Young went to the scene to find Peter, Thomas Williams, and two others quarreling. It seems that Haws had given Williams some bogus money, on shares, which he was to use to buy goods from settlers along the line of march, and Williams had not paid Peter his share of the profits.

Young reproved them all for dealing in base coin and criticized Haws for his inability to govern either himself, his family or his company. Unless he "repented and forsook such dishonesty," said Brigham, "the hand of the Lord would be against him and all those who partook of such corruption."[9] According to one of Haws' associates, the counterfeiters buried two bogus presses at Garden Grove, which one of them had been carrying in his wagon.

After enduring incredible hardships, the Mormon companies began reaching Council Bluffs, Iowa, where they made a semi-permanent camp called "Winter Quarters." Peter located his family at Trader's Point, the principal post for commerce with the Pottawattamie Indians.

In a reminiscence written in later years, Albert Haws said that these Indians were very kind to the Haws family, and he, Albert, "soon became a favorite among them, being quick to learn their language." He even dressed in Indian garb and frequently took part in their dances. The 16-year old was also a favorite with the local half-breeds and traders—nearly all of them gamblers, drinkers, smokers and horse racers—and he said that this environment, "had a strong effect" on a person of his "disposition."[10]

In July, a U. S. Army officer arrived at Council Bluffs and asked Brigham Young to provide 500 men to fight in the war that had just begun with Mexico. Young agreed, desirous of using the men's advance pay to carry his flock through the coming winter.

A "Mormon Battalion" was quickly raised, in which Peter's oldest son, Alpheus, was enrolled as 4th Sergeant of Co D. Alpheus had performed quasi-military duty at least once before, in 1842, when he had joined O. P. Rockwell, John Redding and others, in an attempt to resist the mobs harassing Mormons around Nauvoo.

Young Alpheus left his wife, Adeline, in his parents' care and marched off with the battalion to California. Accompanying him was another young Mormon recruit, Sgt. Luther Tuttle, who just before leaving had married Alpheus' coffee-throwing, soiled sister, Abigail.

The army officer approved by the Mormons to lead the battalion became ill and died shortly after the march began. When his replacement, Lt. Andrew

J. Smith, joined the battalion, he brought with him a contract surgeon, Dr. George Sanderson.

Sanderson was from Missouri, the hated state where Mormons had been so cruelly treated, and this caused the men to fear his potions. Having a great deal of sickness in the ranks, Sanderson tried to force the afflicted men to take large doses of calomel, and when they refused, Lieutenant Smith denied them permission to ride in the wagons. Smith even personally yanked a few of the sick from the wagon beds.

Soon the Mormon men became contemptuous of both officers, and near mutinous. They began referring to Sanderson as "Doctor Death." And, in one instance, Sergeant Thomas S. Williams, faced Smith down, grabbed his whip and threatened him with it. On September 6, when the battalion was passing though Kansas, Luther became very sick. Having refused any medicine, his friends hid him with his blankets in an empty pork barrel, which was carried in a wagon for several days.[11]

When the battalion stopped for a rest at Santa Fe in October, Alpheus sent a letter back to his family at Council Bluffs telling of the hunger and sickness they had endured. He cursed Smith and Sanderson, saying "...i think when i enlist again it will be [to] kill some of the Deavils [sic] that is with us...Smith and the Doctor treated our sick boys worse than mules but i will remember them when my day comes. i ask the lord to curse them daily."

Alpheus asked Adeline to pray for them, and to tell his brother Albert "that he must be a good boy and help father all he can." Having sent some money home, he advised his father to lay in all the flour and clothing that he could, against the coming winter, and to get "plenty of antelope and bufalow [sic] meat" if he had a good horse. Alpheus reminded everyone that it was his birthday, and asked for news of his new baby.

Though a vengeful man, Alpheus seems to have had deep religious convictions. He ended his letter by saying he prayed daily for the Lord to bless all his family, and signed himself "your unworthy husband forever."[12]

Like most of the battalion members, Alpheus saw no combat, and was mustered out at Los Angeles on July 16, 1847. He traveled with Luther Tuttle and others to Sutter's Fort, and then across the Sierra Nevada Mountains to Salt Lake City, arriving October 16. A few of the discharged soldiers found their families in the Salt Lake valley, but most were still in the Council Bluffs area.

Alpheus was one of about thirty men who were healthy enough to continue the journey. After resting just two days, and despite the season, these men left Salt Lake in two groups. Alpheus, under P. C. Merrill, traveled via Fort Bridger, in bitter cold weather, and with little food, trudging through two feet of snow for the final 350 miles to Winter Quarters. They were eight days in finding a passable ford across the icy waters of the Loup Fork. Haws, who had left California with five animals, lost his last one, with part of his outfit, while crossing the river. His last pair of shoes he lost in the quicksand. Fortunately, friendly Pawnee Indians gave the suffering young Mormon men food, and Council Bluffs was finally reached in mid-December, 1847.[13]

Little is known about the Haws family for the next few years. Peter is mentioned as being one of some "prominent citizens" invited to a political caucus held at Council Bluffs by Brigham Young in March 1848.[14] But it is evident that he, and his close friends, Bishop Miller, Lyman Wight, and Lucien Woodward (known as the "Pagan Prophet") were rebelling against Young's authority. These men believed that the Council of Fifty—not Young and the Quorum of Twelve—held supreme authority, at least over secular and political matters. Since all of them had been chosen to the Council by Joseph Smith, they considered themselves equal in authority to Brigham.

Miller and Wight split off from the church and went to Texas to form a colony. Peter stayed on in Iowa, while Young and a small party trekked westward to begin building a new Mormon kingdom in the Salt Lake Valley. In the autumn of 1848, when many of the people at Council Bluffs migrated to Salt Lake City, Peter and Woodward journeyed to Texas to visit Wight and Miller, perhaps to see if his dissident movement was worth joining. But both men soon returned, reporting that the experiment had failed.

It was shortly after this that Peter's association with the Brigham Young faction ended. Peter's son Albert would confirm, long after Peter's death, that his father had:

> ...denounced Brigham and his confreres as deserters from the faith, doctrines and practices taught by Joseph the Seer. For this he was summarily excommunicated by vote of the conference, without due process of law. He was probably the first person who publicly denounced Brigham Young and the course pursued by him and the Twelve.[15]

Albert tells us the excommunication was ordered by Young, and was done at a conference in the log tabernacle at Council Bluffs. Although there is little accessible evidence of it, other persons have declared that Peter was tried and cut off from the church by that conference not only for his rebellious statements, but for selling whiskey to the Indians.

A few years afterward, however, Peter would state that *he* had made the decision to leave the church, after becoming totally disgusted with Brigham Young and his interpretation of doctrine.[16] In confirmation of this, the Mormon apostle, George Q. Cannon, wrote that Haws, the "chief actor" in the bogus operations, along with his whole family, became "apostates, and very disreputable people, and the hand of the Lord was visibly against him."[17]

Whatever the circumstances may have been, Peter and his family did not take part in the grand Mormon migration to the Salt Lake Valley. Instead, they moved eastward from Council Bluffs, in the summer of 1849, to settle on the West Nishnabotna River, near Macedonia, Iowa. Here Peter built a gristmill which, in the spring of 1850, was destroyed by a flood.

In early 1852, Albert was married to Maria Jane Cox, and in June the newlyweds started overland with Alpheus and his family for California to seek their fortunes. Despite a severe cholera outbreak along the trail, the two brothers and their families reached Salt Lake City safely on July 23, and, after a short rest, pushed on to reach Nevada City, California in September.[18] Here they remained for several years, mining and working as teamsters.

Peter, with his wife and daughters migrated to Salt Lake City at about the same time and, after living there some months, in May 1854 moved westward out into the desolate wilderness of what would become northern Nevada. In June of that year, the *Sacramento Daily Union* noted that a man from Salt Lake City had established a homestead and begun farming on the south bank of the Humboldt River, about 60 miles below the natural wells from which the main stem of the Humboldt takes its source.

That same spring, Alpheus and Albert left their families in California and established an outpost on the south fork of the Humboldt, close by their father's place, and began trading with emigrants and Indians. According to report, they and their father intended making their living mainly from buying clapped-out livestock from emigrants, then recruiting and reselling it.

The Haws family had barely arrived in Nevada when rumors arose to the effect that white men in the area were in league with local Indians, stealing livestock at every opportunity. Brigham Young commented in mid-July that, based on what he had learned by the last California mail, a "numerous and well organized band of white highwaymen, painted and disguised as Indians," were driving off stock and perhaps even murdering immigrants along the Humboldt road.[19]

Col. E. J. Steptoe, arrived in Salt Lake City on August 31, with 175 soldiers and a herd of horses and mules, en route to California. It wasn't long before the colonel and his men were aware of these same rumors. Steptoe's quartermaster, Captain Rufus Ingalls, reported to his superiors in Washington that the "native propensity" of the Indians to rob and murder had been "sharpened" and "excited" by contact with "white men of notoriously bad character...who had gone among them."[20] They were being induced by traders to steal horses and cattle, and then exchange them with these persons for trifles.

That fall, more light was shed on the identity of these men of bad character. Colonel Steptoe, having decided to winter in the Salt Lake Valley, hired Oliver B. Huntington and his nephew, Clark Allen Huntington, to explore for a shorter route from Salt Lake City to the Carson Valley of Nevada. The two Huntingtons, John Reese, and several other Mormons started September 18, generally following the route pioneered by Lt. E. G. Beckwith, 3rd Artillery, earlier that summer.

Upon reaching Nevada's Ruby Valley, on September 28, the Huntington party encountered a band of White Knife Shoshoni, whom they reckoned were the same "very bad Indians," who had killed so many men along the Humboldt over the years. The White-Knife (To-sow-witch) territory centered around Stony Point on the Humboldt, a few miles from where Battle Mountain, Nevada now is situated. The band derived its name from a beautiful flint found in the mountains to the north which, at one time, was used by them as knives.

The leader of the band, who spoke English, made some sort of a secret sign as he shook hands with the whites. Later, Huntington's group went to the White Knife camp and used this same sign as a greeting, and found that it had a magical effect, the chief warmly throwing his arms around them. When Oliver Huntington told the chief that he was a longtime friend of the Haws family, the chief talked freely and favorably about them, even referring to Peter Haws as his "father." The natives were given presents, and in turn, they displayed a large array of jewelry, coins and pocket knives—booty which, Huntington said, they had recently robbed from a company of whites on the Humboldt.

Oliver had seen Alpheus Haws before leaving Salt Lake City, and some sort of ugliness had passed between them. The encounter with the White Knives led Oliver to believe that Alpheus had banded with them to rob emigrants, using secret signs and passwords for identification. The Huntington party went on to Genoa and returned, unharmed by Indians, but Oliver was sure that discovery of the secret sign had saved him from being murdered, as planned by Alpheus.[21]

But, aside from Huntington, none of the several men who encountered Peter, Alpheus or Albert Haws during their first few years on the Humboldt named them as doing any wrong, or of being in collusion with the natives.

Indeed, during that same autumn when Oliver Huntington felt so threatened, George Greathouse, who was guiding a party from Salt Lake City to California, obtained two beeves from Alpheus, and gave no hint of any nefarious activities.

The following year, 1855, Peter was visited by three men who recorded the experience. The first of these was Orson Hyde, president of the twelve apostles of the Mormon Church. In those days, most of what would later become Nevada was a part of Utah Territory, and the territorial legislature, sitting in Salt Lake during its January session, had organized the Carson Valley into a county. Hyde was appointed its probate judge and was tasked by Brigham Young to organize the new district. He and some forty other Mormon colonizers left Salt Lake City for the new Carson County on May 17. Their route took them via the Bear River ferry, and thence northwest to The Wells of the Humboldt.

Marching close by Hyde's party was Col. Steptoe and his army detachment bound for California. Steptoe had decided to take the old Humboldt route to California, not being willing to trust Huntington's report of having found a shorter road the previous autumn. About five miles from The Wells the emigrant road forked, one passing down each side of the river. While Steptoe and his men traveled on down the north bank, Hyde and his Mormon colonizers took the south side road, which ran along the foot of the mountains and avoided the swampy regions present in wet years. This trail had been first used by a Mormon pioneer, Howard Egan, a few years earlier.

About eight miles beyond The Wells, Peter Haws met Hyde's party, and piloted them to his ranch some 35 miles farther on. From the point of rendezvous, Hyde noted that there was an abundance of good grass, and, every few miles, pure rivulets of water flowed down from the mountains, with fine speckled trout in all of them.

The Haws homestead was nestled at the foot of the highest mountains in the area, the Rubies, close to one of these clear little brooks. The stream was described as running at right-angles to the main stem of the Humboldt, whose banks could be traced along the plain, in the distance, by a narrow sinuous line of verdure. The brook flowed to the river through a prairie, and here and there its banks were dotted with clumps of willows and poplars.

The exact location of Peter Haws' home can't be determined but, from the various descriptions, it probably lay near where now sits the little village of La Moille, Nevada, and was on the creek bearing the same name.

Arriving at the Haws home on May 31, Hyde was ushered into Peter's cabin, which had been built of poplar trees, and had two large chimneys. Nearby were two smaller huts, a small tract of woods, mowed meadows and

Lamoille Nevada, at the foot of the Ruby Mountains
(*Author's Collection*)

a herd of cattle. All in all, the scene presented an aspect of prosperity and comfort.

Hyde was treated to a fine supper prepared by Mrs. Haws, consisting of "the best of potatoes and beets of their own raising, some fresh antelope meat, nicely broiled and served up according to 'gunter.'" He even got a choice of tea or coffee, and cream to go in it.

It is difficult to understand why Hyde, Brigham Young's apostle, should have been so generously treated by Haws, who had supposedly been cut off six years earlier by the church. Perhaps the two men had formed a strong friendship, during the days in Nauvoo, that overcame any bitterness.

The Haws family was living smack in the midst of several bands of Western Shoshoni, comprising about 500 families. One group, usually found along the river, seems to have been led by an old chief called Nemetickey or Ne-me-te-kalt. Another band, that ranged mostly in Ruby Valley, was under the leadership of a young chief, whose name was variously mangled by whites as Chyukup-ichya, Cho-kup, Shokub, Sho-cup-ut-see, Sokopitz, or Tsokkope. We shall call him Cho-kup, since that is easiest. His likeness is shown at the beginning of this chapter.

Hyde observed that Haws had managed to secure the confidence of these Shoshoni, and appeared to "apprehend no danger from them."[22] He traded for furs, tended his garden and bred cattle. His livestock roamed, unguarded, without molestation; he kept no locks upon his doors, and the latchstrings hung out day and night.

The apostle also concluded that Haws had succeeded in restraining these Shoshoni to a large degree from committing depredations upon the whites as they passed. But, Hyde acknowledged that the natives were still very annoying to emigrants. They had even tried for several nights to steal animals from his party of church colonizers.

Peter knew that some persons had censured him as being a collaborator with the Indians in robbing emigrants, and he told Hyde he wanted the new agent, Dr. Garland Hurt, to come to his ranch with his Shoshoni interpreter, and stay during the season of emigration, so that he could see how things really were.

Hyde agreed that this should be done, and judged the allegations against Haws to be unjust and cruel. Haws had been feeding many Indians and had induced them to do some farming. Since nearly all of the game had been killed or frightened away by emigrants, the natives would have to turn to farming, or they surely would steal and rob in order to live. Hyde thought the government should open farms for the natives, under the management of judicious men, furnishing seed grain and farming utensils. He believed the Shoshoni would like such an arrangement.

Alpheus Haws echoed this same sentiment when he visited Salt Lake City about June 20, claiming there were 2,000 Indians living near his father's ranch, who wished to learn to farm because the emigration to California had scattered away the game.[23]

The next to record a visit to Peter Haws in 1855 was Howard Egan, who stopped on July 15 while returning after delivering a large herd of cattle to California. He and Peter were long-time acquaintances who had both served in the Nauvoo Legion.

Egan adjudged the Haws ranch to be well cultivated, and noted that Peter was growing grains, corn, potatoes and other vegetables very successfully and profitably. These he disposed of to emigrants, traders and Indians. But Egan took pains to mention that Peter carried on "no or very little trade" with the natives "in the way of exchanges of firearms, ammunition, etc..."[24] Peter had also had raised some 300 head of stock the previous year, which he had driven into Salt Lake City. One can't help but wonder just how Haws "raised" so many animals in his first year on the Humboldt.

The trail-blazing Egan, on this return trip from California, was seeking a shorter route to Salt Lake City that would eliminate the need to traverse the Goose Creek Mountains. Accordingly, after leaving the Haws place he traveled northward some 25 miles, where he stopped briefly at the camp of a fellow named Carlos Murray. He then passed through the Ruby Mountains southeastwardly, through what is now called Secret Pass, and into the north end of Ruby Valley, thence westward to his destination.

Carlos Murray was also well known to Egan. Both men were numbered amongst those renowned Mormons who had made the first trip, in 1847, with Brigham Young from Winter Quarters to the Salt Lake valley. Murray's camp consisted of a tent on the Humboldt prairie near the Humboldt Wells, where, ostensibly, he was trading with emigrants. With him was his bride, Peter Haws' 22-year old daughter, Lola, who was once described as being short and "thick-set...with enormous hips, a rather an ugly face, and eyes with a disagreeable expression."[25]

Also rather undersized in stature, Carlos had a fresh, ruddy complexion, a red beard and a bad character that was perfectly matched to that of his in-laws. And, like his relatives, the misanthropic Carlos was suspected of being involved with Indians in depredations against emigrants.

Peter Haws' next visitor that summer was Utah's Indian agent, Dr. Garland Hurt, who was based in Salt Lake City. Hurt and twelve others left that place on July 16, and struck out on the trail to the Humboldt. Near the ford of Bear River, he overtook Alpheus Haws, who had been hired as an interpreter.

Alpheus had with him his "lady," whose name was not given. It may have been his first wife, Adeline Dunn Haws, or her sister, Betsy Dunn Haws. He is known to have married both women and, sometime about 1849, Adeline either died or became the lesser wife, dropping from view, as did the child she had born Alpheus in 1846. Betsy, who was fourteen years younger than Alpheus, had given birth to a child, Laura, at Salt Lake City in January 1855.

Hurt's party reached the Humboldt Wells on July 27, and arrived at Alpheus' trading post the next day. Here the agent met with a few Shoshoni and asked them to gather their people and meet him at Peter Haws' ranch. He wanted to deal with as many natives as possible at that place.

The agent received a friendly reception from Peter when he arrived on July 30. He bought cattle from the elder Haws to feed the hungry Shoshoni that began straggling in, and, on the tenth day, 300 of them having gathered, Hurt offered them a treaty of peace. After Alpheus had interpreted its terms, the principal chief present, Ne-me-te-kalt, and the other headmen agreed to and signed it.

Hurt smoked a pipe with his charges, and distributed blankets, clothing, knives and other goods to everyone present. He also presented several of the chiefs with small American flags, made by Catherine and Lola, the latter of whom was evidently taking a break from her life in a tent with Carlos Murray. That evening the Shoshoni entertained the agent with "an amusing serenade and dance," which continued until midnight.

Hurt bade goodbye to the Shoshoni on August 5—old Ne-me-te-kalt shedding a tear at the parting—then he and Alpheus returned to Salt Lake via Alpheus' trading post.[26]

Peter Haws' last visitor of record during 1855 was a Frenchman, Jules Remy, who, with a friend, George Benchley, was traveling from Sacramento to Salt Lake City. Along the Humboldt, they met some westbound emigrants who told them of the recent murder of a white man by Shoshoni, not far up river from their present position. Upon hearing this, Remy and his friend traveled only at night and reached Peter's farm on August 30.

The Frenchman left us a wonderful picture of Peter and his homestead, which was the first established in northeastern Nevada. Upon arriving, the first thing to strike Remy's eye was a Shoshoni man squatting on Peter's roof. Looking around, he was astounded to see that the whole place was awash in Shoshoni, lounging about, rifles in hand.

Remy overcame his initial fright to the extent that he stayed eleven days, during which time he found Peter to be a cordial and hospitable host. He described Haws as being a stout, good-natured man, of about fifty years (actually he was 60), with a dignified countenance. Mrs. Haws was adjudged to be about the same age.

For some reason, Remy got the impression the couple only had three children. There was a ten-year old girl, whom Remy called Harriet (not Catherine); the daughter, Lola, who had married Carlos Murray; and a son who was seeking his fortune in California. No mention was made of a second son or the third daughter, Abigail.

Remy was fascinated by the vigor of Peter's religious faith, describing how he offered prayer and lectured his guests every evening in favor of Mormonism. Remy was delighted with these evening sessions. Peter's voice would invariably rise to a high, fevered pitch and, one night when he got carried away, the Indians, "believing he had gone mad, raised a tumult round the house as though they had been devils let loose from hell." To calm them, the Shoshoni were told that Peter was "exorcizing evil spirits."

Haws, who had known Joseph Smith intimately, had a profound veneration for his memory; he hated the murderers of Smith, whom he thought were now in California. And Mrs. Haws, when her husband spoke of the martyred prophet "went into a kind of ecstasy, and thanked the gods for having allowed her to know one perfect man on the earth."

Remy said Haws had no "feeling of nationality" other than that which he derived from his religious opinions. He was "neither English nor American, but solely and simply Mormon."[27]

As to the Indians, Peter held to the belief that they were the "Lamanites" spoken of in Joseph Smith's *Book of Mormon*—a fallen people who, along with the "Nephites," were once part of a great American civilization. Although these Lamanites had rebelled against Christ's word, they could, and must, be redeemed by the Mormons. Naturally, the Saints held a fairly pacifistic attitude toward these errant brothers and they followed Brigham Young's imperative that it was "cheaper to feed them than fight them."[28]

Haws told Remy that agent Hurt, during his recent visit, had authorized him to use the Indians to punish any emigrants committing offenses against the natives, but it is hard to imagine Hurt having given Haws this power.

Haws spoke favorably of the Shoshoni in the valley. He said they had no form of worship, but were honest and trustworthy, and the women exceedingly virtuous. They were not warlike, thanks to the pacific disposition of their young chief, Cho-kup, who was just then absent on a hunting expedition. Since Haws didn't speak their language, he communicated with the natives through his daughter, "Harriet."

Remy, however, was not so impressed with the Shoshoni character. He was shocked by the Indian practice of killing a wife of any chief that died, and he thought the Indians often took advantage of any whites who were generous and kind to them.

He told of Mrs. Haws, in the absence of her husband, being ordered by a Shoshoni man to give him whatever food he desired, or receive a bullet through her head. According to the Frenchman, tough old Charlotte Haws made up her mind not to submit to either alternative. Seizing a revolver, she faced the man down, saying she would shoot him at the first movement he made, and, upon this, the fellow took to his heels.

During the time Remy was there, Carlos Murray had come nearer to his father-in-law, camping on the prairie nine miles distant, under the pretense of making hay. Remy said that Murray had frequent relations with the aborigines, whose language he spoke fluently. He had recently, without any provocation, killed a Shoshoni in Thousand Spring Valley, without experiencing himself any "disagreeable result."

Later, at Salt Lake, Remy would learn that Carlos did not confine himself to killing Indians. He was known to have murdered two white men for their money, and the Mormons suspected that he had killed other victims whose deaths had been attributed to the Shoshoni. In fact, when Remy and Benchley didn't appear at Salt Lake at expected time, it was thought they had been done in by the much-dreaded Carlos. Remy reckoned that Peter had no idea his son-in-law was such a ruffian.

Remy had planned to leave on September 7, but his companion was taken ill. That evening an old Indian man told them that some Shoshoni, encouraged by the small number of emigrants who were crossing the plains that year, were attacking all white travelers in the neighborhood of Goose Creek, and blocking the route to Salt Lake. They had just completely stripped seventeen Mexicans of their goods, and had murdered several Americans.

Accordingly, Remy postponed his departure and Peter Haws sent for Chief Cho-kup, who soon arrived with his band of "hunters," as Remy called them. Cho-kup was about 25 years old, rather thin and small, with a countenance that indicated "cunning and ferocity." He wore a revolver on his hip.[29]

Haws proposed that Cho-kup raise a small force and set out to punish the Indians who had been murdering and plundering. The chief declined, saying simply that his own people were peaceable. After thinking about it for two days, however, he did agree to accompany Remy and Benchley to the Mormon capital, and while there visit the Indian agent. Peter also decided to make the trip, and thus Remy and his friend were safely escorted to their destination. Both came away from their encounter with Peter thinking him among the worthiest of men.

At about the same time that Peter and his guests arrived at Salt Lake City, certain Indians told the authorities about Carlos Murray having killed that Shoshoni in the Thousand Spring Valley. In late October, Carlos was indicted by a Salt Lake City grand jury, and a large posse under command of the infamous William A. "Wild Bill" Hickman went out to take him prisoner. Murray was brought in on December 10, 1855, and deputy marshals were sent out to fetch the Indian witnesses to testify against him.

Murray faced a jury in district court the following February, but was acquitted, in short order, for lack of evidence, although there were those who reckoned his dismissal had more to do with the influence of his uncle, Heber Kimball, a high official of the Mormon Church.

As events proved, the brooding friends of the murdered Shoshoni man were not so fussy about a lack of evidence, and, for his crime Carlos Murray would, after all, experience a "disagreeable result." He, his wife Lola, and a younger man named George Redden, had scarcely returned to his camp at the head of the Humboldt, in early May, 1856, when they were set upon and killed by a Shoshoni "grand jury."

Indians friendly to Alpheus Haws told him about the murders, not long

The notorious Bill Hickman
(*Utah State Historical Society*)

after he arrived on the river to begin the season's trading. Alpheus, profoundly affected by the loss of Carlos and Lola, went to give the grim news to Indian agent Garland Hurt, who was making his annual visit to the tribes within his jurisdiction.

On the morning of June 1, Alpheus entered Hurt's camp on the Humboldt, some twenty miles downstream of French Bridge (near today's Winnemucca). Alpheus had been told that the killings had taken place about three weeks earlier, somewhere between Hurt's camp and the head of the river. He and Hurt traveled together upstream and found the murder scene, but got no clue as to who the assassins had been. The only property discovered at the site was a gold pencil and an earring which Haws identified as having belonged to Lola. Alpheus had also seen Murray's pistols in the possession of some emigrants, who claimed to have bought them from the Indians.[30]

It was soon learned that the killers of Carlos, Lola and Redden had been White Knife Shoshoni. Ten days after visiting the murder scene, Hurt had seen a party of about 50 of them near Gravelly Ford, and on the return leg of his journey, he encountered several more fierce-looking groups of the same band, but learned nothing from them. All of these natives were well supplied with guns and horses. They claimed they were on the emigrant road to trade for ammunition, and blamed any troubles on the reluctance of emigrants to deal with them.

Eventually, a friendly Shoshoni chief, *Setoke*, came to Hurt in Thousand Springs Valley, and told him the details of the killings. He confirmed that they had taken place about May 2, and were done by the one of the bands of White Knives Hurt had recently encountered.

The Murray murders marked the beginning of a rash of Shoshoni-Bannock attacks on the annual emigration. Hurt heard from various groups of travelers that Indians had been "attacking them both day and night."[31] From one party he learned of the murder of three whites 14 miles below Gravelly Ford. The E. C. Forshee train, saw, in the same area, the bodies of six men killed while asleep by Indians. And, according to report, a band was at the head of the Humboldt, stealing stock from nearly every train. The agent personally saw six Californians, walking eastward, having just lost all of their animals in an Indian stampede.

That year of 1856 would be the last for Peter Haws in Nevada. Some of chief Cho-kup's people had farmed fifteen acres at Peter's ranch that summer, and had made small crops of wheat, potatoes and squashes. They had used hoes, which Hurt had sent them, and seed furnished by Haws. But after these crops were harvested, Peter—perhaps because things were getting out of hand and he was concerned for his family's safety—packed his wife, daughter and goods into a wagon, abandoned his homestead, and left for the more congenial environs of California, where he settled at Auburn. Soon people traveling the Humboldt were referring to his pioneer Nevada outpost as "the old Haws place."[32]

By the time Peter arrived in California, his two boys, Alpheus and Albert, had moved their families from Nevada City onto a ranch near Bear Creek, about six miles north of Placerville. Alpheus and wife Betsy had a one-year old daughter, Laura, whom he had begun calling "Lola," in remembrance of his murdered sister. Albert's clan now included wife Maria and three children—three-year old Rose Ella, two-year old Charles, and a new baby boy, Francis, all of whom had been born in California.

If, indeed, Peter was fearful for his safety, it is perhaps fortunate that he abandoned Nevada, because the summer of 1857 proved to be one the most dangerous for whites ever recorded along the Humboldt. Alpheus and Albert were still "trading" with the Indians and, that year, they would be directly named as being in league with the Shoshoni.

Peter's two sons left Placerville on May 20, taking with them as an employee a rascally fellow from Nevada City called "California Jim" Tulley.[33] The trio arrived and set up shop on the Humboldt, just below Gravelly Ford, on June 9. Nearby, was another set of traders, a certain Brown, and two brothers from Carson Valley named Jones. Soon after the Haws boys got on station, the advance of the annual emigration began arriving, and all hell broke loose.

From the head of Goose Creek to the Humboldt Sink—but most

especially in the Stony Point and Gravelly Ford region frequented by the White Knives—there were relentless raids on the emigrants for their livestock, clothing and other possessions. In retaliation, Indians were sometimes shot down indiscriminately, and this led, in a brutal cycle, to more raids and killing. Friendly Paiute Indians would claim that, during that summer of 1857, the Shoshoni murdered over 85 people. An emigrant who passed down the Humboldt at the end of the season said he had seen 100 new graves, in just the vicinity of Gravelly Ford and Stony Point.

This was also the year in which the "battle" was fought which gave a Nevada town its name. Under contract with the government, John Kirk was improving the emigrant wagon road that summer. Near Stony Point, he and his 70 employees had a brief skirmish with Shoshoni, but drove them off. Nine years later, when the Battle Mountain diggings were discovered, they were named either for Kirk's skirmish, or an alleged fight that same year between Paiutes and a group of emigrants under a certain Captain Pierson.[34]

We shall make no attempt to catalogue all of the many reported depredations of 1857, but simply relate the ones in which the Haws brothers seem to have been implicated.

In a number of the attacks that summer, white men were seen amongst the Indians and distinctly heard to be speaking English. This was the case when a cattle herd belonging to a man named Holloway, and his brother-in-law, Rector, was raided on July 19, at the head of Goose Creek, by Indians using modern rifles.

Upon arriving at Gravelly Ford, Holloway accused the Haws boys and Jim Tulley of having a wagon load of guns, powder and lead that they had been selling to the natives. He threatened to "hang every trader in that vicinity,"[35] if any more cattle were stolen, believing that Alpheus, Albert and Tulley were surely in league with the Indians, otherwise they couldn't live amongst them.

No less a personage than "major" William M. Ormsby—a pioneer merchant of Carson City—was also sure that the Indians making attacks that summer were led by "white traders and directors."[36] Like Holloway, he believed the Haws brothers and Tulley were those directors.

A day or two after threatening the traders, Holloway and his train reached Stony Point and camped for the night. Theirs was a small outfit—three wagons, a large herd of livestock, six men, one woman and a child. In the morning, just after the travelers had arisen and were beginning to stir about, most of the men were struck down by a volley of gunshots and a deadly flight of arrows coming from nearby willow bushes.

The only woman, Mrs. Holloway, who had seen her husband and her brother, Rector, fall with the others, hid herself under a tent, hugging her baby girl to her breast. But, when the Shoshoni rushed in amongst the wagons and killed a man who lay sick, she jumped up and started to run with her baby.

The Indians hit her in several places with their arrows, and she dropped to the ground. Believing she was dead, the Indians scalped her and stripped the nightgown from her body. But, in reality, she was feigning death all the while, and was perfectly conscious of what they were doing.

When the natives left her for a moment, she moved slightly to ease her discomfort. The Indians noticed this change, and they grabbed the arrows in her body and worked them deeper into her flesh, while stomping on her with their heels. She endured this torture without a groan or drawing a breath that could be perceived. Even when they took her baby girl and dashed its brains out against a wheel she forced herself to keep motionless and quiet.

The Shoshoni looted the wagons and were starting to round up the livestock, but the approach of another wagon train, the Roundtree outfit, caused them to retreat hastily. The Roundtree men recovered most of the cattle, killing one Indian in the process. Mrs. Holloway was found to be barely alive, and the only man to have survived the attack was found lying wounded and hidden under the riverbank. The wounds of the two survivors were dressed, and the Roundtree train took them to Carson City.

Mrs. Holloway's scalp had been dropped as the Indians fled the scene. It was found, and later she had a wig of her own hair made from it. It is said that eventually her mind failed and that she died at Napa, California.[37]

After the Holloway attack, near the end of July, the M. W. Buster party of Missouri, comprising three families with 330 head of cattle, camped some twelve miles below Gravelly Ford, near the two trading outposts. Buster told the Haws boys, as well as Brown and the Jones brothers, that if he lost any cattle that night he would take their scalps. Despite the threat, a good number of his cattle were taken, and, after recovering some of them the next day, Buster and his hired men came across a band of Shoshoni who bantered them to fight. In the ensuing skirmish, the emigrants claimed to have killed 18 Indians and a white accomplice. Buster said that he wished he had also killed the white traders.

As events proved, someone did rid the world of the Jones brothers—who were never seen again after July 30—and their partner, Brown, whose body was found by some of Buster's men, shot and scalped, presumably by Indians. Some people, however, suspected that the Haws boys and Tulley might have killed them.[38]

Not long after the foregoing events, and in the same area, another vicious attack took place. The wagon of a man named Woods—in which he was carrying his two brothers, his wife and child—had lagged behind the others of his train when, suddenly, 20 mounted men—Indians and whites painted as Indians—came galloping down from the hills on the attack. Woods said he cried out: "...take all I have but spare my wife and child!" But one of the attacking whites coldly responded, "We will take what we want!"[39]

Woods quickly cut two mules out of their harness, and put his wife and child on one of the animals, and, with himself on the other, and they made a dash for the safety of the wagons ahead. But, the child was shot and killed in Mrs. Woods' arms, and the distraught woman, in attempt to flee back to her wagon, was herself fatally shot down. Woods and his two brothers were wounded, but managed to overtake the other wagons.

When the emigrants went back to bury the dead, it was discovered that three mules had been taken, along with $700 in English gold coins, which had been concealed in the bottom of Woods' wagon.

On the day after the attack, three men—strangers to the emigrants—came up to the train in a small wagon drawn by two handsome horses. They told the travelers they were mountaineers, well acquainted with Indians and their habits. And, because the Shoshoni were upset over acts of certain whites, the men thought themselves no longer safe amongst the tribe. They wanted to join the train for protection while getting out of the area. Their request was granted, and the three traveled in the rear of the train. The questions these strangers asked, most of which concerned the emigrants' ability to defend themselves, led the people to think they were being sized up for an attack.

On the second day of travel with the emigrants, the three strangers displayed a white flag from a pole on their wagon. When asked about it, they said it was to enable any outriders going beyond view to see the train at a distance. The captain of the train, suspecting that the flag might, instead, be a signal to confederates in the hills, ordered it to be taken down.

At the noon stop, the wounded Woods, who was being carried in a wagon, recognized one of the three as a man who had been with the Indians on the day his wife and child had been killed. Perhaps sensing that they had been recognized, later that afternoon the three said they were safely out of Shoshone country and they left.

But the next day the strangers were back and, when they heard of the accusation against them, one of them warned Woods that if he made it again, he would be shot down like a dog. Another of the three declared that they were honest men, whose business was buying weak stock from emigrants, putting them on range and driving them to California to sell. The one Woods had recognized said his name was James Tulley, and his two companions were the Haws brothers. Tulley threatened the emigrants with a pistol but was faced down by one of the emigrant men. After this, the Haws boys and Tulley rode out of camp.

When Woods and his companions reached the Humboldt Sink, they found Tulley at Tyler and Blackford's trading post, drinking heavily while boasting that he had recently "done up" some emigrants. Tired of such arrogance, the Woods party united with some other travelers who were camped nearby, and organized a kangaroo court, complete with a "judge" and "sheriff." Tulley was arrested and disarmed, and a jury selected. Woods confronted Tulley and reaffirmed that the latter had been with the group that had killed his wife and child. But, since Tulley denied everything, the jury refused to convict him.

The judge then ordered a search of Tulley's person, upon which was found a money belt containing a large quantity of English gold coins, believed to be part of those stolen from Woods' wagon. The jury quickly voted for conviction, and the judge gave Tulley his choice of being shot or hanged from the uplifted tongue of a wagon. Not much liking either choice, Tulley made a break for it, and he was gunned down by a volley of shots from the emigrants' guns.[40]

The above account, based on the recollections of pioneers, is somewhat different than that reported in newspapers at the time. The latter say only that Tulley was associated with the Haws boys, ostensibly buying stock from emigrants, and that he was guilty of leading the Indians who had killed Mrs. Woods and her child, and of stealing a horse and $700.

The papers further relate that, on August 24, the day after the attack, Tulley rode up to another train on the stolen horse, and the fact being known of the robbery the day before, he was searched, and the money found on him. He was then told that he must die, and, given a choice of hanging or shooting, he chose the latter. He was allowed to write a farewell letter to his mother, and while doing so, he jumped up and tried to escape, but was shot dead by some of the emigrants.[41]

In the fall, from Nevada City, there came a report that specifically named the Haws brothers, former residents of that town, as having been connected with the Indians in the massacre of immigrants and stealing of stock. They were also accused of selling arms to the natives.[42]

Alpheus felt obliged to answer these charges. In statements made to several newspapers, he painted his clan as just plain folks. He and Albert, and their families—as well as his father, Peter—were all living quietly in California. For several years he and Albert had been carrying on a legitimate business of buying stock from emigrants and trading with the Indians. He showed one editor a trading permit issued to him by Garland Hurt, the Indian

Agent for Utah.

Alpheus recounted his version of the summer's events, saying that he had only taken six guns with him up the Humboldt. He blamed much of the trouble on whites who had shot down innocent natives in revenge for incidents of thieving. Haws seemed quite knowledgeable of most of the depredations, and of the Indians' motivations for them.

He said it had been a party of nine Indians, bent on revenge for the killing of a friend, that had come into the trading camp of the two Jones brothers and Mr. Brown, while they were asleep, and brutally cut their throats. Alpheus didn't mention the Holloway massacre, but he identified the attackers of the Woods train as being of the same band responsible for killing the traders.

About the time of the attack on Woods' party—so said Alpheus—he, Albert and Tulley decided it was not safe for such a small party as theirs to remain in the area and so, on August 10, they had started down the Humboldt. On their way in, they stopped at Walden and Tutt's trading post, where Tulley became intoxicated and acted so badly that the next morning Haws paid him off and dismissed him.

Alpheus said Tulley was paid in gold coins that had been received from Indians in payment for blankets and other goods, but he claimed to have been unaware, until after receiving them, that these coins had been taken from murdered emigrants.

Soon after being dismissed, Tulley had gone down river to Tyler and Blackford's trading post at the Sink, where he remained drunk for two days, as Haws said he afterwards learned. While in that condition, Tulley told some of the immigrants that he had sold guns and ammunition to the Indians, and swore if they didn't like it he would "put some of their lights out." Because of this threat, and the fact of his having some of the gold coins, the emigrants at the trading post became excited and arrested him.

Upon trying Tulley, said Alpheus, there was not evidence enough to convict him, and he was released, but was accidentally killed when a number of drunken emigrants began shooting at him, intending merely to scare him. Haws denied that Tulley, while in his employ, had ever traded firearms with the Indians, because he, Haws, didn't allow it. Furthermore, he and Albert, at the time of Tulley's death, were 150 miles distant.

It was Alpheus' opinion that emigrants had never acted so recklessly toward the Indians as they had that summer, and he thought the government should build a fort near the head of the Humboldt to keep white men in subjection as well as red ones.[43]

It can't be said with any certainty that the sons of Peter Haws were involved in the robberies and killings along the Humboldt in 1857, but, if in truth they were, their motive might have been as much revenge as profit. For that was the year the "Utah War" began, prompted by the resignations that spring of Justice W. W. Drummond of Utah's territorial supreme court, and other non-Mormon appointed officials.

Drummond accused the Mormons of complicity in several murders and claimed knowledge of secret, oath-bound societies of Mormon men, which existed to resist the laws of the country and take the lives and property of persons who might question church authority. These were the so-called "Danites," or sons of Dan.[44]

With Utah represented to him as being in rebellion by Drummond and others, President Buchanan replaced Brigham Young as governor with Alfred Cumming of Georgia, and ordered a military force to march immediately to the territory to sustain the authority of the new man. Advance elements of a 2,500-man army left Fort Leavenworth in July.

Surely the Haws boys learned of the government's invasion plans by mid-summer. Brigham Young was recalling his flock to Salt Lake City from colonies all over the West. A company of Mormon families under P. G. Sessions abandoned their homes in Carson Valley and trekked to Salt Lake from mid-July to mid-August, and when these people passed up the Humboldt they must have spoken to Alpheus and Albert of the trouble.

The Hawses, of course, had no love for Brigham Young, but many of his followers were their old friends, and perhaps the crisis inflamed their passions against their former persecutors, the Missourians. The Holloway and Woods trains were, after all, from that state.

The infamous massacre of the Fancher emigrant party, at Mountain Meadows in southern Utah that September, proved that such old animosities still existed. In that instance, a combined force of Ute Indians and Mormon militiamen, disguised as Indians, murdered an entire train of over 120 persons, sparing only eighteen small children. The emigrants' crime was that some of them had, supposedly, bragged of helping to kill Joseph Smith.[45]

The year 1857 was the last for Alpheus and Albert as traders along the Humboldt. They remained in California until late 1862 when Albert and his family moved to the Carson River valley, and Alpheus with his brood relocated to the booming Reese River mining region near Austin, Nevada.

Albert worked variously at herding stock, mining, farming, horse racing and hotel keeping. He is listed in 1862 as being proprietor of the Half-Way House, on the toll road between Carson City and Silver City; he was also the "Bert" Haws who, in 1864, was proprietor of Haws' Station, on the 12-mile desert about 35 miles from Dayton, Nevada.[46]

Alpheus took up farming. First, he was reported to have paid $700 for some grass and tillable lands situated in Marshall's canyon, a mile south of Austin. Then, in June 1863 he sold that ranch to some Californians and took up land in Grass Valley, to the northeast of Austin. There, he and a partner, Zeke Robinson, began raising vegetables for the Reese River market.

Alpheus was still cultivating the Grass Valley farm in 1864, and by then, he and his wife—the only woman in the valley—had three children. About this time Alpheus also became involved in mining and, in a meeting at his ranch, helped organize the Wall Street District. He was, seemingly, a good citizen—his house was the designated voting place for the Grass Valley precinct; he served on a committee for a "Calico Party," held in 1868 at Austin for the benefit of a man injured in a gun accident; and he was reportedly very much affected by the preaching of a visiting minister.

Brother Albert was not so prosperous, nor so fortunate. Much of what we know about him comes from a short autobiography of his eventful life written in his old age. Albert seems to have composed it to tidy up his reputation for future generations.

He admitted to having been a "rebellious and revengeful man," who was "doing evil and associating with evil persons," but he claimed that the "good seed sown" in his childhood, and the knowledge received at his baptism as a Latter-day Saint, acted as a check upon his "reckless nature," and called him "back to a better life."[47]

Albert told of writing to Joseph Smith III in 1860, just at the time when young Joseph had, with his mother Emma's help, assumed his place as head of the Reorganized Church of Jesus Christ of Latter-day Saints. Albert told Joseph that he would support him, if he intended to follow the original pattern set by his father, Joseph Smith Jr., when he had begun the Mormon Church. "Little Joseph" replied, assuring Albert that this would be the case.

Albert also maintained that his father, Peter, had wanted to join the Reorganized Church movement, but that he had died in 1859, just before young Joseph took his place.

Albert then began to reform, or so he said. He stopped associating with bad company, and waited for someone to come and baptize him. As events proved, it would take seven years and a debilitating, life-transforming accident to get Albert down to the river for baptism.

In January 1867 he was hauling wood to the Washoe crushing mills, while also running his small hotel, the Half-Way House. One day, while coming down from the hills with a load of wood, he fell from the wagon and over a ledge, breaking his collar and pelvic bones, as well as his right hip bone and its socket.

Friends carried him to his house, where for weeks he lay near death, having also contracted typhoid fever. During this crisis Alpheus came to Carson City for a month and a half, expecting his brother to die.

In the previous few years, there had been several "Josephite" (Reorganized Church) missionaries active in California and Nevada. Three months after Albert's accident, one of them came from Carson City and prayed with the invalid and, in May, carried him to the Carson River and baptized him. A slow recovery began, accompanied by an impassioned commitment to the Reorganized Church. Later that year, the entire families of both Albert and Alpheus were similarly baptized.

At the time, Albert and his wife Maria had a brood of six children, the eldest being in her 13th year. The family had to depend on charity for over a year, and then the county paid to move them to Alpheus' home near Austin. Finally, two years after the accident, Albert was able to walk unassisted.

Once in Austin, where he had "been known as a pretty hard case," Albert began to proselyte for his church. He tells us of his first attempt at public speaking:

> Oh, what a trial it was for me to think of praying and speaking to that houseful of people, many of them my old associates in gambling and drinking and rowdyism, all ready to take up and make fun of any mistake or slip of the tongue! [48]

But, despite his past failings, Albert was ordained an elder and took charge of the small church organization at Austin, keeping Joseph Smith III informed of his activities.

Several historians have confused our Albert Haws with an Albert H. Haws who was a resident of Clover Valley, to the south of Ruby Valley in Elko County. This latter Albert, who was also a rough character, murdered a man in Clover Valley in August 1869. He was eventually cornered by a posse near Grantsville, Utah and gunned down. But, Albert Haws—the brother of Alpheus—was nowhere near Clover Valley in those years.[49]

Both families continued living at Grass Valley until 1871, when the entire clan moved to Battle Mountain. By this time Alpheus' cattle and mining interests had made him a wealthy man. He, or perhaps Albert, also ran a stage line from Battle Mountain to Austin for a time in 1871, in partnership with a certain Woodruff.

In October, 1872, an Elko newsman noted how fortune had smiled on "Alf," and how his efforts in the wilds of the state had been rewarded by a "goodly share of the world's goods," including a band of 2,000 cattle grazing on a range north of the river between Elko and Battle Mountain. The writer recollected Haws' pioneer entry into the Humboldt Valley in 1854.[50]

But neither wealth nor religious renewal could prevent the tragedy that struck both families in 1875 and 1876. Within a six-month period, five Haws offspring died at Battle Mountain, four of them victims of scarlet fever. Alpheus and Betsy lost two-year old Effie Maud and ten-year old Emma. Albert and Maria lost an infant daughter, Perla Belle; 21-year old Rose Ella Arthur, and an infant grandson, Eddie Phelps.[51]

Perhaps due, in part, to this terrible loss, Alpheus and Betsy separated from one another not long afterward. He went to live in the booming mining town of Tuscarora, while she stayed in Battle Mountain with their three remaining children—Don Carl, Lola (Laura), and Martin Luther.

At about the same time, Albert moved to California. The last mention of him at Battle Mountain was when he ran, unsuccessfully, as an independent, for justice of the peace in the fall of 1876.

Though separated, Alpheus provided well for Betsy and the children. They lived in a comfortable house, and she and her bright, industrious children attended many of the little town's social functions. Over the years, they occasionally visited Betsy's elderly father, who was living in Brigham City, Utah as well as friends and relatives in Salt Lake City. Teen-aged Carl and pre-pubescent little Luther spent a few summers with their father in Tuscarora.

At age 56, on January 16, 1881, Alpheus married 40-year old Hannah Eleanor Bradbury of San Francisco. Where the couple lived isn't certain, but it is believed they moved to the Bay Area shortly after their marriage. When, or if, Alpheus ever got a divorce from Betsy is a mystery. She remained in Battle Mountain until at least 1886, but, by 1896, was living in Ogden, Utah. That year, in response to a request from Joseph Smith III, she provided financial support for Graceland College at Lamoni, Iowa.[52]

As to Albert, in his later years, he began traveling in California, Oregon and Washington as a Reorganized Church missionary, passing out tracts door to door, starting up reading rooms, and baptizing converts. He also became a prolific writer, contributing moralistic homilies to church publications.

And, in an attempt to put the events of that bloody summer of 1857 in an innocent light, he penned the autobiography previously noted. Like his brother, Albert denied having incited the Indians to theft and murder, and placed most of the blame for the troubles of 1857 on the shooting of an innocent Indian boy by a white man.

Alpheus had never admitted to any contact with either the Woods or Holloway parties, but Albert claimed to be six miles away, traveling with a large emigrant company, when one of the attacks occurred, although he was confused about which party was which. He would have us believe that the Indians had really intended to attack his party, because they thought that Jim Tulley, who could speak no Indian language, was an emigrant.

Albert also claimed to have been the person who found Mrs. Holloway's scalp and returned it to her. He said the emigrants were very angry at them, supposing them to be aligned with the Indians, and that the derogatory reports continued to such an extent that he feared being hanged as a desperado, so he finally left the Indian country and returned to California. He made no mention of Tulley's demise at the hands of the Woods party.

Albert died at Oakland on November 22, 1902, at age 72, of heart trouble. His church praised his works, noting that he had been "faithful unto death."[53]

Alpheus survived his brother by a few years. One of the last glimpses we have of this enigmatic man was provided by Oliver B. Huntington, who visited him in Oakland, California in 1899. Huntington recalled Alpheus having banded the Indians together in 1854, on the Humboldt and in Ruby Valley, and having hatched a plan to murder him and his traveling partners when they were headed for Carson Valley. Said Huntington of Alpheus:

> I could not but keep thinking how the Lord delivered me from the death he had planned for me by the Indians. He told us what a sufferer he had been for 15 years, how he had been cut open 13 times for stones in the bladder... We chatted together like other men but he could not hold his eyes on mine—was uneasy under my gaze, for he had sought my life yet I felt no bitterness towards him for he was a terrible sufferer.[54]

Alpheus divorced Hannah Haws in 1901. In early October, 1906, at age 81, he entered Burke's Sanatorium at Santa Rosa for some treatments, which didn't work. The "well-known mining man of Berkeley"—as the tabloids labeled him—realized that he was going to die, and his yearning for Hannah swept away the bitterness that was in his heart, so he begged that she be sent for. Hannah, by then 65 years old, responded at once and, upon her arrival at the sanatorium, the pair quickly reconciled and were remarried by a Baptist minister, in the presence of the attending physicians and nurses. This "deathbed romance" caused an improvement in Alpheus' spirits and he gasped his last breath peacefully on November 2. He left a large estate, and was buried at Berkeley.[55]

Uncle Billy

Nevada's most intriguing pioneer character was surely Colonel William H. Rogers. Known to his many friends as "Uncle Billy," this old-timer was a bit of a scoundrel, but his pluck and generous good will toward his fellow man more than made up for his faults.

Billy Rogers lived most of his life in Kentucky, Indiana and Illinois. He was 56 years old when news was first received of the discovery of gold in California, but, possessed of an adventurous spirit, he struck out across the plains, and arrived in the Golden State amongst the earliest of the "forty-niners."

Despite his age, citizens of El Dorado County, in 1850, elected Rogers as their first sheriff. In those troublous early days of crime and vigilantism in California, he proved to be a firm but respected officer, who scrupulously maintained the force of law.

The old man's mettle was tested often. In one instance he faced down a mob about to lynch a thief who had been ordered to leave the area. Despite considerable difficulty, Billy and his deputy—backed by a few citizens of Coloma—rescued the man so that he might be dealt with by proper authority.

A short time later, Rogers' grit, good sense and determination helped him defuse another crisis, caused by refusal of the owners of a certain dam to remove it, as required by mining district law. The owners, and 150 of their friends, all armed, collected at the dam, prepared to resist Billy. The sheriff, who had only a small posse with him, backed off, saying he would return that evening, fully ready to enforce the law. He went to the surrounding towns and recruited nearly 200 miners to help him do his duty, and the news of his activity proved enough to make the dam owners obey the law.[1]

But Rogers was best known during this period as an Indian-fighter. Conflict with the natives was inevitable, what with gold-seekers swarming over the landscape. In early May 1851, a small war was set off by Indians killing a prospector on the south fork of the American River. The men who went out to retrieve the body were also attacked, and one of them slain.

California's governor promptly appointed Rogers a major of volunteer militia and, had him raise an initial volunteer force of sixty men. Sent out to punish the natives, Billy and his men got into a fierce skirmish with the Indian band thought to be responsible for the killings. After losing two of his men in a lengthy fight, Billy declared victory and withdrew, claiming to have done in some fourteen of the enemy.

Rogers sortied from Placerville several more times, with a force varying from two to three hundred men, recruited from the surrounding mining camps. On June 4, near Kyburz, he routed the occupants of a large Indian *rancheria*, burned their possessions and, soon thereafter arrested six of the chiefs involved in the disturbances. California's Indian commissioner came to Placerville, and set Billy's prisoners free, after getting their promise to bring in all the hostile tribes for treaty making. But, ultimately, continued violence on both sides spoiled these plans.

Meanwhile, under pressure to stop spending state money, Rogers discharged 175 of his men. His battalion had cost about $4,000 per day since coming into existence. Added to this was the expense of maintaining the "Mariposa Battalion," which was fighting the Yosemites and other tribes farther to the south.

While the remainder of his subordinates continued chasing Indians— clear across the Sierra Nevada Mountains to Mormon Station—Billy Rogers resumed his duties as sheriff. Late in that summer of 1851, the incoming emigration had reached western Utah (today's Nevada), and was said to be under constant attack by hostile natives. With the permission of his military superior, Major Rogers enrolled thirty mounted militia, under command of Lt. J. P. Fyffe, and sent them to Mormon Station, as reinforcements to the other California forces operating there.

According to Fyffe, he and his men had one minor skirmish with the Indians, while escorting the mail from Carson Valley to Diamond Springs. However, the owner of the "Grand Panorama of the Plains," who was passing through Carson Valley at the time, taking his troupe of artists to Salt Lake City, said that the militia had only "succeeded in killing an old squaw and a dog, which were too old to run away." Most of the volunteers returned to Placerville "after drinking the valley dry of liquor, and kicking up a few rows."[2]

After the militia was disbanded that fall, many of Rogers' men returned to Carson Valley and became involved in the first prospecting and settlement there. About 100 miners took up lands near Mormon Station, hired an engineer to survey the valley, and organized themselves into a kind of squatter-style civil government, with its own laws and leaders.

As for Uncle Billy, he left El Dorado County late that year and went to San Jose, where, briefly, he ran a hotel, called the Mansion House. By the spring of 1854 he had drifted back to El Dorado, and was running an "express" mule train between Placerville and Carson Valley, via Johnson's cutoff. He made the trip some 40 times that year, and, in late July, began taking saddle passengers through for $12. A big booster of Carson Valley, he heartily endorsed plans which were then afoot to improve and shorten the road, so it would be capable of carrying stagecoaches.

Billy had been dabbling for some time with a copper claim he had located in Hope Valley, five miles above Carson Valley. In 1856, in connection with the "San Francisco Company," he hired a small crew, sank a shaft and began mining operations. By mid-August, the company had raised 300 wagonloads of ore. The vein being worked, Billy said, was a big one, and he continued mining until deep snow and bitter cold prevented it.[3]

In those days there was an indomitable man of Norwegian descent, named J. A. Thompson, who carried the mail and express over the Sierra Nevada between Placerville and Carson Valley. In the dead of winter he wore seven-foot long so-called "Norwegian snowshoes," that were used like skis.

This "Snowshoe" Thompson encountered Rogers in Carson Valley in late December, 1856 and learned that one of Billy's miners, Benjamin Fenwick, had frozen to death a few days earlier. It seems that Fenwick had gone to Carson Valley and was returning to the mine site, when the cold overwhelmed him a mere 300 yards from Rogers' cabin. There, he sat down on the snow and perished. He wasn't found until five days afterward, when his faithful dog, emaciated and starved, came to the cabin, and Billy followed its tracks to the body.

Billy himself had his feet badly frozen while returning to his mine from Carson Valley in February, 1857. He was forced to leave the site and get care at Mormon Station, where some friendly Latter-day Saints looked after him. By late April he was well enough to work the mine again and start hauling ore to Sacramento. He made three trips, each time dropping in on the editor of the *Sacramento Union* to extol his enterprise.

On a visit in June, Rogers announced that he would run a trading post at Hope Valley, while continuing to work his mine. He wanted his creditors to know that he was an honest man, and although at present he was "somewhat involved," if they would "wait 'till he cuts and comes again," they would all get their money. From those who were *his* many debtors he expected little, and would not be disappointed if they should fail to meet his expectation. The "old gentleman" also wanted his friends know that he would always "have a clean bed and spare plate" for them, provided they didn't outstay their welcome. His latchstring was long, and would "never be pulled in," while there was a friend on the outside who desired to hake hold of it.[4]

By this time, Carson Valley was booming. There were better roads, gold had been discovered on the Carson River, and a large contingent of Mormons had come from Salt Lake City to settle in the region. Mormon Station had grown, and was now known as Genoa. Sensing an opportunity, Billy and a former Placerville friend of his, William B. Thorrington, built a hotel.

Earlier, Thorrington had helped cut a toll road to Carson Valley through Woodford Canyon, along with the merchants John Reese and E. L. Barnard. He had then brought his family to Carson Valley from the East, and located on a ranch. In September 1854 he had taken control of the considerable property of Reese and Barnard when Barnard absconded with $80,000, causing the firm to fail.

Shortly after this, Thorrington took a stagecoach over the Sierra Nevada Mountains, and from this trip comes the only description we have of this colorful character. Bill's "innards" having caused him some uneasiness, he traded seats with an outsider and perched himself on the upper deck, alongside our observer, "Boz," where he immediately cheered up, and even became musical.

Boz described Thorrington as "a complete man of the world," more than six feet high, rosy-cheeked, who was always telling jokes and laughing as heartily at them as anyone else. His good spirit made the time pass most agreeably on the long ride to Placerville.

Thorrington was said to have prospered in all of his ventures and, for this trait, he had been dubbed "Lucky Bill." At the gaming table he could outsmart the professionals; if he were to buy a sick horse, which, with any other person, would be certain to die, it would recover, and Lucky Bill would double his money on him; on his Carson Valley ranch, he raised the fattest stock in the whole region. And so it went, it was said, with everything he touched.[5]

Well—perhaps not.

On August 20, 1857 Uncle Billy and Lucky Bill held a ball in their new hotel at Genoa, attended by about seventy men and thirty ladies. One editor called the affair "the most fashionable, largest party every given in the valley." Everything went swimmingly until 10 P.M., when a young fellow named William Sides and some friends were asked by the door attendant to leave, because they were in company with a woman of ill repute, well known in Sacramento as Miss Lamb, alias "Bukes."

The drunken Sides became indignant and went into kitchen to complain to Rogers. But Billy himself was steaming mad because the difficulty was causing his female guests to begin leaving. When he harshly insisted that Sides leave, the latter knocked him down and left the house. Rogers also left the hotel to get himself a pistol, and when he returned he found Sides, and his friend Bowen Abernathy, and others, outside, ready to resume the quarrel.

After more arguments, Abernathy threw a rock at Billy at the same instant Billy fired his gun at Abernathy. Billy was struck below the eyes, but his shot grazed Abernathy's forehead, and both men fell to the ground at the same instant. Abernathy, the younger man, arose first and proceeded to kick Billy in the face, then took the pistol from him and beat him with it. Finally, Billy's friends stopped the fracas and took the battered old man away. Reportedly, "Lucky Bill" acted as the friend of Rogers through the entire matter, but the odds were too great.

Needless to say, Genoa's "most fashionable party" was over.

The following morning, the friends of Abernathy assembled en masse determined to lynch Rogers, but couldn't find him. They then decided to tear down the hotel and burn the town, but some citizens deterred them. Some time later, the hotel was opened under a new owner, D. E. Gilbert of Placerville, the two Bills having abandoned their careers as hoteliers.[6]

The much-battered Billy went back to tending his copper mine, but his troubles continued. On September 4, some of "Captain Jim's" tribe of Washoe Indians robbed his cabin and killed his dog. The following day, two Genoans, John McMarlin and James Williams, while traveling on the road from Placerville, were murdered near Slippery Ford. Williams, was packing goods for "Dutch Nick's" trading post east of Genoa. Four of the men's animals were carried off, and their other belongings either stolen or destroyed.

The sheriff found both bodies, stripped of clothing and pierced with arrows and balls. Suspicion immediately fell on the Washoes, about sixty of whom were camped nearby. A hat found near the murder scene was identified by several citizens as belonging to a well-known member of Captain Jim's band.

About a week after the murders, three Washoes came to Genoa, and were recognized by Rogers and one of his workmen as having been among those who had robbed the cabin at the mine. One of these Washoes was wearing a shirt recognized by Billy as being his own, and another had a gun, which Billy seized. In the ensuing attempt by Billy to obtain the names of the murderers and robbers of McMarlin and Williams, the Indians made their escape. Rogers, however, wounded two of them as they fled, one of whom was a brother of Captain Jim, and a suspect in the murders.

After this incident, the camp of Washoes near Genoa moved to the head of the Carson Valley, and the Paiute chief, Young Winnemucca (Numaga), came to Genoa and offered to help the whites fight their common enemy, the Washoes. A contingent of Numaga's braves rode through the town, singing their war song, and expansive plans were made for a joint offensive, but the idea was soon dropped.

Two more men—William Larkin and Charles Stewart—were murdered by Washoes on September 30, along the East Fork of Carson River, about eight miles from Genoa. Rogers was in town, preparing to go to California on business, when one of the murder victims was brought in. A crowd collected around Billy, and asked him to take a petition to the governor of California, J. Neely Johnson, asking for assistance in fighting the Indians.

The request told of the recent murders and stated that there were now over fifty families living in Carson Valley, with more coming over from California all the time, and their case would be quite desperate when the snows came, unless assistance was received. The inhabitants had very few arms, and the 300 or so Washoes camped within a few miles of Genoa had said they intended killing all whites in the valley.

Billy carried the settlers' appeal across the Sierra Nevada and presented it to Johnson at Sacramento on October 6. He received from the governor twenty-five Yager muskets, with the proviso that they be used strictly to aid in the capture of the murderers. It was expected that the arms would be returned in the spring. The governor also issued a proclamation offering a reward of $250 each for the arrest and conviction of the murders. Several citizens of Sacramento donated $110, which was spent for ammunition and transportation.

For his part, Billy promised to raise the requisite number of men, and pay their expenses during the winter, trusting that the state would properly reimburse him. He promptly recruited twenty-five volunteers, most of whom were from San Francisco. On October 17, he left with them for Carson City, having finagled free steamboat tickets to transport everyone as far as Sacramento.

Upon arrival back in Carson Valley with his recruits and arms, Billy learned that Captain Jim of the Washoes had come into Genoa and entered into a compact with the settlers, agreeing to shoot any member of his tribe that molested a white man, and asking only that justice be meted out to offenders among the whites.[7]

With Jim's help, a search was begun for the three supposed murderers of Williams and McMarlin. On some pretense, the chief induced one of them, "Charley," to visit the ranch of "Lucky Bill" Thorrington, where Rogers' posse captured him. At the time, he was wearing a pair of the murdered Williams' trousers.

Rogers took Charley to Genoa, where, on October 27, he acknowledged being present when the two whites were shot, but claimed the other two suspects had done the shooting, and that they were now at Yankee Jim's in California. It was decided to send Charley to that state for trial. But, on the way to a blacksmith's shop to be put into irons, he broke from his keepers and ran for the mountains. Two or three men followed him, firing as they ran. Several of the balls struck home, killing Charley.[8]

Because of this incident, some California papers criticized Rogers for misusing his "Army of Occupation." But a Genoa correspondent of the *San Francisco Herald*, Richard N. Allen—whose *nom de plume* was "Tennessee"—defended Billy as an "upright and honorable old man." At a well-attended meeting of Genoans held at Major Ormsby's store, a resolution was unanimously carried, approving Rogers' leadership. "No family in this place would feel secure if Uncle Billy's men were not here," said Allen.[9]

Allen also mentioned Billy's effectiveness in dealing with those natives that had agreed to peace. Large numbers of them were now coming into town every day, making Billy's quarters their rendezvous, and they seldom left his place hungry.

Billy and his force were never able to capture the other two men concerned in the murder of McMarlin and Williams, and so, with the Washoes at peace, the remainder of Billy's little army was soon disbanded, and most of them left on foot for California. Billy made plans to build a sawmill about a mile below Genoa.

There now occurred an event that would impact Billy's life as well as abruptly end the serendipity of his friend "Lucky Bill" Thorrington.

Near the end of February 1858, the Paiute chief, Numaga, came to Genoa to tell of two whites who were stopping with his tribe, whom he thought had been killing other whites. One of these men answered the description of a fellow who had mysteriously disappeared from the Carson River the previous fall, leaving his partner murdered in their cabin. In response to Numaga's statement, Bill Thorrington raised a posse of five or six citizens, and started out in company with the chief, about March 5, to search for and arrest the two suspects.

Uncle Billy was not one of Thorrington's party, being preoccupied with cutting a road to the site of his sawmill. One evening, after work, he attended another of those "grand cotillion" parties, such as had destroyed the hotel he and Thorrington had owned. At this dance, once again, a terrible row was kicked up—one man was stabbed in the back and arm, and another in the hand. During the melee, the doors of the house were barricaded, and the ladies were poked out through the windows. There is no knowing how the affair might have ended had not Billy and others promptly intervened to halt the hostilities.

Shortly after this high point of Genoa's social season, Bill Thorrington returned from his search for the white desperadoes named by Numaga. The trail of the outlaws had been lost in Honey Lake Valley, near Susanville, California. To get back to Carson Valley, Bill had had to borrow fifteen dollars from William Edwards, a man who had lived for a time with him earlier that year. Also, before he returned, Thorrington had gone to look at some cattle offered for sale by a certain Harry Godier, and had left Honey Lake Valley saying that he had made arrangements to buy them.[10]

Several weeks after Thorrington returned, Godier was murdered, and his cattle were stolen. Subsequently, the people of Honey Lake Valley caught a fellow name Snow and, before they hanged him for Godier's murder, he confessed to being part of a regular gang of thieves, and revealed the names of several men living in Carson Valley who had also been involved.

To avoid tipping their hand, the Honey Lakers kept quiet about Snow's evidence given on the scaffold. Two men from the area were sent to Carson Valley, where they remained for a month, ingratiating themselves with the gang members and prying out their secrets. When they had learned what they needed, a large joint party of armed Honey Lakers and Genoans rode into Carson Valley before daylight of June 14, 1858, and cut off egress from the valley by taking possession of all the roads and trails leading from it.

Seven residents of the area were arrested and charged as being principals or accessories in the murder of Harry Godier, and in the theft of his cattle. They were Bill Thorrington; Bill's 17-year old son, Jerome; Orrin Gray; a gambler named John H. McBride; Luther Olds, and two of his hired men known as "Little Ike" Gandy and Calvin Austin.

The posse offered Bill's son, Jerome, his freedom if he would help them entrap another suspect, William Edwards—the man who had lived for a time with "Lucky Bill" The young man agreed, found Edwards, on June 16, and told him that his father wished to see him at his house, as he had escaped from the posse and wanted help in getting away. Edwards took the bait, went in, and was promptly seized by several posse men posted inside.

Edwards was bound hand and foot and taken to the Sides and Abernathy ranch on Clear Creek, where some 150 people had assembled in a barn to try all of the prisoners. Edwards' captors knew that he stood accused of a murder at Snelling's Ranch, California, and that a $1,500 reward had been offered for his apprehension. Nevertheless, they decided not to deliver him up to the Californians for trial, and take the chance that he might be released. They vowed that he would never leave their hands alive.

The trial took several days. Edwards freely admitted to the killing in California, but claimed that it had been a case of self-defense. As to murdering Godier, Edwards said that he and a certain John Mullen had done it. He seems to have absolved "Lucky Bill" of any part in the commission or planning of the murder, although the suspicion existed that Bill, when he had been at Honey Lake, had proposed that Edwards entice Godier to Carson Valley and then murder him, which would allow Thorrington to buy Godier's livestock at much below its value.

Edwards said he had come to Carson Valley after the Godier murder, and had told Thorrington about having done it, and that Bill didn't let him stay around him. Bill told Edwards that he had befriended him once when in difficulty, but he wanted Edwards out of the way, to go over the mountains. Instead, Edwards went back to Honey Lake.

Despite having no direct evidence to convict Thorrington, the citizen jury found him guilty of having planned Godier's murder, and of having harbored the murderer, Edwards. Then too, Thorrington was a gambler, and had acquired property with suspicious ease.

Luther Olds and another man were both found guilty of harboring horse thieves, fined a certain amount and were banished from the country, under penalty of being shot. J. H. McBride and Orrin Gray were discharged, as was young Jerome Thorrington. Edwards was taken to Honey Lake Valley and hung at the scene of Godier's killing on June 23.

"Lucky Bill" was hung at his farm one mile from Clear Creek on June 19, some three hours after conclusion of the trial. He made no confession, but behaved coolly, putting the rope around his neck. His last words were, "If they wanted to hang him, to hang; he was no hog."[11]

A year later, Captain James H. Simpson, U. S. Army, in command of a corps of topographical engineers, passed on the road between Carson City and Genoa. Upon seeing that the gallows from which Thorrington had hung, was still standing, Simpson expressed amazement that "such a relic of such a season of popular agitation and excitement should be left to be harped upon by every passer-by."[12]

There was no hint, of course, that Billy Rogers was in any way connected with any shady activities of his friend "Lucky Bill" Thorrington. But, perhaps the vigilante activity worried the former sheriff, or soured him on the Carson Valley citizenry. Or maybe Billy's business ventures simply went bust. In any case, that autumn of 1858 he left for Utah, where a large contingent of the U. S. Army had recently arrived.

The "Utah War" had just been resolved. As the reader may recall from reading the misadventures of the Haws family, this conflict had been brought on, in early 1857, by the resignations of most federally appointed Utah officials. These dignitaries had accused the Mormons of complicity in several murders and claimed knowledge of secret, oath-bound societies of Mormon men, which existed to resist the laws of the country and to take the lives and property of persons who might question church authority. These were the so-called "Danites," or sons of Dan.

With Utah represented to him by the officials as being in rebellion, President Buchanan had removed Brigham Young as governor and had sent a new one, Alfred Cumming of Georgia, to the territory with a 2,500 man military force to sustain the new man's authority. But, harassed by Mormon militia, the army had been required to spend a bitter winter on the prairie near Fort Laramie.

By the spring of 1858, a peaceful solution had been found. A presidential pardon for the inhabitants of Utah had been issued, and the army had marched through Salt Lake City on June 26 to the agreed-upon site, forty miles beyond the city. Here, Camp Floyd was established, and nearby a satellite village called "Frogtown" (now Fairfield, Utah) sprang up, whence grog and other essentials were dispensed to thirsty soldiers.

Billy arrived in Utah hoping to reap some federal patronage. He had in his pocket a recently-obtained letter of recommendation, signed by Governor

John Weller and thirty other prominent Californians. This missive, addressed to the officers of the army in Utah, mentioned the prominent part Rogers had played in California affairs.

In November Billy fitted up a large building in Salt Lake City for a hotel. By January of 1859, he had two such establishments in operation, catering mostly to the carpetbagging non-Mormon population. Noted for his gentlemanly conduct, Rogers was highly recommended by "a legion of friends"[13] at Camp Floyd. About this time he took a wife, whose name, alas, is not known.

Rogers also got himself appointed deputy U. S. Marshal for Utah Territory. In this capacity he traveled with Utah's new superintendent of Indian affairs, Dr. Jacob Forney, in March and April, 1859 to southern Utah to take custody of sixteen of the 18 children who had survived the infamous massacre of the Fancher emigrant party at Mountain Meadows, Utah.

In the poisonous atmosphere of the Utah War, there had been bitter words exchanged between the Fancher emigrants and Mormons as they passed through the Utah settlements toward southern California. Supposedly, some of the travelers had bragged of helping to kill the Mormon prophet Joseph Smith in Carthage, Missouri. The Fanchers were also accused of giving poisoned oxen meat to some Indians.

On September 11, 1857, while the Fancher party had been resting its animals a few days at Mountain Meadows, in preparation for the final push to California, a combined force of Ute Indians and Mormon militia disguised as Indians had swooped down on them. After a lengthy siege, and after three of the emigrant men were killed trying to reach Cedar City for help, the Mormon leaders at the scene decided that all the emigrants old enough to talk had to be killed.

One of the assailants, John D. Lee—having removed his disguise, and to the emigrants an apparent savior—was allowed into the camp with a white flag where he persuaded the people to surrender their arms and march back to the settlements for protection. As the beleaguered emigrants abandoned the protection of their wagons to their expected salvation, they were instead slaughtered by the Mormons and their Indian allies. The entire train of over 120 persons was killed, save only the above-mentioned small children.

The bodies had been hastily buried, the emigrant plunder distributed, and the surviving children sent to Jacob Hamblin's ranch, intending that they be assimilated into Mormon homes. Though the true story soon became known, the whites involved would deny and cover the affair up for years to come.

Deputy Marshall Billy Rogers and Superintendent Forney were escorted south by Major Carleton and his Company K, U. S. First Dragoons, reaching

Mountain Meadows on April 14. The soldiers disinterred the bones of the emigrants and buried them in one hole and built a 15-foot high monument of rough stones. After this, Forney went on to Santa Clara to collect the children, who had been assembled there by Jacob Hamblin, one of Forney's agents.

Having seen the emigrant remains, and then the surviving children, Billy and the others were determined to bring the suspected leader of the outrage, John D. Lee, to justice. Billy let it be known that he would pay a reward of $5,000 for Lee's arrest, and an officer of the escort offered to give another $500 out of his pocket for the same cause.

Billy urged Jacob Hamblin to get some Indian help and go with him into the mountains to hunt up John D. Lee and help bring him in, dead or alive. Being a loyal Mormon, Hamblin, of course, refused, saying that he had already searched for Lee and couldn't find him; that he was well-armed and lives would be lost in trying to take him. Though Billy said he didn't care about that, Hamblin held fast, using as his ultimate excuse that it was contrary to his instructions from Forney to encourage Indians in any way to interfere with whites.

And so, Billy was unable to see justice done. He returned to Salt Lake ahead of Forney, carrying a list of names of those thought to have participated in the massacre. Years later, John D. Lee would be brought to trial, as a scapegoat for all of the others who had been involved in the Mountain Meadows affair. He would be executed by a firing squad at the scene of the massacre.[14]

The trip to southern Utah marked the end of Billy Rogers' short career as a deputy marshal. Soon after his return to the Utah capital, he was given a new political plum, when he was appointed Indian agent to the band of Shoshoni that ranged in and around Ruby Valley, Nevada. This was the band led by Cho-kup—the same chieftain who, several years earlier, had been on such good terms with Peter Haws on the Humboldt.

Only a few months before Billy's appointment, the first agent this band, Robert B. Jarvis, had been sent out by Superintendent Forney with some cattle and a few basic implements to start a model Indian farm and locate a reservation. Jarvis had laid out a 36-square mile reserve, but did little else before resigning in May 1859 when Billy was named to replace him.

Several other enterprises had recently begun in Ruby Valley. In December, 1858, a few weeks before Jarvis' arrival there, George W. Chorpenning, the Salt Lake City to California mail contractor, had abandoned his old route along the Humboldt River to begin running the mails and passengers over a new, shorter road, which passed through the lower end of the valley, some thirty miles south of the new reservation. Chorpenning had come out that month with Howard Egan—his agent for the eastern end of the line—and personally treated with the Shoshoni to build a relay station there.

Later, in February 1859, while Egan was building the log shed that would serve as Ruby Valley station—the first house in the valley—Chorpenning had also been there, passing out presents to a large gathering of Shoshoni camped nearby.

In May, Captain James H. Simpson had passed through the valley, leading a corps of topographical engineers whose mission was to explore the southern route across Nevada to California. And, that summer, William H. Russell and Alexander Majors, the freighting contractors supplying the army in Utah, established a depot, consisting of workshops and houses, for handling their livestock in the valley. Howard Egan was preparing to take a large herd of their cattle and mules to California.

It isn't known just when Billy Rogers took up residence on the Ruby Valley reservation, or how long he stayed that first year, but one supposes he was there when Superintendent Forney visited in late August. Nothing was grown on the farm in 1859, and Billy would later blame Forney for not furnishing the means to keep the operation going.

The Indians all the way from Salt Lake City to the Humboldt were dissatisfied with the superintendent because of unfulfilled promises he had made on an earlier trip. One chief, with whom Forney dealt in August, called him an "old woman," and a liar.[15] Frequent raids on the mail company's livestock, which began that summer, were blamed on Forney's failure to furnish the suffering natives with provisions. With the coming of autumn and hunger, the raids intensified.[16]

The loss of livestock—and to a greater extent, poor management—soon led to the failure of George Chorpenning's mail company. For a number of months, Howard Egan and others kept it going at their own expense, but, in March of 1860, Chorpenning's contract was annulled, and a new one made with the recently-incorporated Central Overland California and Pikes Peak Express Company.

William H. Russell, Alexander Majors, John S. Jones, William B. Waddell, and others were directors of the new company, which had also just acquired the stage line running the mail from Salt Lake to the East. Thus, the acquisition of Chorpenning's failed contract gave them control over the entire central mail route to the Pacific coast.

Their contract was for a semi-monthly service. Wishing to secure an expanded one, Russell and his partners instituted a "pony express" from St.

Ruins of Ruby Valley Pony Express Station
(Northeastern Nevada Museum)

Joseph on the Missouri, to Sacramento. It was a stunt, more than a practical means of carrying mail, but its originators wanted to demonstrate that the central route was feasible for year-round travel. They had the good sense to retain Howard Egan as manager of the eastern end of their line.

From Salt Lake City to Placerville, the company would run the express and the regular mail coaches on the route surveyed the previous summer by Captain Simpson, which George Chorpenning had begun to use before going broke. In March and April, stations were established every 20-25 miles across Nevada, and the first of the scheduled semi-weekly expresses started simultaneously on April 3, 1860 from San Francisco and St. Joseph.[17]

The Overland Company's pony express had barely begun operations when Indian unrest manifested itself again throughout Nevada. From Carson City to Salt Lake, Paiutes and Shoshoni alike responded to white incursions and perceived wrongs by engaging in open warfare. Communications between California and Utah were blocked.[18]

Uncle Billy, who had spent the winter in Frogtown with his wife, apparently had not been given money by Forney to operate his Indian farm, and didn't go out to Ruby Valley until early June, 1860. The first report of his activity that year has him at Butte Valley Station, east of Ruby Valley, as that place came under attack and was burned. Billy and an associate had been trying to distribute a store of blankets and shirts from a wagon, but had been forced to defend themselves.

The old man returned immediately to Salt Lake City after this incident, incensed at Superintendent Forney for having, by his neglect, caused the Indian turmoil. Forney was already being investigated by the Interior Department for misuse of government funds. About the time Billy arrived back in the city—six weeks into the inquiry—word arrived by Pony that Forney had been removed from office by President Buchanan.

Forney was to the north of Salt Lake on his way to visit some Shoshoni when he received this unwelcome news. He returned immediately to Salt Lake City and, on June 22, boarded the mail stage, intending to go to the nation's capital and fight the charges. But, in the same coach he discovered Uncle Billy, who was going east to testify against him. Since Forney and Rogers wouldn't ride in the same coach, the doctor got out and laid over until the next stage.[19]

Forney made several trips to Washington, D. C. over the next five months, trying to clear his name. In late September, Capt. E. Ruth, a special Indian Bureau agent, was sent to Salt Lake City to inventory the government property held by Forney, and hand it over to the new Utah superintendent, Benjamin Davies. Forney left Utah for good on November 9, 1860. Ruth reported having found no malfeasance, only incompetence and poor record keeping. But, one resident of Salt Lake City said the earlier commission had found evidence of vast expenditure of public money for personal use.[20]

As summer progressed, army detachments went out from Camp Floyd, but were ineffective in stopping the ongoing rampage along the Overland road. Nonetheless, Billy went back to Ruby Valley for a short time, trying to calm natives in his charge. When camped one night while returning to Salt Lake City, he and the several soldiers with whom he was traveling, were fired upon by Goshiute Indians, without doing any damage, except wounding a soldier's horse with an arrow.[21]

Much can be learned of Uncle Billy from the visit of the world-renowned adventurer and explorer, Richard Francis Burton. In late summer, 1860, Burton arrived in Salt Lake City, bound for California. William Russell's stage coaches were still not running beyond Salt Lake because of the Indian troubles—three drivers had been shot, several stations burned and their occupants killed or wounded. The Pony Express was running only intermittently and the company had been compelled to pack the regular mails on mules, once a fortnight, making Placerville in 16 days.

At Camp Floyd, west of Salt Lake, Burton tried, unsuccessfully, to get the army to provide him an ambulance and escort. He and several other travelers were finally able to strike a deal with a certain Mr. Kennedy who was about to drive a band of horses to California. For $150 each, Kennedy agreed to convey Burton and the others in wagons, and promised to collect a sufficient armed party. Burton prepared himself for possible Indian difficulties by having his hair "shingled off" until his head resembled a "pointer's dorsum,"[22] and he expressed deep regret at having left all his wigs behind in England. He also wished he had purchased one the new Maynard carbines.

Before leaving, Burton met and had a few drinks with the notorious, Orin Porter Rockwell, who was herding cattle for Russell's company near Camp Floyd. Known as a Mormon enforcer, or Danite, Rockwell was nonetheless preferred by the army officers "to the slimy villains" who would drink with a man and then murder him.

Rockwell gave Burton all kinds of advice on how to survive the trip: always keep his eyes skinned—especially in canyons and ravines; carry a double-barreled gun loaded with buckshot; always make a dark camp—that is, unhitch for supper and then hitch up and turn a few miles off the road. Burton should be especially alert for attack when animals were being inspanned and outspanned, Rockwell said. He advised avoiding "White Indians" by shunning the direct route.[23]

But, the Indian troubles of that year had pretty well subsided by the time Burton left Salt Lake, and his trip across Nevada would prove to be without incident. He reached the Ruby Valley pony and stage station on October 7. Billy Rogers was living at or near the station in a stone hut, and he offered Burton and his party such hospitality as he could.

Chief Cho-kup and many of his Ruby Valley Shoshoni tribe were camped around Billy's house. During Burton's visit, the chief was collecting a large party of his men for an autumn hunt. A keen observer, Burton visited the Shoshoni camp and described the natives and their mode of living. He was amazed that such a thinly-clad people could remain relatively healthy in the harsh climate of northern Nevada. Most wore only breech cloths and scanty capes or tippets of wolf and rabbit skin. Some families lived in wickiups shaped like conical tents, but the abodes of the poorer clansmen were merely three-quarter circles of earth, sticks and sagebrush, designed to keep off the prevailing winds.

Uncle Billy fed Burton and his party dinner and then Cho-kup and five of his men—Burton called them "the lions"—sat down with knife and fork before a huge tureen full of soft pie, "amongst which they did terrible execution, champing and chewing with the noisiness of wild beasts, and eating each enough for three able-bodied sailors..."

The remainder of the evening was spent in listening to Uncle Billy's adventures amongst both whites and Indians, and his many hairbreadth escapes. The old man also railed against governmental waste and corruption, particularly in the administration of Indian affairs. Billy, whose salary was $600 per year, said he managed to make his job as agent pay by trading for the pelts of mink, wolves, woodchucks, badgers, antelope, and deer. He spoke highly of the Shoshoni, especially of their affection and fidelity in married life. Burton said the Ruby Valley tribe seemed to look upon Billy as a "Big Hearted Father."

Soon after the Englishman's visit, Billy returned to Frogtown and then to Salt Lake City, where, in an attempt to end the frequent depredations, he signed, as Indian agent, along with Governor Cummings and others, a petition to the Commissioner of Indian affairs in Washington. It asked for immediate steps to make treaties with all of the tribes in Utah Territory.[24]

From late November to mid-January, 1861, Billy went to Ruby Valley with the new superintendent of Indian affairs, Benjamin Davies, to hold peace talks with the bands in that region, taking along a six-mule team carrying a load of flour and presents. Due to the lateness of the season Davies was unable to visit any Indians farther west than Ruby Valley, but he promised to come out again in the spring with provisions, clothing and various presents.[25]

It was a hard winter, with deep snows, and, when spring came, the mail line's Howard Egan, and Indian agent Billy Rogers both predicted a repeat of the previous year's troubles, since the natives had not received any presents, and superintendents had not kept their promises over the past two years. Goshiutes had threatened to attack Deep Creek station in Utah's Ipepah Valley, when the snow was gone. And, a few of them, under a notorious hater of whites, "Jack," were lying round Willow Springs. Another band had appeared at Simpson Springs and tried, unsuccessfully, to commandeer the station keeper's provisions.

Cho-kup, the chief in Ruby Valley, had revealed that the Indians in his vicinity, and all along the line, had also been talking of rising and "cleaning out" all the stage stations. The chief had said he would do all he could to prevent trouble, but that he couldn't control them all.

Rogers hoped that Davies would keep his word to the many Indians who had been congregating at stations all along the road, awaiting his arrival. Billy had been feeding many of them, and said they had about eaten him out of house and home, leaving him nearly as destitute as they were. But, he supposed Davies would say as he had on another occasion—"Make an official statement to me and I will take cognizance of it."[26]

As predicted, Davies failed to provide any subsistence, claiming to be "entirely destitute of funds," and having gotten no response to a request for more money from his superiors. He went East to "lay the state of the case as existing" in Utah "before the proper Department," but he never came back to Utah. In August of 1861, he was replaced by Henry Martin of Wisconsin, who himself lasted only a few months before being replaced by James D. Doty.[27]

Fortunately, no Indian depredations occurred along the stage route in eastern Nevada that year, save one raid on Cold Spring Station. This was due, in large part, to the efforts of transcontinental telegraph contractor James Street to gain the support of the Indians. Street conferred with the major chiefs west of Salt Lake City, and distributed gifts of food and clothing. Cho-kup, after listening to Street, became greatly interested in the white man's "wire rope express."

That summer, the line was pushed eastward from Fort Churchill by a large party of workmen, who reached Ruby Valley on September 27. Ruby remained the easternmost transmitting station until the final link-up was made between it and Schell Creek on October 21, 1861. At that time the Pony Express came to a close. Also, Russell, Majors and Waddell had been superceded, and a daily mail was being carried west of Salt Lake City by the Butterfield Overland Mail Company.

In December, 1861, Chief Cho-kup died of consumption at Ruby Valley, precipitating a small crisis. What part Billy might have played in resolving it is not recorded, because, by then, he had been superceded as Indian agent. Nevada had become a territory, breaking its ties with Utah, and Governor James W. Nye at Carson City had assumed duties as superintendent of Indian affairs, appointing his own men as agents.

Before he died, Cho-kup had named a man known as "Buck" to succeed him as chief, and inherit not only his possessions, but also his wife, Julia. These arrangements weren't in accord with the custom of the tribe, so immediately upon Cho-kup's death his friends slew his horses, collected his arms and other effects, and prepared to add the frantic widow to the funeral pyre, that she might accompany her husband on his journey.

But Julia, who didn't care to be sacrificed, fled to the Ruby mail station, asking for protection, which was granted. The Indians demanded her surrender, threatening to burn the station and kill every white man in the valley unless they gave her up, which the whites wouldn't do.

A month or so earlier, Governor Nye had become aware of the needs of the Indians along the mail route in Nevada, and had convinced the army to

Fort Ruby Nevada
(Bancroft Library)

provide some provisions to feed them. On December 16, the governor was at Fort Churchill, arranging to forward this food, when urgent dispatches were received from the employees of the mail and telegraph companies at Ruby Valley, saying that they hourly expected an attack. Nye immediately ordered Indian agent Warren Wasson to proceed there by stagecoach. He also instructed the commander of Fort Churchill, to send a cavalry detachment to the valley and report to Wasson. More soldiers would follow with the Indian provisions.

By the time Wasson arrived in Ruby Valley on December 22, the excitement had died down. A young White Knife man had shot and killed Cho-kup's favorite Indian doctor, which perhaps obviated the necessity of fricasseeing his widow. In any case, upon a promise of the Shoshoni that they would not kill her, Julia was given up to the new chief, Buck, by the whites. Wasson talked to Buck, and about 100 natives, the rest having left for White Knife Shoshoni country, to the northwest, when the trouble started.[28]

In the autumn of 1862, with America's Civil War in full bloom, a regiment of California Volunteer Infantry, under the command of Colonel Patrick E. Connor marched across the Sierra Nevada mountains and the Nevada desert, from Stockton, en route to Utah. Their mission was to protect the mail and telegraph routes, and to keep an eye on the Mormon leader, Brigham Young, who had been recently been worrisome to the federal government.

During a one month stopover in Ruby Valley, Connor's regiment built Fort Ruby on the southwestern side of the valley, 2.5 miles northeast of the mail company's stage station (near today's Hobson, Nevada). Rude cabin-style quarters were fashioned using hand-hewn logs, taken from nearby canyons. Stables were made by setting logs vertically, stockade fashion, in a trench, and corrals were made of adobe bricks.

After the fort was mostly completed, Colonel Connor and the majority of his men continued on to Salt Lake City, where he established Fort Douglas. Left behind to garrison the cold and lonesome new post were Companies C and F of the Nevada volunteer infantry, under Major Patrick A. Gallagher.[29]

By the following summer of 1863, Billy Rogers was working in Austin, Nevada building some stables for a road contractor, and erecting a mill house in nearby Jacobsville. By that time, Colonel Connor had subdued most of the tribes in the region, except the Goshiutes, who remained unbowed. That season they made a number of fierce raids on the coaches and stations of the Overland Company, killing, in all, two drivers, two civilians, and seven soldiers. One of Connor's cavalry leaders, Captain Sam Smith and his company operated ruthlessly against these Goshiutes all summer long, using friendly Indians living in Ruby Valley as informants and guides.

During this time, the Ruby Valley Shoshoni remained peaceful, drawing praise from Billy Rogers for their good deeds, such as standing guard against the Goshiutes while the whites of the valley cut their hay. Billy said there was no fear of trouble with them if whites would just treat them civilly "and pay them for what they do without taking advantage of their ignorance." Billy's words should be heeded, said one newsman, because what he "didn't know about Indians isn't worth learning."[30]

The Utah governor made a treaty at Ruby Valley, in the autumn, with the two principal bands of Western Shoshoni living in Utah and eastern Nevada —the Tosowitch (Tosawi), or White Knives, and the Unkoahs (Ankoahs). A pact was also finally made with four Goshiute chiefs about the same time, in the Toelle Valley of Utah Territory.[31]

Billy Rogers apparently spent the rest of his life under the protective wing of Chester A. Griswold and his family. "Chess" Griswold had been a "lightning slinger"—a telegraph operator—at Ruby Valley until 1864, when he went into partnership with Judge Sam Woodward to farm a choice piece of land on Overland Creek, some ten miles north of where Harrison pass enters Ruby Valley, and at, or near, the place where Billy had built himself a crude cabin when he first came to the region.

The Wines brothers—Len and Ira—may also have had an interest in the farming enterprise, but Griswold was in charge of it, while Woodward took care of the pair's other joint ventures, which, at various times, included several stores, a hotel, and a freighting business. Woodward was a handsome man, seemingly always combing his hair and curling his moustache. Griswold often accused him of being too high-toned for sagebrush country.

That first year, 1864, Billy helped Griswold grow a large tract of vegetables and 30 acres of barley. Seeing the good results that could be obtained, Griswold and his partners made a deal with the Overland Stage Company, in the spring of 1865, to raise grain and foodstuffs for the company at a set price. For several years, Griswold farmed on a scale larger than ever seen in the state, employing hundreds of people and producing fine yields. The first year alone the venture produced a profit of $50,000.[32]

But Billy Rogers wasn't cut out to be a farmer, nor to lay up wealth. He spent most his time, in his latter years, wandering the country, prospecting with his constant companion and good friend, Captain Frank of the Ruby Valley Shoshoni. Frank was the same chief who, in 1865, had been a guide for Fort Ruby soldiers, both on Colonel McDermit's expedition and at the battle of Cottonwood Creek (see "A Hard Road to Jordan," herein).

In 1870, when Billy was 77 years old, he and Frank spent the summer looking, fruitlessly, for a silver ledge in the Goose Creek Mountains, which Billy had noticed while first crossing the plains. That October, Frank was thrown from a horse, and died from internal injuries. He was buried with great pomp by his tribe. Billy told the papers that the chief had always been generous and kind, and a true friend to the whites.

Billy was himself nearly killed while riding about a month later. His horse fell and turned a complete somersault, before falling on the old man. The animal then got up and began bucking, with one of Billy's feet hung-up in the stirrup. Several friends came to his aid, but not before one knee and ankle were twisted almost out of joint. The tough old pioneer managed to ride to the Overland Ranch where he was cared for by a doctor, and within a month was up and about, visiting in the new railroad town known as Elko.[33]

In September 1871, Rogers was making bricks for a hotel being built on the Overland Ranch, which place, by then, was owned solely by Chester Griswold. Billy had a garden about 300 yards from Griswold's buildings, and to be more independent, he had built a willow house and arbor nearby. He had a lot of visitors to his "harbor," as he called it. On one afternoon, he was seen entertaining several ladies and children, doing the honors at table, "with as much grace and dignity as any Prince in his mansion."

Billy was reportedly upset by the dishonesty of the era, and by people trying to see how much money they could make out of an election. If the country got much more corrupt, he warned, it would "fall in pieces" like his "shanty" would when the winter winds came on it.[34]

But Rogers was himself accused of dishonesty in December of that year. An article appeared in the Petaluma, California *Crescent*, accusing the "old vagabond loafer" of causing the Indian war of 1851, by shooting, without provocation, the chief of the Coloma tribe when he came into town to buy a pair of pants. Further, that Billy had presented a bill for $80,000 to the state, of which $70,000 was paid.

This led a Carson City paper to defend Rogers, saying that possibly the *Crescent* was correct in repeating the allegations of some previous writers regarding Roger's part in the Indian troubles of 1851, but in Nevada his great influence with the Indian tribes had always been used for the preservation of peace. In eastern Nevada, he had long been "a sort of a white chief" among the Shoshoni, "and his influence [had] undoubtedly saved the lives of many of the pioneers of that section."[35]

With his rifle and his pick, said the editor, Uncle Billy was still living smack in the middle of the bands of savages, exploring and prospecting with absolute immunity in localities far from safe to most white men. And, he was still hale and hearty as when he first started down the Mississippi on a flat boat about 60 years ago.

But Billy didn't need any help in defending himself. Responding to the accusations, he wrote the *Elko Independent*, saying:

> Now I am an old man, eighty years of age, and have always hoed my own row and rowed my own boat; and I pronounce the author of that article a liar, a scoundrel and a coward and he can not dance...it is true I was sheriff of El Dorado County and led the troops against the Indians, and the bill against the State instead of being $80,000, was $349,742, which was allowed and paid in State bonds, for which the government paid the state in gold and silver. I have now in my possession all the receipts and documents to prove my statements true...
>
> I have to my knowledge not done a mean act, nor wronged an individual, state or the General Government out of a dollar. I can look any man in the face with a clear conscience. I do not like to leave this world with the stigma upon my character...[36]

Indeed, newspapers reported, at the time, that the cost of the El Dorado Indian expeditions was about $300,000. Billy also sent, with his letter to the editor, statements made in 1858 by the California senate, secretary of state, and comptroller, clearing him of any defalcations in his expedition accounts.

After an absence of 25 years, Rogers took the new transcontinental railroad to visit his hometown of La Moille in Bureau County, Illinois, in 1873, and went there again two years later. It was here he had first been married and, he said, he still had old friends who welcomed him with open arms.

When Billy's friend, the editor of the *Independent*, saw him upon his return from the second visit, all scrubbed-up and barbered, he remarked that "the subdued air of humility surrounding him like a halo, together with the peculiar cut of his hair and store clothes led us into the natural mistake of taking him for Methodist missionary."[37]

Small, but meaningful honors were given Billy Rogers during his final years. He was named marshal of the 1874 Independence Day celebration held at the Overland Ranch, which by this time was owned by the Wines brothers, the Griswolds having moved to Starr Valley. A tall liberty pole was erected, from which, "proudly floated the star-spangled banner." And, in the custom of that era, an anvil chorus "announced to the slumbering patriots of the valley that another glorious fourth had dawned..." The many attendees, including residents of Starr Valley, held a picnic on a small willow-shaded island in the creek just above Wines' house. The Declaration of Independence was read, an oration was given, and Len Wines read some poetry. Those present feasted on delicacies imported from Elko, and strawberries from the nearby Egan ranch. In the evening, fireworks were set off and there was dancing.[38]

That fall, Billy attended, along with Griswold, the Elko County Democratic Party convention. A committee waited on "the old pioneer of Nevada, and the patriarch among men and the Democracy," and requested him to come forward and place himself under the protecting wing of the convention. Before taking his seat Uncle Billy made one of his "happy little speeches," which was received with hearty applause.[39]

In early 1876 Billy went to live with members of the Griswold family in Starr Valley, Len Wines having sold the Overland Ranch. By the end of that year, he had grown quite feeble and lost most of his sight. As December approached, the editor of the *Independent* noted that the old man was poor and helpless, and had no relatives in the West from whom to draw assistance; he asked that friends make donations in the form of Christmas presents so Billy could be made comfortable in his decline.

On Wednesday, September 5, 1877, the vicissitudes of his eventful life caught up with Col. William Rogers. He died peacefully, at age 84, among friends in Elko, and departed for "that bourne from which no traveler returns." His well-known generosity, in former years, kept him poor, but at the same time made him fast friends, and drew respect and esteem from all who knew him. The news of Billy's death caused "a feeling of sorrow to invade every hamlet and ranch within a circuit of an hundred miles."[40]

Billy was buried in the Elko cemetery. About two years after his death, a tombstone for his grave was made. When taken to the burying ground to be placed in position, it was discovered that the board that had temporarily marked the grave was missing. To avoid a mistake as to the correct locality, Billy's casket was dug up and its lid opened. Observers said that the countenance of the old pioneer still looked as natural as though he had just fallen asleep, the only change noticeable being that the beard had grown several inches in length since his interment.[41]

The stone his friends placed can still be seen, standing under a large pine tree, and inscribed with a most fitting tribute—"Here lies a man."

Notes to the Chapters

NOTES TO "JOSEFA AND THE SENATOR"

1. John Daggett, Scrapbooks, 4:4; also see Irving McKee, ed., *Alonzo Delano's California Correspondence*, 62.
2. Franklin A. Buck, *A Yankee Trader in the Gold Rush*, 102.
3. New Orleans *The Daily True Delta*, Apr. 11, 1850.
4. San Francisco *Alta California*, Aug. 2, 1849.
5. San Francisco *Placer Times and Transcript*, July 29, 1850.
6. *Alta*, Steamer ed., July 13, 1850.
7. McKee, 123.
8. San Francisco *Daily Herald*, Aug. 21 and 25, 1851.
9. Sacramento, California, *Sacramento Daily Union*, Aug. 2, 1852.
10. Weekly *Alta*, April 3, 1852; San Francisco, California *Daily Evening Picayune*, Apr. 2, 1852.
11. Major William Downie, *Hunting For Gold*, 146.
12. *Picayune*, Jan. 26, 1852.
13. *Ibid.*
14. *Ibid.*
15. *Ibid*, Jan. 27, 1852.
16. *Ibid*, Jan. 26, 1852.
17. *Alta*, Jan. 29, 1852 and July 14, 1851 respectively.
18. *Picayune*, Jan.26, 1852; also see *Nevada Journal*, Jan.31, 1852; S. F. *Herald* Jan. 27, 1852.
19. *Dictionary of American Biography*, s.v. John B. Weller; Boise *Statesman*, August 27, 1864.
20. Nevada City, California, *Nevada Democrat*, Oct. 9, 1860.
21. Buck, 167. More on Josefa can be found in J. D. Borthwick, *Three Years in California*, 182; William B. Secrest, *Juanita*, 31; S. F. *Herald*, Oct. 5, 1853; San Jose, California, *The Pioneer*, Oct. 22, 1881; San Francisco, California, *The Pacific*, July 9, 1852; *Picayune*, Jan. 29, 1852; Merced, California *Star*, May 22, 1890; Marysville, California *Daily Evening Herald*, June 28 and July 8 and 12, 1851.

NOTES TO "BROTHER JONATHAN"

1. Hubert Howe Bancroft, *History of California*, 7: 135; also see *Sac. Union*, Oct. 20, 1854, June 4, 1858.
2. San Francisco, California *Daily Evening Bulletin*, Aug. 25, 1862; see also *Alta*, steamer ed., Feb. 20, 1856; Stockton California, *San Joaquin Republican*, Apr. 27, 1855.
3. David G. Robinson, *Comic Songs*, 33.
4. *Sac. Union*, Oct. 12, 1854; also see Portland, Oregon, *The Oregon Weekly Times*, Oct. 27, 1855.
5. Albert D. Richardson, *Beyond the Mississippi*, 419.
6. Salt Lake City *Daily Union Vedette*, July 25, 1865.
7. Portland, Oregon, *Oregonian*, Mar. 4, 1864; also New York *Herald*, Nov. 27, 1850; *Alta*, Mar. 3, 1851.
8. *Alta*, Jan. 15, 1852.
9. Ellison L. Crawford Letter of Oct. 4, 1852, MS-0476, Calif. Hist. Society, MS-0476: *Oregon Times*, June 26, Dec. 18, 1852. The *Oregon Times*, Oct. 9, 1851, lists *Jonathan* as one of Vanderbilt's Atlantic steamers as of Aug. 22, 1851, or earlier, with Captain H. Squier as her commander.
10. Other details of *Jonathan's* early history are in Bancroft, *California* VI: 140-44; San Francisco *Daily Evening Journal*, Feb. 2, 1853; "Continuation of the Annals of San Francisco," *C. H. S. Q.* 15: 164, 169, 172, 178; *OregonTimes*, Oct. 9, 1851, Mar. 27, 1852, Mar. 13, 1853, Oct. 14, 28, 1854, Mar. 21, Apr. 11, 18, June 6, 20, 27, July 25, Aug. 8, Sept. 5, 19, Oct. 10, 17, 31, Nov. 7, 14, 26, 1857, Jan. 23, Mar. 6, Apr. 10, 1858; Elizabeth Martin, "The Hubert-Walker Letters," C.H. S. Q., 36:134; *Alta*, Apr. 10, 1853, Apr. 14, 1858; *Sac. Union*, June 11, July 31, Aug. 31, Sept. 29, Oct. 9, 10, 16, 19, 1854, Dec. 19, 1855, Jan. 7, Feb. 9, Mar. 6, Apr. 7, 11, 14, May 2, 27, Oct. 23, 24, Nov. 27, Jan. 28, Feb. 2, 4, 9, 18, 27, 28, Mar. 20, Apr. 7, 11, 14, 25, June 11, Nov. 2, 15, 1857, Jan. 25,1858; Seattle, Washington, *Marine Digest and Transportation* News, May 24, 1958, 13; *Oregonian*, Aug. 4, 1935.
11. *Sac. Union*, July 15, 1858.
12. *Oregon Times*, July 31, 1858.
13. *Sac. Union*, July 15, 1858: also see eds. of May 21, June 4, 10, 22, July 7, 9, 10, 21, 1858.
14. *Oregon Times*, July 31, 1858.
15. *Ibid*, Mar. 19, 1859; also see eds. of Apr. 9, 30, 1859.
16. *Alta*, May 4, 1861; also see Alfred L. Lomax, "Brother Jonathan." O. H. S. Q. 67: 338-343.
17. *Oregonian*, Oct. 21, 1861.
18. *Alta*, October 16, 1861 and *Oregonian*, Oct. 21, 1861, resp.
19. *Oregonian*, Oct. 19, 1861.

20. *Ibid.*, Oct. 4, 11, 12, 14, Nov. 20, 21, 23, 25, 1861. James H. Hawley, *History of Idaho*, 1:864-65; W. J. McConnell, *Early History of Idaho*, 261-287; Charles Abbot Tracy, "Police Function in Portland, 1851-1874, Part II." *O. H. Q.* 80: 2, 141-42. Staples was a native of Maine, and had been on the Pacific Coast since 1849. He was survived by a wife and child in San Francisco.
21. *Alta*, Dec. 15, 1861 and *Oregonian*, Dec. 25, 1861, resp. Also Nicholas C. Polos, "John Swett: A Stranger in the Southland," *C. H. S. Q.* 42: 146-47.
22. *Oregonian*, Feb. 1, 1862; also eds. of Dec. 24, 27, 28, 1861, Jan. 15, 29, Feb 4, 1862.
23. *Oregonian*, Oct. 22, 1861.
24. *Sac. Union*, Aug. 3, 1865; also ed. of July 15, 1858; *Oregonian* Feb. 12, Mar. 4, 1864, July 18, 1931; E. W. Wright, *Lewis and Dryden's Marine History*, 66; *Alta*, Feb. 27, Apr. 7, Aug. 18, 1864.
25. *Oregonian*, Oct. 29, 1864; also see *Sac. Union*, Mar. 7, 14, 22, 31, May 20, Apr. 25, Sept. 12, 27, Oct. 13, 14, 1864.
26. *Alta*, July 16, 21, 1865; *Oregonian*, Dec. 7, 28, 1864; Aug. 12, 1865.
27. *Sac. Union*, June 28, Aug. 4, 5, 1865; *Alta*, Feb.1, 1855, July 26, 1865; The Dalles, Oregon *Weekly Mountaineer*, July 21, 1865.
28. *Sac. Union*, August 3, 1865; also see eds. of Aug. 7, 12; *Oregonian* Aug. 4, 14, 1865; Salem, *The Oregon Arena*, Aug. 21, 1865.
29. Carl P. Schlicke, *General George Wright*, 175; *Sac. Union* Oct. 8, 15, 18, 25, 27, 1858.
30. Kent D. Richards, *Isaac I. Stevens; Young Man in a Hurry*, 310.
31. *Sac. Union*, June 17, July 6, 19, 1865; Virginia City, Nevada, *Virginia Daily Union*, June 18, 1865.
32. Wright, 132; also see Mrs. Laura E. Shipman, "Recollections of the Wreck of the Brother Jonathan," 1.
33. *Oregonian*, Aug. 3, 1865.
34. *Mountaineer*, Aug. 25, 1865; also *Oregonian*, October 26, 1865.
35. *Oregonian*, Aug. 18, 1865.
36. *Sac. Union*, Aug. 12, 1865.
37. *Ibid.*, Aug. 24, 1865.
38. Jacksonville, Oregon, *The Oregon Reporter*, Aug. 5, 1865; also *Oregonian*, Aug. 19, 1865.
39. *Sac. Union*, Aug. 24, 1865; also see eds. of Aug. 4, 10, 15, 1865.
40. New York *Tribune*, Oct. 13, 1865; also see Richardson, 418-19; *Alta*, Aug. 3, 1865.
41. *Vedette*, Aug. 21, 1865.
42. *Reporter*, Aug. 5, 1865.
43. *Oregonian*, Aug. 25, 1865; see also ed. of Sept. 8, 1865.
44. *Oregonian*, Aug. 14, 1865.
45. *Sac. Union*, Aug. 24, 1865.
46. *Reporter*, Aug. 12, 1865.

47. *Oregonian*, Aug. 4, 25, 1865; also eds. of July 4, 1932, July 18, 1931; Aug. 4, 1935; newspaper clipping in De Wolf scrapbook, Del Norte County Museum, Crescent City, California.
48. S. F. *Bulletin*, Aug. 28, 1865 and *Sac. Union*, Aug. 26, 1865, respectively.
49. S. F. *Bulletin*, Aug. 28, 1865; also John A. Hussey, ed. "The California Recollections of Casper T. Hopkins," *C. H. S. Q.* 26: 360; W. H. Hutchinson, "Never Forget," *Westways*, Feb., 1952, 8-9: Hopkins was manager of the California Mutual Marine Insurance Co. Ditat, Belle, Nellie and baby Myra were the Hopkins children.
50. *Reporter*, August 5, 1865.
51. James A. Gibbs, *Shipwrecks of the Pacific Coast*, 183; San Fran. California *Times-Gazette*, Aug. 9, 1890; *Alta*, July 13, 28, Aug. 2-4, 8, 10, 14, 1865; Oct. 13, 18, 22, 1865; *Mountaineer*, Aug. 25, Sept. 1, Nov. 10, 1865; *Sac. Union*, Aug. 11, 17, 21, 25, Oct. 20, 23, 1865; Mary F. Ackley, *Crossing the Plains*, 58-59; Anthony J. Bledsoe, *History of Del Norte County*, 79-83; Wright, 133-134; *Oregonian*, Aug. 25, 29, Sept. 6, Oct. 6, 26, Nov. 8, 1865.
52. *Alta*, Aug. 2, 1865; Schlicke, 229-31, 337-38; *Sac. Union*, Aug. 12, 18, 1865; Merle W. Wells, *Gold Camps*, 32; Alfred L. Lomax, "Ellendale Woolen Mill, 1865-71." O. H. S. Q. 31; Dorothy O. Johansen and Frank B. Gill, "A Chapter in the History of the Oregon Steam Navigation Co." O. H. S. Q. 38.
53. Mrs. M. E. De Wolf, *Account of the Loss of the Steamship Brother Jonathan*; *New York Times* Aug. 26, 1865; Keith and Donna Clark, "William McKay's Journal," 152n. *Sac. Union* Nov. 24, 1865; Boise, Idaho *Tri-Weekly Statesman*, Aug. 15, 1865; *Oregonian*, July 18, 1931. The amounts insurance companies paid were: California Insurance Co., $20,000; California Lloyds, $13,670; Merchants Mutual, $10,000; Bigelow Brothers, $2,600; Faulkner & Bell, $2,300.
54. Opinion of the Supreme Court of the United States, 96-1400, April 22, 1998; also see Crescent City, California *The Triplicate*, July 19, 1996, June 10, July 4, 1997; San Francisco, California *Chronicle*, July 18, 1996; Nash, "Canadian Gold." 9; National Park Service, National *Register* of Historic Places Registration Form for *Brother Jonathan*, July 5, 1995.
55. S. F. *Chronicle*, March 19, 1999; *Triplicate*, Sept. 21, 1999.

NOTES TO "SAGEBRUSH STEAMBOAT"

1. Lewiston, Idaho Territory, *The Golden Age*, Aug. 2, 1862; Hubert Howe Bancroft, *History of Oregon*, 2:480-81; S. F. *Bulletin*, Feb.-Mar., 1862. Ainsworth was president of the company.
2. *Sac. Union*, June 8, 1865; also see ed. of May 20, 1864.
3. Alexander Ross, *The Fur Hunters of the Far West*, 205-206.
4. *Golden Age*, Feb. 5, 1863.
5. *Golden Age* in *The War of the Rebellion*, Series I, Vol. 50, Part 2: 259 (hereafter

cited as "O.R.")
6. *Golden Age*, Mar. 12, 1864; see also *Oregonian*, Nov. 4, 1863.
7. *Oregonian*, Feb.20, 1864; also see Idaho City, Idaho, *Boise News*, Mar. 12, 1864; Idaho City, Idaho Territory, *Idaho World*, May 6, 1865; Hubert H. Bancroft, *History of Washington, Idaho and Montana*, 407-08.
8. Lockley, Fred, ed. "Reminiscences of Captain William P. Gray," *O. H. Q.* 14:321-54. The passengers were Gray's father, W. H. Gray, and J. M. Vansyckle, a merchant of Wallula. The younger Gray later became a renowned Columbia River pilot.
9. Austin, Nevada, *Reese River Reveille*, July 28, 1865; also Lewiston, Idaho *Morning Tribune*, Mar. 20, 1927; *World*, July 1, 1865; *Mountaineer*, July 7, 1865; Bancroft, *Oregon*, 2: 462; Wright, 80. Tom Stump served the O. S. N. for nearly 20 years; he died in 1881 aboard the steamer *Spokane* on a down river run from Lewiston.
10. *Oregonian*, Nov. 7, 1865; *Statesman*, Dec. 18, 1865; Hawley 1: 419. Stump also inspected some mining property in the Owyhee district, owned by officers of the O. S. N. (*Sac. Union*, Aug. 18, Sept. 13, 1864).
11. *Alta*, Oct. 28, 1865; *Statesman*, Nov. 16, 1865.
12. Johansen and Gill, O. H. S. Q., 38: 304
13. Silver City, Idaho, *The Owyhee Avalanche*, Dec.16, 1865.
14. *Oregonian*, Jan. 6, 1866.
15. *Laws of the Territory of Idaho, Third Session*; Hawley 1: 426.
16. *Avalanche*, Sept. 9, 1865.
17. Wright, 101, fn. 33. Gates died in 1888 while serving as mayor of Portland.
18. *Alta*, Oct. 28, 1865; also *Avalanche* Aug. 26, Dec. 23, 1865; *World*, Sept. 9, 1865; Bancroft, *Washington, Idaho and Montana*, 437; *Oregonian*, Aug. 7, 12, 30, Sept. 23, 1865; Hawley 1: 695.
19. *Statesman*, Dec. 23, 1865, Jan. 6, 1865.
20. *Avalanche*, Mar. 31, 1866; also ed. of Mar. 10, 1866.
21. *Ibid.*, Apr. 14, 1866
22. *Statesman*, Jan. 6, Mar. 24, 31, Apr. 26, 1866; *Mountaineer*, May 10, 1870; *Avalanche*, Feb. 24, 1866.
23. *Avalanche*, May 12, 1866.
24. *Statesman*, Jan. 4 1866; also eds. of Dec. 15, 22, 1864; Thomas Donaldson, *Idaho of Yesterday*, 125-7; Placerville, California, *Mountain Democrat* Sept. 27, 1856. English and Scottish forces recaptured Lucknow, India during the Mutiny of 1857.
25. C. Aubrey Angelo, *Sketches of Travel in Oregon and Idaho*, 105.
26. *World*, July 1, 1865.
27. *Statesman*, Oct. 14, 1865; also see ed. of Jan. 2, 1866. Record's Station was an adobe house, 15 miles out of Boise, near a spring. The Cold Springs "stage house" consisted of a tent pitched in a ravine, just before Reynolds' Creek was reached (*Oregonian*, July 12, 1865).

28. *Statesman*, May 19, 1866.
29. *Ibid.*, May 22, 1866.
30. *Ibid.*, Feb. 20, 1866; also see *Oregonian*, Mar. 27, 1866.
31. *Statesman* May 22, 1866; see also eds. of May 24 and 26, 1866.
32. *Avalanche* June 2, 1866.
33. *World*, July 7, 1866; also see ed. of April 14, 1866; *Statesman*, June 21, 28, 1866; *Avalanche*, July 7, 1866; Angelo, 73.
34. Johansen and Gill, O. H.S. Q., 38: 398.
35. *Oregonian*, Sept. 21, 1866; also *Statesman*, July 19, 21, Sept. 8, 1866; *Avalanche*, Mar. 9, 1867; Bancroft, *Washington, Idaho and Montana*, 437; *World* July 20, 1867.
36. *Statesman*, Oct. 31, 1867; *Avalanche*, Oct. 26, 1867.
37. *Statesman*, Nov. 2, 1867.
38. Sebastian Miller learned the marine engineer's trade on the Ohio River and came to Oregon in 1852. After getting his master's papers, he commanded nearly 40 different steamers on the Willamette, Columbia and Snake. Buchanan had previous experience as both master and engineer of a small steamboat. In later life he worked as a government engineer, superintending navigation improvements on the Columbia until 1889. (Wright, 45 fn.33 & 181-2, fn.1)
39. Wright, 183; also *Mountaineer*, May 10, 1870; Treasure City Nevada, *White Pine Daily News*, July 9, 1869.
40. Captain Stump had run *Okanagan* through the Dalles in October 1866. (*Statesman*, Oct. 30, 1866).
41. Wright, 18, 145. The steam propeller, *Celilo*, was the first to be taken successfully from Lewiston down to Portland. She ran the Dalles in the summer of 1863 and the Cascades in August, 1864. (*Sac. Union*, Sept. 2, 1864).

NOTES TO "OLD KALE"

1. Hawley, 1: 153.
2. Miriam Drury, "The Jeffers-Willey Wedding," *C. H. S. Q.*, 35: 1-4.
3. Jacob H. Bachman, "The Diary of a Used-Up Miner," *C. H. S. Q.*, 22: 69; Bancroft, *California*, 6: 285, fn. 63, 289; *Sac. Union*, Mar. 17, 1858.
4. *Sac. Union*, July 25, 1867.
5. *Ibid.* To trace Lyon's early years see also ed. of Mar. 12, 1858; *Golden Age*, Mar.12, 1864; *Statesman*, Feb. 27, 1866; Donaldson, 231-242; *Dictionary of American Biography*, s. v. Caleb Lyon; *Biographical Directory of the American Congress*, 1319; N. Y. *Times*, Dec. 11, 1858, Sept. 9, 1875.
6. Elmo R. Richardson, "Caleb Lyon: A Personal Fragment." *Idaho Yesterdays*, vol. 1-4: 5; also see S. F. *Bulletin*, Oct. 24, 1862. No election had been held at Fort Laramie, so the 479 votes for Wallace from there were fraudulent. But, as it turned out, Wallace would have won the election without these votes. (*Idaho State Historical Society Reference Series*, No. 264, "Idaho Territorial Election

Returns, Oct. 31, 1863," 1985, 1).
7. This set of laws was published by James A. Glascock, Territorial Printer (*Sac. Union*, Aug. 4, 1864)
8. *Sac. Union*, Feb. 27, 1864; also see ed. of Feb. 29.
9. *Oregonian*, Aug. 2, 1864 and *Sac. Union*, Dec. 30, 1864, respectively; also see E. Richardson, 2-4; *Golden Age*, Mar. 12, 1864.
10. McConnell, 288; also see N. Y. *Times* Dec.11, 1858; Lyon to Seward (two letters), 10 Aug. 1864, in National Archives Microfilm Publications, State Department Territorial Papers, Idaho, 1863-1872, Record Group 59, Microcopy M445 Roll 1. (Cited hereafter as RG 59, M445, Roll 1) Downer to Sec. of Interior 31 December, 1866 in Bureau of Indian Affairs, Letters Received, National Archives RG 75, M234, Roll 337.
11. Cochran had been seeking the secretary's job since December, 1863. But, by this time, both he and Daniels had lost out to Clinton De Witt Smith, a former New York lawyer (*Idaho State Historical Society Reference Series* No. 375).
12. *Oregonian*, Sept. 7, 1861, Jan. 23, 1862; *Statesman*, Aug. 30, Sept. 3, 29, 1864; *Golden Age*, Aug. 2, 1862; Merrill D. Beal and Merle W. Wells, *History of Idaho*, 1:347; Ronald H. Limbaugh, *Rocky Mountain Carpetbaggers*, 48; Alvin M. Josephy, Jr., *The Nez Perce Indians and the Opening of the Northwest*, 416, 432. The U. S. Marshal for Idaho, Dolphus S. Payne, was in the East lobbying to become governor; he had left the territory under a cloud of suspicion for having been involved in the Laramie vote fraud.
13. Clifford M. Drury, *Henry Harmon Spalding*, *Pioneer of Old Oregon*, 380 and *Golden Age*, Nov. 16, 1864, respectively; also see O'Neill to Indian Commissioner, June 4, 1864 in RG 75 M234 Roll 337.
14. Elmo Richardson, 4-5; also see Lewiston, Idaho Territory, *North Idaho Radiator*, Feb. 25, 1865; C. M. Drury, "Grievances of the Nez Perce," *Idaho's Yesterdays*, 4-3: 6-7 quoting *Golden Age*, Aug. 27, 1864; Drury, *Henry Harmon Spalding*, 379. The land Lyon wanted was included in the reservation defined by the 1855 treaty, but was not within the 1863 treaty boundaries; all Indian lands north of the Clearwater were relinquished. (Charles J. Kappler, *Indian Affairs: Laws and Treaties,* II, 843-48)
15. Lyon to Indian Office, Aug. 18 and 24 in National Archives RG 75 M234 Roll 337; also see telegrams from Lyon, June 21 and 24, 1864 to J. P. Usher, Secretary of Interior in RG 48, M191, Roll 3; Acting Ind. Commissioner to Lyon, June 22, 1864 in RG 75, M832 Roll 1; Lyon to Cooley Dec.14, 1865 and O'Neill to Cooley May 10, Oct. 18, 1866, in RG 75, M234, Roll 337.
16. *Radiator*, Mar. 4, 1865: also see Limbaugh, *Carpetbaggers*, 49-50.
17. *Golden Age* Nov.19, 1864; *Sac. Union*, Dec. 30, 1864; O.R. 50-1:388; *Statesman*, Oct.11, 13, 18, Nov. 3, 8,12, 26, 1864, Feb. 6, 1866; *Reveille*, Nov. 9, 1864; *World*, Mar. 13,1865; Lyon to Seward, Nov. 26, 1864 in RG 59 M445, Roll 1.
18. Hawley 1: 159; also see *World*, Jan. 26, 1865; Bancroft, Washington, Idaho,

463-4; *Oregonian,* Jan. 30, 1865; *Statesman,* Dec. 8, 13, 22, 1864; Eugene B. Chafee, "The Political Clash Between North and South Idaho Over the Capital," *Pacific Northwest Quarterly,* XXIX, 260-62.
19. *Statesman,* Jan. 19, 1865.
20. *Oregonian,* Feb. 8, 1865.
21. E. Richardson, 6.
22. Silver City, Idaho, *Owyhee Bullion,* Feb. 7, 1867.
23. *Statesman,* Mar. 25, 1865; also *Radiator,* Jan. 28, Feb. 18, 25, Mar. 4, 1865; Smith to Seward Mar. 4, 1865 in RG 59 M445, Roll 1.
24. *Statesman,* Jan. 26, Feb. 7, 14, 18, Mar. 7, 14, 21, Apr. 13, May 2, 6, Aug. 24, 1865; Beal and Wells, 1: 350-3; *Sac. Union,* May 5, June 20, 1865; *Oregonian,* Jan. 12, 30, Feb. 7, 1865; *World,* Mar. 4, 13, 25, Apr. 1, 1865, Feb.10, 11,1866; Merle W. Wells, "Clinton De Witt Smith, Secretary, Idaho Territory, 1864-1865," *O. H. Q.,* 52: 38-53. Alonzo Leland came to Oregon in 1850. He started the first three daily newspapers in the Pacific Northwest, and spent many years trying to get a new territory established that would encompass northern Idaho.
25. *Radiator,* Mar. 11, 1865.
26. *World,* Apr. 15, 1865; also eds. of Apr. 8, 1865, Feb. 10, 1866.
27. *Radiator,* Apr. 1, 1865.
28. *Statesman,* Apr. 15, 24, 1865, July 29, 1865, June 16, 1866; *Sac. Union,* Apr. 21, 1865; *World,* July 29, 1865 *Oregonian,* Sept. 25, 1865; *Radiator,* Apr. 8, 1865; Smith to Seward Apr. 15, 1865 in RG 59 M445, Roll 1.
29. Telegram and letter from Amos Reed, acting Governor of Utah, to Sec. of State Seward, Aug. 28, 1865 in RG 59 M445, Roll 1.
30. Limbaugh, "Ragged Dick In a Black Hat," 10; *Statesman,* Sept. 21, 30, 1865, Aug. 12, 1866; Limbaugh, *Carpetbaggers,* 57; De Witt Smith to Seward, Dec. 28, 1864, RG 59 M445, Roll 1.
31. Lyon to Acting Sec. of State Wm. Hunter, Aug. 3, 1865, and Lyon to Pres. Lincoln, Mar. 1, 1865, both in RG 59 M445, Roll 1; also see *World,* Apr. 22, 1865; Beal and Wells 1: 354-56.
32. Sec. of Interior, James Harlan, to Robert B. Van Valkenberg, Acting Commissioner of Indian Affairs, Sept. 22, 1865 in RG 75 M234 Roll 337.
33. Lyon to Van Valkenberg, Sept. 25 and 26, 1865, in RG 75 M234 Roll 337.
34. Lyon to James Harlan, Oct. 20, 1865, in RG 75 M234 Roll 337.
35. Howlett to Town and Bacon, June 25, 1866, in RG 59 M445, Roll 1; *Statesman,* July 29, Aug. 17, 1865, Feb. 3, 6,1866; N. Y. *Times,* Sept. 21, 1865; Lyon to Van Valkenberg, Sept. 28, 1865, in RG 75 M234 Roll 337.
36. *Statesman,* Mar. 14, 1867; also see Downer to Sec. of Interior, December 31, 1866 in RG 75 M234 Roll 337.
37. *Statesman,* Apr. 17, 1866; also see eds. of Sept. 19, 1865, Aug. 7, 1866, Jan. 31, 1867; *World,* Dec. 3, 1864, Sept. 23, 1865; *Radiator,* Mar. 4, 1865; *Oregonian,* Nov. 26, 1864. O'Neill himself would later abscond with $10,000, much of it supposed to be salaries for teachers, when there were no schools. (House Exc.

Doc. No 198, 42nd Cong., 2nd Sess., p. 3).
38. O'Neill to D. N. Cooley, Oct. 5, 1865 in RG 75 M234 Roll 337.
39. In *World*, Nov. 11, 1865.
40. *Avalanche*, Nov. 18, 1865 and *Statesman*, Nov. 9, 1865 respectively; also see *Statesman*, Oct. 31, Nov. 7, 1865.
41. A. D. Richardson, *Beyond the Mississippi*, 507.
42. *Avalanche*, Nov. 25, 1865.
43. *Ibid.*, Also eds. of Sept. 23, Oct. 7, 28, 1865; *Statesman*, Dec. 5, 1865.
44. *Ibid*, Dec. 2, 1865; also see *Statesman*, Nov. 21, 1865, Feb. 21, 1867; Beal and Wells, 1: 329.
45. *Statesman*, Jan. 16, 1866. Fogus would later be twitted endlessly by his friends over his enthusiastic involvement.
46. *Avalanche*, Dec. 9, 1865.
47. *Ibid*, Feb. 3, 1866; also see ed. of Dec. 23, 1865; *Statesman*, Dec. 2, 1865.
48. *Avalanche*, Dec. 2, 1865; also see *World*, Dec. 9, 1865.
49. Cooley to Lyon Nov. 14, 1865, and Lyon to Cooley, Dec. 14, 1865, both in RG 75 M234 Roll 337; also see *Statesman*, Dec. 5, 1865; Ballard to Cooley, July 10, 1866, and O'Neill to Nesmith, Dec. 10, 1865, both in RG 75 M234 Roll 337.
50. *Avalanche*, Dec. 16, 1865.
51. *World*, Dec. 30, 1865; *Statesman*, Aug. 23, 1864, Nov. 30, Dec. 5, 9, 21, 1865; *Avalanche*, Dec. 30, 1865, Jan. 6, 20, 27, 1866; Hawley 1: 160.
52. *Golden Age*, Aug. 8, 1863. The various seals used can be seen in the front matter of the annual Laws and Resolutions.
53. *Statesman*, Jan. 27, 1866; see also eds. of Jan. 16, 18, Feb. 6, Aug. 23, 1866; *World*, Dec.16, 1865, Jan. 13, Feb. 24, 1866; Limbaugh, *Carpetbaggers*,55, 61; McConnell, 327.
54. Gilson to Seward, Dec. 12, 1865, in RG 59 M445, Roll 1.
55. *World*, January 6, Mar. 10, 1866; *Statesman*, Feb. 10, 1866. There is no written evidence of this act, except in the *World*; it may have been deliberately expunged from the published laws for that session. Its legal status remained in doubt until the next year.
56. *Avalanche*, Jan. 27, 1866; *World*, Feb. 3, 1866.
57. *Statesman*, Feb. 6, 1866; also see *World*, Mar. 17, 1866.
58. *Ibid.*, Feb. 6, 1866; also ed of Feb. 3.
59. In RG 59 M445, Roll 1.
60. Lyon to Seward, Dec. 21 and Dec. 10, 1865, resp., in RG 59 M445, Roll 1.
61. *World*, July 28, 1866; see also eds. of Feb. 10, 17, July 28, 1866; *Statesman*, May 12, 1866.
62. *Statesman*, Aug. 23, 1866. Gilson had not yet received any of the government salary due him. (C. Lyon to F. Skinner, Treasurer of the U. S., Jan. 31, 1866, in RG 59 M445, Roll 1).
63. *Statesman*, Jan. 31, 1867; *World*, Feb. 24, Aug. 25, 1866; Office Designated Depository, Oregon City, Jan. 17, 1869, to Howlett in RG 59 M445, Roll 1.

64. *Avalanche*, Feb. 17, and 24 respectively.
65. *Statesman*, May 12, 1866; also see ed. of Feb. 17, 1866.
66. *Avalanche*, Feb. 24, 1866.
67. *Ibid.*, Mar. 3, 1866; also see ed. of Feb. 24.
68. *Statesman*, May 10, 1866; also *Avalanche*, Mar. 10, 1866; *World*, Mar. 10, 1866.
69. *Statesman*, Feb. 22, 1866.
70. *Avalanche*, Mar. 17, 1866; see also *Statesman*, Feb. 20; Virginia City, Nevada, *The Virginia Daily Union*, Mar. 17, 1866; *Radiator*, Apr. 8, 1865.
71. *Avalanche*, Feb. 24, 1866.
72. *Statesman*, Feb. 13, Mar. 1, 6, 1866.
73. *Ibid.*, Mar. 25, Sept. 30, Oct. 5, 7, 1865.
74. *Reveille*, Sept. 7, 1868. In 1868, Ridgley would be shot dead by Thomas Carberry ("Irish Tom.") in front of the Lick House Saloon at Austin, Nevada. He had been in Montana and White Pine, Nevada, since leaving Idaho. (*Reveille*, Sept. 5, 1868).
75. *Avalanche*, Mar. 3, 1866.
76. *Ibid.*, Mar. 10, 1866; also see ed. of Feb. 3, 1866; *Statesman*, Mar. 3, 8, 1866.
77. *Avalanche*, Mar. 3 and 10, 1866, respectively.
78. *Statesman*, Mar. 13, 1866; *World*, Mar. 31, 1866; Lyon to Seward, Mar. 10, 1866, in RG 59 M445, Roll 1. The Freedman's Bureau had been established a year earlier to supervise refugees, freedmen and abandoned lands in the south, which it gave to freed slaves. The Congress overrode Johnson's veto on July 16, 1866.
79. *Statesman*, Mar. 13, 1866.
80. *N. Y. Times*, May 21, 1866; also see *Statesman*, June 14, 1866.
81. *Statesman*, Mar. 15; see also ed. of June 28, 1866; Lyon to Cooley, Feb. 6 and Mar. 1, 1866, in RG 75 M234 Roll 337.
82. *Statesman*, Mar. 18 and 21, 1866 respectively.
83. *Statesman*, Mar. 27; also eds. of Mar. 22, 24, 1866; *Avalanche*, Mar. 24, 31, 1866.
84. McConnell, 245.
85. *Statesman*, Apr. 17, 1866; also eds. of Sept. 19, 1865, Mar. 31, Apr, 5, 16, 1866, Jan. 31, Mar. 14, 1867; *Avalanche*, Apr. 7, 1866.
86. *Statesman*, Sept. 3, 1865. Patterson had also killed Captain George Staples in Portland in 1862, and had scalped his own doxy, whom he suspected of being disloyal.
87. *Statesman*, Apr. 7, 1866.
88. *Ibid*.
89. *Ibid.*, Apr. 17, 1866; also see Bancroft, *Washington, Idaho*, 460, 489-91; Donaldson, 166-67.
90. *World*, April 21, 1866; also see ed. of May 5.
91. *Statesman*, Apr. 17, 1866; also ed. of May 1, 1866.
92. *Ibid.*, April 19, 1866.

93. *Avalanche*, Apr. 14, 1866 and *Statesman*, June 23, 1866, respectively; also see Lyon telegram to Indian Office, April 12, 1866, in RG 75 M234 Roll 337.
94. "Caleb Lyon's Bruneau Treaty, April 12, 1866," *Idaho Yesterdays*, 13-1 (Spring, 1969), 16-19, 32.
95. *Statesman*, June 23, 1866.
96. *Avalanche*, Apr. 21; *Statesman*, Mar. 29, Apr. 5, 10, 1866, Feb. 21, 1867.
97. *Statesman*, Apr. 26, 1866.
98. *Avalanche*, Mar. 31 and May 5, 1866, respectively.
99. *Statesman*, June 2, 1866.
100. *Avalanche*, Apr. 7, 1866; also ed. of Apr. 28; *Sac. Union*, Feb. 3, 1866; Jacksonville Oregon, *The Oregon Sentinel*, Jan. 20, Mar. 10, 1866.
101. A. S. Downer to Cooley, May 9, 1866, and to Sec. of Interior, Dec. 31, 1866, both in RG 75 M234 Roll 337. Downer had been Lewiston's first postmaster.
102. Ballard to Seward, July 18, 1866, in RG 59 M445, Roll 1.
103. *Statesman*, Jan. 31, 1867 and Aug. 7, 1866, respectively; also see ed. of Sept. 11, 1866; Beal and Wells 1: 357, 372; W. Turrentine Jackson, "Indian Affairs and Politics in Idaho Territory," 14:311-313; *Avalanche*, Oct. 28, 1865, June 30, 1866; Treasury Department to Commissioner of Indian Affairs, Nov. 26, 1866, and James O'Neill to Lyon, Nov. 28, 1865, both in RG 75, M234, Roll 337.
104. Caleb Lyon Jr. to Cooley, Aug. 6, 1866; also see Ballard to Cooley, Sept. 1, 1866; Sec. of Interior to Sec. of State, Oct. 2, 1866, all in RG 59 M445, Roll 1; Sec. of Interior to Sec. of Treasury, Oct. 17, 1866 in RG 75 M234 Roll 337.
105. *Owyhee Bullion*, Feb. 28, 1867.
106. Lyon to Cooley, Dec. 24, 1866; McCall to Cooley, Oct. 8 and Nov. 22, 1866, all in RG 75 M234 Roll 337.
107. *Statesman*, Jan.10 and 8, 1867 respectively; also see eds. of May 29, 31, Dec. 20, 1866, Jan. 17, 31,1867; *Oregonian*, Jan. 30, 1867.
108. Treasury Department Auditor's office to Lyon, Feb. 6, 1867, in RG 59 M445, Roll 1; also see Merle W. Wells, "Caleb Lyon's Indian Policy," 200.
109. *Statesman*, Sept. 21, 1875; also see *Sac. Union*, July 25, 1867; *Avalanche*, Sept. 2, 1865; N. Y. *Times*, Sept. 9, 1875.

NOTES TO "A HARD ROAD TO JORDAN"

1. McDermit's early history can be found in *Yreka Union*, Sept. 19, 29, 1855, July 24, 1859, Feb. 11, Apr. 5, Aug. 30, Nov. 10, 1860, Sept. 19, 1861; *Alta*, Aug. 26, 1851, Sept. 14, 1852, Aug. 10, 12, 1865; San Jose, California *The Pioneer*, Oct. 19, 1878, Oct. 14, 1882; *Sac. Union*, Feb. 28, May 4, Nov. 19, 1853, July 14, 1856; S.F *Transcript*, Jan. 17, 1853; Sacramento, *Transcript*, July 23, Oct. 28, 1850; S. F. *Herald* Oct. 9, 1854.
2. O. R. 50-2, 630.
3. In Elko, Nevada *Elko Weekly Independent*, Mar. 19, 1870; also *Virginia* City D. *Territorial Enterprise*, Oct. 6, 1866; Gold Hill, Nevada *Daily Evening News*,

Sept. 18, 1866.
4. *Sac. Union*, Feb. 1, 1864.
5. *Union*ville, Nevada, *The Humboldt Register*, Feb. 11, 1865. Beachy had opened the first hotel in Lewiston, Idaho in 1861.
6. Elias D. Pierce, *The Pierce Chronicle; Personal Reminiscences of E. D. Pierce*, 101-105; *Register*, Feb. 2, 11, Mar. 4, 1865; Victor O. Goodwin, "William C. (Hill) Beachy," 18-19; *Sac. Union*, Jan. 31, Feb. 17, 1865; O. R. 50-2, 1125, 1129, 1130, 1136, 1156, 1160; Pierce had a charter from the territorial legislature for the Idaho end of such a road. He had been the leader of the group that had made the first gold discovery in the Clearwater region of Idaho.
7. Va. *Union*, Mar. 18, 23, 1865; *Sac. Union*, Feb. 24, 1864, Mar. 16, Apr. 3, 1865.
8. O. R. 50-2, 1166. The story of Wallace's expedition and his captives can be found in Va. *Union*, Mar. 4, 16, 25, Apr. 13, 22, 1865; O. R. 50-1, 404-08; *Reveille*, March 14, 1865; Dayton, Nevada *Lyon County Sentinel*, Mar. 25, 1865; O. R. 50-2, 1161; *Sac. Union*, Apr. 1, 1865.
9. Va. *Union*, Mar. 26 and Mar. 28, 1865 resp. Also see eds. of Mar. 22, 30, 1865.
10. Gold Hill *News*, Mar. 25, 1865.
11. Va. *Union*, Mar. 25, 1865; also eds. of Mar. 15-17, 19, 1865; O. R. 50-1, 403-04; *Reveille*, Mar. 20, 23, 1865; *Sentinel,* Apr. 1, 1865; Gold Hill News, Mar. 16, 17, 1865; O. R. 50-2, 1161-62, 1165-66; *Register*, Mar. 18, Apr. 15, 1865; *Sac. Union*, Mar. 18, 1865.
12. *Reveille*, Mar. 31,1865; also ed. of May 30, 1865.
13. Va. *Union*, Mar. 26, 1865; also ed. of Mar. 24.
14. Va. *Union*, Mar. 25, 1865; also *Register*, Apr. 1, 1865.
15. Va. *Union*, Mar. 26, 1865.
16. Gold Hill News, Mar. 29, 1865; also *Reveille* May 30, 1865; Philip Dodd Smith, Jr., "The Sagebrush Soldiers," 3-4, 62.
17. *Register*, May 2, 1863.
18. *Ibid.*, Aug. 1 and 8, 1863, respectively.
19. Mark Twain (Samuel Clemens), *Roughing It*, 684.
20. *Sac. Union*, Feb. 23, 1864 and *Register*, May 16, 1863, respectively..
21. *Register*, Mar. 25, 1865; also see ed. of Apr. 1, 1865; Va. *Union*, Mar. 18, 25, 28, 1865; Gold Hill News, Mar. 18, 1865.
22. *Register*, Apr. 15, 1865; Va. *Union*, May 17, 1865; Albert Simmons was Humboldt County's representative in the 1863 and 1864 state legislatures. He was house speaker for the latter session.
23. *Register*, Apr. 8, 1865; also see eds. of April 22, July 22, 1865; *Reveille* Apr. 15, 1865. Ragan, who had come across the plains with his wife and sons, was one of the founders of Dun Glen. Forbes called him a brave, noble man, because of his perseverance the previous winter in getting through the mountains, despite having a frozen foot.
24. *Reveille*, Apr. 8, 12, 1865; Va. *Union*, Apr. 21, 1865.
25. Samuel P. Davis, ed., *The History of Nevada*, 1: 168.

26. One of the wounded was Thomas Raper, whose arm was nearly shot off. He and his wife lost all their property to the Indians, and, due to his disability, lived thereafter at Dun Gen, in penury. (*Register*, Feb. 12, 1867).
27. O. R. 50-2, 1177-78, 1181-83, 1187; *Sac. Union*, Apr. 18, 1865; Gold Hill *News*, Apr. 17, 1865; Va. *Union*, Apr., 8, 14, 18 1865.
28. O. R. 50-2, 1192.
29. *Register*, Apr. 15, 1865; also see *Sac. Union*, Apr. 12; Aug. 10, 1865; Gold Hill News, Apr. 8, 1865; O.R. 50-2, 1209-10, 1215-16.
30. John Cradlebaugh, "Report of the Adjutant-General," 11-12. Safford, who stood a mere 5 feet high, was county recorder and a mining speculator. When he came home to Humboldt in September,1867, after a long absence, Captain Sou and many of his tribe came down out of the pine forests, where they were gathering nuts, to greet him. In 1869, he was appointed governor of Arizona. (*Register*, Sept. 7, 1867).
31. *Register*, Apr. 22, 1865; also see eds. of Apr. 8, July 30, Aug. 6, 1864; Hubert Howe Bancroft, History of Nevada. 207-211; Davis 44-49; 160-61; *Enterprise*, Oct. 20, 1866; Sentinel, Oct. 21, 1865; *Reveille*, Jan. 28, 1868.
32. O. R. 50-2, 1204-05, 1214-15; Va. *Union*, Apr. 7, May 10, 1865; *Sac. Union*, Apr. 5, 27; 1865.
33. O. R. 50-1, 409-10; also Va. *Union*, May 11, 18, 1865; *Register*, May 27, 1865.
34. Va. *Union*, May 18, 1865; *Register*, May 13, 1865; Col. George Rhulen, "Early Nevada Forts," 53.
35. Va. *Union*, May 17, 1865.
36. Twain, *Roughing It*, 677.
37. Va. *Union*, May 18, 1865; also see ed. of Aug. 10; *Register*, May 13, Oct. 28, 1865; Gold Hill *News*, Oct. 15, 1865.
38. *Register*, Oct. 28, 1865; also see eds. of May 14, June 3.
39. *Register*, May 13, 1865; also see ed. of May 6; Va.*Union*, May 7, 1865; Granville Stuart, *Prospecting for Gold* ,114.
40. Va. *Union*, Aug. 10, 1865; also see *Register*, May 20, 1865.
41. Va. *Union*, Aug. 10, 1865
42. O. R. 50-2, 1245; also see Sessions S. Wheeler, *The Black Rock Desert*, 164; *Reveille*, May 29, 1865.
43. *Register*, May 27, 1865; also see Va. *Union*, June 1, Aug. 10, 1865; Carson City, Nevada *Daily Appeal*, May 27, 31, 1865.
44. *Register*, June 3, 1865; also eds. of May 13, 20; Va. *Union*, May 14, 1865.
45. Appeal, June 3, 1865 and Washoe City, Nevada *Washoe Weekly Times*, June 3, 1865, respectively; also see Gold Hill *News*, Jan. 31, 1865.
46. *Reveille*, May 4-6, 11, 12,15, 16; Gold Hill *News*, Jan. 3, 1866.
47. *Ibid.*, May 18, 20, 1865.
48. *Ibid*, May 24 and 25, 1865 resp; also Va. *Union*, May 28; O. R. 50-1, 412-14.
49. *Reveille*, May 26, 1865.
50. Gold Hill *News*, June 14, 1865; *Register*, June 3, 1865; *World*, June 24, 1865; O. R. 50-2, 1245-46; *Reveille*, May 29, 1865.

51. Instead of Starr, Captain Street with Co. K of the 2nd left Camp Union on July 25, 1865 to establish Fort Bidwell. Maj. Smith of the 2nd was to command both Co. K and Knight's company at Smoke Creek and patrol the roads as far as Puebla and Granite Station. (*Avalanche*, Aug. 26, Oct. 7, 1865; Va. *Union* Aug. 8, 1865; *Sac. Union*, July 26, 1865; O. R. 50-2, 1168-73, 1195, 1259)
52. Va. *Union*, May 30, 1865.
53. O. R. 50-1, 410-11; also see Va. *Union*, April 20, 22, May 10, 11, 26, June 2,3, 8, 11, July 23, 25, 1865, Aug. 1, 15, 1865; Gold Hill *News*, Jan. 3, 1866; *Sentinel*, May 27, 1865; *Reveille*, May 8, 1865; O.R. 50-2, 1176-77, 1218-29, 1226, 1230, 1241, 1244-45, 1249- 51, 1258; *Sac. Union* May 10, June 1, 1865.
54. *Reveille*, June 7, 1865; also see David M. Goodman, *A Western Panorama*, 204, 210-12; *Reveille*, May 13, June 16, 1865; Sam Gilson was a cattleman and express rider who discovered the mineral Gilsonite in 1882. Later, as a deputy U. S. Marshal he supervised John Lee's execution.
55. *Register*, June 17, 1865.
56. *Reveille*, May 8, 31, June 3, 1865. In early May, a large camp of Bannocks had been seen camped on the South Fork of the Humboldt.
57. O. R. 50-1, 410-11; also see O. R. 50-1, 412-14.
58. Va. *Union*, June 15, 1865; also see eds. of June 8, Aug. 10; *Register*, June 3, July 22, 29, 1865; *Reveille*, June 28, 1865.
59. *Reveille*, June 17, 1865.
60. *Register*, July 1, 1865; also O. R. 50-1, 411-12; Gold Hill *News*, June 24, 1865.
61. *Sac. Union*, Aug. 11, 1865; Brig. Gen. Richard H. Orton, ed., *Records of California Men in the War of the Rebellion*, 168-69.
62. *Report of the Adjutant General of the State of Oregon, for the years 1865-6*, 50- 58, 81, 104-106, 156; O. R. 50-2, 1264-5, 1257-58, 1278-80; *Avalanche*, Aug. 26, 1865; Pierce 106-08; *Oregonian*, July 7, 12, 27, 1865; *Sac. Union*, May 4, 8, 17, 19, 22, June 8, July 1, 1865; Va. *Union* June 7, 14, 15, 17, July 8, 18, 1865; Gold Hill *News*, June 16, 1865; *Sentinel,* June 17, 1865; *Statesman*, June 24, July 15, 1865; *Register*, June 10, Jul 1, 1865. A few years earlier, Mullan had laid out a wagon road from Ft. Walla Walla to Ft. Benton on the Missouri.
63. Va. *Union*, July 13, 1865; also eds. of July 16, 25, 1865; *Reveille*, June 6, 1865.
64. Orton 184-85; also Va. *Union*, July 1, 9, 16, 1865; *Sentinel*, July 15, 1865.
65. Wheeler, 165; also Gold Hill *News*, Aug. 11, 1865; O. R. 50-2, 1274-75.
66. *Union*, July 29, 31, Aug. 12, Nov. 3, 1865; *Appeal,* Aug. 11, 1865; *Register*, June 24, 1865, July 22, 1865; Va. *Union*, July 9, 23, 1865; Gold Hill *News*, July 17, 1865; *Independent,* May 11, 1870; *Enterprise*, August 9, 1866.
67. Va. *Union*, July 25; *Register*, July 22, 1865; *Sac. Union*, July 7, 17, 1865; *Reveille*, July 27, 1865; O.R. 50-2, 1259-60, 1285-86; O. R. 50-1, 414-15.
68. *World*, Aug. 5, 1865. Thomas J. Butler and his brother J. S. Butler had previously published the *Red Bluff Beacon* and the *Boise News*. They later edited the *Helena Radiator*. Thomas Ewing, in an interview as an old man, said it was Old Winnemucca who had led the Indians attacking the Jackson party. (Winnemucca,

Nevada, *The Humboldt Star*, June 14, 1911).
69. *Register*, July 8, 1865; also see *Reveille*, July 11, 1865.
70. *Register*, July 15, 1865; also see O. R. 50-2, 1279-80; *Statesman*, June 27, July 13, 15, 1865.
71. Va. *Union*, Aug. 18, 1865.
72. Winnemucca, Nevada *The Silver State*, Apr. 10, 1888.
73. *Register*, July 22, 1865.
74. *Ibid*, July 29; also see *Alta*, July 23; *Reveille*, July 25, 1865. "Mac" Bonnifield, a Virginian, was a schoolteacher, newspaper editor. In June 1862 he opened a law office in *Union*ville, and later edited the *Register* and *Silver State*.
75. Gold Hill *News*, August 11, 1865; also see Va. *Union*, August 24, 1865; *Sac. Union*, Aug. 12, 1865.
76. *Register*, Aug. 5, 1865; also see ed. of Sept. 23; *Alta*. July 30, 1865; *Sac. Union* Nov. 3, 1865.
77. Va. *Union*, Aug. 10, 12, 1865; *Appeal*, Aug. 11, 1865; *Statesman*, June 24, Aug. 10, 17, 1865; *Avalanche*, Aug. 26, 1865; *Oregonian*, Aug. 15, 1865.
78. Va. *Union*, Aug. 9, 15, Oct. 5, 1865; *Reveille*, Aug. 14, 1865; *Enterprise*, Aug. 9, 1866; *Independent*, Nov. 2, 1870. After being mustered out in January 1866, Lt. Seamonds became involved in mining, and owned a ranch in Clover Valley. He became Elko county assessor in 1870, and, a few years later was arrested in Pioche, charged with embezzlement. (Gold Hill *News*, Jan. 6, 12, 1866; *Independent*, Mar. 29, 1873).
79. Letter from 2nd Lt. Wm. Gibson Overend, in Smith, 75-78. Overend said he wrote it "In compliance with the request of the widow of my late and much beloved Colonel." See also Va. *Union*, Jan. 30, 1864.
80. *Alta*, Aug. 10, 1865; also *Sac. Union*, Aug. 18; *Register*, Aug. 12, 1865.
81. *Register*, Aug. 19, 1865.
82. Va. *Union*, Aug. 22, 1865; Gold Hill *News*, Aug. 26, 1865. Later, McDermit's remains were re-interred at Carson City. Almond B. Wells was mustered out of Nevada service in November 1865 and went into the regular army; he died in 1901 as a colonel of the 1st U. S. Cavalry. (Francis B. Heitman, *Historical Register and Dictionary of the U.S. Army*, 1: 1016).
83. *Register*, Aug. 12, 1865; *Statesman*, Sept. 7, 1865; *Sac. Union*, Aug. 10, 1865; Va. *Union*, Aug. 15, 18, 31, 1865; *Silver State*, June 29, July 2, Sept. 19, 1889; *Alta*, Aug. 11, 1865; *Vedette*, Aug. 12, 1865. Camp McDermit was on the north bank of the East Fork of Quinn (Queen's) River, close to the Oregon border, two miles east of U. S. Highway 95. In 1879 it was designated a fort. In 1889 the post was closed and turned over to the Interior Department. In the 1890s it was designated as an Indian reservation.
84. *Appeal*, Aug. 27, 1865.
85. *Sac. Union*, Nov. 13, 1865.
86. *Ibid*. Also see ed. of Sept. 28, 1865.
87. Gold Hill *News*, Nov. 11, 1865.

88. *Register*, Sept. 2, 1865; also ed. of Sept. 9, 30, 1865; *Sac. Union*, Sept. 18, 1865.
89. Va. *Union*, Sept. 21, 1865; also *Register*, Sept. 23, 1865.
90. *Register*, Nov. 25, 1865; also eds. of Nov. 11, 18; Wheeler, 117-120; Va. *Union*, November 16, 1865; *Sac. Union*, Nov. 20, 1865.
91. *Register*, Dec. 30, 1865; also Gold Hill *News*, Feb. 26, 1866; Wheeler, 120-122.
92. *Register*, Jan. 20, 27, 1866; *Vedette*, Jan. 20, 1866.
93. *Avalanche*, Oct. 28, Dec. 30, 1865; *Statesman*, Oct. 12, 1865; Gold Hill *News*, Oct. 5, 1865; Pierce 109; *Sac. Union*, Aug. 12, 1865; *Oregonian*, Oct. 20, 1865.
94. Va. *Union*, Sept. 22, 1865; *Sac. Union*, Aug. 23, Sept. 8, 1865; *Reveille*, Aug. 19, 1865; *Avalanche*, Sept. 2, 9, 1865; *Statesman*, Sept. 5, 1865; O. R. 50-2, 1290-93;*World*, July 15, 1865; *Register*, July 1, 1865.
95. *Report of the Adjutant General of the State of Oregon*, 79-81; *Mountaineer*, July 21, Sept. 15, 1865, July 31, 1868; *Oregonian*, Nov. 24, 1865.
96. *Register*, May 6, 1866; also see eds. of Feb. 10, June 2, 1866.
97. *Register*, July 7, 1866; *Reveille*, Jan. 28, 1868.
98. *Register*, Feb. 2, 1867. Two years after Forbes left, *Union*ville died, due to the decline of mining and the coming of the railroad, which bypassed it. After the last issue of the *Register* on May 29, 1869, the press and materials were taken to the new railhead of Elko, and used in starting up the *Independent*.
99. *Register*, Jan. 25, 1868.
100. In *Reveille*, Jan. 28, 1868
101. Myron Angel, ed., *History of Nevada*, 302.
102. *Reveille*, May 13, 1869.
103. Angel, 302; also see *Independent*, Jan. 25, Mar. 30, Nov. 7, 1872, Jan.12, Feb. 8, 1873; White Pine *D. News* Apr. 23, 6, May 2, 1872; Richard E. Lingenfelter and Karen R. Gash. *The Newspapers of Nevada*, 76.
104. *Silver State*, Sept. 20, 1875; *Independent,* Oct. 18, Dec. 27, 1873; Aug. 1, 1875.
105. Angel, 302; see also *Silver State*, Nov. 1, 1875; *Register*, Sept. 10, Oct. 1, 1864.

NOTES TO "SLAUGHTER AT BEAR RIVER"

1. *Vedette*, Feb. 1, 1864.
2. Orton, 508.
3. Salt Lake City, Utah, *The Deseret News*, Jan. 7, 1863.
4. O. R., 50-2: 61-62; *Deseret News*, Nov. 26, 1862. Accounts of the Otter-Van Orman saga can be found in *Deseret News*, Oct. 31, 1860; Oregon City, Oregon *Argus*, Nov. 24, 1860.
5. Orton, 173; also see Orton, 509; S. F. *Bulletin*, June 27, 1863.
6. Col. J. H. Martineau, "Military History of Cache Valley," *Tullidge's Quarterly Magazine*, 2-1: 125.
7. Newell Hart, *The Bear River Massacre*, 84; also see *Deseret News*, Nov. 26, Dec. 3, 1862.
8. *Deseret News*, Dec. 17, 1862

9. *Ibid.*, Dec. 31, 1862.
10. *Ibid.*, Jan. 14, 1863; also see ed. of Feb. 4.
11. O. R., 50-1: 185.
12. Richard F. Burton, *The City of the Saints*, 503.
13. Captain Charles H. Hempstead as quoted in *Vedette*, Jan. 30, 1864.
14. Fred B. Rodgers, *Soldiers of the Overland*, 70-71.
15. Lee's oral history, in Hart, 130.
16. *Deseret News*, Feb. 11, 1863.
17. Orton, 176-177.
18. *The Passing of the Redman*, 14.
19. *Sac. Union*, Feb. 17, 1863.
20. Rodgers, 74; Blackfoot, Idaho *Daily Bulletin*, June 11, 1929.
21. Edward W. Tullidge, *History of Salt Lake City*, 289.
22. Daughters of the Utah Pioneers, *The Trail Blazer: History of the Development of Southeastern Idaho*, 13.
23. Mae T. Parry, "Massacre at Bia Ogai," in *The Trail Blazer*, 128.
24. *The Passing of the Redman*, 14.
25. *Sac. Union*, Feb. 13, 1863.
26. Hiram S. Tuttle, "Account of Service in Utah," 7.
27. *Sac. Union*, Feb. 13, 1863.
28. *Ibid.*
29. O. R. 50-1: 187.
30. Tullidge, 288.
31. *Ibid.*

NOTES TO "THE LAST BATTLE"

1. Elko, Nevada *Elko Free Press*, Mar. 3, 1911.
2. Twin Falls, Idaho *News*, Feb. 28, May 1, 1908.
3. Rice had been involved on the fringes of the "Diamondfield Jack" Davis affair, testifying at a pardon hearing for Davis in February 1898 after Rice's friend, Jeff Gray, confessed to a killing which had been blamed on Davis. (Twin Falls, Idaho *Times-News* May 16, 1965; *A Folk History of Twin Falls County*, 19).
4. Twin Falls *News,* May 1, 1908; see also ed. of August 7, 1908.
5. In February 1907, J. Frank Tranmer married Jeanette Dopp in Twin Falls County. Ed Diffendarfer is listed as a "stockman" in the 1910 *Twin Falls City Directory*. His father, Frank Diffendarfer, was a lime burner and was also connected with the Shoshone Basin irrigation project. (T. Falls *News*, Aug. 30, 1907, Oct. 30, 1908.) Nimrod Urie was also from a large, respectable family. (T. Falls *News*, Nov. 17, Dec. 8, 1905; Feb. 9, July 6, Oct. 18, Nov. 9, 1906; Nov. 8, 1907) Gordon Girdner had been a clerk in Perrine & Burton's grocery; he married in 1906. (T. Falls *News*, July 6, Feb. 23, 1906, Dec. 17, 1909; *City Directory of Twin Falls for 1908-09*). Girdner's parents ran a boarding house in Twin Falls and farmed. (T. F. *News*, Feb.

22 and June 21, 1907).
6. G. A. Gutches, U.S. Indian Service, Fort Hall, report of Feb. 6, 1911 to E. P. Holcombe, Chief Supervisor, Denver Indian Office in Shoshone Mike Papers, Humboldt County Historical Museum, Winnemucca, Nevada; Twin Falls, Idaho *Times*, March 17, 1910, Wells, Nevada, *Nevada State Herald*, May 6, 1910.
7. Elko *Independent*, May 13, 1910.
8. N. R. Urie statement at Winnemucca, Nevada before Judge E. J. L. Taber, and James Dysart, District Attorney, and Sheriff Lamb in Shoshone Mike Papers.
9. T. Falls *Times*, Mar. 17, 1910. Henry Harris (1863-1937) was a black cowboy whom John Sparks had brought from Texas to Nevada as a houseboy. In his free time Henry learned to be a skilled cowboy, and was employed as such by several outfits—the Sparks-Harrell, Shoesole, Miller and Lux, and the Utah Construction companies. Henry died at San Jacinto at age 69 and is buried in Twin Falls. (James L. Holloway, *Families of the Salmon Tract and Some of Their History*, 198; Nora L. Bowman, *Only The Mountains Remain*, 215, 249-50).
10. T. Falls *Times*, May 12, 1910.
11. Washoe Sheriff Ferrell in Reno Nevada, *Nevada State Journal*, Mar. 3, 1911.
12. *Independent*, May 6, 13, 1910; Wells *Herald*, May 6, 1910; *Nevada State Journal*, Feb. 24, Mar. 3, 1911; *Star*, Jan. 13, 1911.
13. Gutches report in Shoshone Mike Papers.
14. C. H. Asbury to Commissioner of Indian Affairs, July 27, 1910; also letter of Aug. 17, 1910, both in Shoshone Mike Papers.
15. Gay Tranmer statement in E. J. L. Taber letter of Sept. 27, 1910, and Urie confession in letter of January 18, 1911, both in Shoshone Mike Papers.
16. Taber to Commissioner of Indian Affairs, Sept. 27, 1910, in Shoshone Mike Papers.
17. Indian Office, Oct. 29, 1910, to George B. Haggett, Supt. of Western Shoshoni Indian School, Owyhee, Nevada; John B. Hoover, Supt. of Fort McDermit Indian school, Nov. 9, 1910, to Indian office; Indian Office, Nov. 26, 1910, to Taber; Elko County Dep. District Attorney, E. P. Carr, Nov. 30, 1910 to Indian Department. All in Shoshone Mike Papers.
18. T. Bailey Lee, to Attorney General, Washington D. C, Nov. 24, 1910, Shoshone Mike Papers; also see T.F. *Times*, Dec. 9, 1910.
19. Attorney General to Sec. of Interior, Nov. 30, 1910,; Indian Office to Taber, Dec. 20, 1910; Indian Office to U. S. Attorney General, Dec. 21, 1910, all in Shoshone Mike Papers.
20. *Free Press*, Dec. 9, 1910.
21. *Star*, Jan. 11, 1911; also ed. of July 12, 1911; *Free Press* Jan. 13, 1911.
22. *Star,* Jan. 18, 1911; T. F. *Times*, Nov. 25, 1910; *Free Press*, Jan. 13, 1911. Lamb was Humboldt County sheriff from 1902 to 1916, and again beginning in 1930. He was shot in the line of duty, in 1933, near Golconda.
23. Taber to Indian Department, Jan. 10, 1911; also see Asbury to Indian Office, Jan. 28, 1911, both in Shoshone Mike Papers.
24. *Star*, Jan. 9, 13, 16, 18, 1911; *Silver State*, Jan.14, 1911; *Independent*, Jan. 13,

20, 1911.
25. Lee to Taber, Jan. 14, 1911, Shoshone Mike Papers.
26. Lee to Asbury, Jan. 20, 1911; also see Lee affidavit Jan. 26, 1911, both in Shoshone Mike Papers.
27. G. A. Gutches, District Forester to E. P. Holcombe, Department of Interior, Feb. 6, 1911, Shoshone Mike Papers.
28. *Independent*, Feb. 29, 1911; also *Silver State*, Feb. 11, 18, 21, 23, 1911.
29. *Sac. Union*, Feb. 28, 1911; *Nevada State Journal*, Feb. 24, 26, Mar. 1, 3, 10, 1911; *Star*, Feb.10, 13, 15, 17, 20, 22, 24, 1911; *Silver State*, Feb. 9, 11, 14, 21, 23, 1911.
30. T.L. Oddie to Sen. George S. Nixon, Feb. 19, 1911, in Shoshone Mike Papers.
31. *Star* February 20, 22, 24, 1911; *Silver State* Feb. 28, 1911.
32. *Nevada State Journal*, Feb. 26, 1911.
33. *Ibid.*, Feb. 27, 1911.
34. James Buckley, Coroner, Inquisition....into the death of Edward Hogle, Golconda, Nevada, Mar. 1, 1911.
35. *Ibid.*
36. *Ibid.*
37. *Star*, Mar. 1, 1911.
38. Frank V. Perry, "The Last Indian Uprising in the United States," 4, 35.
39. *Star*, Feb. 27, 1911.
40. Wells *Herald*, Mar. 3, 1911.
41. Buckley, Inquisition of Mar. 1, 1911.
42. James Buckley, Coroner. Inquisition by Coroner's Jury, State of Nevada, County of Humboldt, in the deaths of [Mike's Band]. Mar. 3, 1911. Humboldt County Clerk's Office, Winnemucca Nevada.
43. *Independent*, June 9, July 14, 1911; *Silver State*, Mar. 7, 1911; J. P. Donnelly, *Biennial Report of the Nevada State Police*, 1911-1912.
44. *State Journal*, Mar. 4, 1911 and Mar. 5, 1911 respectively; also see Asbury to Indian Office, Mar. 8, 1911, Shoshone Mike Papers.
45. *State Journal*, Mar. 6, 1911.
46. *Ibid.*, Mar. 8, 1911; Owyhee District Agent George B. Haggett to Indian Office, Mar. 17, 1911, in Shoshone Mike Papers.
47. *State Journal*, Mar. 3, 1911."Salmon River Jim" Lewis was born in the Boise Valley. Known also as "Rock Creek Jim," he was respected by his neighbors. He died in September 1924 and is buried in the Twin Falls cemetery. (*A Folk History of Twin Falls County*, 19).
48. Owyhee Indian School Superintendent, John B. Hoover, to Indian Office. Feb. 2, and Sept. 12, 1911, Shoshone Mike Papers.
49. *Silver State*, Apr. 27, 29, 1911.
50. Supt. Asbury to Commissioner of Indian Affairs, March 8 and Apr. 27, 1911, both in Shoshone Mike Papers.
51. Winnemucca, Nevada *Humboldt Sun*, Mar. 26, 1993; Frank Bergon, *Shoshone*

Mike, 287; *Nevada State Journal*, Nov. 17, 1911; Census of Fort Hall Indian Agency for years 1911-18, National Archives, RG 75, M595, Roll 140.
52. *City of Twin Falls Directory for 1912-13.* Draft registrations for T. Falls County, 1917, Twin Falls Public Library; Twin Falls *News*, July 13, 1952.
53. *Nevada State Journal*, Oct. 30, Nov. 8, 11, 1911; J. Howard Moon, *Early History of Filer, Idaho Schools*, 377; T. Falls *News*, July 13, 1911; *Silver State*, Jan. 21, Feb. 6, July 26, 1913; Sept. 10, 1912, Jan. 4, 1916; *Star*, Jan. 12, 1912, Mar. 7, 1913, Sept. 18, 1918; Prison Records of J. Frank Tranmer and Nimrod Urie; Second Judicial District Court of State of Nevada, Order 8442 of Jan. 25, 1913. All in Nevada State Library and Archives, Carson City.
54. T. F. *Times*, Mar. 3, 10, 1910; Indian Commissioner to Attorney General, May 27, 1911, in Shoshone Mike Papers. More of Mike's story can be found in *Silver State*, Mar. 1, 2, 4, 9, 1911, Sept. 10, 1912, Jan. 7, Feb. 15, Mar. 6, 8, Nov. 6, 1913; *Independent*, Dec. 9, 1910, Feb. 24, 25, Mar. 4, Apr. 21, 28, June 2, 23, July 21, Aug. 25, 1911; *Nevada State Journal*, Apr. 14, 28, Oct. 27, 1911; Wells *Herald*, Mar. 17, Aug. 18, Sept. 15, 1911; Burley, Idaho *Burley Bulletin*, Mar. 17, 1911; *Star*, May 11, 1910, Mar. 3, 1911; T. F. *Times* May 21, June 24, July 16, 1908, Feb. 11, 1909; Effie Mona Mack, *Nevada, a history of the state*, 139-143; Dayton O. Hyde, *The Last Free Man*.

NOTES TO "FIRST FAMILY"

1. Dallin H. Oaks and Joseph I. Bentley. "Joseph Smith and Legal Process: In the Wake of the Steamboat *Nauvoo*," 3: 735-82; see also Albert Haws. "In Pioneer Days," *Autumn Leaves*, 37: 348.
2. Albert Haws, 348; Susan E. Black, Early Members of the Reorganized Church of Jesus Christ of Latter Day Saints, 376. Reorganized Church of Jesus Christ of Latter-Day Saints Membership Record Book A, Carson City, Nevada Branch, 397, 398; Austin Nevada Branch, Jan. 1, 1871, 622, 623.
3. Fawn M. Brodie, *No Man Knows My History, The Life of Joseph Smith*, 356-57.
4. Church of Jesus Christ of Latter day Saints, Journal History of the Church (hereafter Journal History), Jan. 3, 1840, Jan.19, Feb. 25, Mar. 20, 1841, Feb. 21, April 23, 24, 29, 31, Oct. 27, 1843, Mar. 4, 11, May 17, 1844; Brodie, 363; Robert E. Lee, Indenture, Sept. 10, 1840, Ms. 2495, Church Historian's Office, Salt Lake City; *The Doctrine and Covenants*, Section 124: 62, 70, 223-224; *Des. News*, Sept. 23, 1857; Stout, *On The Mormon Frontier*, I: xvii, 89, fn. 47.
5. Hubert H. Bancroft, *History of Utah*, 145, 402; Richard E. Bennett, *Mormons at the Missouri*, 55, 182, 247; Susan W. Easton Black, comp. *Membership of the Church of Jesus Christ of Latter Day Saints*, 21:849, 915-17; Andrew Ehat and Lyndon W. Cook, eds. *The Words of Joseph Smith*, 265; Journal History, Sept. 16, 24, Oct. 11, Dec. 9, 1845; Stout, I, 91. Donald Q. Cannon and Lyndon W. Cook, eds. *Far West Record*, 266.
6. Journal History, Apr. 5, 1846.

NOTES TO THE CHAPTERS 335

7. *Ibid.*, March 15, 1843.
8. "Diary of Lorenzo Dow Young," *Utah Hist. Quarterly,* 14:138; also Stout, I: 160.
9. Journal History, May 12, 1846; also see regarding the exodus: William Clayton. *William Clayton's Journal,* 9-15, 18, 20, 24; Stout, I, 14; Journal History, Mar. 26, 27, 30, Apr. 23, 1846; Elden J. Watson, comp., *Manuscript History of Brigham Young,* 131.
10. Albert Haws, 349.
11. Norma B. Ricketts, *The Mormon Battalion,* 51.
12. Alpheus P. Haws to Adeline Haws, October 11, 1846, in Mormon Battalion Correspondence Collection; also see Journal History, Sept. 18, 1842.
13. Daniel Tyler, *A Concise History of the Mormon Battalion,* 1881. Wallace Stegner, *The Gathering of Zion,* 193 fn.; Hubert H. Bancroft, *California Pioneer Register and Index,* 182; Kate Carter, *The Mormon Battalion,* 12.
14. Journal History, Mar. 27, 1848.
15. Albert Haws, 350.
16. *The Latter-day Saints' Millennial Star,* XI: 14, 54; Stout I, 6 fn.12, 220; Stegner, 103; San Francisco, California, *The Wide West,* Oct. 11, 1857.
17. George Q. Cannon, "History of the Church," *Juvenile Instructor,* XVII: 293.
18. Albert Haws, 350-51.
19. *Des. News,* July 13, 1854; also ed. of Aug. 24; *Sac. Union,* July 3, Nov. 13, 1854; *Sacramento Democratic State Journal,* Oct. 5, 1857; *Mountain Democrat,* June 10, 1854; *Wide West,* Oct. 11, 1857.
20. Capt. Rufus Ingalls' report regarding his trip with Col. Steptoe, contained in *Report of the Secretary of War, 1855,* 34th Cong. 1st sess, Senate Ex. Doc. No. 1, Part 2, 162-63; also see *Des. News,* Aug. 3, 1859; *Sac. Union,* Oct. 20, 1854.
21. Huntington, Oliver B., *Diary and Reminiscences,* 2:83-85; also *Sac. Union,* June 11, 1857; *Des. News,* Oct. 19, Dec. 7, 1854; Edna B. Patterson, Louise A. Ulph and Victor Goodwin, *Nevada's Northeast Frontier,* 443.
22. *Des. News,* July 4, 1855; also eds. of May 29, June 12, 1852, Aug. 1, 1855; *Sac. State Journal,* Mar. 16, 1855; Captain J. H. Simpson, *Report of Explorations Across the Great Basin,* 64-67.
23. Journal History and *Des. News,* both of June 30, 1855.
24. *Sac. Union,* Oct. 11, 1855; Howard R. Egan, Pioneering The West, 196-97.
25. Jules Remy and Julius Benchley. *A Journey To Great-Salt-Lake City,* I: 122-149.
26. *Des. News,* Aug. 29, 1855 also see ed. of Feb. 8, 1855.
27. Remy and Benchley, I: 122-149.
28. Brigham Young, "Message to the Legislative Assembly of the Territory of Utah," Dec. 11, 1855.
29. Remy and Benchley, I: 122-149; also see *Sac. Union,* Jan. 3, 1856.
30. *Sac. Union,* July 31, 1856; Kate B. Carter, comp., *Our Pioneer Heritage,* 2:589; Stout II: 563, 570, 571, 586, 591.
31. Davis, 1:32.
32. *Des. News,* Oct. 28, 1857; also see Oliver B. Huntington, "Eighteen Days on the

Deserts," 266; *Sac. Union*, Aug. 4, 18, 25, Oct. 28, 30, 1856; *Des. News*, Sept. 3, 1856.
33. *Sac. Union*, Oct. 17, 1857.
34. *Alta*, May 7, 1866; Helen S. Carlson, *Nevada Place Names*, 47; S. Fran. *Herald*, Oct. 14, Nov. 15, 1857; W. T. Jackson, 174-205; *Sac. Union*, Sept. 28, 1857; Leroy R. and Ann W. Hafen, *The Utah Expedition*, 122-23, 151.
35. *Sac. Union*, August 17, 1857; also see ed. of Sept. 22.
36. *Ibid.*, also see *Sac. State Journal*, Sept. 9, 1857.
37. William A. Maxwell, *Crossing the plains*, 53, 73; *Alta*, Sept. 1, 1857; *Sac. Union*, Aug. 31, Sept. 10, 18, 22, 1857.
38. *Sac. Union*, Aug. 17, 31, 1857; *Alta*, Sept. 1, 1857; *Sac. State Journal*, Aug. 20, 1857; Weaverville Trinity Journal, Sept. 5, 1857.
39. *Sac. Union*, Sept. 17, 1857.
40. Maxwell, 116-134; George R. Stewart, The California Trail, 314-16. For more on the summer's depredations see *Sac. State Journal*, Oct. 5, 6, 1857; *Alta*, Sept. 10, Oct. 8, 1857; San. Fran. *Herald*, Nov. 15, 1857; *Des. News*, Aug. 19, Oct. 28, Nov. 4, 1857; *Sac. Union*, Aug. 6, 8, 12, 15, 22, Oct. 5, 6, 12, Nov. 2, 1857; *Trinity Journal*, Aug. 22, 1857; "Arthur M. Menefee's Travels Across the Plains, 1857" N. H. S. Q. 9-1: 22-25.
41. *Alta*, Sept. 10, 1857; *Sac. Union*, Sept. 10, 1857.
42. Nevada Journal in Wide West, Oct. 11, 1857.
43. *Sac. Union*, Oct. 17, 1857; *Sac. State Journal*, Oct. 5, 1857.
44. W. W. Drummond to Jeremiah Black, Attorney-General of the U.S., March 30, 1857, 35th Cong., 1st sess., H. Exec. Doc. 71, 212.
45. *Deseret News*, Aug. 19, 1857.
46. *Reveille*, June 17, 20, 22, July 11, 1863, Apr. 5, 1864, June 5, Sept. 20, 1865; Va. *Union* Mar. 2, 1864; Carlson, 131; J. Wells Kelly, *First Directory of Nevada Territory*, 225.
47. Albert Haws, 356 and 352 respectively; also see *Reveille* Feb. 4, Mar. 18, 1867, Sept. 12, 23, 1868.
48. Albert Haws, 356-57; also Reorganized Church of Jesus Christ of Latter-day Saints, *True Latter Day Saints' Herald*, 13:157; *Reveille*, June 21, July 6, 1867, Nov. 26, 1869.
49. *Independent*, Aug. 18, 1869; May 7, 14, 1870; White Pine D. News, May 10, 1870; *Reveille* Oct. 23, 1868, April 6, 1869.
50. *Independent*, Oct. 5, 1872; also see *Humboldt Register*, May 20, 1871, March 30, 1876; *True Saints' Herald*, 19:249.
51. *True Saints' Herald*, 22:541. Alpheus and Betsy's other children were 20-year old Laura (Lola) A., 18-year old Adelia (Ardelia) G., 12-year old Don Carlo and 7-year old Leland Ann. Albert and Maria's other children were 20-year old Charles M., 18 year old Francis, 15-year old Hette L., 13-year old Ida Jane, 10-year old William Dale and 7-year old Oscar (1870 Nevada Census Index).
52. Tuscarora, Nevada *Times-Review*, Oct. 25, Dec. 24, 28, 1880, Jan. 18, 1881;

Independent, Jan. 23, 1881; Battle Mountain, Nevada *Messenger*, Aug. 23, 1879; Nevada Census, 1880; *Silver State* Nov. 2, 1876; *True Saints Herald*, 33: 730; Reorganized Church of Jesus Christ of Latter-day Saints, Joseph Smith Letter Book #6, 441, 485.
53. Reorganized Church of Jesus Christ of Latter-day Saints, *Zion's Ensign*, December 3, 1902; see also *True Saints Herald* 36: 38, 831-32; 48: 567, 647; 25: 39; Albert Haws, 351, 352.
54. Huntington, *Diary*, 436.
55. Oakland, California *Tribune*, October 23, Nov. 3, 1906.

NOTES TO "UNCLE BILLY"

1. *Alta*, May 3, 1851; Elko *Independent*, Sept. 9, 1877.
2. *Deseret News*, Aug. 19, 1851; also *Alta*, July 3, 26, 1852; May 14, 15, 19, 28, 29, 31, June 7, 14, 18, 19, 28, July 3, 6, 25, 26, 29, 31, Aug. 8, 27, 1851; *San Joaquin Republican,* Sept. 20, 1851; Bancroft, California, 6: 319; Wren, *A History of the State of Nevada*, 27-29.
3. San Francisco *Placer Times and Transcript* July 1, 1852; *Sac. Union*, Nov. 25, Dec. 1, 1854, Feb. 7, 1855; Aug. 18, Dec. 10, 1856; Placerville, California *Mountain Democrat*, July 22, 1854.
4. *Sac. Union*, June 10, 1857; also eds. of Jan. 10, Feb. 14, Apr. 14, 28, July 3, 1857.
5. *Ibid* , Nov. 11, 1854; also ed. of Sept. 29, 1854.
6. *Ibid*., Aug. 8, 26, 29, Sept. 7, 8, 1857.
7. Sac. *Union*, July 2, Sept. 14, 28, Oct. 5, 1857; Sac. *Dem. State Journal*, Oct. 6, 7, 1857; S. F. *Herald*, Oct. 9, 1857, Sept. 30; May 19, June 5, 1860; *Alta*, Oct. 10, 1857; Marysville, California *Daily Herald*, Sept. 11, 1857.
8. *Sac. Union*, Oct. 17, 28, 31, Nov. 2, 1857; S. F. *Herald*, Nov. 15, 1857.
9. S. F. *Herald*, Dec. 3, 1857.
10. *Sac. Union*, Feb. 15, Mar. 3, 8, April 18, June 25, 1858; S. F. *Herald*, Jan. 11, 1858.
11. *Sac. Union*, June 22, 1858; also eds. of June 17, 18, 19, 25, July 2, 1858; Van Sickles, "Utah Desperadoes," 190-91; Bancroft, *Nevada*, 84.
12. Simpson, 92.
13. Salt Lake City, Utah *Valley Tan*, Dec. 10, 1858.
14. *Deseret News*, Feb. 16, Mar. 30, May 11, Aug. 17, 1859; Virginia City, Nevada. *Territorial Enterprise*, Jan. 8, 1859; S. F. *Herald*, February 24, 1859; Moorman and Sessions, *Camp Floyd and the Mormons*, 143; *Journal History*, June 1, 3, 1859; Elko Ind Feb 3, 1872; Brooks, *The Mountain Meadows Massacre*, 74; Beadle, *Western Wilds*, 515.
15. *Sac. Union*, Sept. 28, 1859 also see Elliot, 120; Patterson 209, 501, 535; S. F. *Herald*, June 5, 15, 1860; S. F. *Bulletin*, Dec. 22, 1858; *Union*, July 15, 21, Sept. 6, 10, 29, Oct. 11, Nov. 12, Dec. 11, 21, 1858, Mar. 9, Aug. 25, 1859; *Enterprise,* Jan. 8, Mar. 26, 1859; Simpson, 35, 62-64, 94; *Valley Tan*, March 15, 22, Aug.

17, 1859; *Des. News*, Jan. 5, 1859, Jan. 11, May 16, 1860; Omer Stewart 256-57; Thompson and West, 148; *Independent* June 18, 1870.
16. *Des. News*, Mar. 16, Aug. 3, Dec. 21, 1859; *Enterprise*, July 2, 1859; *Sac. Union*, Nov. 22, 1859.
17. *Sac. Union*, May 12, Nov. 4, 22, Dec. 19, 1859, Mar. 22, 23, June 15, 1860; Hafen 135, 150, 157, 165-66, 179; S. F. *Bulletin*, Oct. 13, 1859, Mar. 17, 1860; Burton, *City of the Saints*, 32-33, 369, 515; S. F. *Herald* Nov. 16, 1859; *Des. News*, Nov. 23, 1859, Feb. 12, Apr. 11, 1860; Egan, *Pioneering the West*, 211-13.
18. *Des. News*, May 16, June 13, 1860; also eds. of Sept. 28, 1859, May 17, 1860.
19. *Des. News*, March 14, April 18, 25, June 13, 20, 27, July 11, 1860; *Sac. Union*, July 21, August 4, 6, 18, 1860; *Journal History*, June 26, 1860.
20. *Sac. Union*, Aug. 25,1862; also eds. of Oct. 3, 17, Nov. 14, 1860.
21. *Des. News*, Aug. 15, 1860.
22. Burton, 495.
23. *Ibid*, 503.
24. *Journal History*, Nov. 1, 1860; Patterson, 15.
25. *Des. News*, Dec. 5, 1860.
26. *Journal History*, April 16, 1861; also *Des. News*, Mar. 13, 1861.
27. *Sac. Union*, Aug. 25,1862; also see *Des. News*, April 17, 1861.
28. National Archives, State Department Territorial Papers, Nevada Series, Vol I. No. 13, Roll 1, Ltr fm Nye to Wm Seward Dec 21, 1861; also Angel, *History of Nevada,* 178-79; O. R. vol. 50-1, 746, 770-71.
29. S. F. *Bulletin*, Oct. 30, 1862; Apr. 17, 1863; Virginia City, Nevada. The Virginia Daily *Union*, Apr. 27, 1865; Austin, Nevada, Reese River *Reveille*, July 24, 1866.
30. *Reveille*, June 3, 1863; also eds. of July 1, Sept. 5, 1863; O. R., vol. 50-2: 420; O. R., vol. 50-1: 230; Egan, 200, 263-64; Orton, 182, 567-69; S. F. *Bulletin*, May 22; June 4, July 10, Aug. 1, 7, Nov. 12, 1863.
31. Trenholm and Carley, 205; Rodgers, 97; S. F. *Bulletin*, Nov. 5 and 6, 1863.
32. *Reveille*, Nov. 1, 11, 1865; V. *Union*, Aug. 22, 1865; *Elko Index* Aug. 3, 1872; N.Y. *Tribune*, Dec. 2, 1865; *Independent*, June 18, 1870, Sept. 9, 1877.
33. *Independent*, July 6, Nov. 1, 16, Dec. 14, 1870.
34. *Ibid.*, Sept. 23, 1871.
35. *Ibid.*, Dec. 23, 1871.
36. *Ibid.*, Feb. 3,1872; also *Star*, Feb. 28, 1852.
37. *Ibid.* May 22, 1875; also see ed. of Dec. 13, 1873.
38. *Ibid.*, July 18, 1874; also ed. of June 18, 1870.
39. *Ibid.*, Sept. 3 and 12, 1874 respectively; also ed. of Sept. 17, 1872.
40. *Ibid.*, Sept. 9, 1877; also *Silver State* Feb. 12, 1876; *Independent*, Dec. 17, 1876.
41. *Independent*, Aug. 24, 1879.

Select Bibliography

UNPUBLISHED MATERIAL

Buckley, James, Coroner. Inquisition by Coroner's Jury, State of Nevada, County of Humboldt, into the death of Edward Hogle. Golconda, Nevada. March 1, 1911. Humboldt County Recorder's Office, Winnemucca, Nevada.

———. Inquisition by Coroner's Jury, State of Nevada, County of Humboldt, into the deaths of [Mike's Band]. March 3, 1911. Humboldt County Recorder's Office, Winnemucca, Nevada.

Condy, Richard. Journal of the March from Camp Halleck, California to Fort Ruby, Nevada, July 12 to September 1, 1862. Haggin Museum, Stockton California.

Crawford, Ellison L. Letter of October 4, 1852, MS-0476, California Historical Society.

De Wolf Scrapbook, Del Norte County Museum, Crescent City, California.

De Wolf, Mrs. M. E. *Account of the Loss of the Steamship Brother Jonathan.* Undated ms. at Del Norte County Museum, Crescent City, California.

Draft registrations for Twin Falls County, Idaho,1917. Twin Falls Public Library.

Haws, Alpheus P. letter to Adeline Haws, October 11, 1846. Mormon Battalion Correspondence Collection, 1846, Ms. 2070, Folder 14. Historian's Office, Church of Jesus Christ of Latter-day Saints.

Huntington, Oliver Boardman. "Diary and Reminiscences, 1843-1900." 3 vols., typescript. Historian's Office, Church of Jesus Christ of Latter-day Saints.

Lee, Robert Edward. Indenture of September 10, 1840. Ms. 2495, L. D. S. Church Historian's Office, Salt Lake City.

National Archives Microfilm Publications. Interior Department. Territorial Papers Relating to Idaho, Letters Received, 1864-1890. Record Group 48, Microcopy 191, Roll 3.

———. State Department. Territorial Papers of Idaho, 1863-1872. Record Group 59, Microcopy 445, Roll 1.

———. Bureau of Indian Affairs. Letters Received, Idaho Superintendency 1863-1880. Record Group 75, Microcopy 234, Roll 337.

———. Bureau of Indian Affairs. Records of the Idaho Superintendency, 1863-1870, Letters Received by the Commissioner, 1863-70. Record Group 75, Microcopy 832, Roll 1.

_____. Bureau of Indian Affairs. Indian Census Rolls, 1884-1940. Record Group 75, Microcopy 595, Roll 140.

_____. War Department, Adjutant General's Office. Returns from U. S. Military Posts, 1800-1916, Fort Churchill Nevada, July 1860-September 1869. Record Group 94, Microcopy 617, Roll 208.

National Park Service, United States Department of the Interior. National Register of Historic Places Registration Form for *Brother Jonathan*, July 5, 1995. Del Norte County Museum, Crescent City.

Prison Records of J. Frank Tranmer and Nimrod Urie. Nevada State Library and Archives, Carson City.

Reorganized Church of Jesus Christ of Latter-day Saints. Membership Record Book A, Carson City and Austin, Nevada Branches, January 1, 1871.

_____. Joseph Smith Letter Book #6.

Second Judicial District Court of State of Nevada, Order 8442 of January 25, 1913. Nevada State Library and Archives, Carson City.

Shipman, Mrs. Laura E. "Recollections of the Wreck of the Brother Jonathan," 1910. Ms. Del Norte County Historical Society.

Shoshone Mike Papers. Humboldt County Historical Museum, Winnemucca, Nevada. Reproduced from National Archives.

Tuttle, Hiram S. "Account of Service in Utah." Photocopy. Fort Douglas Military Museum, Salt Lake City, Utah.

BOOKS, MONOGRAPHS, PAMPHLETS AND ARTICLES

A Folk History of Twin Falls County. Twin Falls, Idaho: Twin Falls County Territorial Centennial Committee, 1962.

A Historical, Descriptive and Commercial Directory of Owyhee County, Idaho. 1898. Reprint. Seattle: The Shorey Book Store, 1966.

Ackley, Mary F. *Crossing the Plains and Early Days in California.* San Francisco, 1928.

Angel, Myron, ed. *History of Nevada, with Illustrations and Biographical Sketches of Its Prominent Men and Pioneers.* 1881. Reprint. Berkeley, California: Howell-North, 1958.

Angelo, C. Aubrey ("Chaos"). *Sketches of Travel in Oregon and Idaho, With Map of South Boise.* 1866. Reprint. Fairfield, Washington: Ye Galleon Press, 1988.

Bachman, Henry Jacob. "The Diary of a Used-Up Miner," *California Historical Society Quarterly,* 22: 69.

Bancroft, Hubert Howe. *History of California.* San Francisco, 1888.

_____. *History of Nevada, Colorado and Wyoming, 1540-1888.* San Francisco, 1890.

_____. *History of Washington, Idaho and Montana, 1845-1889.* San Francisco, 1890.

_____. *History of Oregon,* 2 vols. San Francisco, 1888.

_____. *History of Utah,* 1540-1887. San Francisco, 1889.

SELECT BIBLIOGRAPHY

_____. *California Pioneer Register and Index, 1542-1848.* Baltimore, Regional Publishing Co., 1964

Beadle, John H. *Western Wilds and the Men Who Redeem Them,* 188.

Beal, Merrill D. and Merle W. Wells. *History of Idaho.* 3 vols. New York: Lewis Historical Publishing Co., 1959.

Bennett, Richard E. *Mormons at the Missouri.* Norman: University of Oklahoma Press, 1987.

Bergon, Frank. *Shoshone Mike.* New York: Viking Penguin Inc., 1987.

Biographical Directory of the American Congress, 1774-1971. Senate Document No. 92-8. Washington: Government Printing Office, 1971.

Black, Susan W. Easton, comp. *Early Members of the Reorganized Church of Jesus Christ of Latter Day Saints.* Provo, Utah: Brigham Young University, 1993.

_____, *Membership of the Church of Jesus Christ of Latter Day Saints.* 21 vols. Provo, Utah: Brigham Young University, 1986.

Bledsoe, Anthony J. *History of Del Norte County, California.* 1881. Reprint. Crescent City, California: Wendy's Books, 1971.

Borthwick, J. D. *Three Years in California.* 1857. Reprint. Oakland, California: Biobooks, 1948.

Bowman, Nora L. *Only The Mountains Remain.* Caldwell, Idaho: Caxton Printers, Ltd., 1958.

Brodie, Fawn M. *No Man Knows My History, The Life of Joseph Smith.* New York: Alfred A. Knopf, 1985.

Brooks, Juanita. *The Mountain Meadows Massacre.* 2nd ed. Norman: University of Oklahoma Press, 1962.

Buck, Franklin A. *A Yankee Trader in the Gold Rush; The Letters of Franklin A. Buck.* Boston: Houghton Mifflin Co., 1930.

Burton, Richard F. *The City of the Saints and Across the Rocky Mountains to California.* Reprint. New York: Alfred A Knopf, 1963.

"Caleb Lyon's Bruneau Treaty, April 12, 1866." *Idaho Yesterdays,* 13-1 (Spring, 1969).

Cannon, Donald Q. and Lyndon W. Cook, eds. *Far West Record: Minutes of the Church of Jesus Christ of Latter-day Saints,* 1830-1844. Salt Lake City: Deseret Book Co., 1983.

Cannon, George Q. "History of the Church," *Juvenile Instructor,* XVII (1882).

Carlson, Helen S. *Nevada Place Names; a Geographical Dictionary.* Reno: University of Nevada Press, 1974.

Carter, Kate B. *The Mormon Battalion.* Salt Lake City: Daughters of Utah Pioneers, 1956.

_____, comp. *Our Pioneer Heritage.* 2 vols. Salt Lake City: Daughters of Utah Pioneers, 1959

Chafee, Eugene B. "The Political Clash Between North and South Idaho Over the Capital." *Pacific Northwest Quarterly,* 29.

Church of Jesus Christ of Latter-day Saints. Journal History of the Church. Church Historian's Office, Salt Lake City.

_____. *The Doctrine and Covenants of the Church of Jesus Christ of Latter-Day Saints.* Salt Lake City, 1974.

_____. *The Latter-day Saints' Millennial Star.* Vol. XI. Liverpool, 1856.

City of Twin Falls, Idaho. *City Directories for 1908-09, 1912-13.* Twin Falls Public Library.

Clark, Keith and Donna. "William McKay's Journal, 1866-67: Indian Scouts, Part I." *Oregon Historical Quarterly,* Vol. 79, No. 2.

Clayton, William. *William Clayton's Journal; A Daily Record of the Journey of the Original Company of "Mormon" Pioneers from Nauvoo, Illinois, to the Valley of the Great Salt Lake.* Salt Lake City, Utah: The Deseret News, 1921.

"Continuation of the Annals of San Francisco." *California Historical Society Quarterly,* 15 (1936).

Cradlebaugh, John. "Report of the Adjutant-General of the State of Nevada for 1865," *The Journal of the Senate of the Legislature of the State of Nevada, 1866.* Carson City, 1866.

Daggett, John. Scrapbooks. Vol. 4 (1919), entitled "Old Time Original Matter." California State Library, Sacramento, California.

Daughters of the Utah Pioneers. *The Trail Blazer: History of the Development of Southeastern Idaho.* Preston Idaho, 1976.

Davis, Samuel P., ed. *The History of Nevada.* 2 vols. Reno and Los Angeles, 1913.

"Diary of Lorenzo Dow Young." *Utah Hist. Quarterly,* Vol. 14 (1946).

Dictionary of American Biography. 20 vols. and 6 supplements. New York: Charles Scribner's Sons, 1928-80.

Donaldson, Thomas. *Idaho of Yesterday.* Caldwell, Idaho: Caxton Printers, 1941.

Donnelly, J. P. *Biennial Report of the Nevada State Police, 1911-1912.* State Printing Office, Carson City, Nevada, 1913.

Downie, Major William. *Hunting For Gold.* 1893. Reprint. Palo Alto, California: American West Publishing Co., 1971.

Drury, Clifford Merrill. *Henry Harmon Spalding, Pioneer of Old Oregon.* Caldwell, Idaho: The Caxton Printers, 1936.

_____. "Grievances of the Nez Perce." *Idaho's Yesterdays,"* Vol. 4, No. 3, Idaho State Historical Society, Fall 1960.

Drury, Miriam. "The Jeffers-Willey Wedding." *California Historical Society Quarterly,* Vol. 35, 1-4.

Egan, Howard R. *Pioneering the West, 1846 to 1878.* Richmond, Utah, 1917.

Ehat, Andrew and Lyndon W. Cook, eds. *The Words of Joseph Smith: The Contemporary Accounts of the Nauvoo Discourses of the Prophet Joseph.* Provo, Utah, 1980.

Gibbs, James A. *Shipwrecks of the Pacific Coast.* Portland: Binfords & Mort, 1962.

Goodman, David Michael. *A Western Panorama, 1849-1875; the travels, writings and influence of J. Ross Browne.* Glendale, California: Arthur H. Clark, 1966.

SELECT BIBLIOGRAPHY 343

Goodwin, Victor O. "William C. (Hill) Beachy, Nevada-California-Idaho Stagecoach King." *Nevada Hist. Society Quarterly,* 10-1 (Spring, 1967).

Hafen, Leroy R. and Ann W. *The Utah Expedition,* 1857-1858. Glendale, California: Arthur H. Clark, 1958.

Hart, Newell. *The Bear River Massacre.* Preston, Idaho: Cache Valley Newsletter Publishing Co., 1982.

Hawley, James H. *History of Idaho, The Gem of the Mountains.* 3 vols. Chicago, 1920.

Haws, Albert. "In Pioneer Days." *Autumn Leaves,* 37: 348-358. Reorganized Latter-day Saints Church Library, Independence Missouri.

Heitman, Francis B. *Historical Register and Dictionary of the U.S. Army, from its Organization, September 29, 1789, to March 2, 1903.* 2 vols. Washington, 1903.

Holloway, James L. *Families of the Salmon Tract and Some of Their History.* Twin Falls, Idaho, 1991.

Huntington, Oliver B. "Eighteen Days on the Deserts." *The Young Woman's Journal,* Vol. 2 (1890-91).

Hussey, John A., ed. "The California Recollections of Casper T. Hopkins," *California Historical Society Quarterly,* 26 (December 1947).

Hutchinson, W. H. "Never Forget," *Westways,* February, 1952.

Hyde, Dayton O. *The Last Free Man; The True Story Behind the Massacre of Shoshone Mike and His Band of Indians in 1911.* New York: The Dial press, 1973.

"Idaho Territorial Election Returns, October 31, 1863," *Idaho State Historical Society Reference Series.* No. 264, 1985.

Jackson, W. Turrentine. "Indian Affairs and Politics in Idaho Territory, 1863-1870." *Pacific Historical Review,* Vol. 14 (September1945).

Johansen, Dorothy O. and Frank B. Gill. "A Chapter in the History of the Oregon Steam Navigation Company." *Oregon Historical Society Quarterly,* 38 (1937).

Josephy, Alvin M. Jr. *The Nez Perce Indians and the Opening of the Northwest.* Boston: Houghton Mifflin Co. 1965.

Kelly, J. Wells. *First Directory of Nevada Territory,* 1862. Reprint. Los Gatos, California: The Talisman Press, 1962.

Laws of the Territory of Idaho, Third Session. Boise, Idaho, 1866.

Limbaugh, Ronald H. *Rocky Mountain Carpetbaggers;* Idaho's Territorial Governors 1863-1890. Moscow, Idaho: Univ. of Idaho Press, 1982.

_____. "Ragged Dick In a Black hat; The Idaho Career of Horace C. Gilson." *Idaho Yesterdays,* 11-44.

Lockley, Fred, ed. "Reminiscences of Captain William P. Gray," *Oregon Historical Quarterly,* 14.

Lomax, Alfred L. "Brother Jonathan." *Oregon Historical Society Quarterly,* 67.

_____. "Ellendale Woolen Mill, 1865-71." *Oregon Historical Society Quarterly,* 31.

McConnell, W. J. *Early History of Idaho,* 1913.

McKee, Irving, ed. *Alonzo Delano's California Correspondence.* Sacramento: Sacramento Book Collector's Club, 1952

Mack, Effie Mona. *Nevada, a history of the state from the earliest times through the Civil War.* Glendale: Arthur H. Clark Company, 1936.

Martin, Elizabeth. "The Hubert-Walker Letters," *California Historical Society Quarterly,* 36 (1957).

Martineau, Col. J. H. "Military History of Cache Valley." *Tullidge's Quarterly Magazine,* Vol. 2, Part 1.

Maxwell, William Audley. *Crossing the plains, days of '57; a narrative of early emigrant travel to California by the ox team method.* San Francisco, 1915.

Moorman, Donald R., with Gene A. Sessions. *Camp Floyd and the Mormons; the Utah War.* University of Utah Press, Salt Lake City, 1992.

Oaks, Dallin H. and Joseph I. Bentley. "Joseph Smith and Legal Process: In the Wake of the Steamboat *Nauvoo,"* *Brigham Young University Law Review,* 3.

Orton, Brig. Gen. Richard H. ed. *Records of California Men in the War of the Rebellion,* 1861-1867. 1890.

Parry, Mae T. "Massacre at Bia Ogai," *The Trail Blazer,* 128.

Patterson, Edna B.; Ulph, Louise A., and Goodwin, Victor. *Nevada's Northeast Frontier.* Sparks, Nevada: Western Printing and Publishing Co., 1969.

Perry, Frank Vernon. "The Last Indian Uprising in the United States." *Nevada Historical Society Quarterly,* Vol. 15 No. 4 (Winter 1972).

Pierce, Elias D. *The Pierce Chronicle; Personal Reminiscences of E. D. Pierce as transcribed by Lou A. Larrick.* Ed by J. Gary Williams and Ronald Stark. Moscow, Idaho: Idaho Research Foundation, Inc. 1975.

Polos, Nicholas C. "John Swett: A Stranger in the Southland." *California Historical Society Quarterly,* 42 (1963).

Remy, Jules and Julius Benchley. *A Journey To Great-Salt-Lake City.* 2 vols. London, 1861.

Reorganized Church of Jesus Christ of Latter-day Saints. *True Latter Day Saints' Herald,* Vols. 13 (1868), 19 (1872), 22 (1875), 25 (1878), 33 (1886), 36 (1889), 48 (1901).

_____, *Zion's Ensign,* December 3, 1902. R. L. D. S Archives, Roll No. 279, Vol. 13. No 49.

Report of the Adjutant General of the State of Oregon, for the years 1865-6. Salem, Oregon. 1866.

Rhulen, Col. George. "Early Nevada Forts." Nevada Historical Society Quarterly,. Vol. 7, Nos. 3 and 4 (1964).

Richards, Kent D. *Isaac I. Stevens; Young Man in a Hurry.* 1979. Reprint. Pullman: Washington State University Press, 1993.

Richardson, Albert D. *Beyond the Mississippi; From the Great River to the Great Basin. Life and Adventure on the Prairies, Mountains, and Pacific Coast.* Hartford, Connecticut, 2nd Ed. 1869.

Richardson, Elmo R. "Caleb Lyon: A Personal Fragment." *Idaho Yesterdays,* Vol. 1 No. 4 (Winter 1957-58).

Ricketts, Norma Baldwin. *The Mormon Battalion; U. S. Army of the West, 1846-1848.* Logan, Utah: Utah State University Press, 1966.
Rodgers, Fred B. *Soldiers of the Overland.* San Francisco, 1939.
Robinson, David G. *Comic Songs; or Hits at San Francisco, by Dr. D. G. Robinson as sung by him at the San Francisco Theatre.* San Francisco, 1853.
Ross, Alexander. *The Fur Hunters of the Far West; a Narrative of Adventures in the Oregon and Rocky Mountains.* 2 vols. London, 1855.
Scammell, Col. J. Marius. "The Siskiyou Cavalry (1861-66)." *The Siskiyou Pioneer in Fact and Folklore,* Vol. 3 No. 2 (1959).
Schlicke, Carl P. *General George Wright, Guardian of the Pacific Coast,* Norman: University of Oklahoma Press, 1988.
Secrest, William B. *Juanita.* Fresno: Saga-West Publishing Co., 1967.
Simpson, Captain J. H. *Report of Explorations Across the Great Basin of the Territory of Utah For a Direct Wagon-Route From Camp Floyd to Genoa, In Carson Valley,* In 1859. 1876. Reprint. Reno: University of Nevada Press, 1983.
Smith, Philip Dodd Jr. "The Sagebrush Soldiers." *Nevada Historical Society Quarterly,* Vol 5, No 3-4, July-December 1962.
"Steamboat Down the Snake; the Early Story of the 'Shoshone.'" *Idaho Yesterdays* 4 (Winter 1961-62).
"Steamboating in Hell's Canyon," *Idaho Yesterdays,* Summer 1957.
Stegner, Wallace. *The Gathering of Zion; the Story of the Mormon Trail.* New York: McGraw-Hill Book Co., 1964.
Stewart, George R. *The California Trail.* New York: McGraw-Hill Book Co., 1962.
Stout, Hosea. *On The Mormon Frontier; The Diary of Hosea Stout, 1844-1861.* Ed. by Juanita Brooks. 2 vols. Salt Lake City: University of Utah Press, 1964.
Stuart, Granville. *Prospecting for Gold From Dogtown to Virginia City, 1852-1864.* Ed. by Paul C. Phillips. Lincoln: University of Nebraska Press, 1977.
"Territorial Governors of Idaho," *Idaho Yesterdays,* 7-1 (Spring, 1963).
The Passing of the Redman. Franklin County Historical Society and Monument Committee, Preston, Idaho, 1917.
The War of the Rebellion: A Compilation of the Official Records of the Union and Confederate Armies. Series 1. Washington, D. C., 1880-1900.
Tracy, Charles Abbot III. "Police Function in Portland, 1851-1874, Part II." *Oregon Historical Quarterly,* Vol. 80, Part 2.
Tullidge, Edward W. *History of Salt Lake City, and Its Founders.* Salt Lake City, 1886.
Twain, Mark (Samuel Clemens). *The Mark Twain Papers; Mark Twain's Letters, Volume 1: 1853-1866.* Berkeley: University of California Press, 1988.
_____. *Roughing It.* 1872. Reprint. New York: The Library of America, 1984.
Tyler, Daniel. *A Concise History of the Mormon Battalion in the Mexican War, 1846-1847.* 1881. Reprint. Waynesboro, Virginia: M. & R. Books, 1964.
U. S. Congress. Senate. *Report of the Secretary of War,* 1855. 34th Cong. 1st sess.

Ex. Doc. No. 1, Part 2.
_____. House. 2nd Cong., 2nd Sess., Exc. Doc. No 198.
_____. House. 35th Cong., 1st Sess., H. Exec. Doc. 71, 212.
Van Sickles, H. "Utah Desperadoes," Nevada Historical Society Papers, 1913-1916. Carson City, 1917.
Watson, Elden J., comp. *Manuscript History of Brigham Young, 1846-1847*. Salt Lake City, 1971.
Wells, Merle W. *Gold Camps & Silver Cities*. Moscow: Idaho Department of Lands, 1983.
_____. "Clinton De Witt Smith, Secretary, Idaho Territory, 1864-1865." *Oregon Historical Quarterly*, Vol. 52 (March 1951).
_____. "Caleb Lyon's Indian Policy." *Pacific Northwest Quarterly*, October 1970.
Wheeler, Sessions S. The Black Rock Desert. Caldwell, Idaho: The Caxton Printers, 1978.
Wren, Thomas. *A History of the State of Nevada*. New York, 1904.
Wright, E. W. ed. *Lewis and Dryden's Marine History of the Pacific Northwest*. 1895. Reprint. Seattle: Superior Publishing Company, 1967.
Young, Brigham. "Message to the Legislative Assembly of the Territory of Utah, December 11, 1855." Photocopy. Utah State Historical Society.

NEWSPAPERS

Austin, Nevada. *Reese River Reveille*, 1863-1869.
Battle Mountain, Nevada. *Battle Mountain Messenger*, 1878-1884.
Blackfoot, Idaho. *Daily Bulletin*, 1929.
Boise, Idaho. *Tri-Weekly Statesman* 1864-1868.
Burley, Idaho. *Burley Bulletin*, 1911.
Carson City, Nevada. *Daily Appeal*, 1865.
Como and Dayton, Nevada. *The Como Sentinel / Lyon County Sentinel*, 1864-1866.
Crescent City, California. *The Triplicate*, 1996-1999.
Elko, Nevada. *Elko Free Press*, 1910-11.
Elko, Nevada. *Elko Independent / Weekly Independent*, 1869-1881; 1910-11.
Genoa / Carson City / Virginia City, Nevada. *Territorial Enterprise*, 1859-66.
Gold Hill, Nevada. *Daily Evening News*, 1864-1866.
Idaho City, Idaho. *Boise News / The Idaho World*, 1863-April 1869.
Jacksonville, Oregon. *The Oregon Reporter*, 1865.
Jacksonville Oregon. *The Oregon Sentinel*, 1866.
Lewiston, Idaho. *Morning Tribune*
Lewiston, Idaho Territory. *North Idaho Radiator*,1865
Lewiston, Idaho Territory. *The Golden Age*, 1864.
Marysville, California. *Daily Evening Herald*, 1851.

Merced, California. *Star*, 1890.
Nevada City, California. *Nevada Democrat*, 1860.
Nevada City, California. *Nevada Journal*, 1852.
New York City. *Frank Leslie's Illustrated Newspaper*, 1868.
New York City. *Herald*, 1850.
New York City. *New York Times*, 1865.
New York City. *Tribune*, 1865.
Oakland, California. *Tribune*, 1906.
Oregon City, Oregon. *Argus*, 1860
Oregon City, Oregon. *Oregon Spectator,* 1846-1855
Placerville, California. *Mountain Democrat*, 1854-1857.
Portland, Oregon. *Morning Oregonian / Daily Oregonian*, 1861-1867.
Portland, Oregon. *The Oregon Weekly Times*, 1851-1859.
Reno, Nevada. *Gazette,* 1882.
Reno, Nevada. *Nevada State Journal*, 1911-12.
Sacramento California. *Sacramento Daily Union,* 1854-1860; 1862-1866.
Sacramento, California. *Sacramento Democratic State Journal*, 1857.
Salem, Oregon. *The Oregon Arena*, 1865.
Salt Lake City, Utah. *Daily Union Vedette*, 1865.
Salt Lake City, Utah. *The Deseret News,* 1850-1862.
Salt Lake City, Utah. *Valley Tan*, 1858-1860.
San Francisco, California. *Daily Alta California,* 1852, 1855-58, 1860-61, 1864-65.
San Francisco, California. *Chronicle,* 1893, 1996.
San Francisco, California. *Daily Evening Bulletin,* 1862.
San Francisco, California. *Daily Evening Journal,* 1853.
San Francisco, California. *Daily Herald,* 1851-54, 1857.
San Francisco, California. *Placer Times and Transcript*, 1853.
San Francisco, California. *The Pacific*, 1852.
San Francisco, California. *The Wide West*, 1857.
San Francisco, California. *Times-Gazette*, 1890.
San Jose, California. *The Pioneer,* 1878, 1881, 1882.
Seattle, Washington. *Marine Digest and Transportation News,* May, 1958.
Silver City, Idaho. *Owyhee Bullion*, 1866-1867.
Silver City, Idaho. *The Owyhee Avalanche*, 1865-1869.
Stockton, California. *San Joaquin Republican*, 1855.
The Dalles, Oregon. *Weekly Mountaineer*, 1861-68.
Treasure City/Hamilton, Nevada. *White Pine News*, 1868-1873.
Tuscarora, Nevada. *Tuscarora Times,* 1877 / *Daily Mining Review,* 1877 / *Daily Times-Review,* 1880-1881
Twin Falls, Idaho. *Twin Falls News*, 1904-1909.
Twin Falls, Idaho. *Times/Times-News*, 1910, 1965
Virginia City, Nevada. *The Virginia Daily Union*, 1863-66.
Virginia City, Nevada. *Virginia Evening Bulletin*, 1863-1864.
Washoe City, Nevada. *Washoe Weekly Times*, 1863, 1865.

Weaverville, California. *Trinity Journal,* 1857.
Wells, Nevada. *Nevada State Herald,* 1909-11.
Winnemucca, Nevada. *Humboldt Sun,* 1993.
Winnemucca, Nevada. *The Humboldt Star,* 1911-1912.
Winnemucca, Nevada. *The Silver State,* 1875-76, 1888-89, 1911-13.
Yreka, California. *Yreka Union,* 1855-1861.

Index

Aden, Joseph, 126
Ainslie, George, 124
Ainsworth, Captain John C., 61, 69, 70, 79, 83
Alvord, Brig. Gen. Benjamin, 100
Alvord, James H., 103
Anderson, Rev. John A., 211, 213
Ankeney, Captain A. P., 63
Asbury, C. H., 224, 230, 253, 256
Austin, Nevada, 151, 162-166, 188, 198, 237, 286-288, 310

Babbington, Joseph, 119, 120
Bacheler, Chauncey D., 119
Baldwin, Captain C. H., 20
Ballard, Gov. David W., 125, 132, 133
Bannack, Montana, 198, 199
Barnes, Charles W., 73-75
Battle Mountain, Nevada, 189, 271, 281, 288-289
Beachy, William C. "Hill," 64, 71, 73, 74, 79, 119-121, 139, 157, 170, 173, 178, 182, 186, 326
Bear Hunter (Shoshoni chief), 193, 195-197, 199, 202, 208, 209
Bernard, James C., 119
Benson, Ezra T., 195, 197
Berry, Captain David G., 200, 201, 206, 213
Berry, John G., 97
Bidwell, John, 16, 64, 73, 139, 156, 186
Blasdel, Gov. H. G. 141, 143-146, 155-156, 162-165, 178
Bohannan, Edward, 119, 121
Boise Basin, 62, 64, 72, 79, 138
Boise, Idaho, vigilante action 126-128, becomes Idaho capital, 97-100
Bonnifield, McKaskia S., 155, 176, 329
Bowles, Samuel, 68-69
Boone, J. C., 111
"Brother Jonathan," & "Uncle Sam," 16-17

Brother Jonathan (steamship), 16, built, 18, Atlantic service, 18-19, Pacific service, 19-25, 28-30, sinking of, 31-33, 36-45, 47-53, salvage of, 53-56
Browne, J. Ross, 86, 165
Buchanan, Captain Daniel E., 81, 83
Buck, Sgt. Frank F. 240, 241
"Buck," (Shoshoni headman), 309
Buckley, James, 247, 248, 251, 252
Butterfield, Henry, 163, 166, 168, 171, 172, 179, 183
Burns, Aaron M., 25, 28, 29
Burton, Sir Richard F., 201, 306-307
Byrnes, Constable Charles T., 241-244

California Infantry, 47, 164, 169, 187
Cambron, Ben F., 234, 238, 242-244, 250
Cambron, Harry, 232-234, 236, 240, 241, 244, 246-247, 251, 252
Camp Lyon, Oregon, 80, 109, 118, 119, 169, 173, 183
Camp Nye, Nevada, 142, 164
Cannon, Jack, miner, 6-11, 13, 14
Carey Land Act, 217
Chase, Lieutenant Darwin, 204, 205, 211, 213
Chico, California, 64, 73, 79, 139, 156, 170, 183, 186
Cho-kup (Shoshoni chief), 273, 277, 278, 280, 303, 307-309
Church of Jesus Christ of Latter-day Saints: See Mormon Church
Church, John, 144, 146, 151
Clark, Sheriff I. G., 222-225, 230
Clark, John, 126-128
Clemens, Samuel (Mark Twain), 148, 158
Cochran, Silas D., 90, 97-99, 101, 114, 321
Colonel Wright (steamship), 61, 64-68
Commodore (steamship), 21-24
Conkling, Roscoe, 89
Connor, Brig. Gen. Patrick E., 107, 185,

and Bear River battle, 192-215, and Fort Ruby, 309, 310
Conrad, Lt. George D., 185, 196, 206-207
Conover, A. H., 199
Cooley, D. N., 110, 113, 124, 125, 131-133
Cummins, John, 97-99

Daggett, Charlie, 217, 219-225, 244, 245, 251, 256, 260
Daggett, Henie "Snake," 245-247, 249-257, 259, 260
Daggett, Jim, 217, 220, 225, 244, 245, 251, 256
Daggett, "Shoshone Mike," 215-217, 219, 222-227, 230-232, 237-248, 251-252, 254, 256, 359-260
Daniels, William B., 88, 90, 321
Delano, Alonzo, 6
Denio, Aaron, 151-153
Denio, William, 233, 235, 237, 238
Denoille, Sgt., murder of, 80
De Wolf, Marie, 52
De Wolf, Captain Samuel, 28-30, 38, 40-43, 48, 52
Diamond, Ray, 206
Diffendarfer, F. Edward, 218, 220, 221, 225, 229, 257, 258, 331
Dixon, Jacob, 127, 128
Donnelly, Captain J. P., 235-238, 240-244, 246-248, 250-253
Dopp, Frank, 219-228, 230-232, 247, 255, 259
Dorsey, Reed, 69
Doughty, Captain James C., 163, 164, 166, 169-171, 175-177
Downer, A. S., 131
Downey, Gov. John, 136
Downieville, California, 8-14
Drake, Lt. Col. John M., 72, 173
Drummond, W. W., 286
Duck Valley, Nevada, Indian Reservation, 240-241, 254
Dun Glen, Nevada, 139, 141, 148, 151, 168, 169, 171, 173, 175, 182-184
Durell, B. M., 69, 76, 127
Duzan, Samuel P., 119-122
Dysart, James, 230

Egan, Howard, 271, 274, 275, 303-304, 308, 314
Erramouspe, Peter, 232-233, 236, 246, 252
Estep, Evan W., 256, 257

Farewell Bend of Snake River, 59, 64, 68, 70, 76, 79
Ferguson, Jack, 242-243, 246
Ferrell, Sheriff Charles P., 234-235, 238, 240-242, 250-254
Fogus, Col. D. H., 111, 323
Forbes, William J., 146-147, 149, 151, 154-156, 159, 162, 165, 174, 176, 178,182, 185-189, 326, 330
Fort Bidwell, California, 164, 225, 328
Fort Churchill, Nevada, 236-237, 139-141, 144, 154, 161-164, 166, 169, 172, 175-178, 181-182, 308-309
Fort Douglas, Utah, 191, 193, 200, 214, 310
Fort Jones, California, 136
Fort Ruby, Nevada, 140, 162-163, 166, 172, 178, 200, 310-311
Franklin, Utah, 195, 199, 202, 203, 208, 210
Francis, J. B., 139, 170

Gallagher, Major Patrick, 200, 204-206, 212, 310
Garnett, Major Robert S., 86
Gates, Captain John, 71-72, 76-77, 319
Getzler, Susan Robinson, 72
Gibbs, Gov. Addison C., 90
Gibbs, Isaac L., 199-200
Gilson, Horace C., 100-104, 115, 117, 118, 132, 133, 323
Gilson, John, 143, 165
Gilson, Samuel H., 165, 328
Girdner, Gordon G., 218-221, 232, 257, 331
Gold Rush, California, 2, 8, 28, 72
Gould, A. S., 86
Gravelly Ford, Nevada, 151, 153, 154, 157, 158, 163, 165, 166, 171, 172, 175, 183, 279-282
Gray, Captain Henry F., 79, 319
Gray, William P., 67, 319

INDEX 351

Griffin, James W., 114
Grimm, George B., 221-224, 230, 231
Gutches, G. A., 227, 230-232

Harding, Gov. Stephen S., 211
Harlan, James, 105, 105, 119, 121, 129
Harris, Henry, 221, 231, 332
Haviland, Mark W., 151, 155
Haws, Abigail, 263, 266, 267, 276
Haws, Albert, 262, 266-271, 280, 281, 284-290, 336
Haws, Alpheus, 263, 265-268, 270-272, 274-276, 278-282, 284-290
Haws, Betsy, 265, 275, 280, 289, 336
Haws, Charlotte, 263, 265, 277
Haws, Hannah, 289, 290
Haws, Lola, 263, 257-76, 278-280
Haws, Peter, at Nauvoo, 261-265, and Brigham Young, 266-270, in Nevada, 270-278, 280, 303
Hell's Canyon of Snake River, 59-64, 68, 81, 82
Hensley, John, 41, 42, 44
Hensley, Samuel J., 25, 26, 28, 30
Hickman, William A., 278, 279
Hog 'em (mining camp), 112
Hogle, Edward, 242-243, 245-247, 249-252
Holladay, Benjamin, steamship owner, 28, 45, 47, stage line owner, 70
Holloway Indian massacre, 281, 282, 285, 286, 289, 290
Hoover, John B., 225, 255
Howlett, Solomon R., 102-103, 118, 132
Hoyt, Captain Samuel N., 200, 203-205, 211
Hull, William, 208
Hurt, Dr. Garland, 274-277, 279, 280, 284
Humboldt Register, Unionville, Nevada, 155, 159, 162, 174, beginnings, 146-147, 149, sold to Bonnifield, 187
Huntington, Oliver B., 271, 272, 290
Hyde, Orson, 272-274

Idaho *City World* (newspaper), 117, 128
Idaho Territory, 61, 114, 135
Indiano, Bertrand "Dominic," 233, 236, 237
Inskip, Dr. G. W., 120

Jacobs, George W., 162, 163, 165
Jane A. Falkenberg (bark), 31, 48, 53
Jenkins, West, 123, 128
Jennings, Isaac, 123-124

Josefa, (Mexican woman), 1-14
Joseph (Nez Perce chief), 91

Kelly, Milton, 104, 117, 134
Kenyon, Frank, 101-103, 117, 118, 132

Lamb, Sheriff Selah G., 228, 229, 234, 238, 240, 241, 247, 248
Lamoille, Nevada, 273
Lapwai, Idaho, 91-94, 100, 102, 106, 121, 125, 134
Lawyer (Nez Perce chief), 91, 92
Laxague, John B., 232, 233, 253
Lee, Private John S., 204, 205, 210
Lee, Robert E., 89, 263
Lee, T. Bailey, 226, 227, 230-232
Leech, Andrew, 149, 150
Lewiston, Idaho, 88, 90-96, 106, river navigation to, 59-65, 68, 81, 83, capital of Idaho, 97-103, 121
Leland, Alonzo, 97, 101, 322
Littlefield, Lt. John., 158-162, 168, 171, 172, 177, 185
Lyon, Caleb, early life, 85-87, as Idaho governor, 88-97, 98-119, 121-126, 129, 134, makes Indian treaties, 94, 95, 105, 106

McCall, William, 106, 130-133
McDermit, Camp, 157, 160, 161, 168, 183, 329
McDermit, Lt. Col. Charles, 132, early life, 136, commander at Fort Churchill, 137-141, 143-146, 151, 153-159, 161. 183, and Indian expedition, 164-186, 311, 329
McDowell, Maj. Gen. Irvin, 36, 51, 89, 139, 141, 156, 163, 164, 182-184
McGarry, Major Edward, 192, 195-200, 204, 205, 212
McLean, Captain Daniel, 204, 205, 211
MacKenzie, Donald, 62
Marshall, Maj. Louis H., 125

Maugham, Peter, 197
Maury, Col. Reuben F., 94, 96
Miller, George, 263, 266, 269
Miller, Captain Sebastian, 80-83
Mills, Edward, ship owner, 18, 19
Moguannoga, see Sou, Captain
Molthrop, Captain George, 64, 79, 80
Monk, Hank, (stagecoach driver), 12
Montez, Lola, 87
Morgan, Sen. Edwin D., 104, 105
Mormon Battalion, 213, 267, 268
Mormon, Book of, 277
Mormon Church, 192, 195, 201, 213, 261-272, 278, 287, "Danites," 286, 300
Morrison, Dr. Sydney K., 235-237
Mosho, Mary J., 257
Mount Shasta, California, 136
Mullan, Captain John, 73, 170, 173, 186, 328
Murrieta, Joaquin, 192
Murray, Carlos, 275-280
Myrick, Captain Josiah, 73, 75-77, 79

Nauvoo (steamship), 263
Nauvoo, Illinois, 262-267, 273
Nauvoo Legion, 262, 264, 274
Nesmith, Sen. James W., 26, 106, 107, 110, 119, 125, 130
Newgard, Sgt. P. M., 242-244
Nez Perce Indians, 91-94, 105-107
Nisbet, James, 32, 43, 50, 51
Numaga (Paiute chief), 144-146, 296, 298
Nye, Gov. James W., 138, 140, 309

O'Brien, Maj. Michael, 169, 171, 181, 182
Olds' Ferry of Snake River, 64, 69, 70, 76, 79
O'Neill, James, 92-94, 102, 106, 107, 113, 132
Oregon Steam Navigation Company, 61-66, 69-73, 75, 79 80, 138, 319
Ormsby, William M., 14, 281, 297
Osmer, Lt. Richard, 163, 169, 171, 173, 179, 183-185
Owyhee Avalanche (Silver City, Idaho newspaper), 70, 72, 73, 77, 110, 111, 118, 122, 131

Paiute Indians, 80, 94, 138-148, 151, 162, 165, 183-187, 228, 254, 281, 305,
Paiute War of 1860, 14, 136, Sidocaw band, 155-157
Paradise Valley, Nevada, 139, 141, 146, 149, 151-156, 159, 161, 162, 164, 171-175, 177, 178, 183, 241-242
Pascal, "Skinny" (Paiute Indian), 228, 238, 242-243, 248, 250, 252
Patterson, Ferd, 26-28, 126
Patterson, James, 40-45, 48
Payne, Captain Robert C., 164, 175-177, 179, 181-183, 185
Perry, Frank, 238, 242, 244, 247, 251
Pierce, E. D.,139, 156, 170
Plummer, Henry, 122-123
Pocatello (Shoshoni chief), 209
Price, Captain George, 204, 207
Providence, Utah, 195, 197
Prussia, Merl, 241-243, 252
Pyramid Lake, Nevada, 14, 136, 141, 143, 157, 187

Queen's River, Nevada, 135, 157, 164, 171, 173-176, 178, 183, 184, 185, 329
Quilici (Eugene and Maria) murders, 227-229, 232, 240, 257-259
Quinn, Lieutenant John, 204, 207

Ragan, M. J., 151, 326
Raymond, Reuben, 126, 128
Reed, Amos, 104
Reese River Reveille, Austin, Nevada, 143, 163, 166, 176, 188, 189
Reid, Dr. Robert K., 205, 210, 212
Remy, Jules, 276-278
Reorganized Church of Jesus Christ of Latter-day Saints, and Albert Haws, 287-289
Reynolds, James S. 73-78, 80, 95, 96, 100, 101, 104, 107, 108, 115-117, 121, 124-130, 133
Reynolds Landing, Idaho, 64, 68, 73-79
Rice, James B. "Buck," 217, 218, 331
Richardson, Albert D., 16, 45, 105, 108
Ridgley, Charles, 123, 324
Riggs, Henry C., 97, 121
Robie, A. H., 69

INDEX

Robinson, David G. "Yankee," 16
Robinson, Susan: see Getzler, Susan
Rockwell, Orin Porter, 201, 202, 210, 211, 267, 306
Ruby City, Idaho, 108, 139, 156, 164, 169, 183
Ruby Valley, Nevada, 163, 303, 305-311

Safford, A. P. K., 155, 174, 176, 327
Sagwitch (Shoshoni chief), 199, 206-210
Salmon Falls (Snake River), 63, 70, 72, 76, 78, 79, 125, 193
San Jacinto ranch, 217-219, 221, 226, 260, 332
Sanpitch (Shoshoni chief), 199, 209
Seamonds, Lt. William G., 163, 164, 166, 168, 171, 172, 178, 179, 329
Seward, William H., 89, 90, 104, 117, 124
Scranton, John H., 163
Shoshone (steamboat, 60, 73, 75-80, passage down Hell's canyon, 81-84
Silver City, Idaho, 70, 74, 79, 94, 97, 110, 111, 114, 118, 119
Silver City, Nevada, 147, 162, 164, 182
Slocum, Alfred, 115
Smith, Sheriff A. Elsy, 235, 242, 244, 250, 252
Smith, Lt. Andrew J., 268
Smith, Aleck C., 97, 98, 103
Smith, Clinton De Witt, 99, 100-104, 117, 321
Smith, Captain Cyrus, 80, 81
Smith, Hyrum, 263, 265
Smith, Joseph III, 287-289
Smith, Joseph Jr., 201, 261-266, 269, 276, 277, 286, 301
Smith, Captain Samuel, 196, 300
Smoke Creek Paiute Indians, 139-143
Smoke Creek, Nevada, 139, 156, 163, 169-170, 183, 328
Sommercamp, William, 118
Sou, "Captain" (Paiute chief), 155-157, 184, 185, and Wm. Forbes, 185-188
Spalding, Eliza, 91, 92
Spalding, Rev. Henry Harmon, 91-93, 106
Spear, William S., 10, 11, 13, 16
St. Mary's, Nevada, 141

353

Star City, Nevada, 119, 138, 139, 141, 148, 153, 156-158
Staples, Captain George W., steamship commander, 21-29, 50, 317, 324
Statesman, Boise Idaho newspaper, 71, 73, 95, 101, 116-117, 121, 132, 134
Steptoe, Col. Edward J., defeated by Indians, 343, in Utah, 270-272
Stevens, Gov. Isaac I., 91
Stewart Indian School, Nevada, 253
Stony Point, Nevada, 158, 159, 271, 281
Street, James, transcontinental telegraph contractor, 308
Stump, Captain Thomas J., 64, 65, 67-70, 319-20
Surprise Valley, California, 141, 232, 233, 237, early roads, 139, 170, army post, 156, 64
Susanville, California, early roads, 139, 141, 156; 164, 298

Taber, E. J. L., 223, 225, 227, 230, 231
Telegraph, transcontinental, 192, 308, 310, 335
Thurston, Captain George A., 162
Tranmer, John Franklin "Frank," 219, 222, 223, 225, 226, 228-232, 240, 257-260
Tranmer, Sarah, 231
Tranmer, William Gay, 218-226, 228-232, 257, 260
Treaties, with Nez Perce Indians, 91-93, 105, 125, 129, 130, 321, with Shoshoni, 213, 275, 311, made by Caleb Lyon, 94, 95, 105, 106
Truax, Major Sewell, 94, 99
Trumbull, Jonathan, 17
Tulley, "California Jim," 280-285, 290
Turner, Archie G., 123-124, 129
Tuttle, Corporal Hiram, 210
Tuttle, Luther, 261-268

"Uncle Sam," 16-17
Underwood, G. B., 72, 76
Unionville, Nevada, 55, 131, 146-151, 153-155, 157-159, 162, 164, 169-171, 173, 174, 176, 182, 184, 187, 198
Updyke, David C., 122-128

Urie, Nimrod R., 218-221, 224, 225, 228-232, 240, 247, 248, 252, 255, 257, 258, 331
Usher, John Palmer, 89, 93, 94, 99, 105
"Utah War," 201, 286, 300, 301

Vanderbilt, Cornelius, and *Brother Jonathan*, 19-21, 316
Van Norman, Otto D., 236
Van Orman, Reuben, 193, 195-197
Van Orman, Zachias, 193, 195-197, 201
Vigilantes, Boise, Idaho,126-129
Vineyard Stock and Cattle Company, 217, 219, 221

Walker, Capt. John H., 110, 119, 122
Walker Lake, Nevada, 139-143, 145, 156, 160
Walker, William, filibuster, 20, 21
Wallace, Gov. William H., 88, 89, 97, 103-105, 113, 320
Wallace, Captain William, Nevada Infantry, 140-143, 156, 164, 166, 171, 172, 175, 176, 326
Warner, Lt. Charles C., Nevada Infantry, 166, 171, 172
Wasson, John, 110-113, 122, 124, 130, 131
Wasson, Joseph, 70-73, 77, 110, 112, 118, 124, 129, 130
Wasson, Warren, 309
Weller, Gov. John B., 8, 10, 12-14, 301
Wells, Captain Almond B., 141-144, 146, 154, 155, 157-163, 168, 171, 173, 175, 178, 179, 182, 183
White Bird (Nez Perce chief), 91
White Knife Shoshoni tribe, 169, 271, 279, 281, 309, 311
Whitman, Eliza, 91
Whitman, Rev. Marcus, 91, 93
Williams, Thomas S., 266-268
Willow Point, Nevada, stage station, 151-155, 157, 240-242, military post, 174, 177
Wilson, Samuel, 111, 131
Winnemucca (Poito-Paiute chief): 142, 144, 186, 328
Winnemucca, Nevada, 79, 225, 227-234, 238, 240, 241, 247-252, 258

Wolverton, Lt. Joel, 146, 149-151, 153-155
Woodward, Lucien, 269
Woodward, Samuel, 311
Wright, Brig. Gen. George, 65, 137, 139, 142, 157, 163, 166, early life, 33-36, and steamship *Brother Jonathan*, 40-43, 50, 51
Wright, John, ship owner, 21-22, 24

Young, Brigham, 192, 202, 265, and Peter Haws, 265-270; 272, 273, 275, 277, 280, 300, 310
Yreka, California, 136